CLASS STRUGGLE

AND

THE COLOR LINE

CLASS STRUGGLE
AND
THE COLOR LINE

AMERICAN SOCIALISM
AND THE
RACE QUESTION
1900–1930

PAUL M. HEIDEMAN

HAYMARKET BOOKS
CHICAGO, ILLINOIS

Published in 2018 by
Haymarket Books
P.O. Box 180165
Chicago, IL 60618
773-583-7884
www.haymarketbooks.org
info@haymarketbooks.org

ISBN: 978-1-60846-777-8

Trade distribution:
In the US, Consortium Book Sales and Distribution, www.cbsd.com
In Canada, Publishers Group Canada, www.pgcbooks.ca
In the UK, Turnaround Publisher Services, www.turnaround-uk.com
All other countries, Ingram Publisher Services International,
IPS_Intlsales@ingramcontent.com

This book was published with the generous support of Lannan Foundation
and Wallace Action Fund.

Cover and text design by Eric Kerl.

Printed in Canada by union labor.

Library of Congress Cataloging-in-Publication data is available.

10 9 8 7 6 5 4 3 2 1

Contents

Acknowledgments

Many people had a role in shaping this book, knowingly or not. At the University of Wisconsin, Craig Werner first showed me the importance of Black history. At Rutgers–Newark, Barbara Foley supervised my dissertation on Black intellectual history and the Russian Revolution, which is where I first encountered much of the material included here.

Matthew Nichter did what he does better than anyone else, pointing me to corners of the archives I had overlooked and asking simple but probing questions. Douglas Williams and Grant Hoppel provided timely research assistance, and Matthew Tucker saved the day with a late-stage tech fix.

The team at Haymarket Books provided support at every step along the way. This book first grew out of conversations with Ahmed Shawki over a half decade ago. Nisha Bolsey shepherded the manuscript along the way, enduring far more missed deadlines than are decent. Tanya Grove from BookMatters undertook the Herculean task of copyediting a book of century-old documents, and the book is considerably more readable for her efforts.

This book is dedicated to my fiancée, Vickie Sliva, who kept believing I would finish this project even as deadlines flew by, who helped get it done with some late-night transcribing, and whose love and support made every step possible.

Introduction

In the history of American radicalism, the struggle against racism looms large. W.E.B. Du Bois, writing in 1913, famously called the race question "the great test of the American socialist."[1] Later generations of socialists tended to agree with him, elevating the antiracist struggle to a place of centrality in left strategy. From the 1930s to the present day, American leftists have seen the struggle against racial oppression, most centrally of black Americans, as one of the key questions radicals face in the movement to remake American society.

At the same time, it is something of a consensus judgment on the left that before the 1930s, when the Communist Party (CP) threw itself into organizing the struggle against Black oppression, American radicals largely failed Du Bois's test. The record of the pre-Depression left is often summed up with Socialist Party (SP) leader Eugene Debs's statement: "We [the Socialist Party] have nothing special to offer the Negro."[2] The SP, which was the largest organization of the American left until the growth of the CP in the 1930s, and the left more broadly, are judged guilty of class reductionism and general neglect of the problems of Black Americans.[3]

The truth is considerably more interesting than this caricatured image. Take Debs, for example. In the same essay from which his infamous statement is drawn, he also declares, "The whole world is under obligation to the Negro, and that the white heel is still upon the black neck is simply proof that the world is not yet civilized." Later he declares, "Socialists should with pride proclaim their sympathy with and fealty to the black race, and if any there be who hesitate to avow themselves in the face of ignorant and unreasoning prejudice, they lack the true spirit of the slavery-destroying revolutionary movement." When an SP member wrote back to Debs, warning him, "you will jeopardize the best interests of the Socialist Party if you insist on political equality of the Negro," Debs replied with scorn that the party would "be false to its historic mission, violate the fundamental principles of Socialism, deny its philosophy and repudiate its own teachings" if it failed to stand strong for Black equality. These were hardly the words of a man who thought his movement should simply ignore Black oppression.[4]

In one sense, Debs was an outlier in early twentieth-century radicalism. Few other white socialists matched his deeply felt commitment to the emancipation of all oppressed groups, and fewer still took the kind of steps he did to bring it about, from fighting his union on the question of racial integration to refusing to speak in front of segregated audiences.[5]

At the same time, Debs's attention to what was then called "the Negro question" was hardly exceptional in this period of American radicalism. From the turn of the century to the advent of the Depression, there was a wide-ranging and extensive debate among American radicals on what the fact of Black oppression meant for socialists. The answers to this question varied tremendously, from Black socialists who argued for emigration to build socialism in Africa to some white socialists who wholeheartedly embraced white supremacy. Whatever might be said about this debate, the one thing early American socialism cannot be accused of is ignoring the race question.

This collection seeks to restore this debate to its proper place in the history of American radicalism. All too often, early socialists' discussion of the color line is treated as little more than a prelude to the more important advances made in the 1930s. The earlier decades are brought up mainly as an example of the time when socialists got it wrong. Rather than a prelude, this collection suggests that the pre-Depression left is better seen as a foundation on which later radicals built.

To this end, this collection reconstructs the scope of the debate on the race question that took place on the American left during the first three decades of the twentieth century. Many of the texts collected here have never before been republished, with some remaining out of print for more than a century. Their relative unavailability has been one factor enabling the lazy generalizations one so often encounters about the American left during these years. Other texts have been luckier, finding their way back into print multiple times in the intervening decades. But even these, like the Du Bois essay from which the above quote is taken, have been distorted as the intellectual context in which they appeared has been lost. It is my hope that republishing this material will allow for a new appreciation of the seriousness with which early American socialists confronted the problem of Black oppression.

In particular, there are two streams of thought I hope to draw attention to. The first is that developed by the Black socialists, most extensively at publications like the *Messenger* and the *Crusader*. While the writers behind these publications, like A. Philip Randolph, Chandler Owen, and Cyril V. Briggs, have long been recognized as pioneering Black Marxists, the full creativity of their contributions has rarely been appreciated. Typically, the *Messenger* writers are treated as "class first" socialists, in accord with their allegiance to the SP, while the *Crusader's* ideology is summarized as Black nationalism drawn to communism through the Communist International's support for anticolonial movements. Both these glosses contain more falsehood than truth, as the material collected here demonstrates. Rather than simplistic exemplars of easily categorized ideologies, these journals contained arguments leading in any number of often contradictory directions. Early black Marxism was, quite simply, more interesting and creative than has been appreciated.

The second stream of thought I hope to highlight is that of the white socialists who treated the race question with real seriousness. From SP members like Isaac Max Rubinow to Communists like Robert Minor and William F. Dunne, there were a number of early American radicals who wrote at length about the problems of Black history and what they meant for the struggle for emancipation. Like the Black Marxists with whom they were in dialogue these writers possessed a political creativity and analytical acumen that has gone unrecognized for too long. Debs may have thought his party had nothing special to offer the Negro, but in the context of Jim Crow America, he and his comrades were something special indeed.

The remainder of this introduction will offer a sketch of the history of early American socialism and its relationship to the race question. Beginning with Marx's writings on the Civil War, it traces the development of socialist thought on the question of Black oppression in the United States and the organizational contexts in which that thought developed.

Marx and Slavery

The caricature of early American socialism as disinterested in race stems in large part from a more basic accusation that Marxism has never paid much attention to issues of racial oppression. Examples of this charge are legion. Cedric Robinson, in his influential work *Black Marxism*, contends that "Marx consigned race, gender, culture, and history to the dustbin. Fully aware of the constant place women and children held in the workforce, Marx still deemed them so unimportant as a proportion of wage labor that he tossed them, with slave labor and peasants, into the imagined abyss signified by precapitalist, noncapitalist, and primitive accumulation."[6] Following a similar path, historian of slavery Walter Johnson argues, "If [Adam] Smith displaced the question of slavery, it might be said that Marx simply evaded it."[7]

These kinds of arguments cannot survive an even cursory confrontation with Marx's writings. From his days as a radical journalist in Germany to his time studying political economy as an exile in England, Marx showed a significant interest in the politics and economics of slavery in the United States. When the Civil War broke out, Marx followed its progress intently, holding that its conclusion would determine the future course of working-class politics. And unlike so many commentators on the war, Marx understood from the beginning that it was about slavery, and that it must, at some point, force the issue of emancipation to the forefront of American politics.

During the late 1840s, when Marx was first emerging as an important presence in European politics and it was still over a decade before the first shots in the Civil War, slavery was already occupying an important place in his thought. In *The Poverty of Philosophy*, a polemic against his anarchist rival Pierre-Joseph Proudhon, Marx pronounces:

> Direct slavery is just as much the pivot of bourgeois industry as machinery, credits, etc. Without slavery you have no cotton; without cotton you have no modern industry. It is slavery that gave the colonies their value; it is the colonies that created world trade, and it is world trade that is the precondition of large-scale industry. Thus slavery is an economic category of the greatest importance.
>
> Without slavery North America, the most progressive of countries, would be transformed into a patriarchal country. Wipe North America off the map of the world, and you will have anarchy—the complete decay of modern commerce and civilization. Cause slavery to disappear and you will have wiped America off the map of nations.[8]

Though today one could disagree with some of Marx's assertions here on the basis of modern econometric evidence, it is clear that for Marx, the system of slavery and cotton production in the Southern United States was of utmost importance for understanding the world economy.[9]

Marx's interest in American slavery was not merely academic. As editor of the *Neue Rheinische Zeitung*, a radical magazine in Germany, Marx ran news stories about the abolitionist movement in the United States, even criticizing one abolitionist meeting for being critical of "the planter and his system" but failing to take "practical steps toward its abolition." In other words, as a German revolutionary embroiled in all manner of political struggles in his own country, Marx still placed such importance on the question of American slavery that he was arguing about the politics of the abolitionist movement developing thousands of miles away from him.[10]

As war between the North and South loomed, American slavery moved to the very center of Marx's attention. In January of 1860, even before Lincoln's election, he wrote in a letter to Engels, "In my view, the most momentous thing happening in the world today is the slave movement—on the one hand, in America, started by the death of Brown, and in Russia, on the other. . . . I have just seen in the *Tribune* that there's been another slave revolt in Missouri which was put down, needless to say. But the signal has now been given."[11] For Marx, the rebellions of the enslaved were key to the development of the contest between North and South.

When war finally came, Marx continued to see slavery as key to the entire conflict. In explaining the war's genesis, Marx pointed to the slaveholders' dominance over the American state. "In the foreign, as in the domestic, policy of the United States," he argued, "the interest of the slaveholders served as the guiding star." Marx placed special emphasis on the planter class's efforts to expand the American state through conquest in order to enlarge the territory available for slavery:

> [T]he acquisition of Cuba, whether by purchase or by force of arms, was proclaimed as the great task of national policy. Under his government northern Mexico was already divided among American land speculators, who impatiently awaited the signal to fall on Chihuahua, Coahuila and Sonora. The unceasing piratical expeditions of the filibusters against the states of Central America were directed no less from the White House at Washington. In the closest connection with this foreign policy, whose manifest purpose was conquest of new territory for the spread of slavery and of the slaveholders' rule, stood the reopening of the slave trade, secretly supported by the Union government. St[ephen] A. Douglas himself declared in the American Senate on August 20, 1859: During the last

year more Negroes have been imported from Africa than ever before in any single year, even at the time when the slave trade was still legal. The number of slaves imported in the last year totalled fifteen thousand. Armed spreading of slavery abroad was the avowed aim of national policy; the Union had in fact become the slave of the three hundred thousand slaveholders who held sway over the South.[12]

For Marx, slavery was not some regional aberration but a fundamental aspect of American society. The slaveholders' need to maintain supremacy in the state—and to bend all policy to their interests—was ultimately what lay behind the outbreak of war.

As the war progressed, Marx grew increasingly impatient with the dithering of Lincoln and the North. Northern generals saw little point in fighting the South and were even less interested in stopping slavery. As they allowed the South to seize the initiative with a string of early victories, Marx began to criticize Lincoln for attempting to evade the slavery issue. The president, who Marx described as "legally cautious, constitutionally conciliatory, by birth a citizen of the border slave state of Kentucky," "escapes only with difficulty from the control of the 'loyal' slaveholders, seeks to avoid any open breach with them."[13] Yet Marx predicted that such a strategy could not but fail. All it would do, he argued, was create conflict between Lincoln and "the parties of the North which are consistent in point of principle and are pushed more and more into the foreground by events"—the abolitionists.[14] Though the North's manifest ambivalence toward fighting a revolutionary war caused Marx much frustration, he still maintained that the North would ultimately win, "for in case of necessity it can play the last card, that of a slave revolution."[15]

When Lincoln finally began to take steps toward abolition, issuing the preliminary Emancipation Proclamation warning that any states still in rebellion by January 1, 1863, would be subject to immediate emancipation, Marx was ebullient. He declared the proclamation "the most important document in American history since the establishment of the Union, tantamount to the tearing up of the old American Constitution."[16] After the passage of the deadline and the issuance of the official Emancipation Proclamation, Marx reflected back on recent Union defeats: "'Politically,' the defeat was good. They ought not to have had good luck before January 1, 1863. Anything of the sort could have caused the 'Proclamation' to be revoked."[17] For Marx, Union military fortunes in this moment took a backseat to the importance of Emancipation.

Marx's most famous commentary on the Civil War came through the letter of the International Workingmen's Association (IWMA) congratulating Lincoln on his reelection in 1864. Marx had founded the IWMA with collaborators in an effort to coordinate the struggle for workers' power across countries. The letter to Lincoln was one of the new organization's first initiatives. Marx wrote the letter himself, confiding to Engels that doing so was "far more difficult than writing a proper book."[18]

The letter begins by measuring the political distance traveled between Lincoln's first and second administrations. "If resistance to the Slave Power was the reserved watchword of your first election," it proclaims, "the triumphant war cry of your reelection is Death to Slavery."[19] Marx then places the Civil War in a global context, arguing that the outcome of the war would decide the future of class struggle everywhere. The slaveholders, in taking up arms for their cause, had "sound[ed] the tocsin for a general holy crusade of property against labor."[20] As such, Marx argued that the workers of Europe were firmly on the side of the Union, feeling "instinctively that the star-spangled banner [the union flag] carried the destiny of their class." Indeed, Marx himself had helped to organize this sentiment a few months earlier, when British workers had demonstrated to prevent their country's ruling class from intervening on behalf of the confederacy.[21]

For Marx, slavery and its abolition were clearly phenomena of massive importance. Some of Marx's critics will concede this. After all, slavery is mentioned in the *Communist Manifesto* as a form of class society. This, they argue, is the rub. Marx, and hence Marxists, can only see slavery as a class structure—as materialists, they necessarily miss or underplay its racial element.

Leaving aside how the reverse mistake—seeing American slavery as primarily a racial structure, and missing its class dynamics—bedevils so much discussion of the issue, even this accusation is plainly false for Marx and, as the documents collected here reveal, for early American socialists as well. Marx saw the racial ideology birthed by slavery as one important factor in shaping the development of working-class politics in the United States. Writing to Engels in late 1862, Marx wrote scornfully of anti-Union sentiment in New York City, which "hitherto an active participant in the slave trade, the seat of the American money market and full of owners of southern plantation mortgages, has always been decisively 'Democratic,' just as Liverpool is still Tory today."[22] Continuing, Marx noted, "The Irishman sees in the Negro a dangerous competitor. The efficient farmers in Indiana and Ohio hate the Negro second only to the slaveowner. For them he is the symbol of slavery and the debasement of the working class, and the Democratic press threatens them daily with an inundation of their territories by the 'nigger.'" Marx understood how racial ideology shaped working-class consciousness.[23]

Marx returned to this point again in his letter to Lincoln. His discussion there of racism and class consciousness is worth quoting in full:

> While the workingmen, the true political power of the North, allowed slavery to defile their own republic, while before the Negro, mastered and sold without his concurrence, they boasted it the highest prerogative of the white-skinned laborer to sell himself and choose his own master, they were unable to attain the true freedom of labor or to support their European brethren in their struggle for emancipation, but this barrier to progress has been swept off by the red sea of civil war.[24]

Here, Marx points quite directly to the way racism retards the development of class consciousness. Free workers who saw in their freedom their superiority to the slave only helped to guarantee their continued inferiority to their employers. One might argue here that Marx was too sanguine about the prospects for interracial working-class alliances after abolition, and there is no doubt some truth to the charge. But here, Marx's error flows from his evaluation of the Civil War's revolutionary nature. It is precisely because Marx thought abolition such a momentous event that he overestimated the possibilities for class struggle in its wake. Regardless of this revolutionary optimism, Marx was clearly sensitive to racism's effects as an ideology.

For Marx, then, slavery in the United States was of world-historic importance. It shaped the development of capitalism across the Atlantic world, and the war fought over it was the decisive event in determining the course of working-class politics during its decade. When the Civil War began, Marx devoted a tremendous amount of time to reading and writing about it—and this at a time when he was at work on the manuscript for *Capital*!

Unfortunately, for all the effort Marx expended in understanding slavery and racism's importance in the United States, his writings on this score did little to shape the early generations of American Marxists. Until the 1930s, American Marxists made little reference to Marx's writings on the Civil War. Few of the authors collected in this volume appear to even have been aware of Marx's body of work on this subject. When American socialists began debating the race question in the years following the turn of the century, they were largely starting from scratch, inventing their own approach to the problem of black oppression and its implications for the class struggle.

All of this, of course, only heightens the irony in the charge that Marx and his followers ignored race. To the contrary, Marx pioneered an analysis that understood racial oppression as interlinked with the development of capitalism, containing weighty implications for working-class struggle. And then, his followers, unaware of his labors, pioneered another such analysis decades later. Twice, in a half-century, Marxists have effectively invented new analyses of racial oppression in the United States.

Black Socialist Forebears

A decade after Marx wrote his analyses of slavery and emancipation, the first Black Marxists appeared in the United States. To call their initial numbers modest would be over-generous. Prior to the founding of the Socialist Party, there were two Black socialists who left their mark in the historical record: Peter H. Clark and George Washington Woodbey. Both testify to the deep roots the tradition of Black socialism has in American history, and Woodbey, in particular, served as a predecessor to later socialists like Hubert Harrison.

Peter Clark was, so far as is known, the first Black socialist in the United States. Clark joined the Workingman's Party of the United States (WPUS), the American affiliate of the International Workingmen's Association, in 1876, shortly after its founding. Prior to this, he already had a long political career. Clark had been a conductor on the Underground Railroad, had written for Frederick Douglass's newspaper, and was the founder of a teachers' union for Black teachers in Cincinnati, where he lived. Indeed, Clark had a long history of participating in the fledgling American labor movement before he became a socialist. When the Colored National Labor Union (CNLU), an effort to unite Black labor activists around the country, put out a call encouraging Black workers to join unions, Clark responded enthusiastically. In 1870, Clark and other CNLU figures attended the National Labor Union convention in hopes of forging interracial solidarity in the labor movement.[25]

Until the mid-1870s, Clark was a sometimes-skeptical Republican. He had been quite active in the Cincinnati abolitionist movement and, after emancipation, argued that Black voters should vote as a bloc for the Republicans. During these years, political parties operated through the spoils system, whereby parties maintained their support by rewarding their advocates with government jobs. Clark operated fully within this system and expected that his vigorous campaigning for Republicans over the years would be duly rewarded. This reward, however, never materialized, feeding a growing disillusionment with the Republican Party.[26]

In 1873, this disillusionment found expression in the Chillicothe Convention. Organized by Clark in Chillicothe, Ohio, the convention attacked the Republican Party for failing to live up to its stated commitments to Black civil rights. In his speech to the convention, Clark issued a scathing indictment of Republican failures. He attacked the central narrative of Black Republicanism, arguing that Lincoln had only freed the slaves out of military necessity, leaving the party no particular attachment to the cause of Black rights. His central argument, however, concerned the party's exclusion of Black Americans from government jobs. White party members hoarding jobs for themselves, Clark argued, showed just how thin their commitments to equality really were.[27]

The Chillicothe Convention set off a period of dispute in Black politics, as Republican Party stalwarts like Frederick Douglass and John Mercer Langston tried to respond to Clark and his followers. As dramatic as these arguments often were, however, they did not lead to a complete break between Clark and the Republican Party. He continued to endorse and campaign for Republican candidates through the election of 1876. After that election, he even defended the Republicans against charges of abandoning Blacks in the South with the Compromise of 1877.[28]

Clark's movement away from the Republican Party was really completed only in late 1876, when he joined the Workingman's Party of the United States. Clark had been familiar with socialist thought for some time before this. Before the Civil War, he had spoken alongside the German communist emigre and sometimes-enemy of Karl Marx, August Willich, who was a militant abolitionist and would become a major general during the war. Cincinnati was, in general, one of the hotbeds of German-American socialism, and those ideas circulated freely in the decades Clark spent in the city.[29]

In the early 1870s, Clark deepened his association with socialist thought through his friendship with William Haller, a socialist newspaper editor and former abolitionist. The two had met at the National Labor

Union convention where Clark had represented the CNLU in 1870; and as Clark became increasingly disillusioned with the Republican Party, he was attracted to Haller's socialism. He joined the WPUS in late 1876. According to Clark's biographer, Nikki M. Taylor, at this point he was still a Lasallean socialist, who believed political action culminating in government ownership of industry was the route to socialism, rather than via working-class struggle.[30]

Clark rose quickly in the Cincinnati WPUS. The skills he had honed during abolitionist agitation and Republican campaigning were put to use spreading the good news of socialism. From almost the moment of his joining, he was one of the party's most prominent lecturers in the city. His rise was greatly accelerated, however, by the 1877 Great Uprising. The strike, which began in response to wage cuts, spread across the country, leading to a general strike in St. Louis. Over a hundred thousand workers struck across the country. In Cincinnati, Clark spoke on behalf of the WPUS to a crowd of thousands, denouncing the state repression the strikers faced:

> The sight of soldiery fired the hot blood of the wronged men [the strikers], and they met force with force. Whether they are put down or not, we are thankful that the American citizens, as represented by these men was not slave enough to surrender without resistance his right to appeal for redress of grievances. . . . These men will be avenged—nobly avenged. Capital has been challenged to the contest; and in the arena of debate, to which in a few days the question will be remanded, the American people will sit as judges, and just as surely as we stand here, their decision will be against monopolists and in favor of the workingmen.

Clark's speech won him praise from the socialists, and obloquy from the city's newspapers, who painted him as a dangerous anarchist. Later that year, he ran as a WPUS candidate for state school commissioner, becoming the first Black socialist in American history to run for political office. While unsuccessful, he did win around 8,000 votes, mostly from black and German neighborhoods in the city. When the party reorganized itself as the Socialist Labor Party (SLP) at the end of 1877, Clark was elected to the national leadership.[31]

Trouble was brewing, however, in the SLP. Clark's friend William Haller became the head of a faction in the party which disdained trade unionism, arguing that political action was the only way forward. The majority of the party disagreed, hewing to an orthodox Marxist line on the necessity of unions. Haller was eventually brought up on charges inside the party for his heresy.[32]

This internal turmoil coincided with new pressure on Clark. The Republican Party in Cincinnati, clearly worried about Clark's popularity as a socialist, had given him an ultimatum: resign from the SLP or lose his job teaching at the Black schools in the city. Looking at the disarray into which the SLP had fallen and the party's general electoral failure, the choice for Clark was not a difficult one. Though he maintained that he remained a socialist, he resigned from the party.[33]

Soon after leaving the SLP, Clark became a Democrat. The move was an unorthodox one for a Black Ohioan in the 1880s, but not unprecedented in Clark's history. Once more, he appears to have been outraged by the Republican Party's failure to reward its Black supporters. Moreover, Democrats in places like Ohio were now attempting to court Black votes, and, as such, the local party was only too happy to subsidize the newspaper Clark and his son published together, which was full of attacks on Republican betrayals of Black rights. Though it was a position that did little to endear him to most of Cincinnati's Black population, it was consistent with his Chillicothe Convention convictions that his race owed no party its vote.[34]

Clark lost his job in the Cincinnati schools in 1886 over a political scandal and taught for a while in Alabama before settling in St. Louis, where he died in 1925. In a period of political upheaval, few Americans found themselves associated with as many different political currents as Clark did over the course of his long life. Of all of these, his time as a leader of the Socialist Labor Party is certainly one of the most distinctive. Yet for all Clark's importance as the first black American socialist, he did surprisingly little to advance the cause of racial equality within socialist ranks. The SLP had, formally, a position for Black equality. Yet the organization, comprised primarily of German immigrants, never lent the issue any importance whatsoever. Within the party, Clark rarely, if ever, mentioned the racial oppression Black workers faced, or talked about the problems a racially divided working class posed for socialist strategy. As a result, as the Socialist Party was being formed around the turn of the century, a gap had grown between Marx's close attention to the problems of race, slavery, and freedom, and the actual thought and practice of American Marxism.[35]

The second major Black American socialist, George Washington Woodbey, would begin the work of mending this gap. Woodbey was born into slavery in Tennessee in 1854. When he was 20, he became an ordained minister in Kansas. Over the next two decades, he became active in Republican politics and various reform movements, most notably prohibition, across the lower Midwest. During this time, he was exposed to the ideas of populism and socialism, both of which had strong followings in these states. The 1900 presidential election found him supporting William Jennings Bryan, who was running on both the Populist and the Democratic tickets. During the campaign, he heard Eugene Debs speak and was won to his ideas almost instantly. When Democratic officials asked Woodbey to speak on behalf of Bryan, he did, but his speeches were full of Debs's ideas. The Democratic Party quickly stopped inviting Woodbey to speak on its behalf.[36]

In 1902, he moved to San Diego and joined the newly formed Socialist Party. Woodbey rapidly became a party favorite in Southern California. He was elected to the state executive board of the California Socialist Party and became one of the party's main speakers on the West Coast. Such was his popularity with his comrades that when a hotel in Los Angeles refused to give him a room on account of his color, the LA Socialist Party issued a leaflet warning fellow workers to stay away: "We demand as trade unionists and socialists, that every wage-worker in Los Angeles bear well in mind these two places that depend on public patronage—the Northern Restaurant and Southern Hotel—keep away from them. They draw the color line."[37]

This would not be the last time Woodbey would challenge the repressive atmosphere of early twentieth-century California. In his public speaking, Woodbey frequently encountered state repression and went to battle, both in the courts and in the streets against it. He was arrested multiple times and sent to the hospital multiple times by police brutality. In 1905, he was stopped by force from speaking on a street corner in San Diego. Woodbey responded by leading a crowd to the police station to protest and was again assaulted there by the same officer. Woodbey pressed assault charges. When the jury acquitted the officer, despite overwhelming evidence against him, Woodbey responded by taking to the street corner once again and holding a massive meeting denouncing the police as "the watch dogs of capitalism."[38]

Woodbey continued to lead free-speech fights over the next decade. In 1908, he was at the center of the ultimately successful Socialist effort to repeal

San Francisco's ordinance restricting the right to hold street meetings. In 1912, he worked closely with the Industrial Workers of the World (IWW) fighting San Diego's ordinance banning street meetings in a 49-square-block area in the center of the city. The ordinance was widely known to be aimed at stopping IWW from organizing efforts in the city, and Woodbey threw himself into the fight against it. Woodbey and his comrades called meetings in explicit defiance of the ban and were met with considerable police violence. The level of repression was so bad that one official looking into the matter for the governor compared it to labor repression in tsarist Russia. Woodbey himself was confronted by armed vigilantes at his house. The fight went on until 1914, when the IWW finally won the right to hold street meetings in the city.[39]

In addition to the free speech fights, Woodbey also distinguished himself for the attention he devoted to race and socialism. Unlike Clark, Woodbey wrote and spoke forthrightly on the race question. Like many of the early socialist race radicals, Woodbey saw the struggle for socialism as an extension of the struggle against slavery. Where the Civil War had destroyed chattel slavery, socialism would finish the work of emancipation by destroying wage slavery. He directly compared the institutions of contemporary capitalism with those of slavery, arguing:

> In the days of chattel slavery the masters had a patrol force to keep the negroes in their place and protect the interests of the masters. Today the capitalists use the police for the same purpose.

In his propaganda for socialism, Woodbey repeated this move over and over again, comparing the capitalist class to the slaveholders, and using this comparison to convince his readers that capitalist power could be overthrown.[40]

Woodbey also wrote socialist tracts specifically addressing the race question. He made a few different arguments on this front. First, he argued that Black Americans should vote socialist because "nearly all [Black Americans] are wage workers," and as such, would benefit disproportionately from socialism. Second, he argued that since the Socialist Party needed workers' votes, it was opposed to any and all methods of disenfranchising workers, including those directed against Blacks in the South. Third, he argued that socialism was not an anti-religious ideology. This last point he pressed repeatedly in a number of tracts. Woodbey understood that it would be impossible for socialism to gain a hearing among early twentieth-century Black Americans if socialists forced them to choose between socialism and their religion.[41]

Perhaps most interestingly, Woodbey noted the development of class differentiation in Black America and warned against relying on upper-class African Americans for the salvation of the race. Woodbey confronted such arguments head on, arguing that while many believed "the accumulation of wealth in the hands of a few Negroes will solve this problem . . . a few white men have all the wealth and the rest of their brothers are getting poorer every day." For Woodbey, the race problem had one solution—"[g]ive the Negro along with others the full product of his labor by wrenching the industries out of the hands of the capitalist and putting them into the hands of the workers."[42]

Woodbey didn't limit his thinking on race to "the Negro question." He was also, unlike most of his West Coast comrades, a dedicated foe of the racist anti-immigrant politics that existed throughout the labor movement during those years. While party leaders rushed to support the attacks on immigrants and calls for restrictions that issued from the American Federation of Labor (AFL), Woodbey stood firmly against the scapegoating. At the 1908 national convention of the SP, at which there was an extended debate over the party's position on immigration, Woodbey declared himself completely opposed to restriction. "There are no foreigners," he proclaimed, "unless some person comes down from Mars, or Jupiter." Turning the logic that immigrants were "unorganizable" on its head, he reminded his listeners that there were socialists in every country from which they were trying to ban immigration:

> Are the Socialists of this country to say to the Socialists of Germany, or the Socialists of Sweden, Norway, Japan, China, or any other country, that they are not to move anywhere on the face of the earth? It seems to me absurd to take that position. Therefore, I hope and move that any sort of restriction of immigration will be stricken out of the committee's resolution. [43]

Though Woodbey was ultimately unsuccessful in persuading the party to stand by the principles of internationalism, he joined the small group of party members—including Eugene Debs and John Spargo—who refused to overlook the racism in the labor movement.

Ultimately, though Woodbey encouraged the party to direct propaganda to Black Americans and to drop anti-clericalism, he never pursued a sustained argument over the party's approach to the race question. In his interventions at national conventions, he never brought it up. Like Debs, Woodbey directed his energy toward arguing outwards, trying to reach Black workers himself. The consequence, however, was that the debate over the race question in the party's early history was left to men like Algie M. Simons, who knew far less than Woodbey and lacked his firm commitment to Black equality.

Woodbey fades from the historical record in about 1915. He left his mark on the party, however, in paving the way for future Black socialists in it. A whole group of Black socialist preachers were recruited to the SP by Woodbey, who continued his work of rendering socialism palatable to church folk. Hubert Harrison, the party's most important Black intellectual in the prewar years, also was familiar with Woodbey's work, judging him "very effective." In his work in the SP, Woodbey continued the legacy of Peter H. Clark, while preparing the ground for later Black socialists, whose numbers would soon grow.

The Socialist Party and the Race Question

The record of the Socialist Party on the race question is one of the most misunderstood dimensions of American radicalism. Again and again, one can find the whole party dismissed for having "nothing special to offer the Negro." Even among the most erudite students of American socialism, this impression reigns. James Weinstein, for example, author of the impressively researched *The Decline of Socialism in America, 1912–1925*, claims that prior to the Great Migration that began during World War I, "the Socialist Party paid little attention to the Negro."[44]

In fact, as Philip Foner has demonstrated, "apart from the question of the farmers' role in the Socialist party, the Negro question was the most widely debated issue in American socialist circles during the opening years of the twentieth century."[45] The actual substance of this debate varied widely—some socialists embraced racist stereotypes of African Americans and argued for segregated socialism, some declared themselves in full solidarity with oppressed Blacks, and many tried to carve out some sort of middle route. The one thing the party cannot be accused of, however, is ignoring the race question.

Debate over how to deal with the color line began at the founding convention of the Socialist Party. The SP was formed out of two groups: Social Democracy of America, led by Eugene Debs and Victor Berger, and Morris Hillquit's group, which had split a few years earlier from the Socialist Labor Party. In July of 1901, these two groups, which had alternated between denouncing one another and calling for unity over the preceding year, finally met in Indianapolis to, in the words of one historian, "form a Socialist Party in which they could quarrel at closer range."[46]

At the convention, the resolutions committee offered a resolution to the assembled delegates declaring the socialist movement in favor of "equal rights for all human beings without distinction of color, race or sex."[47] The resolution proceeded to identify Black Americans in particular as the victims of oppression and exploitation, and called for their being organized into the socialist movement and the trade unions.[48]

The resolution met immediate opposition from a number of white delegates, who argued that no special appeal to Black workers was necessary. Of the three Black delegates at the convention, two, John H. Adams and Edward D. McKay, agreed. However, the third, William Costley, disagreed strongly, pointing out that "the Negro as a part of the great working class occupies a distinct and peculiar position in contradiction to other laboring elements in the United States."[49] In response to delegates' attacks on the original resolution, Costley introduced an even more strident one, this time including language denouncing the "lynching, burning and disenfranchisement" that Black Americans were subject to.[50]

This resolution provoked a new storm of opposition but also attracted new allies. For the opposition, A.M. Simons, who had been a "maximalist" on other issues at the convention, attacking the endorsement of any reform short of revolution, said the adoption of such a resolution would "make a great deal of trouble in the South" if the references to lynching and disenfranchisement were not eliminated.[51] Perhaps incensed by the naked opportunism of Simons's position, John H. Adams announced his support for the new resolution, with the proviso that it be clear the resolution promised no special favor for Negroes over other workers. Adams was joined by a number of white delegates, particularly those representing unions. Members of the United Mine Workers, the machinists' union, and the printers' union all supported the new resolution. One white socialist, the Reverend George D. Herron, made the basic point of principle clear. He declared, "I would prefer that we lost every white vote in the South than to evade the question which is presented today in the resolution."[52] Ultimately, the language on lynching and disenfranchisement was eliminated by committee, but the resolution itself passed. It read as follows:

NEGRO RESOLUTION Whereas, The Negroes of the United States, because of their long training in slavery and but recent emancipation therefrom, occupy a peculiar position in the working class and in society at large;

Whereas, The capitalist class seeks to preserve this peculiar condition, and to foster and increase color prejudice and race hatred between the white worker and the black, so as to make their social and economic interests to appear to be separate and antagonistic, in order that the workers of both races may thereby be more easily and completely exploited;

Whereas, Both the old political parties and educational and religious institutions alike betray the Negro in his present helpless struggle against disfranchisement and violence, in order to receive the economic favors of the capitalist class. Be it, therefore,

Resolved, That we, the Socialists of America, in national convention assembled, do hereby assure our Negro fellow worker of our sympathy with him in his subjection to lawlessness and oppression, and also assure him of the fellowship of the workers who suffer from the lawlessness and exploitation of capital in every nation or tribe of the world. Be it further

Resolved, That we declare to the Negro worker the identity of his interests and struggles with the interests and struggle of the workers of all lands, without regard to race or color or sectional lines; that the causes which have made him the victim of social and political inequality are the effects of the long exploitation of his labor power; that all social and race prejudices spring from the ancient economic causes which still endure, to the misery of the whole human family, that the only line of division which exists in fact is that between the producers and the owners of the world—between capitalism and labor. And be it further

Resolved, That we the American Socialist Party, invite the Negro to membership and fellowship with us in the world movement for economic emancipation by which equal liberty and opportunity shall be secured to every man and fraternity.[53]

The Socialist Party came into being declaring itself in sympathy with oppressed Blacks, inviting them to join its struggle, and blaming capitalists for Black oppression and white racism. In the United States of 1901, there is no avoiding the conclusion that this was something special.[54]

Far from settling the issue of the new party's stance on the race question, however, the resolution at the founding convention only opened up a debate that would run from its founding through to the split of 1919 that signaled the end of the SP's hegemony on the American left. The first to respond to the resolution were the elements of the party who opposed it, many of whom gave voice to the vilest sorts of turn-of-the-century racism. Victor Berger, leader of the party's right wing and party boss in Milwaukee, propounded on the "scientific" basis for Black inferiority in a party paper, declaring, "There can be no doubt that the negroes and mulattoes constitute a lower race. . . . [M]any cases of rape . . . occur whenever negroes are settled in large numbers. . . . [F]ree contact with the whites has led to the further degeneration of the negroes, as of all other inferior races." In the *International Socialist Review*, William Noyes offered a similar lesson in race science, informing his readers that "the negroes are as a race repulsive to us. . . . The odor, even of the cleanest of them, differs perceptively [sic] from ours." Even Julius Wayland, publisher of the *Appeal to Reason* and an opponent of lynching and disenfranchisement, argued that a socialist society would be a segregated one, where "Negroes" would "live in communities of their own just as Caucasians do."[55]

These views did not go unopposed in the party. Debs, the leading light of the young party, announced his views in the same spirit as the original resolution. He confessed, "I feel a burning sense of guilt for [the Negro's] intellectual poverty and moral debasement that makes me blush for the unspeakable crimes committed by my own race." At the same time, however, Debs argued for repealing the resolution, contending that it served only "to increase rather than diminish the necessity for explanation." A southern SP member wrote back to Debs, arguing "[I]f the resolutions are adopted to give the African equality with the Anglo-Saxon," then Debs would lose more votes than he thought he would. He also encouraged Debs to read white supremacist novelist Thomas Dixon. Debs did not hold back in his reply. If the SP followed his interlocutor's advice, Debs argued, it would not simply fail, "but forfeit its very life, for it would soon be scorned and deserted as a thing unclean, leaving but a stench in the nostrils of honest men."[56]

Debs was not alone in continuing the spirit of the 1901 resolution. One of the most remarkable—and least noticed—early comrades of his was the Philadelphia writer Caroline Hollingsworth Pemberton. The niece of a confederate general, Pemberton had written articles on the race question around the turn of the century, as well as a novel about a Black Tuskegee graduate who tries to organize a southern Black community only to fall victim to vigilante violence. After she joined the SP sometime shortly after its founding, Pemberton began to write in the socialist press. In late 1901, she published a series of articles in the *Worker*, a New York socialist paper. Pemberton began with a history of slavery, reminding her readers that slavery hadn't been the solution to a race problem, but rather a labor one, as Black slaves and workers had been "the basis of every form of industrial enterprise south of the Mason and Dixon's line."[57] She recounted the oppression of slavery, puncturing the myth accepted by some socialists that slavery had been a benign institution. Especially unusual for a white socialist at the time, Pemberton also discussed the history of Black resistance to slavery, declaring "every fugitive slave was a whole insurrection in itself."[58] Moving forward to the early twentieth century, Pemberton argued that the real Negro problem was "the labor problem plus the inherited prejudices of employer and fellow workmen in the North, plus the bitter jealousy in the South of a proud people who were conquered by the sword while defending their beloved dogma that 'the negro is not a man.'"[59] More forthrightly than any other socialist in the early years of the party, Pemberton argued that the race question was actually a question of racism.[60]

The practical upshot of these debates soon became clear, as state parties in the South began drawing up their constitutions. In Louisiana, the party adopted a "Negro clause," which opposed disenfranchisement, declaring that "the State has no right to disbar any citizen from the franchise," while endorsing segregation, including in the SP itself, arguing for "separation of the black and white races into separate communities, each race to have charge of its own affairs."[61]

The Louisiana party's explicit endorsement of segregation opened a new round of debate in the party. A number of southern socialists disapproved of the "Negro clause" not because it accommodated the party to racism, but because it put the party on record as having done so. John Kerrigan of the Texas party pointed out that while they practiced segregation in Texas, the party did not openly declare itself for it, and thus did not open itself up to charges of hypocrisy from the bourgeois press. Other southern socialists wrote in to various publications declaring their full-throated support for the clause. Throughout the country, most socialist papers reacted largely with embarrassment. Unwilling to stand forthrightly for full equality, they mainly wished the issue would simply go away. A few months after the publication of the Louisiana state party's constitution, they got their wish. The National Committee persuaded the Louisiana party to withdraw the clause, and when the party went on to establish segregated branches, it encountered no further controversy from the rest of the SP.[62]

In the rest of the South, the party's position varied. In Texas, the party was, if anything, even more brazenly racist. Tom Hickey, editor of the Texas socialist weekly the *Rebel*, used the opportunity of news about a Black socialist running for office in Los Angeles to launch a tirade against social equality, denouncing capitalism for creating workplaces where one could see "negro and white men alternating with the scrapers and drinking out of the same cups. . . . Capitalism has driven the workers into a social equality that would not be possible in Socialism."[63] Elsewhere the situation was somewhat better. The 1912 platform of the Tennessee party declared that "the question of white supremacy" was injected into white workers' minds by the "capitalist class to keep the workers divided on the economic field." In 1909, Virginia socialists adopted a resolution directing the party "as a whole to pay more attention to the solidarity of the white and colored workers," and "to break down the race prejudice existing in their own state by particularly inviting colored workers into the organization."[64]

The most exceptional group of southern socialists were in Oklahoma. There, the state party waged a determined battle against Black disenfranchisement, winning substantial Black support in the process. The roots of this unusual commitment lie partially in the peculiarities of Oklahoma history. There, Black voters retained full legal rights until 1910. Unlike most of the South, Black voters there were a potential constituency for the SP during the first decade or so of its existence. Equally important, however, was the presence of Oscar Ameringer in the Oklahoma party. Originally from Germany by way of Wisconsin, Ameringer moved South to work as a union organizer in New Orleans. Later, he credited his experience there with convincing him of Black equality. When he moved to Oklahoma, he began editing the state party's leading organ, the *Oklahoma Pioneer*.[65]

In 1910, the Oklahoma legislature moved to disenfranchise the state's Black population with a literacy test and a grandfather clause, which would then be voted on in a statewide referendum. The state party immediately moved into action against it. Party leaders formed a committee to campaign against the referendum, and launched a lawsuit to prevent it from reaching the ballot. In their propaganda, the Oklahoma socialists issued a warning that Black socialists would pick up time and again in the coming years: "If the white section of the working class abandons the negro he will become a scab and strike breaker on the industrial fields and in times of unrest the armed and uniformed mercenary of the ruling class."[66]

The party ultimately failed to stop the referendum, which was won with the sort of violence and fraud that was typical of southern elections in those years. Yet it did win the attention and respect of a number of Black voters and writers in the state. A convention of Black voters met to declare their disappointment with the Republicans, issuing a resolution that concluded, "Therefore, Be It Resolved, That we hereby endorse the platform put out by our Socialist brothers and recommend that all the colored people of Oklahoma vote the Socialist ticket and align themselves with our Socialistic brethren."[67] Throughout the state, socialist papers proudly carried news of the resolution. As the *Pioneer* put it, "We welcome this action on the part of the negroes, not because it will increase our voting strength in the fall election, but because the negro is part of the working class and we stand for the whole of it."[68]

The party's resolute stand against disenfranchisement did provoke some debate in the party. One socialist accused the party of costing itself 10,000 votes by standing for Black voting rights. A Black socialist, John B. Porter, replied that abandoning Black voters to line up racist white votes would be "the tactics of the curbstone politician, putting the office above principles. Such a victory is in reality a defeat for International Socialism."[69] A white socialist also replied, accusing his opponent of trying to build "The Socialist Jim Crow Car." When the original party critic declared that the party had no right to "fix a social standard for its members," and that he would quit if it did, Ameringer happily closed the debate in the pages of the *Pioneer*, ending it with "Good riddance, then."[70]

After their defeat on the referendum, the Oklahoma socialists continued to fight against black disenfranchisement. In 1915, partially as a result of socialist litigation, the Supreme Court struck down the Oklahoma law.

When the legislature responded by passing a new literacy test, the party launched a massive campaign to defeat it, forming a coalition with state Republicans. At the height of their campaign, Oklahoma socialists were gathering 2,000 signatures a day against the new test. The state party brought Eugene Debs in to tour the state for a week, explicitly to campaign for defeating the referendum. When election day came, the state Democrats suffered a surprise defeat, losing by some 40,000 votes.[71]

As Oklahoma socialists were waging their struggle for Black voting rights, socialists elsewhere in the country were growing dissatisfied with the party's vacillating stance on Black rights. The immediate impetus for this dissatisfaction was the Springfield, Illinois, race riot of 1908. Over 2,000 Black citizens were forced from the city, and several were killed. The socialist journalist William English Walling went to Springfield to investigate for a Chicago socialist newspaper and was horrified by what he saw. Walling had joined the party in 1908, immediately becoming a partisan of the party's left wing, which supported the IWW against the AFL. The IWW itself strongly supported Black equality, and its main representative in the party, Big Bill Haywood, was a steadfast proponent of Black inclusion in the labor movement.[72]

Walling was astounded by the naked, unrepentant racism he found in Illinois. His report on the race riot, "The Race War in the North," caught the attention of Mary White Ovington, a socialist and former settlement-house worker, who wrote to Walling in hopes of founding a new organization of Blacks and whites together dedicated to Black equality. Walling and Ovington gathered around themselves a small group of like-minded socialists, centered in New York City, and began organizing. The fruits of their efforts were revealed in early 1909, when a call for a "Lincoln Emancipation Conference to Discuss Means for Securing Political and Civil Equality for the Negro" was circulated, signed by the white socialists, as well as prominent Black leaders, including Ida B. Wells-Barnett, W.E.B. Du Bois, and Mary Church Terrell. The socialists promoted the conference in the socialist press, and the resulting conference, in June of 1909, led to the formation of the Ovington, Mary WhiteNational Association for the Advancement of Colored People.[73]

Inside the party, both Walling and Ovington were intensely critical of the failure to steadfastly support Black equality. They were increasingly joined in this criticism in the years before World War I. In 1910, the pioneering Black socialist Hubert Harrison wrote a series of articles in the New York

Call challenging the party to make a choice between "Southernism or Socialism." Around the same time, the New York economist I.M. Rubinow was publishing a very long series of articles in the *International Socialist Review*, covering Black history in the United States and arguing that the party needed to organize black workers if it was to have any hope of succeeding. Throughout the country, evidence slowly mounted that the party was taking the task of organizing Black workers more seriously. A chapter of the Intercollegiate Socialist Society was chartered at Howard University. In West Virginia, the party press called to Black workers: "As Socialists, and as a party organization, you are welcome to become one of us and we exclude none on account of color, race or previous conditions."[74] In the socialist press, discussions of the race question began to take on a different character. The *Call*, for example, proclaimed: "The whole Negro race is suppressed, robbed, outraged, insulted, debauched, ground down in a manner that makes the blood of those not blinded by race passion to boil. And this is a regular thing, not in isolated cases of passion."[75] Slowly, but perceptibly, the party was beginning to take the task of opposing racism more seriously.

Unfortunately, World War I cut this process short. Wartime repression crippled the party; the Oklahoma state party, so distinguished by its commitment to Black equality, dissolved itself to avoid repression. Across the country, socialist papers were kept from the mails, and socialists were subject to vigilante violence. In this atmosphere, the race question slipped from the party's attention.[76]

Even worse, the war brought to the fore tensions in the party that had lain dormant for years. The fight between the left and right wings of the party had been subdued since 1912, when the right scored a decisive victory in removing Big Bill Haywood from the party leadership. The war and the collapse of the Second International into parties backing their respective countries brought this conflict roaring back. Much of the party right stood only half-heartedly against the war, and when the United States entered the conflict, dropped their opposition entirely. At the same time, the left's efforts to organize more robust antiwar sentiment in the party were met by repression from the party leadership. Tensions escalated, and in mid-1919, the party leadership moved to expel the left wing from the party, in the process purging the bulk of the party's membership.[77]

Race played little role in this conflict, though it simmered beneath the surface of many of the polemics. Black socialists in the party found

themselves on both sides of the split. A. Philip Randolph and Chandler
Owen, who had founded the Black socialist journal the *Messenger* in
1917, stayed with the party, becoming bitter anticommunists in the early
1920s. Others, like Otto Huiswoud and Lovett Fort-Whiteman, would,
respectively, help found the Communist Party or join it soon thereafter.[78]

The 1919 split, combined with wartime repression, vastly reduced the
Socialist Party's ability to act on any issue, let alone the race question,
which had caused such internal divisions. During the period of the
party's dominance on the left, any honest judgment of its record must
pronounce it mixed. The party gave voice to the worst kinds of prejudice
found in American society, in both its northern and southern branches.
At the same time, at no point from its founding did it lack principled
members who stood steadfastly for Black equality. In this regard, it is
simply incomparable to any other predominantly white organization in
the United States in these years. Whatever the accomplishments of these
members, however, it must be said that they failed utterly to give the fight
for a proper position on the race question the prominence it deserved inside
the party. While figures from Caroline Pemberton to Hubert Harrison
wrote brilliantly on the necessity for the party to take a strong position,
the question rarely came up at party conventions. There was, quite simply,
no organized effort to win the rest of the party to a commitment to Black
liberation. Contrary to the judgment of generations of critics, the party
did not ignore the race question. Early American socialists got further
than that. Where they failed was in agreeing among themselves on the
nature of the question—or a solution to it. The Communist Party would
soon surpass the Socialists in this regard, and on many others as well, on
the question of the color line.

The Communist Party

There was no indication when the Communist Party was born that only
a decade later it would be playing a leading role in the struggle for Black
liberation in the United States, or in anything else, for that matter. Born out
of the groups expelled by the SP leadership in mid-1919, the Communist
Party actually began life as two separate groups, both claiming to be
the proper representatives of American Bolshevism. Only through the
intervention of the Communist International (or Comintern) were these

groups gradually cajoled into unity, and even then, factionalism would wrack the party until the completion of its Stalinization at the end of the 1920s extinguished factionalism, or any internal disagreement with the party leadership whatsoever.

Historians looking back on the CP's first decade have, not without reason, judged it harshly, seeing a group totally incapable of confronting the realities of American society in the 1920s. This judgment has extended to the party's treatment of the race question. Not until the Black Belt Thesis came down from the Comintern in 1928, the story goes, did the party really pay attention to the problems of Black liberation in the United States. (The Black Belt was a series of counties in the deep South named for its rich black soil and for its predominant Black population.) While the notion of an oppressed Black nation in the South, comparable to an oppressed nation like Poland in Europe, was a strange one, historians of American communism have often pointed out that, at the very least, it got the party to grasp the centrality of the Black liberation struggle for the project of socialist revolution in the United States.

Like the standard judgment on the Socialist Party's record on race, this narrative obscures easily as much as it reveals. From quite early on, American Communists had an orientation toward Black struggle and an understanding that the color line in organized labor had to be smashed in order for the working class to advance. Within five years of the left wing's expulsion from the SP, American Communists, Black and white, were writing texts on the history of slavery, racism, and Black struggle that surpassed anything to come out of the Socialist Party in their theoretical and political acuity. Long before the Black Belt Thesis was conceived, the Communist Party was devoting significant attention to the race question, and were also attempting to play a role in organizing antiracist struggle. The party's organizing efforts, in particular, would fall short throughout the 1920s, but as the texts collected here reveal, the intellectual energy the party devoted to understanding the race question was not in vain and produced real advances over the Socialist Party. Most centrally, the CP came to understand that the black struggle for equality was itself a potentially radical force in American society, whether or not it was being led by socialists or communists.

The CP's roots did not suggest that such advances lay in store. While left-leaning SP members like Haywood, Harrison, and Walling had been among the party's most advanced thinkers on the race question, the formation of an organized left wing in 1919 did not indicate that it had anything special to offer. The "Left Wing Manifesto," published in May 1919, which became the basis for the left's program, did not mention Black Americans or the race question. One future Black communist, Otto Huiswoud, attended the National left wing Conference, and was later a founding member of the Communist Party. As the Left Wing was expelled from the SP over the course of 1919, two distinct currents within it emerged. The first, composed mainly of native-born Americans, wanted to try fighting within the SP as long as possible, and to orient toward radicalism in the union movement. The second, largely foreign-born, agitated for immediate revolutionary activity, scorning both the labor movement and SP as dead-ends. At the beginning of September, two separate communist parties were created: the first group formed the Communist Labor Party (CLP), while the second formed the Communist Party of America (CPA).[79]

Early on, neither group seemed to be moving much beyond this early neglect. The Communist Labor Party did not mention the race question in its initial program, while the Communist Party of America simply declared its intent to conduct propaganda among Black workers. Commenting on the race riots of 1919 in its newspaper, the CPA argued that the riots were a product of competition between wage workers but failed to distinguish between oppressed Blacks and rampaging whites. The riots, the paper sneered, were an "exhibition of assinity on the part of the wage slaves."[80] In another venue, the CPA declared: "The race problem is simply a phase of the general social problem, which the Communist revolution alone can solve."[81] The CLP, meanwhile, simply did not address the race question in its main publication, the *Toiler*. Indeed, it seemed to go out of its way to avoid the question, as in an article describing how "[t]he year 1919, gave us more lynchings than were ever recorded in one year before."[82] The article decried mob justice but never mentioned race. Offering arguments such as these, it is little surprise that neither of the two communist parties succeeded in expanding its influence among Black Americans.[83]

In May of 1920, a substantial section of the CPA broke off to join the CLP, which had been agitating for unification since the split. The new group was called the United Communist Party, and it soon began to address the race question with more seriousness. It assigned an organizer to make contact with Black radicals. At its party convention, the UCP called for organizing direct action bodies among Black Americans to fight back against racial violence. Its press also began printing articles dealing with the race question.[84]

The most important step the UCP took, however, was to begin a relationship with Cyril V. Briggs, editor and publisher of the *Crusader*. Briggs was a Caribbean-born Black nationalist who sympathized with socialism and the Russian Revolution. By early 1921, the UCP was aware of and beginning to promote the *Crusader*. In the middle of that year, after the last rump of the CPA had been convinced, under Comintern pressure, to join the UCP, Briggs was convinced to join the Communist Party. He brought with him his publication, as well as the radical secret society he had founded, the African Blood Brotherhood (ABB). From the ABB would come many of the early Communist Party's most important Black cadre members, including the brothers (and later rivals) Otto Hall and Harry Haywood, as well as the powerful orator Richard B. Moore. More than any other single initiative in the CP's first decade, the recruitment of Briggs and his ABB comrades provided the party with a foundation for winning over Black radicals to communism.[85]

The newly united Communist Party's halting efforts to orient more seriously to the race question were much enhanced by the intervention of the Communist International in 1922. [86] At the Comintern congress of that year, the body established a Negro Commission and subsequently passed "Theses of the Fourth Comintern Congress on the Negro Question." These theses, while less famous than the Black Belt Thesis of 1928, were arguably more important in steering the party toward a greater focus on antiracist struggle. The theses began by connecting the Black struggle in the United States with anticolonial struggles worldwide. They argued that colonialism had provoked a wave of rebellion across the colonized world and that the Black movement in the United States should be seen in that context. Referencing the history of Black revolt against slavery and oppression, the document declared it the duty of communists to link up the struggle for Black liberation with the struggle against capitalism. Doing so, it declared, was a "vital question of the world revolution."[87]

The Comintern's incisiveness on the race question at the Fourth Congress was in no small part thanks to the interventions of Black communists. Otto Huiswoud was a delegate and addressed the convention with a speech on the difficulties posed by antiracist organizing in the United States. Even more significant than Huiswoud, however, was the Jamaican-born poet Claude McKay, who was part of Black radical circles around 1918 and 1919. McKay wrote "If We Must Die," the anthem that arguably launched the New Negro movement, and helped edit the Greenwich Village radical journal, the *Liberator*. He went to Russia as a delegate from the United States, but unattached to the CP, of which he was not a member. Overcoming CP suspicions and jealousy of his independent recognition by the Comintern, McKay flourished in Russia, giving a major speech at the congress accusing the American communist movement of failing to take its proper place in the Black liberation struggle in the United States. His speech was quite well received by the congress (not as much by the American delegation), and McKay followed it up with a book on the race question, *The Negroes in America*. Between the proddings of McKay and Huiswoud, and the congress's general support for anticolonial movements, the stage had been set for the Comintern to place a new priority on Black liberation struggles.[88]

Part of the reason Huiswoud and McKay's interventions were so successful was that their arguments about the party's need to decisively combat white racism were deeply congruent with arguments Lenin had made about the right of nations to self-determination almost a decade earlier. In 1914, as part of a larger debate with other Second International leaders about nationalism, Lenin had argued that there was a decisive difference between the nationalism of oppressor nations, such as Russia, and the nationalism of oppressed nations, like Poland. The nationalism of the oppressors, he argued, was everywhere and always a brake on the development of class consciousness, while the nationalism of the oppressed, insofar as it was part of a struggle against their oppression, merited support. Though the analogies with the race question were clear, it took Huiswoud and McKay to make plain that the Leninist position on national self-determination could easily be extended to the color line.[89]

The party adapted to this new perspective only slowly. Evidence suggests that the leading faction in the party, that behind Charles Ruthenberg, were not enthused with the Comintern's line. A few months after the "Theses on the Negro Question" were passed, the American representative on the Comintern's executive body reported that the party was having difficulty implementing the theses, and that the party's leadership disagreed with them. Ruthenberg himself wrote to the Comintern claiming that the theses were not helpful in the United States. More disturbingly, Ruthenberg appears to have had a deep hostility to the ABB, accusing the group of fomenting scabbing with its encouragement of Black workers to leave the South. At one point, the

CP's Central Committee even passed a resolution declaring that future work on the race question would go through neither Briggs nor Huiswoud.[90]

However, at the same time that the party leadership was digging in its heels, events were developing that would render such obstinacy irrelevant. Around the same time as the Fourth Congress, Robert Minor had been put in charge of the CP's Negro Committee. As Mark Solomon has noted, though it says a great deal that the party still didn't see the need for Black leadership on this front, Minor was surely the most qualified white person in the party for the job. Born in Texas, Minor rebelled against the racism of southern life and became an anarchist. Working in New York as a cartoonist for the socialist press around 1917, he became friends with Lovett Fort-Whiteman, a fellow Texan and Black radical who would become one of the early CP's most important Black organizers. Minor developed an interest in the race question and, by 1924, he had read classic pieces by Frederick Douglass, as well as work from more contemporary writers, including W.E.B. Du Bois and James Weldon Johnson. That year, Minor wrote a series of articles in the *Liberator* that were more advanced than anything that had previously come from the pen of a white socialist or communist in the United States.[91]

The first article was a two-part essay entitled "The Black Ten Millions," which ran in the February and March issues of the *Liberator*. The article began with a history of slave revolts, going through not only well known episodes such as those led by Nat Turner, Gabriel Prosser, or Denmark Vesey, but more obscure ones as well, including Mark Caesar's revolt in Maryland and the German Coast Uprising in Louisiana. From the beginning, Minor made clear that the history of Black Americans was not only a history of oppression, but of resistance as well. From there, Minor went through the history of Black struggle from Emancipation to the 1920s. Commenting on the meteoric rise of Marcus Garvey's Universal Negro Improvement Association (UNIA), Minor argued that even though Garvey could be called a "monarchist" and a "Bolshevik-baiter," his organization was revolutionary.[92] To make this argument, Minor drew on Lenin's distinction between the nationalism of oppressor nations vs. the nationalism of oppressed nations, and applied it to race consciousness:

> Race consciousness in a dominant race takes the form of race arro-
> gance, and we are accustomed to despise it as reactionary (which it
> is). But race consciousness in a people who have just emerged from

slavery and are still spurned as an inferior race may be—and in this
case *is—revolutionary*.[93]

By building the UNIA, even on the basis of a fantastical and unworkable
program, Garvey had "in five years destroyed the tradition that the American
Negro masses cannot be organized."[94] The article ended by reprinting key
passages from the "Theses of the Fourth Comintern Congress on the Negro
Question" and arguing that communists were ready to stand as allies to the
Black struggle for liberation.[95]

Over the rest of the year, Minor wrote several more articles on the state
of Black struggle. In August, he wrote a report on the NAACP's annual
convention praising the organization's fighting spirit and encouraging it to
break from the Republican and Democratic parties. In October, he followed
this up with a much longer piece on the politics of Garveyism, taking a
more polemical approach to Garvey as he had become more and more
hostile to the left. Together, these texts offered a narrative of Black history
that focused on the Black struggle against oppression and advanced politics
that were based on joining that struggle with the communist movement.[96]

Minor's intellectual efforts were accompanied by initiatives to engage
in organizing alongside groups like the UNIA. The ABB had pioneered
this kind of work in 1921 with an intervention at the UNIA convention.
There, Briggs convinced Garvey to allow Rose Pastor Stokes, a white
communist, to address the convention. While her address, which called for
an Africa free of imperialism and proclaimed the communist movement
in solidarity with this struggle, was well received, Garvey was dismissive,
saying the group would make up its mind about communism later. When
the communists challenged Garvey to take a stand, he expelled them from
the conference and launched a long-running and deeply personal feud
between himself and Briggs.[97]

In 1924, the party intervened at the Negro Sanhedrin, a conference
organized by Howard University dean Kelly Miller, composed of
representatives from more than 60 black organizations. At the conference,
the party representatives put forward resolutions calling for Black-white
labor unity, condemning lynching and segregation, and recommending
armed defense against lynching. Under Miller's conservative hand,
however, the conference rejected the CP's proposals.[98]

That same year, the party once more attempted to reach out to Garvey's
rank-and-file followers. At the 1924 UNIA convention, party representatives

once more distributed its literature and spoke from the floor. At this point, however, Garvey had moved to a position of non-confrontation with white supremacy. In 1922, he famously met with leaders of the Ku Klux Klan (KKK), declaring the two groups had similar perspectives on the race question. At the 1924 convention, he declared that the race question in the South could easily be solved to the satisfaction of all involved through separatism. When the CP representative challenged this perspective, accusing Garvey of demoralizing the struggle against racism by meeting with the Klan, the communists were once more shown the door.[99]

During these years, the party also began launching its own first efforts to organize Black struggle. Most of these efforts centered on Chicago, where the party headquarters was. There, in 1924, the party dove into a strike by Black women garment workers. The party set up a storefront office in the neighborhood, and as party activists won over more supporters employers began to come to the table. That same year, the party launched the Negro Tenants Protective League in Chicago, in an attempt to organize rent strikes against exploitative landlords. Though these efforts were small and localized, they heralded a new approach to the race question, one that prioritized direct participation in the struggle against racism.[100]

In 1925, the party took its biggest step yet in confronting the color line, organizing a new body—the American Negro Labor Congress—to advance Black working class radicalism. The organization was largely the vision of one man—Lovett Fort-Whiteman. After joining the CP shortly after its founding, Fort-Whiteman had spent time in Russia as a student at the Comintern's University of Toilers of the East, a school for revolutionists from oppressed countries. When he returned to the United States, Fort-Whiteman was ready to put what he had learned into action. He was, however, disappointed with the half-hearted attempts the party had made so far at building a base among Black workers. In late 1924, he complained to the Comintern that the American party had not made "any serious or worthwhile efforts to carry communist teaching to the great masses of American black workers." He proposed the ANLC to remedy this failure, and the Comintern enthusiastically agreed.[101]

The ANLC was launched in mid-1925. Though entangled in the party's arcane faction fights, it made something of a splash upon its launch. The Black press greeted the new organization enthusiastically, impressed by the vigor with which the communists supported Black equality. W.E.B.

Du Bois himself greeted the congress with optimism. From an opposed perspective, William Green, leader of the AFL, condemned the congress, arguing Black workers had all they needed in the AFL, while conveniently leaving unmentioned the segregation or outright exclusion practiced by most of its member unions. Green was joined in his attacks on the new organization by Randolph and Owen's *Messenger*, which had by that time learned to live with the AFL's limitations on the race question.[102]

Despite this auspicious start, the ANLC never managed to become what Fort-Whiteman envisaged. Organizing Black workers into a radical labor organization in the mid-1920s was, quite simply, a Herculean task. A well-organized group would have found the task daunting, and the CP of the mid-1920s was hardly well organized. Though the ANLC managed to intermittently publish a newspaper, the *Negro Champion*, and hold forums in places like New York and Chicago, it never became a mass organization. In 1927, the CP's Central Committee, fed up with the ANLC's lack of success (and encouraged by leading Black Communists), removed Fort-Whiteman from leadership of the group, replacing him with former ABB member Richard B. Moore.[103]

Around the same time that Moore came in to lead the ANLC, big changes were afoot in what was coming down from the Comintern. In Russia, Harry Haywood, a student at the Lenin School, and Charles Nasanov, a Russian communist who had spent time in the United States in the Young Communist League, were developing a new approach to the race question that broke radically with anything previously proposed on the American left. Haywood and Nasanov argued that blacks in the South were trapped in semi-feudal conditions for the foreseeable future, locked in by economic underdevelopment and segregation. In these conditions, Black Americans became an oppressed nation, and the politics of national self-determination came to the foreground. Communists should therefore raise the demand for self-determination in the Black Belt and support the ambitions for nationhood that naturally grew out of the oppression Blacks suffered there.[104]

At the Sixth Congress of the Comintern, in the summer of 1928, Haywood and Nasanov put this theory forward. It quickly became entangled in the factional fights still wracking the American party. After Ruthenberg had died in 1927, his apprentice, Jay Lovestone, had inherited both his faction and leadership of the party. Still opposed by William Z. Foster and his faction, Lovestone hoped to consolidate his position through the Sixth Congress. Lovestone had the singular misfortune, however, of having argued recently that American capitalism was stabilizing, that insurrectionary tactics were outdated there, and in particular, that little could be accomplished in the South, so progress on the race question would have to wait until the Great Migration had moved the race question to more modern conditions.[105]

Foster and his allies immediately saw the Black Belt Thesis as a valuable weapon against Lovestone and embraced it immediately. Some Black communists were more ambivalent. Otto Hall, Harry Haywood's brother, was particularly opposed to the thesis. He argued that it ignored class differences among Black Americans and that its advocates were guilty of seeing

> the American Negro problem only through the eyes of their experience with national minorities in Europe and the East. The American Negro problem has many unique features that make it necessary to examine the special facts as they exist in the United States. In no other country in the world have we a parallel situation.[106]

James Ford, who had been recruited through the ANLC, was similarly skeptical. Discussions about whether the race question was really a national question, he argued, were distractions from the party's actual failure to establish a real base among Black workers. Ford also accused the Foster faction of embracing the thesis for purely factional reasons.[107]

These doubts were not enough to derail the thesis after the Comintern leadership got behind it, however. By 1928, Joseph Stalin had largely succeeded in extinguishing all opposition to him within Russia and the Comintern. The Black Belt Thesis, with its perspective of self-determination for the Black nation, dovetailed nicely with Stalin's general perspective on revolution in the colonized world, which held that such countries had to first go through a bourgeois-democratic revolution, and then a socialist one. Just as capitalist development was arrested in colonial countries by imperialism, so the Black South was kept in semi-feudal conditions by analogous forces. With the Comintern leadership behind it, the thesis became official Comintern policy.[108]

Though occasionally featured in party propaganda, the thesis itself was largely left on the shelf when it came to actual organizing. As national self-determination was, after the implosion of Garveyism in the mid-1920s, far from the agenda of most of the struggles against racism in the United States, the party found little political space to agitate around the demand of self-determination in the Black Belt. While acknowledging this, historians have often concluded that the thesis at least got the party focused on the race question. Yet as the history described above and the documents included in this collection reveal, the party had begun to turn serious attention to the problem of the color line well before Haywood and Nasanov even began discussing self-determination for the Black nation. By the mid-1920s, the party was already attempting to build a mass base for itself among Black workers. As black communists from Fort-Whiteman to James Ford pointed out, its efforts on this score were often lacking. But credit for the party's decision to throw itself into the black liberation struggle in the late 1920s then surely rests as much with figures like Fort-Whiteman and Ford, both of whom opposed the Black Belt Thesis and constantly prodded the party to devote more resources to their work, as it does with the thesis itself.

The Black Belt Thesis, then, did not play the role of focusing the party's attention for the first time on the race question. Like SP members before them, early members of the CP figured out quite early that confronting the color line would be of the utmost importance to their party. By 1925, they had already surpassed the SP in their attention to the dynamics of Black politics and in their analysis of the relationship between the fight against racism and the fight against capitalism. The politics that allowed the CP to play such an important role in the Black liberation struggle during the 1930s were forged, not in Moscow of 1928, but in the United States in the mid-1920s by Black and white American communists.[109]

Conclusion

The record of early American socialism when it comes to race is far more interesting than generally presented. Overall, it is fair to say that both the SP and CP, in their early years, failed in developing a strategy for confronting the race question. Yet their failures, in both instances, were not sterile but laid the groundwork for future advance. The most perspicacious and militant commentators on race in the SP—Rubinow, Harrison, Randolph, and Owen—pointed toward a socialist strategy built on merging the fight for Black equality with the fight against capitalism. Building on this legacy, early CP members like Minor, Dunne, and Fort-Whiteman came to understand that there was a Black movement for equality, whether socialists recognized it or not, and that its success, as well as the success of American communism, would be dependent upon CP members playing a leading role in that struggle, pushing it toward a broader confrontation with capital.

In doing so, they rekindled the legacy of Marx, who had first understood that the battle against slavery in the Civil War was intimately connected with the fate of the workers' movement, in the United States and around the world. Despite the obloquy heaped on socialists for supposedly ignoring the race question, or subordinating it to class, American socialism has a record in confronting Black oppression that is unmatched by other political traditions. As this collection demonstrates, the intellectual roots of this tradition run back to its founding.

The political ideas pioneered in these years by American socialists would exert a profound influence on the trajectory of Black struggle for much of the twentieth century. The CP's attempt to decisively unite the Black struggle for equality with the revolutionary workers' movement became, by the mid-1930s, a strategy contending for hegemony in the Black movement. For decades to follow, American radicals of many stripes saw the development of radical Black workers' organizations as a key task.[110]

At the same time, the Black Belt Thesis and its positing of Black Americans as an oppressed nation seeking self-determination found afterlives long after the CP officially dumped it in 1958. In the radicalization of the 1960s, Black nationalism returned with a force not seen since Garvey's movement in the 1920s, and analyses drawing on the framework of nations and self-determination once more were common currency. The national framework was bolstered both by black nationalists—who analogized black oppression in the United States to the struggle of the decolonizing nations of Africa—as well as Marxists. From the Black Panthers to the League of Revolutionary Black Workers, Black Marxists drew on metaphors of colonialism to describe the source of Black oppression.[111]

This strain of analysis carried with it both strengths and severe limitations. Its strength was identifying the causes of Black oppression as resolutely structural, rooted in economic relationships of exploitation. Its weaknesses, however, were devastating. While the analogy with national oppression had, since Lenin's time, helped socialists to understand the strategic importance of the Black liberation struggle, the purveyors of the colonial analysis tended to treat it less as an analogy and more as an equivalence. The result was a tendency to treat both the Black and white populations monolithically, as though white capitalists and workers alike benefited from Black exploitation, whereas Black workers and Black elites were bound together in a common subordinate status. This papering-over of class structures within each racial group served not only to cut black radicals of this era off from potential alliances with radicalizing white workers, but it also tended to obscure the threat posed by a rising Black elite class to liberation movements of all kinds. If the race-nation analogy in the early 1920s enabled socialists to approach the race question with new creativity, the identification of the two categories in the '60s and '70s became an ossified dogma that obscured some of the most basic facts about racial formation in the United States.[112]

Today, these frameworks have faded from the foreground of racial politics. The Black Lives Matter movement, at its height in 2014–15, brought radical activism against racial oppression back into American politics. At the same time, however, the long retreat of the American left was evident in the movement's politics. Strategic perspectives like internal colonialism or interracial workers' solidarity were, by and large, absent, replaced by academic frameworks such as "Afro-Pessimism," which achieved far wider currency. Even as the movement confronted spectacles like a Black mayor and Black district attorney in Baltimore crushing popular protest, the analytic frameworks that would allow it to analyze such processes failed to find popular articulation.[113]

In a moment like this, it is more necessary than ever to look back at the history of the left's attempts to confront the color line for perspective. To be sure, a number of points that were the subject of intense debate in the period covered in this book are, thankfully, dead letters today. For contemporary radicals, there is no debate over whether Black equality is a demand to be supported. Yet other debates from this period point to political problems that remain unsolved today. In particular, the vision that animated socialists from Hubert Harrison to Claude McKay to Robert Minor—the fusion of the movement for Black equality with radical workers' movement—remains elusive.

Today, as socialism finds new resonance with a nation confronting a dismal future of inequality, ecological devastation, and continued racial oppression, radicals have a chance to recover this perspective. I hope the words of those who pioneered this perspective can prove useful today to those who would continue their work. If socialists today can be as open, creative, and militant as their comrades were a century ago, a dark future can, perhaps, be brightened.

Part I
The Socialist Party

Eugene V. Debs

Introduction

Eugene V. Debs (1855–1926) was the single most important figure in the Socialist Party during its heyday. Four-time presidential candidate and perennial representative of the party on the lecture circuit, Debs carved out a political space as an American socialist beloved by workers far beyond party ranks that has not been occupied since his death. Throughout his long career, Debs distinguished himself through his tireless devotion to the working class, Black and white. In party debates on race, Debs was inevitably on the left wing, a fact that has been somewhat obscured by his infamous line, "We have nothing special to offer the Negro, and we cannot make separate appeals to all the races."

Debs began his political career as a railroad unionist. He distinguished himself as an advocate for industrial unionism, arguing that the different positions workers held in the industry—engineers, brakemen, and others— should amalgamate into one union as a way of enhancing bargaining strength and overcoming the tendencies toward sectionalism within the existing unions. Toward that end, he helped found the American Railway Union (ARU) in 1893. As head of the ARU, Debs argued for eliminating the color line in the union, an effort that was defeated by the union's white membership. In 1894, the union went to battle with the Pullman Company, one of the leading manufacturers of railway cars. The strike grew to involve a quarter of a million workers, prompting the federal government to intervene on the side of the company with an injunction against Debs and the union. Though it succeeded in crushing the strike, it also elevated Debs to the leading representative of American workers against rapacious nineteenth-century capitalism.

Years later, looking back on the Pullman strike, Debs would often note that the ARU's racism was a factor in its defeat. It was a lesson he would learn well, and for the rest of his life, Debs would be a forceful advocate for racial equality in the workers' movement.

While he was in prison for the Pullman strike, Debs was approached by Victor Berger, who convinced the jailed unionist to join his efforts to build a mass American socialist party. The two got to work immediately, going through a few organizations before finally, in 1901, founding the Socialist Party of America.

It was in the course of responding to the debates at the SP's founding that Debs would write his two most important statements on socialism and the color line. The resolution adopted at the 1901 founding convention professed the party's sympathy with the oppression Blacks faced, and invited Black workers to join the party. Southern delegates, in particular, were incensed by the resolution and made it the subject of some controversy over the following few years.

Debs responded to this controversy with a forceful defense of Black equality. His first article, "The Negro in the Class Struggle," from which the "nothing special to offer" line comes, is a full-throated condemnation of white racism. At the same time, Debs combines this opposition to racism with a decidedly underdeveloped sense of how the party should respond to racial oppression. While Debs is clear that party members would not suffer themselves "to be divided by any specious appeal to race prejudice," he also argued that there is no "Negro question" outside of the labor question and that the party cannot make special appeals to every race. This is the context in which his famous quote appears, and while it is certainly an unsatisfactory account of the relationship between Black liberation and class struggle, it is far indeed from the "colorblind" view often ascribed to Debs.

Debs's opposition to racism was unyielding for the rest of his career. He refused to speak before segregated audiences in the South and excoriated the hypocrisy that overlooked white men's abuses of Black women while lynching black men at the suggestion of interracial romance. Debs was also a radical on the subject of immigration, a topic that divided the socialist movement even more deeply than "the Negro question." Especially on the West Coast, socialists, along with most of the union movement, espoused a violent anti-Chinese racism that often manifested in race riots and violence. Debs denounced this accommodation to racism in no uncertain terms, declaring, "Away with the 'tactics' which require the exclusion of the oppressed and suffering slaves who seek these shores with the hope of bettering their wretched condition and are driven back under the cruel lash of expediency by those who call themselves Socialists."

Though Debs himself was a dedicated foe of racism in the party, he failed to ever force a real decision by the SP regarding where it stood on the issue. Thus, even as the party ran Debs for president election after election, it maintained in its leadership men like Morris Hillquit, a devotee of Chinese exclusion, and Victor Berger, an out-and-out racist against Black people. Over the period covered in this book, the party's ambivalence on the race question would cost it dearly, not least with the Black socialists who sought to make it their home.

Further Reading

Ginger, Ray. *The Bending Cross: A Biography of Eugene V. Debs.* Chicago: Haymarket Books, 2007.

Jones, William P. "'Nothing Special to Offer the Negro': Revisiting the 'Debsian View' of the Negro Question." *International Labor and Working-Class History* 74, no. 1 (2008): 212–24.

Salvatore, Nick. *Eugene V. Debs: Citizen and Socialist.* Champaign: University of Illinois Press, 1982.

The Negro in the Class Struggle (1903)

I t so happens that I write upon the Negro question, in compliance with the request of the editor of the *International Socialist Review*, in the state of Louisiana, where the race prejudice is as strong and the feeling against the "nigger" as bitter and relentless as when Lincoln's proclamation of emancipation lashed the waning Confederacy into fury and incited the final and desperate attempts to burst the bonds that held the southern states in the federal union. Indeed, so thoroughly is the south permeated with the malign spirit of race hatred that even Socialists are to be found, and by no means rarely, who either share directly in the race hostility against the Negro, or avoid the issue, or apologize for the social obliteration of the color line in the class struggle.

The white man in the south declares that "the nigger is all right in his place"; that is, as menial, servant and slave. If he dare hold up his head, feel the thrill of manhood in his veins and nurse the hope that some day may bring deliverance; if in his brain the thought of freedom dawns and in his heart the aspiration to rise above the animal plane and propensities of his sires, he must be made to realize that notwithstanding the white man is civilized (?) the black man is a "nigger" still and must so remain as long as planets wheel in space.

But while the white man is considerate enough to tolerate the Negro "in his place," the remotest suggestion at social recognition arouses all the pent-up wrath of his Anglo-Saxon civilization; and my observation is that the less real ground there is for such indignant assertion of self-superiority, the more passionately it is proclaimed.

At Yoakum, Texas, a few days ago, leaving the depot with two grips in my hands, I passed four or five bearers of the white man's burden perched on a railing and decorating their environment with tobacco juice. One of them,

---

Originally published in the *International Socialist Review* 4, no. 5 (November 1903): 257–60.

addressing me, said: "There's a nigger that'll carry your grips." A second one added: "That's what he's here for," and the third chimed in with "That's right, by God." Here was a savory bouquet of white superiority. One glance was sufficient to satisfy me that they represented all there is of justification for the implacable hatred of the Negro race. They were ignorant, lazy, unclean, totally void of ambition, themselves the foul product of the capitalist system and held in lowest contempt by the master class, yet esteeming themselves immeasurably above the cleanest, most intelligent and self-respecting Negro, having by reflex absorbed the "nigger" hatred of their masters.

As a matter of fact the industrial supremacy of the south before the war would not have been possible without the Negro, and the south of today would totally collapse without his labor. Cotton culture has been and is the great staple and it will not be denied that the fineness and superiority of the fibre that makes the export of the southern states the greatest in the world is due in large measure to the genius of the Negroes charged with its cultivation.

The whole world is under obligation to the Negro, and that the white heel is still upon the black neck is simply proof that the world is not yet civilized.

The history of the Negro in the United States is a history of crime without a parallel.

Why should the white man hate him? Because he stole him from his native land and for two centuries and a half robbed him of the fruit of his labor, kept him in beastly ignorance and subjected him to the brutal domination of the lash? Because he tore the black child from the breast of its mother and ravished the black man's daughter before her father's eyes?

There are thousands of Negroes who bear testimony in their whitening skins that men who so furiously resent the suggestion of "social equality" are far less sensitive in respect to the sexual equality of the races.

But of all the senseless agitation in capitalist society, that in respect to "social equality" takes the palm. The very instant it is mentioned the old aristocratic plantation owner's shrill cry about the "buck nigger" marrying the "fair young daughter" of his master is heard from the tomb and echoed and re-echoed across the spaces and repeated by the "white trash" in proud vindication of their social superiority.

Social equality, forsooth! Is the black man pressing his claims for social recognition upon his white burden bearer? Is there any reason why he should? Is the white man's social recognition of his own white brother such as to excite the Negro's ambition to covet the noble prize? Has the Negro any greater desire, or is there any reason why he should have, for social intercourse with the white man than the white man has for social relations with the Negro? This phase of the Negro question is pure fraud and serves to mask the real issue, which is not social equality, BUT ECONOMIC FREEDOM.

There never was any social inferiority that was not the shrivelled fruit of economic inequality.

The Negro, given economic freedom, will not ask the white man any social favors; and the burning question of "social equality" will disappear like mist before the sunrise.

I have said and say again that, properly speaking, there is no Negro question outside of the labor question—the working class struggle. Our position as Socialists and as a party is perfectly plain. We have simply to say: "The class struggle is colorless." The capitalists, white, black and other shades, are on one side and the workers, white, black and all other colors, on the other side.

When Marx said: "Workingmen of all countries unite," he gave concrete expression to the socialist philosophy of the class struggle; unlike the framers of the Declaration of Independence who announced that "all men are created equal" and then basely repudiated their own doctrine, Marx issued the call to all the workers of the globe, regardless of race, sex, creed or any other condition whatsoever.

As a social party we receive the Negro and all other races upon absolutely equal terms. We are the party of the working class, the whole working class, and we will not suffer ourselves to be divided by any specious appeal to race prejudice; and if we should be coaxed or driven from the straight road we will be lost in the wilderness and ought to perish there, for we shall no longer be a Socialist party.

Let the capitalist press and capitalist "public opinion" indulge themselves in alternate flattery and abuse of the Negro; we as Socialists will receive him in our party, treat him in our counsels and stand by him all around the same as if his skin were white instead of black; and this we do, not from any considerations of sentiment, but because it accords with the philosophy of Socialism, the genius of the class struggle, and is eternally right and bound to triumph in the end.

With the "nigger" question, the "race war" from the capitalist viewpoint we have nothing to do. In capitalism the Negro question is a grave one and will grow more threatening as the contradictions and complications of capitalist society multiply, but this need not worry us. Let them settle the Negro question in their way, if they can. We have nothing to do with it, for that is their fight. We have simply to open the eyes of as many Negroes as we can and bring them into the Socialist movement to do battle for emancipation from wage slavery, and when the working class have triumphed in the class struggle and stand forth economic as well as political free men, the race problem will forever disappear.

Socialists should with pride proclaim their sympathy with and fealty to the black race, and if any there be who hesitate to avow themselves in the face of ignorant and unreasoning prejudice, they lack the true spirit of the slavery-destroying revolutionary movement.

The voice of Socialism must be as inspiring music to the ears of those in bondage, especially the weak black brethren, doubly enslaved, who are bowed to the earth and groan in despair beneath the burden of the centuries.

For myself, my heart goes to the Negro and I make no apology to any white man for it. In fact, when I see the poor, brutalized, outraged black victim, I feel a burning sense of guilt for his intellectual poverty and moral debasement that makes me blush for the unspeakable crimes committed by my own race.

In closing, permit me to express the hope that the next convention may repeal the resolutions on the Negro question. The Negro does not need them and they serve to increase rather than diminish the necessity for explanation.

We have nothing special to offer the Negro, and we cannot make separate appeals to all the races.

The Socialist Party is the party of the working class, regardless of color—the whole working class of the whole world.

The Negro and His Nemesis (1904)

Since the appearance of my article on "The Negro in the Class Struggle" in the November Review I have received the following anonymous letter:

Elgin, Ill., November 25, 1903.

Mr. Debs:

Sir, I am a constant reader of the *International Socialist Review*. I have analyzed your last article on the Negro question with apprehension and fear. You say that the South is permeated with the race prejudice of the Negro more than the North. I say it is not so. When it comes right down to a test, the North is more fierce in the race prejudice of the Negro than the South ever has been or ever will be. I tell you, you will jeopardize the best interests of the Socialist Party if you insist on political equality of the Negro. For that will not only mean political equality but also social equality eventually. I do not believe you realize what that means. You get social and political equality for the Negro, then let him come and ask the hand of your daughter in marriage, "For that seems to be the height of his ambition," and we will see whether you still have a hankering for social and political equality for the Negro. For I tell you, the Negro will not be satisfied with equality with reservation. It is impossible for the Anglo-Saxon and the African to live on equal terms. You try it, and he will pull you down to his level. Mr. Lincoln, himself, said, that "There is a physical difference between the white and black races, which I believe will forever forbid them living together on terms of social and political equality." If the Socialist leaders stoop to this method to gain votes, then their policy and doctrine is as rotten and degraded as that of the Republican and Democratic parties, and I tell you, if the resolutions are adopted to give the

Originally published in the *International Socialist Review* 4, no. 7 (January 1904): 391–97.

African equality with the Anglo-Saxon you will lose more votes than you now think. I for my part shall do all I can to make you lose as many as possible and there will be others. For don't you know that just a little sour dough will spoil the whole batch of bread. You will do the Negro a greater favor by leaving him where he is. You elevate and educate him, and you will make his position impossible in the U.S.A. Mr. Debs, if you have any doubt on this subject, I beg you for humanity's sake to read Mr. Thomas Dixon's "The Leopard's Spots" and I hope that all others who have voiced your sentiments heretofore, will do the same.

I assure you, I shall watch the INTERNATIONAL SOCIALIST REVIEW with the most intense hope of a reply after you have read Mr. Thomas Dixon's message to humanity.

Respectfully yours,
So far a staunch member of the Socialist Party

The writer, who subscribed himself "A staunch member of the Socialist Party" is the only member of that kind I have ever heard of who fears to sign his name to, and accept responsibility for what he writes. The really "staunch" Socialist attacks in the open—he does not shoot from ambush.

The anonymous writer, as a rule, ought to be ignored, since he is unwilling to face those he accuses, while he may be a sneak or coward, traitor or spy, in the role of a "staunch Socialist," whose base design it is to divide and disrupt the movement. For reasons which will appear later, this communication is made an exception and will be treated as if from a known party member in good standing.

It would be interesting to know of what branch our critic is a member and how long he has been, and how he happened to become a "staunch member of the Socialist Party." That he is entirely ignorant of the philosophy of Socialism may not be to his discredit, but that a "staunch member" has not even read the platform of his party not only admits of no excuse, but takes the "staunchness" all out of him, punctures and discredits his foolish and fanatical criticism and leaves him naked and exposed to ridicule and contempt.

The Elgin writer has all the eminent and well recognized qualifications necessary to oppose Negro equality. His criticism and the spirit that prompts it harmonize delightfully with his assumed superiority.

That he may understand that he claims to be a "staunch member" of a party he knows nothing about I here incorporate the "Negro Resolutions" adopted by our last national convention, which constitute a vital part of the national platform of the Socialist Party and clearly defined its attitude toward the Negro:

NEGRO RESOLUTION

Whereas, The Negroes of the United States, because of their long training in slavery and but recent emancipation therefrom, occupy a peculiar position in the working class and in society at large;

Whereas, The capitalist class seeks to preserve this peculiar condition, and to foster and increase color prejudice and race hatred between the white worker and the black, so as to make their social and economic interests to appear to be separate and antagonistic, in order that the workers of both races may thereby be more easily and completely exploited;

Whereas, Both the old political parties and educational and religious institutions alike betray the Negro in his present helpless struggle against disfranchisement and violence, in order to receive the economic favors of the capitalist class. Be it, therefore,

Resolved, That we, the Socialists of America, in national convention assembled, do hereby assure our Negro fellow worker of our sympathy with him in his subjection to lawlessness and oppression, and also assure him of the fellowship of the workers who suffer from the lawlessness and exploitation of capital in every nation or tribe of the world. Be it further

Resolved, That we declare to the Negro worker the identity of his interests and struggles with the interests and struggles of the workers of all lands, without regard to race or color or sectional lines; that the causes which have made him the victim of social and political inequality are the effects of the long exploitation of his labor power; that all social and race prejudices spring from the ancient economic causes which still endure, to the misery of the whole human family, that the only line of division which exists in fact is that between the producers and the owners of the world—between capitalism and labor. And be it further

Resolved, That we the American Socialist Party, invite the Negro to membership and fellowship with us in the world movement for economic emancipation by which equal liberty and opportunity shall be secured to every man and fraternity become the order of the world.

But even without this specific declaration, the position of the party is so clear that no member and no other person of ordinary intelligence can fail to comprehend it.

The Socialist Party is the congealed, tangible expression of the Socialist movement, and the Socialist movement is based upon the modern class struggle in which all workers of all countries, regardless of race, nationality, creed or sex, are called upon to unite against the capitalist class, their common exploiter and oppressor. In this great class struggle the economic equality of all workers is a foregone conclusion, and he who does not recognize and subscribe to it as one of the basic principles of the Socialist philosophy is not a Socialist, and if a party member must have been admitted through misunderstanding or false pretense, he should be speedily set adrift, that he may return to the capitalist parties with their social and economic strata from the "white trash" and "buck nigger" *down* to the syphilitic snob and harlot heiress who barters virtue for title in the matrimonial market.

I did not say that the race prejudice in the South was more intense than in the North. No such comparison was made and my critic's denial is therefore unnecessary upon this point. Whether the prejudice of the South differs from that of the North is quite another question and entirely aside from the one at issue, nor is it of sufficient interest to consider at this time.

The Elgin writer says that we shall "jeopardize the best interests of the Socialist Party" if we insist upon the political equality of the Negro. I say that the Socialist Party would be false to its historic mission, violate the fundamental principles of Socialism, deny its philosophy and repudiate its own teachings if, on account of race considerations, it sought to exclude any human being from political equality and economic freedom. Then, indeed, would it not only "jeopardize" its best interests, but forfeit its very life, for it would soon be scorned and deserted as a thing unclean, leaving but a stench in the nostrils of honest men.

Political equality is to be denied the Negro, according to this writer, because it would lead to social equality, and this would be terrible— especially for those "white" men who are already married to Negro women and those "white" women who have long since picked the "buck nigger" in preference to the "white trash" whose social superiority they were unable to distinguish or appreciate.

Of course the Negro will "not be satisfied with equality with reservation." Why should he be? Would you?

Suppose you change places with the Negro just a year, then let us hear from you—"with reservation."

What now follows it is difficult to consider with patience: "You get social and political equality for the Negro, then let him come and ask the hand of your daughter in marriage."

In the first place *you* don't get equality for the Negro—*you* haven't got it yourself. In the present social scale there is no difference between you and the Negro—you are on the same level in the labor market, and the capitalist whose agent buys your labor power doesn't know and doesn't care if you are white or black, for he deals with you simply as *labor power*, and is uninterested save as to the quality and quantity you can supply. He cares no more about the color of your hide than does Armour about that of the steers he buys in the cattle market.

In the next place the Negro will fight for his own political and economic equality. He will take his place in the Socialist Party with the workers of all colors and all countries, and all of them will unite in the fight to destroy the capitalist system that now makes common slaves of them all.

Foolish and vain indeed is the workingman who makes the color of his skin the stepping-stone to his imaginary superiority. The trouble is with his head, and if he can get that right he will find that what ails him is not superiority but inferiority, and that he, as well as the Negro he despises, is the victim of wage-slavery, which robs him of what he produces and keeps both him and the Negro tied down to the dead level of ignorance and degradation.

As for "the Negro asking the hand of your daughter in marriage," that is so silly and senseless that the writer is probably after all justified in withholding his name. How about the daughter asking the hand of the Negro in marriage? Don't you know this is happening every day? Then, according to your logic, inferiority and degeneracy of the white race is established and the Negro ought to rise in solemn protest against political equality, lest the white man ask the hand of his daughter in marriage.

"It is impossible," continues our critic, "for the Anglo-Saxon and the African to live upon equal terms. You try it and he will pull you down to his level." Our critic must have tried something that had a downward pull, for surely that is his present tendency.

The fact is that it is impossible for the Anglo-Saxon and the African to live on *unequal* terms. A hundred years of American history culminating in the Civil War proves that. Does our correspondent want a repetition of the barbarous experiment?

How does the Anglo-Saxon get along with the Anglo-Saxon—leaving the Negro entirely out of the question? Do they bill and coo and love and caress each other? Is the Anglo-Saxon capitalist so devoted to his Anglo-Saxon wage-slave that he shares his burden and makes him the equal partner of his wealth and joy? Are they not as widely separated as the earth and sky, and do they not fight each other to the death? Does not the white capitalist look down with contempt upon the white wage-slave? And don't you know that the plutocrat would feel himself pretty nearly, if not quite as outrageously insulted to have his Anglo-Saxon wage slave ask the hand of his daughter in marriage as if that slave were black instead of white?

Why are you not afraid that some Anglo-Saxon engine-wiper on the New York Central will ask the hand of Vanderbilt's daughter in marriage?

What social distinction is there between a white and a black deck-hand on a Mississippi steamboat? Is it visible even with the aid of a microscope? They are both slaves, work side by side, sometimes a bunch of black slaves under a white "boss" and at other times a herd of white slaves under a black "boss." Not infrequently you have to take a second look to tell them apart—but all are slaves and all are humans and all are robbed by their "superior" white brother who attends church, is an alleged follower of Jesus Christ and has a horror of "social equality." To him "a slave is a slave for a' that"—when he bargains for labor power he is not generally concerned about the color of the package, but if he is, it is to give the black preference because it can be bought at a lower price in the labor market, in which equality always prevails—the equality of intellectual and social debasement. To paraphrase Wordsworth:

"A wage-slave by the river's brim
A simple wage-slave is to him
And he is nothing more."

The man who seeks to arouse prejudice among workingmen is not their friend. He who advises the white wage-worker to look down upon the black wage-worker is the enemy of both.

The capitalist has some excuse for despising the slave—he lives out of his labor, out of his life, and cannot escape his sense of guilt, and so he looks with contempt upon his victim.

You can forgive the man who robs you, but you can't forgive the man you rob—in his haggard features you read your indictment and this makes his face so repulsive that you must keep it under your heels where you cannot see it.

One need not experiment with "sour dough" nor waste any time on "sour" literature turned into "Leopard Spots" to arrive at sound conclusions upon these points, and the true Socialist delights not only in taking his position and speaking out, but in inviting and accepting without complaint all the consequences of his convictions, be they what they may.

Abraham Lincoln was a noble man, but he was not an abolitionist, and what he said in reference to the Negro was due regard to his circumscribed environs, and, for the time, was doubtless the quintessence of wisdom, but he was not an oracle who spoke for all coming ages, and we are not bound by what he thought prudent to say in a totally different situation half a century ago.

The Socialist platform has not a word in reference to "social equality." It declares in favor of political and economic equality, and only he who denies this to any other human being is unfit for it.

Socialism will give all men economic freedom, equal opportunity to work, and the full product of their labor. Their "social" relations will be free to regulate to suit themselves. Like religion this will be an individual matter and our Elgin Negro-hater can consider himself just as "superior" as he chooses, confine his social attentions exclusively to white folks, and enjoy his leisure time in hunting down the black spectre who is bent on asking his daughter's hand in marriage.

What warrant has he to say that the height of the Negro's ambition is to marry a white woman? No more than a Negro has to say that the height of a white woman's ambition is to marry a Negro. The number of such cases is about equally divided and it is so infinitesimally small that any one who can see danger to society in it ought to have his visual organs treated for progressive exaggeration.

The normal Negro has ambition to rise. This is to his credit and ought to be encouraged. He is not asking, nor does he need, the white man's social favors. He can regulate his personal associations with entire satisfaction to himself, without Anglo-Saxon concessions.

Suppose another race as much "superior" to the white as the white is to the black should drop from the skies. Would our Illinois correspondent at once fall upon his knees and acknowledge his everlasting inferiority, or would he seek to overcome it and rise to the higher plane of his superiors?

The Negro, like the white man, is subject to the laws of physical, mental and moral development. But in his case these laws have been suspended. Socialism simply proposes that the Negro shall have full opportunity to develop his mind and soul, and this will in time emancipate the race from animalism, so repulsive to those especially whose fortunes are built up out of it.

The African is here and to stay. How came he to our shores? Ask your grandfathers, Mr. Anonymous, and if they will tell the truth you will or should blush for their crimes.

The black man was stolen from his native land, from his wife and child, brought to these shores and made a slave. He was chained and whipped and robbed by his "white superior," while the son of his "superior" raped the black child before his eyes. For centuries he was kept in ignorance and debased and debauched by the white man's law.

The rape-fiend? Horrible!

Whence came he! Not by chance. He can be accounted for. Trace him to his source and you will find an Anglo-Saxon at the other end. There are no rape-maniacs in Africa. They are the spawn of civilized lust.

Anglo-Saxon civilization is reaping and will continue to reap what it has sown.

For myself, I want no advantage over my fellow man and if he is weaker than I, all the more is it my duty to help him.

Nor shall my door or my heart be ever closed against any human being on account of the color of his skin.

A.M. Simons

Introduction

Algie M. Simons (1870–1950) was a socialist writer and editor who was an important figure in the pre–World War I Socialist Party. Simons edited the *International Socialist Review* (*ISR*) for its first few years, helping to establish the journal as one of the premier socialist publications in the country. As factional disputes in the party heated up, Simons moved to the right, eventually working with Victor Berger on the *Milwaukee Leader*. Even Berger proved to be too far left for Simons during the war, however, and Simons was expelled from the party for his pro-war activism. The last few decades of his life were spent working as an economist for the American Medical Association.

Simons was born on a farm in Wisconsin and attended the University of Wisconsin at a time when socialist and progressive ideas had a strong presence on campus. After a few years working in social services, he joined the Socialist Labor Party (SLP), convinced that capitalism had to be eliminated. Simons's talents as a writer allowed him to rise through the ranks of the SLP rapidly, becoming a rival of the group's notoriously intemperate leader, Daniel De Leon. When Simons sided with the factions of the SLP, led by Morris Hillquit, who wanted unity with Eugene Debs's Social Democracy of America, he and his allies were driven from the party.

Pursuing unity with the Debsians, Simons was a delegate to the 1901 Socialist Unity conference that established the Socialist Party. There, he sided with the far left of the conference, arguing against the struggle for reforms. In Simons's view, capitalism had run out of room to provide reforms to the working class, and calling for reform would only divert the class from its goal of revolution. At the conference, Simons's view lost out, and the SP endorsed a number of reform planks.

Around the same time, Simons was invited to become editor of *International Socialist Review* by Charles H. Kerr, the journal's publisher. Simons would remain editor until 1908, nurturing the journal through its formative years to establish it as the leading intellectual journal of American socialism.

In 1908, political conflicts between Simons and Kerr, who had become increasingly sympathetic to the IWW, came to a head, and Simons was forced to resign. Over the next few years, he worked as editor of a number of different socialist publications, eventually settling in Milwaukee at Victor Berger's *Milwaukee Leader*. Simons had moved from opposing reforms altogether to allying himself with a socialist who identified socialism with reform and nothing more.

When World War I broke out, Simons initially supported the SP's antiwar stance. As the war progressed, however, he moved fairly quickly to a pro-British position. He took a job with a pro-war organization in Wisconsin, and began explicitly working against his SP comrades. When the party passed its 1917 St. Louis Manifesto against the war, Simons tried to use it as evidence to have the party repressed. He was quickly expelled.

From there, Simons moved steadily to the right, refusing even to ally himself with the large group of pro-war socialists who had left the party. By the mid-1920s, he had left the socialist movement behind altogether.

Simons's article "The Negro Problem" was part of an exchange in the early issues of the *ISR*. Simons's essay was followed by articles by Charles H. Vail, Clarence Darrow, and William Noyes. Of these, Simons's is the most analytically substantive. The essay is distinguished primarily by two main lines of argument. First, Simons is quite clear that Black Americans are the victims of prejudice and oppression. Second, in Simons's analysis, black people are victims only. Throughout his essay, he sees Black Americans as being manipulated by Northern politicians during the Civil War and Reconstruction, and by capitalists in his contemporary society. The struggle for freedom by African Americans themselves simply plays no part in his analysis. As such, his endorsement of Black equality in the essay is profoundly limited by a paternalistic conception of how that equality could be achieved.

Further Reading

Glaser, William A. "Algie Martin Simons and Marxism in America." *Mississippi Valley Historical Review* 41, no. 3 (1954): 419–34.

Kreuter, Kent, and Gretchen Kreuter. *An American Dissenter: The Life of Algie Martin Simons 1870–1950.* Lexington: University Press of Kentucky, 2015.

Marti, Donald B. "Answering the Agrarian Question: Socialists, Farmers, and Algie Martin Simons." *Agricultural History* 65, no. 3 (1991): 53–69.

The Negro Problem

A series of events running through several years and leading up to a climax within the last few months have served to bring the "negro question" prominently before the public. The succession of terrible outrages committed in the Southern states—the burning and torturing of defenseless negroes, often innocent, and always without form of trial—have attracted universal attention. The horrible barbarities accompanying these scenes—the slow roasting alive of human beings, the tearing to pieces of the still quivering bodies and the distribution of portions of them among the mob as "souvenirs"—all this bore witness to the fact that capitalism had developed within itself a body of demons more ferocious than African head-hunters or prehistoric savages.

Perhaps the feature of these horrors that impressed the ordinary observer trained to capitalist methods of thought was that throughout the portion of the country in which these ghastly orgies took place the so-called "respectable" or bourgeois element of society, who are supposed to be the especial conservators of "morality" and "law and order" apologized for, excused or openly encouraged such acts. Still further, at the same time that these outrages were being inflicted upon a helpless people these same bourgeois pillars of society were conspiring to take away their only means of legal defense—the ballot. Apparently more remarkable still, although the votes thus destroyed were almost wholly Republican, that party made no emphatic or significant protest against such action. On the contrary, the last few weeks have seen the beginning of a series of outbreaks against the negroes in Northern cities, that for unreasoning brutal violence rival those that have gained so much notoriety for the Southern states. New York, Brooklyn, and Akron, Ohio, have been the seats of "race riots" as ferocious as those of the South, and it was apparently only the lack of opportunity that prevented

Originally published in the *International Socialist Review* 1, no. 4 (October 1900): 204–11.

the perpetration of equally hideous barbarities. Here, too, the "authorities" and "respectable citizens" lent open sympathy, if not active assistance, to the perpetrators of the outrages. In New York City it was especially noted that the police often lent assistance in the beating of the helpless negroes.

These are the phenomena with which we are confronted. It now remains to find an explanation. To do this it will be necessary to pass hastily in review the various phases that the "negro problem" has assumed in American history.

During the pre-revolutionary period those who sought to live upon the labor of others found themselves confronted with the problem which always arises in a new country where natural opportunities are not yet wholly monopolized by a possessing, employing class. Such opportunities being open to all and capable of utilization with simple individually-owned tools, everyone can secure the full product of his labor in this crude form of production, and there is no class whose members are compelled to sell themselves to the owning class in order to live. This is the situation at present in the S. African diamond fields, and the Philippine Islands. In all of these cases it was found necessary to introduce some form of chattel slavery until the natural opportunities could be sufficiently monopolized to make it impossible for anyone possessing nothing but his labor power to exist without selling himself into wage-slavery.

In America all attempts to reduce the Indians to slavery having failed, recourse was had to Europe and white "indentured servants" and negro slaves were imported. Owing to a variety of circumstances, such as the long Winters, an increasingly intensive system of agriculture, a more concentrated population, hemmed in by natural features and hostile Indian tribes, and the growth of a trading class, there soon arose in the North a body of men who were compelled to sell themselves into wage-slavery while at the same time life ownership of the slave became unprofitable.

Under these circumstances chattel slavery became "immoral" and the New England Puritans "freed their slaves," and thus avoided the burden of their support at unprofitable periods of the year, while they well knew that monopolized opportunities would keep them close at hand eager to sell themselves for a limited period when needed. This left the highly moral New Englander free to organize "abolition" societies and carry New England rum to the Gold coast with which to buy the "black ivory" so much in demand in the Southern states.

With the settling up of the great West the two systems came into conflict, and, the Northern capitalist being in the ascendant in Congress, cut off one source of supply to the slave market by forbidding the further importation of chattel slaves. At the same time he began in every possible way to encourage the importation of wage-slaves for the Northern labor market. The following table, giving the number of immigrants by ten-year periods from 1821, will show the extent to which this form of labor was imported:

Years	Number immigrants.
1821–1830	143,439
1831–1840	599,125
1841–1850	1,713,251
1851–1860	2,598,214
1861–1870	2,314,824
1871–1880	2,812,191
1881–1890	5,246,613
Grand total, 1821–1890	15,427,657

Since that time the economic conditions here having become practically identical with those of Europe, and there consequently being no particular incentive to the immigrant upon the one hand to come, nor to the capitalist upon the other to encourage his coming, immigration has fallen off considerably.

By the late '50s the two forms of labor in the United States were in sharp conflict. Each owner was eager for new fields for his slaves to exploit. The resulting struggle was a testimonial to the wisdom of the Northern capitalist in choosing wage in preference to chattel slavery, for he was able to inspire a portion of his "hands" with "patriotism" and send them forth to fight his battles, while those who remained at home to work for him were immensely more profitable than the Southern chattel slaves.

At the close of the Civil War, when the victory was won the conquerors wished to revel in the spoils of the conquered and complete the humiliation of their fallen foe. As instruments to that purpose they chose the former chattel slaves, and through a series of constitutional amendments gave them full political equality with their late owners. With the mock morality that has ever marked all dealings with the helpless negro since the time he was brought from Africa to "enjoy the blessings of a Christian civilization" this was nominally done for the protection of the former chattel slaves. But precious little good it has done him up to the present time, and when he does show some signs of using it for his own good it is promptly taken away.

In the "reconstruction period" immediately following the war the negro was but the helpless tool of the horde of Northern "carpet-baggers" who rode upon his back through the prostrate, defenseless South to a career of plunder and pillage that had scarce been equaled since the days of Alaric or Atilla. And this period, when the helpless blacks were but mute tools in the hands of a new and more unscrupulous set of masters, is known in history by the bitterly ironical name of the "period of negro domination."

With the passage of time the South too began to be capitalistic and the interests of the ruling classes of the two sections, North and South, became the same. Both desired submissive wage-slaves. The troops were withdrawn from the South by President Hayes and the Southern employers were left to treat their black wage-slaves as they chose. Steps were at once taken to disenfranchise the negroes. At first this was accomplished by the clumsy methods of intimidation and fraud. These were the days of the Ku Klux Klan, the "tissue ballot" and the "shot-gun campaign."

But shortly after this, great industrial changes began to take place in the South. The great superiority of wage over chattel slavery from the point of view of the employer began to make itself felt. Factories of all kinds sprang up throughout the South. A quotation from the "Textile World" of July, 1900, will give some idea of one phase of this movement:

> The Southern group of states now operated 5,815,429 spindles and the Northern mills 15,242,554. In 1890 the South had 1,828,982 and the North 12,721,341. The actual increase in the number of spindles in the South in ten years is 3,986,447, a gain of 217 per cent. The actual increase in Northern states is 2,521,213, a gain of 19.8 per cent.

These figures and the movement they represent offer one more proof of the fact that when slaves are bidding against one another in the labor market for a job they are much more docile and profitable to the slave owner than when masters are bidding against each other to secure possession of the slaves. They will work harder to fit themselves for their masters' work and are no expense to him save when actually engaged in production. At first only white laborers were used in the new Southern industries. The "poor whites" and "crackers" who fought so valiantly from '61 to '65, that their rich neighbors might have the right to own black laborers for life, are now pouring into the cities to fight each other for the chance to sell their own bodies and brains for such periods as they can make themselves profitable to their buyers. Unorganized, composed mostly of women and children, helpless, untrained to resistance, with a low standard of life in a semi-tropical climate, wages are soon forced down to the subsistence point, hours lengthened to the limit of endurance, and abuses of all kinds multiplied until the terrible horrors of the early days of the English factory system are almost duplicated today in many a Georgia, Alabama or Mississippi cotton factory.

But the black can live even cheaper than the white, and so another phase is given to the "negro question." Says a writer in the *Forum* for June, 1898:

> A notion is abroad in the South that the negro could not work in the cotton mill. . . . But there is no rational ground for this belief. Negroes now work day and night in the tobacco factories and display marvelous dexterity and deftness in the use of their fingers. Of course unusual risks must attend the first venture with dark labor in a cotton mill. All new mills must employ some experienced hands to start with; and if a manufacturer undertook to start with negro help he could not bring in white laborers to teach them, owing to the unwillingness of the whites to commingle with the other race. He would have to start with all raw workers; and if the business failed, the fact that negroes had lived in the tenement houses would render it almost impossible to get decent white laborers to occupy them. However, the ice will soon be broken. A mill in Charlestown is already running with dark labor, and another is now building at Concord, North Carolina, to be run exclusively by the same kind of labor. If these experiments prove successful, then indeed will the South have a never-failing fountain of cheap labor.

These experiments have proven successful, as anyone who had followed the course of capitalist development could have foretold from the beginning. Deficiency of education and incompetency will not long prove serious obstacles. Lured on by the will-o'-the-wisp hope of economic advance that has for these many years sufficed to lure the white worker into the swamps of capitalism, the negro is crowding into Tuskegee, Berea, Hampton, and a host of other "colleges" and "training schools," where he is fitted to better serve the purposes of his new capitalist masters.

These developments have for the first time made the negro an essential element of the capitalist system. The "negro question" has completed its evolution into the "labor problem." This at once made itself felt in two directions. Of one of these, the introduction of the developed factory system into the South, we have already spoken. The other was the use of the negro by Northern capitalists to break the resistance of organized labor. At Pana, Virden and the Chicago Packing Houses, and at various other points, strikes of organized white labor have been followed by the wholesale importation of negro "scabs." Their presence added the fury of race prejudice to the natural hatred of union and non-union men and was the occasion of bloody race riots.

This race hatred was in itself a valuable thing for the capitalist class. When the negro entered the field of modern industry as a wage-slave his interests were for the first time in his history completely identical with those of his fellow white laborers. It was of the utmost importance to the laborers that the two races should act together in harmonious, united resistance to the demands of the employing owning class. But, as is always the case, the class interests of the capitalists and laborers being diametrically opposite, it was of the greatest importance to the material interests of the capitalist class that this race hatred and prejudice be fomented and increased in every manner possible.

Hence it is that whenever the two races are introduced to each other in the course of capitalism, it is under conditions tending in every way to embitter their natural hatred. The negro is brought in as a scab at a time when passion is running high against any who dares to betray the cause of labor, or else, as in the Coeur d'Alene, he comes as a part of the regular army to act as the tool of oppression and capitalist outrage upon his fellow white worker. In the South there was little need of active encouragement of race hatred. It was only necessary to give natural savagery full sway whenever a negro was accused of any crime and occasionally permit a few of the "best citizens" to take part in a "negro hunt" with all its accompaniments of brutal bestiality.

This fact that the material interests of the ruling class are in accord with the excitation and continuance of race hatred accounts for the comparative acquiescence by the Northern people in outbreaks of savage ferocity throughout the South, which did they occur in Turkey or China would at once be considered as grounds for "armed intervention" on the part of capitalist government. The capitalist interests of the North and South are now in accord with the prejudices of the old plantation owners in opposition to "negro domination"—as if the dice had ever dominated the hand that threw them, or it was of any advantage to the spades in a pack of cards to be used as trumps.

But if something is not done it will not be very long before the negroes, who are now meeting the same problems, bearing the same burdens and groaning beneath the same form of slavery as their white fellow toilers, will begin to realize the fact of the solidarity of interests which unites the workers of the world. The history of the world has shown that no difference of race, religion, color or politics is able to maintain itself permanently against the terrible leveling influence of capitalism. Hence the time cannot be far away when the white and black laborers of the United States will join hands in their unions to resist economic tyranny (indeed, the process is already well advanced), and there are even signs that the time may be closer than we think when the fact of the common economic interests will find expression in common political action and a joint protest against the entire capitalist system.

Under these circumstances every material interest of the ruling class both North and South pointed to one course of action—the excitation of race hatred, followed by disenfranchisement of the negro before he could intelligently protest. Hence the open encouragement or silent approval of negro lynchings, burnings and torturings, the quiet acquiescence by the "authorities" in negro riots in Northern cities, and, most significant of all, the general acceptance of wholesale disenfranchisement of the black laborers. Ten years ago any suggestion of such a disenfranchisement on the part of the Democratic party would have been met with a howl from every Republican spell-binder or editorial scribbler from Maine to Oregon. Today the party of Bryanism can stand upon the proposition that "all governments derive their just powers from the consent of the governed" and at the same time take away from 500,000 American citizens all opportunity of protest or participation in the government beneath which they must live, and the Republican party scarcely utters a growl.

To anyone foolish enough to think that the Republican Party really desires the enfranchisement of the negro it can be shown that, on the contrary, it would much rather see William Jennings Bryan elected to the Presidential chair than to in any way interfere with the economic or political slavery of any portion of the laboring class. Did they really desire to defeat Bryan or defend the negro they could accomplish both at one stroke by wiping 34 electoral votes completely off the Bryan side of the slate.[†] The Constitution provides that "when the right to vote at any election . . . is denied to any of the male members of such state, being twenty-one years of age, and citizens of the United States, or in any way abridged, except for participation in rebellion or other crime, the basis of representation therein shall be reduced in the proportion which the number of such male citizens shall bear to the whole number of male citizens twenty-one years of age in such state." But no step has been or will be taken to enforce this provision because ever since the time when the Democratic party ceased to be semi-feudalistic and became purely capitalistic, the two parties have agreed to perfection upon the point of keeping the worker in helpless subjection. When the "negro question" became the "labor problem" both parties joined hands against the worker.

---

[*]   In the *North American Review* for 1899 complete figures of the extent of disenfranchisement up to that time are given. The following table giving the vote in three of the Southern states in 1876 and again in 1898 is taken from this article and shows to what extent both white and black laborers have been disenfranchised. —PH

[†]

VOTE OF 1876	Republican	Democratic	Total
Louisiana	75,315	70,508	145,823
Mississippi	52,705	112,143	164,848
South Carolina	92,981	91,540	184,521
Totals	220,001	274,191	495,192
VOTE OF 1898	Republican	Democratic	Total
Louisiana	5,667	27,629	33,296
Mississippi	3,573	23,804	27,377
South Carolina	2,823	28,970	31,793
Totals	12,063	80,403	92,466

This indicates a falling off during these 22 years in the Republican vote of 807,938 or over 94 percent, and in the Democratic vote of 183,788 or 67 percent or a total falling off in votes of 401,826, or over 81 percent. But this does not tell the whole truth, as this has been a time of rapid growth in population in these states especially since the new industrial development. Says the writer in the North American Review quoted above: "According to the census of 1890 there were 797,249 males of voting age in these three states, of whom 854,016 were whites and 403,233 were colored. The natural increase from births and immigration must have brought the total up to 900.000 and the white voters to about 400,000."

I.M. Rubinow

Introduction

saac Max Rubinow (1875–1936) was an American statistician and economist who was also a member of the Socialist Party. Known primarily for helping inspire Social Security, Rubinow was also a prolific author with the socialist press before World War I, contributing the longest discussion of the race question the SP press published during those years.

Rubinow was born in Russia and came to the United States as a teenager, shortly before the turn of the century. Originally intending to become a doctor, Rubinow found that the poverty in which his patients lived was at least as injurious to their health as the diseases they suffered, and switched to studying economics instead.

By 1904, Rubinow had joined the Socialist Party. In that year, he wrote to W.E.B. Du Bois, sounding out the Black intellectual for his feelings on socialism. Rubinow argued that "the actual foundation of the race prejudice is the desire of the stronger to exploit the weaker, though of course historical causes have contributed to the survival of these prejudices." He also shared his opinions on Booker T. Washington, suggesting that Washington's strategy of accommodation provided remedy "for the *few*, while what is necessary is relief for the *many*." Du Bois, though confessing sympathy with the socialists, replied that he was still some way off from embracing Rubinow's beliefs.

In 1908, Rubinow began his series of articles on the race question in the *International Socialist Review*. Eventually running to well over a hundred pages, Rubinow's articles provided a detailed history of Black Americans through slavery and emancipation. The series concludes with a challenge to socialists, arguing that though the connection between Black liberation and socialism was not obvious or automatic, it was necessary, and that the party would have to work to build a base among black workers.

After the beginning of World War I, Rubinow's links to the socialist movement become less clear. His work as an economist continued to bring him attention, and in the 1930s he was pivotal in making the case for Social Security. In the socialist press, his work disappears.

Further Reading

Brown, Theodore M., and Elizabeth Fee. "Isaac Max Rubinow: Advocate for Social Insurance." *American Journal of Public Health* 92, no. 8 (2002): 1224–1225.

Dorrien, Gary. *The New Abolition: WEB Du Bois and the Black Social Gospel*. New Haven: Yale University Press, 2015.

Foner, Philip S. *American Socialism and Black Americans: From the Age of Jackson to World War II*. Westport, CT: Greenwood Press, 1977.

Economic Aspects of the Negro Problem The Solution: A Prophecy and a Remedy (Part I) (1910)

WAS IST der langen Rede kurzer Sinn?

This is to be the last installment of the drawn out series of my studies on the Negro problem. I can almost hear both the editor and the patient reader of the entire series (if there be any such person) drawing deep sighs of relief. I sometimes feel as if I had played a successful confidence game upon both the editor and the reader. For surely Comrade Kerr would never had agreed to accept a series of fifteen articles about the forsaken negro, for whom we have until now shown so very little concern.

Ah, but there is the rub. Has the socialist done his duty by the Negro in this country? And what may perhaps appeal more strongly to the class-conscious socialist, has he done his duty by the American working class and by the socialist movement in thus neglecting the negro? And even if my articles have accomplished nothing more than to continually remind the American socialists of this tremendous social and economic problem, a problem of exploitation of labor, I still cannot help flattering myself that my efforts were worth while. For it is unfortunately true that in the North the vast majority of the socialists are entirely oblivious to the existence of the problem, while in the South the socialist's attitude often characterizes Southerner rather than him as a socialist.

But surely the socialist attitude on this problem cannot be a purely academic one. To him, as to every thinking American for that matter, it must not only be an interesting problem but one of tremendous vital importance. The question is not only: "What will the Southerner do to solve that problem?" or

---

Originally published in the *International Socialist Review* 10, no. 11 (May 1910): 1010–20.

"What will the negro do to solve the problem?" or "What will happen to solve the problem?" but "What will we do to help solve it?" And what will the problem bring to the struggle of the American working class for his emancipation? What will the effect of the ten million negroes be upon the social evolution of the country? In short, what will be the solution of the Negro Problem? And what can and ought the socialist contribute to this solution?

It was for the very object of formulating an answer to these questions that I have planned my series of studies, but now that I have reached the final stage, I confess that I face the duty of giving a solution with a good deal of apprehension. It is an accepted maxim of medical science that when a long list of remedies is recommended for a disease, the disease is probably an incurable one, or at least that remedy has not yet been discovered. For the real remedy is usually found, when discovered, to be a simple and specific one.

What is a solution to a social problem, anyway? And to go back one step further, what is a social problem? In the entire vernacular of the publicist there is scarcely a more useful, more convenient and more abused word.

A social problem, we take it, is a condition of social maladjustment. Its manifestations are discomfort and pain, finding outward expression in dissatisfaction and complaints. A problem is therefore a truly objective social fact, in so far as the subjective impression of pain or discomfort find objective expression. To some white southern gentlemen the position of the negro in the South may present no problem at all, for they may feel that they "have got the negro just where they want him." But even if all the millions of white persons inhabiting the South thought so (which they don't), the problem would still persist, as long as the ten millions of negroes still remain dissatisfied, still suffer discomfort and pain.

From this point of view there never will cease to be problems in social life, and efforts at their solution will forever agitate the minds and hearts of sentient beings, for only in death would there be complete adjustment and absence of all friction. Nevertheless, individual problems must some day be solved, for, in the words of the immortal Spencer, unstable equilibrium constantly tends to become a stable equilibrium. For life (social as well as individual) is a continuous process of adjustment of internal relations to external relations, and the adjustment is not perfect, as long as some pain exists.

As my previous articles have to some extent indicated, an enormous literature on the negro question exists in this country, and seldom a book or even an article is written, without containing a "solution" of the problem carefully outlined, and a very long list of such "solutions" may easily be quoted. That the problem still exists, that the pain and discomfort still exist, may be claimed by these physicians of the ills of the body politic to be due to the fact that in its blindness society has not yet resolved to apply this or that solution. But the difficulty of applying this or that "remedy," and the vast difference between the "remedies" lie in the fact, that not only the "remedies" but also the results accomplished vastly differ as between one self-appointed doctor and another. And just here lies the great difference between bodily and social ills. Physicians may differ in their remedies, but the object which they strive to accomplish is presumable a definite one—to bring the suffering patient to health and vigor. But the aims of the many solutions of the negro problem are different and contradictory.

When a discussion of an important social problem is led up to the final "solution"—one of the three methods may be pursued:

1. We may simply picture things as they ought to be, in contrast to things as they are, we may picture the social ideal and stop at that. This method is used more frequently than the reading public is conscious of, and when clothed in sufficiently eloquent phraseology, often receives a cordial welcome, especially when the wishes of the writer agree with those of the reader. Socialists and other honest social idealists have more frequently sinned in that direction than practical politicians. "Some time, when I do not know, or how, or where, but some time, there will be perfect equality upon the earth," concludes C.S. Darrow in his article on "the Problem of the Negro" (*International Socialist Review*, Nov, 1907).

2. A specific plan of action for the solution of the negro problem may be offered. Obviously this plan will depend upon what is considered the desirable solution of the problem. And in actual practice these plans are so strongly influenced by what appears to be desirable from an individual or class point of view that all considerations of probability or feasibility are forgotten. Thus a big volume of nearly 600 pages recently appeared (*The Negro Problem. Abraham Lincoln's Solution*. By William P. Pickett) which carefully elaborates in all its minutest details the plan of forcible deportation of the negroes—a plan economically unthinkable, legally impossible, ethically monstrous in the twentieth century.

It is the only scientific solution, but unfortunately it is impossible—quoth a student in biology. What a fruitful conception of sociological science, that permits the impossible to be scientific!

3. An effort may be made to throw a glance into the future, to give a forecast as to the probable development of the social relation under the influence of conditions and forces studied. To one who accepts the doctrine of economic interpretation of history, or at least believes in the applicability of the law of causation to social as well as to physical phenomena—such a glimpse promises some results, though the virtue of accuracy may not be claimed for it. It is true that often "the wish is the father of the thought," but on the other hand, prophecies are not always necessarily hopeful ones. Spencer, after fighting the doctrines of Socialism for many years nevertheless finished by writing a book on the "Coming slavery" admitting thus that the Cooperative Commonwealth was coming, though to him it was slavery nevertheless.

Thus a solution of a social problem as usually given, is either an ideal, a remedy or a prophecy, but a true solution should be all these things together. It should draw an ideal that is practical, present a remedy that should be useful, and make a prophecy that should be acceptable to our sense of justice as well as satisfy our curiosity as to the future, for unless it does satisfy our sense of justice, the prophecy may be a true prophecy, yet it fails to be a solution.

Before we start at the constructive part of our conclusions, however, it is necessary to pass the solutions offered in a rapid review.

What are the ideals offered concerning the future of the race relations in this country and the future of the negro race?

Three, and only three solutions, may offer themselves as final, i.e., such solutions as will do away with the negro problem. Of course, I am fully conscious of the fact, that such a complete solution, no matter what it is, will not be for a great many years or decades. But theoretically that is immaterial. We must have the final ideal not because we can immediately strike out for it, but so that we may know what to do, in order to keep getting nearer to it, and not away from it. This—in our opinion—is equally true of socialism itself.

The future of the negro may be imagined to assume one of the three following ideal forms: 1) a definite relegation of the negro to the position of an inferior, and acquiescence in that situation by everybody concerned; 2) the elimination of the negro from the life of the American people either by removal or by territorial segregation, and finally, 3) the absolute destruction of all discrimination against the negro, and the achievement by the negro of full civic political and social rights.

The faithful may be surprised at the failure to mention socialism. But, formally at least, these two problems are unrelated. Their connection, if any, is not logical, but historical and must be established. It is easy to conceive of a solved negro problem in a capitalist society, or at least the absence of all racial friction in such a society; it is also possible to conceive, though perhaps somewhat less easily, of a negro problem, or some race discrimination surviving after the introduction of a cooperative commonwealth, as for instance the relegation of all negro citizens to the worst paying occupations. This is all hypothetical of course, but it is purposely stated here to underscore the fact that the connection between race justice and socialism is not self-evident. It is not enough to assert, "Socialism is the only remedy," as did Charles H. Vail in his article in the *Intern. Soc. Review* for Feb, 1901—the historical and economic connection of it exists, must be established.

Let us therefore meet the solutions offered in a fair spirit, forgetting for the time our Socialist hopes and aspirations, and see which one of the three is at all feasible and offers the promised solution.

1) **Recognition of and acquiescence in inferiority.** That, according to the practically unanimous Southern opinion, is the only acceptable solution. Acceptable to whom? Why, to the white Southerner of course. Do the negroes like it? Some do, and some don't. The old antebellum darkeys, or the ignorant, illiterate, brutal plantation hands are willing to accept this, perhaps. But the new, "impudent" negro, the college negro, the professional negro, the business negro and the industrial negro worker do not accept it, and their number is growing all the time, while the antebellum negro and even the next generation will have died out in another 30–50 years. Education and economic growth in their mutual interaction, will rapidly increase the number of dissatisfied and rebellious negroes. And even if it was possible to repress the rebellious 10,000,000 negroes by armed force, can that be considered a "solution"?

Can that result ever, if possible, be considered desirable from any point of view of human progress? Can repression by brutal force of the desires and aspirations of millions of human beings, be thinkable in a democratic society? Human beings, to whom, as we have conclusively shown, nothing human is foreign, who have shown themselves fully fit to partake of all the fruits of our culture and civilization? Even among the Southerners, or at least the most intelligent of them, the consciousness is growing that this effort to hold half of their citizenship in suppression, is no less destructive of their moral and mental growth, than was slavery up to fifty years ago. The recognition-of-inferiority theory may be claimed to be a true prophecy, and it certainly is that, if only the immediate future is considered, but it is utterly devoid of all elements of a social ideal. It is not a thing worth striving for.

2) **The elimination of the negro.** In a purely abstract way, this has the elements of a true solution. That is, were it possible to actually remove all the persons of African descent to some other country, this would bring about a complete solution of the negro problem in this country. In the same way, the killing off all these 10,000,000 negroes would be a true solution. Spain once solved its Jewish problem by forcibly ejecting all its Jews. Russia tried to solve its Jewish problem by killing off its Jews. I suppose this is what my friend the biologist meant by his statement that the elimination of the negro would be the only true scientific solution if it were possible. Of course, from the point of view of Justice, we might as well propose to kill them, as to eject them forcibly from a land, in which they have acquired a proprietary interest by a longer residence than the majority of the white persons inhabiting it.

If it were possible! Is it possible? In a democratic country, whose entire social and political philosophy is based upon the recognition of certain inalienable rights of the individual? For to all the proposals for voluntary emigration the simple reply is sufficient that such emigration is not contemplated, is not given even a serious thought to.

But even supposing that all the organic, constitutional difficulties in the way of such plan were removed, could this solution by accomplished? Spain removed the Jews because it feared their economic power. Russia, (barring the demagogic reasons for Jew baiting) has the same fear of the commercial abilities of the Jews. But what is the greatest objection to the negro now? Not only in this country, but in the African colonies as well? That he does not want to eliminate himself? No, just the opposite, that he does not stay in one place, that he does not always prove himself a patient and reliable source of exploitation! Not only forcible removal, but even a peaceful propaganda among the Southern negroes for voluntary emigration to Africa would not be tolerated by the vast majority of Southerners.

The proposal of elimination is neither an ideal nor a prophecy, though it is a remedy,— it is only a quack remedy.

3) **Territorial Segregation.** Most of these arguments are applicable against the proposed segregation of the negroes within some of the states within

this Union, a solution, which the famous English critic William Archer has recently advocated with a great deal of enthusiasm and conviction characteristic of a very superficial knowledge of the problem. Because of the weight of Archer's name and the eloquence of his plea, a popular monthly has readily published and probably handsomely paid for this contribution. But neither the South nor the North, neither the negro nor the white has shown any enthusiasm or even any interest for the plan. And for a very good reason—for it is a remedy that has neither the qualities of an ideal for any considerable element of the population, nor is there the slightest indication that historical tendencies are moving in that direction. It is an invented prescription, and no such prescriptions have been worth the paper they were written on in sociological problems. It was shown in one of the preceding installments of the series that the tendencies were exactly in the opposite direction, toward a scattering of the negro population. Not only does it contain all the unsatisfactory elements of forcible emigration, in depriving Southern capital of a large supply of cheap labor,—but it is much more open to attack, for even abstractly does it not produce the desired "solution," but by concentrating the negro power, would give stronger expression to their dissatisfaction. And as for constitutional difficulties—only a foreign mind, utterly oblivious to the legal foundations of the structure of this nation, could suggest the introduction of the Russian "Pale of Settlement" doctrine, brought down from the Middle Ages to a twentieth century democratic republic,—a "pale of settlement" doctrine with the concomitant feature—the denial of personal right of free travel, perhaps a passport system, and local police boards for rendering ethnographic decisions as to the racial status of doubtful individuals.

4) **Equalization of the negro status** with that of the white man, is evidently the only solution that can be classed as such—that will really solve the problem, i.e., receive this one problem as a source of social friction. It is the only solution that meets the requirements of a social ideal. It is the only solution, of which ten million negroes are dreaming, to which all their leaders are leading, no matter what different roads they chose, no matter how carefully they disguise their ultimate hopes.

But if satisfactory to the oppressed racial element, is it, or can it ever be satisfactory to the oppressing Caucasian Race? Is it, can it ever become the ideal of both sides to the controversy? That is, of course, the crucial point upon which our ideals must depend. Not that our opinions or wishes are really decisive of historical and sociological processes. But surely they are not without some influence, either of a stimulating or of a retarding nature. And in any case, disregarding blind elemental social forces, we are now discussing the ideal.

Enough has been said in the preceding chapter about the Southern attitude on this problem, and the facts of the negro's growth during the fifty years of freedom in this country were rapidly pictured. To avoid repetition we must assume as true all those deductions which in the previous chapters we tried to establish. It has been demonstrated that the American negro is capable to absorb all the fruits of Caucasian culture and civilization. This being so, how can the negro's emancipation from his present status interfere with social progress? How can it injure the interests of his white neighbor?

Let us make this question quite clear to the reader. That it is to the interest of the white employer to "keep the negro down" and to keep his wages down, that a deep prejudice against the negro, and his legitimate demands for civic rights exist, all this is recognized. Thus there is a real economic interpretation of the negro's plights both in the economic relations of the present, and the psychologic aftermath of the economic relations of the past. But neither of these is evidently a basic, organic, unsurmountable difficulty. Economic relations of the present must change, the psychologic effects of past economic relations must wear off. If economically, and biologically the white race cannot be injured by the emancipation of the negro, then it surely will not succumb to the psychological effects of the shock.

For what does the civic emancipation of the negro race mean, when reduced to its component elements? It means opportunity, economic, educational, cultural, social. It means the chance to rise intellectually, morally, economically, politically, socially. Why should the rise, the growth of any of my neighbors hurt me, unless I want to profit by his ignorance and weakness?

Ah, but this means social equality, and that is something the South will never agree to, many a southerner exclaims (Socialists, unfortunately, not excluded. But of this later). Yes, social equality, of course. That is really a splendid, telling phrase, when confined to its proper meaning. That is something the negro lacks, the negro, like every free citizen, must have.

Now, what is "social equality?" What do you understand by it, my southern friend? Is it the right to enter your parlor against your wishes, to marry your daughter against her wishes? Those are decidedly individual and not social acts. Your home is your castle, you frequently repeat. Even the officer of the law dare not enter it without a special warrant. Why, all that means that the home is the least social of our existing institutions. It is primarily the retreat of the individual, and personal fancies and caprices, prejudices and favoritism frequently rule there supreme. It is because in the swift current of socializing influences we nevertheless remain individuals, and therefore of necessity, individualists, that we appreciate our home just because it is the place for the expression of caprices, fancies, moods and irrational or supra-rational manifestations of life.

Evidently, with this institution social equality has absolutely nothing to do. No sensible, cultured negro wants to force his way into a private parlor, by whose owner he is hated and despised; and no law on earth can force the negro upon this unwilling parlor. The Jews in this country never suffered from discriminating legislation, and in most European countries they have been free from it for many decades. But in this country as well as in Europe, an overwhelming majority of the parlors is by a silent understanding closed to the Jews. Have you ever heard of a concerted effort of the Jews to legislate themselves into your parlor or into your family?

No, this is not social equality, and, moreover, I strongly suspect that even the bigoted Southerner understands this distinction. He is for Jim Crow cars, and Disenfranchisement acts, and for vagrancy laws, and against negro schools, not because he is afraid of the negro's intrusions against his parlor, but for other much more material, much more sordid reasons.

It is social equality that a negro has a right to demand, and to expect, and that he must have before we may claim to have solved the negro problem, i.e., equality at the hand of organized society, equality in all social institutions, equality before the election officers, equality in the civil service, equality in a library, built at public expense, to which at present he is not admitted, equality in the jury, when one of their race is on trial, equality in representation and the making of laws, under which he must live, equality at the hands of the school board, when money is appropriated for schools, equality in railroads, street cars, steamers, theatres and stores, which are truly public even if owned by private capital. Give the negro these, and he will not make any effort to force his way into your parlor, any more than the Jew forces or can force his way.

Now, I don't want to be misunderstood for a moment as trying to justify Caucasian snobbishness concerning the African or Yellow races. Personally,

I think it silly, though I can understand its origin. There are other things, logically silly, but historically inevitable, whether we mention long skirts, boiled shirts, or excessive sexual modesty. In a limited way I practice social, or rather "parlor" equality, and I do it in no spirit of bravado, but because I found a few highly intelligent negroes whom I enjoy meeting. To tell the truth, I found it much easier to force my way into an intelligent negro's house, than to get him into mine, possibly because there always lingers in the minds of the negro a suspicion as to the motives of the exceptionally cordial white man.

But I also know that it will be a long time before all the white folks will get rid of this prejudice as well as of many other prejudices and superstitions, and I also know that an organized effort to overcome this prejudice forcibly would be the surest way to give it new life. Only slowly, unconsciously do these large changes in mass psychology take place, but they are inevitable when the logic of events destroys the bases for existing beliefs.

The final argument against the full emancipation of the negro remains: the fear of miscegenation, the necessity to fight for racial purity. In a previous chapter I have shown, how frequently, as in the work of Professor Smith of Tulane University, this was made the justification and explanation for the entire policy of negro repression, with absolute disregard of the actual facts of life. Of all the different aspects of the negro problem, that known as amalgamation has caused the greatest amount of hysteria, and it has become a topic of greatest difficulties for calm and rational consideration by a Southerner. But here hysteria must be discarded, and the problem must be approached calmly, and without prejudices, if we are to arrive at reasonable results.

The charge of the negro's desire to carry on a forcible amalgamation through rape is too silly to deserve more than a possible mention, even if it did move John Temple Graves to advocate the wholesale castration of all bad negroes as a preventative measure. The question of amalgamation is therefore a question of voluntary miscegenation.

What are the facts? First, that forcible miscegenation was for centuries practiced by the white man and he is therefor primarily responsible for the degree of amalgamation accomplished thus far, and no small degree it is, to be sure.

These results were achieved without any "parlor" equality of which the South is so fearful, in fact were accomplished while the negro, as slave, was at the bottom of the social ladder. There is one important factor to be taken into consideration. The charge is often been made by Southern writers, Tillinghast for instance, that it was really the immorality of the negro woman and not the voluptuousness of the Southern man that was responsible for this miscegenation. Supposing this were true—then evidently the rise of the negro would decrease rather than increase the cause of amalgamation. For it must not be forgotten, that "amalgamation" of the races proceeded almost exclusively through illicit intercourse.

It is often claimed by Southerners that all this is a thing of a past. In the nature of things no statistics of illicit sexual intercourse is possible. But a series of articles in Pearson's Magazine recently published, urging the Southern white youth to limit itself to white prostitutes, so as to avoid further amalgamation (this is no exaggerated misstatement, but the actual advice given by the author) seems to indicate that with all the supposedly natural, biological antagonism between the races, the southern gentlemen is not averse to concoursing with a negro prostitute, and continues to practice miscegenation, social equality or no social equality. And it is quite natural to suppose that in the simple psychology of a negro prostitute or semiprostitute a white client represents the more affluent and therefore more desirable class.

In the opinion of Prof. Smith, however, there are two different kinds of amalgamation vastly differing as to their Social effects. The woman, he insists, is the carrier of racial purity. The illicit relations of white men with negro women bring white blood to the negro race. The reverse relations, between negro men and white women, would contaminate the white race.

Granting this difference, miscegenation has not interfered with the purity of the Caucasian race, but has infused a good deal of Caucasian blood into the African race, and from the Southern point of view, could but improve the latter. To use a crude colloquialism, "Where is the kick coming?"

But, says Prof. Smith, if social equality (in his sense of "parlor" equality) is granted, it will be followed by mixed marriages of both types, and the American people will become a mongrel people.

Is the danger of such marriages real? And if they should really take place, would they represent a serious danger to the racial evolution of the white race in the United States?

I might as well admit it: to me, individually, a mixed marriage between a caucasian and a real negro, seems monstrous, biologically as well as esthetically. I'd much rather eat at the same table with a negro woman than marry her. Southern practice seems to take the diametrically opposite view. But socially, I see no danger in such marriages. The Southerner objects to them from a social point of view, while conniving at them individually. I refuse to admit the social danger, first because I assume that my esthetic objections are shared by the vast majority of men and especially women, when a marriage relation is contemplated. As a result the mixed marriages are extremely rare. When they do occur, unless in the very bottom of social structure, the negro has usually more white than African blood, and is a negro constructively only.

Economic Aspects of the Negro Problem The Solution: A Prophecy and a Remedy (Part II) (1910)

If amalgamation is to continue, it is evidently probable only at the very fringe of the negro race among those members of it, among whom "crossing the hue" is frequent, to whom the entire status of the negro applies most cruelly, most unreasonably. There a racial prejudice often rises to destroy the happiness of innocent people, as for instance in the splendid play, the Nigger, which was presented to the New York public at the New Theatre last winter. Where biological and esthetical reasons no longer exist, there the emancipation of the negro race will make further amalgamation possible.

It is possible to imagine that in the indefinite future such a legitimate amalgamation at the fringe will lead to completed amalgamation of the negro race. Professor Giddings a few years ago made that prediction, to the horror of the Southern Aristocracy, the same aristocracy, which often secretly gossips about the drop of African blood in this or that exclusive family. Of course, it is quite evident, that as a practical problem this far delayed process need not cause any one sleepless nights at present. Whether the light increase of legitimate amalgamation will overcome the decline in illegitimate relations, consequent upon the moral, intellectual and economic improvement of the negro race, is a statistical problem with too many unknown quantities to permit of an exact solution. But supposing such a result is inevitable, what are its historical horrors?

The 10,000,000 negroes represent scarcely more than 10 per cent of our population. Were we able to estimate the exact proportion of white blood in the veins of these ten million negroes then the proportion of

Originally published in the *International Socialist Review* 10, no. 12 (June 1910): 1106–17.

negro blood to the entire sum total of ethnic elements of this country would dwindle down perceptibly. Add to this the continuous flow of white immigration, which is a constant factor, depressing the percentage of negro blood. In another century the negroes, even including all the quasi-negroes, will represent no more than four or five percent. Their entire amalgamation would introduce one twentieth or one twenty-fifth into the Caucasian race. Is our conceit really so great as to actually make us believe that this is a danger to our national efficiency? There are hundreds and perhaps thousands of "white" men and women, highly esteemed by their friends, who have more than that amount of negro blood.

The scare of amalgamation is a phantom, which consciously or unconsciously, the Southerner holds before our eyes, in justification of his anti-negro policy and in furtherance of his brutal exploitation of negro labor.

Our ideal has been defined and defended. Is there any historical justification for it? Is it a dream or a prophecy? Thus we come to the second element in the solution of the negro problem.

It is quite easy to put a wet blanket over the hope of ultimate negro emancipation. As we have shown repeatedly, recent years have brought about a decided aggravation of the negro's position. The curtailment of his rights goes on, and anti-negro riots become more frequent, the specific southern sentiment is no longer local—it gradually extends over the rest of the country, because of the diffusion of the negro population, as A.H. Stone insists, and often even in advance of it, by direct psychological infection following the diffusion of the white southerners through northern cities. Even Booker Washington in the privacy of his study is discouraged and pessimistic at times, though insisting on the platform and in interviews that everything must turn out well in the end. The protests of the few radical negro leaders remain voices in the wilderness thus far. History does not favor the negro at present.

But . . . history does not move in straight lines. Under pressure of economic forces it follows the line of least resistance, no matter how roundabout and crooked. The logic of social evolution is not the logic of a human mind shaping itself to a purpose. And a careful analysis of the social forces, blindly acting, does to my mind, point at one sign of hope and promise for the negro. And that is the negro's resistance, the negro's reaction to the white man's oppression.

In her lectures to the American audiences Mrs. Pankhurst very wisely pointed out that no element in society succeeded in gaining its rights in face of the opposition of the oppressors until it has made a nuisance of itself. This conforms with the socialist philosophy that the emancipation of the downtrodden must be the result of their own efforts, or as our Russian socialist friends eloquently express it in their motto: "Through struggle shall thou gain thy rights."

Dissatisfaction and protest is the first step to resistance and struggle, and the dissatisfaction of the American negro must inevitably grow. All educational activity among the negroes tends to increase this dissatisfaction, the agitation of the radical negro tends to increase it, and even the sermon of economic betterment so meekly taught by Booker Washington, works in the same direction, in so far as it produces more efficient, more intelligent and more prosperous negro workmen.

We may therefore assume that the forces of negro dissatisfaction must eventually be measured by the entire strength of the negro population. It is perfectly clear however, that by themselves the negroes will ever be in a hopeless minority, and therefore unable to influence legislation, or forcibly acquire their rights, which are unjustly denied them. It is because of this evident helplessness that the negroes have been forced to hold tenaciously to the Republican party as their only ally, and as with the growth of industrialism and the protective spirit, the South is rapidly turning republican, all interest for the negro has entirely been lost, and the negro for the first time feels that he is without white friends.

But in political struggles sentimental friends are very much less to be depended upon than business allies. Were a united white race confronting the negroes of this country, his position, in view of the present attitude toward the negro, would appear to be almost a hopeless one. But the 80 million white men and women are not so united, and among the struggling factions of the white race the negro must look for his most trustworthy ally.

Thus far this is cool and business-like politics. When the question is asked, what element of the white population will want to join hands with the negro, the answer is: only that element which will be forced to do so, that element which will find itself on the same side of the fight as the negro: the American working class.

The present relations between these two social groups are such that our prophecy will seem to the negro but an idle dream, and the white workingmen, the vast majority of them, and practically all of them in the South, will dismiss it with disgust. The present antagonism between the white and the negro workingmen may be said to represent the most acute aspect of the negro problem. For barring, perhaps, the occasional outburst of violence and bloodshed, nothing hurts the negro so much, and nothing raises his wrath so as does the opposition of white labor to his efforts to obtain a footing in the industrial field, or to retain it after having won it. "Granted that you do not want us in your parlor, nor in your cars, theaters, libraries, nor on juries, or in your civil service; and granted that you have decided to keep us out of all political life, and to deny us ally and help in the preparation of laws under which we must live, or the levying of taxes, which we must pay—surely, surely, you must give us an opportunity to pursue peacefully our trades and earn a living."

This very thing the white workingmen, whether organized or not, do deny the negro laborer, unless he is willing to remain satisfied with the lowest and least remunerative employment.

Thus the white and negro workmen are not only not allied in their economic struggle, but are actually engaged now in suicidal struggle, a struggle, it must be admitted, of the white man's making.

And right here the philosophy of political struggle comes in. In this peculiar struggle between white and negro labor, capital will invariably be found on the side of negro labor. This struggle furnishes the only opportunity for southern capital to become fond of the negro, and appreciative of the negro's rights. Thus with the help of southern white capital, negro labor is enabled to become a very great nuisance and danger for white labor.

Unless we are ready to deny all intelligence in the American workman, we must admit that the only possible way to counteract this nuisance, to avoid that danger, is for the American workman to enter into an alliance with the negro competitor and thus realize the principle, that "when combination is possible, competition becomes impossible." It is because I can look a little further into the future, and see the inevitable developments, that I welcome such struggles as the one that recently arose on the Georgia Railroad, for they help to clear the issues. And personally, I confess, that I can not repress my satisfaction when the negro laborer succeeds in beating his white brother, even if it be with the help of his employer. For the childish attitude of the southern white workman needs that lesson.

It is idle for the white workman to depend upon the negro hater's fairy tales of the negro's inability to enter industrial life. Southern capital is willing to defend this theory—on paper, until a real labor struggle sets in.

And, of late, northern capital has learned to depend upon negro scabs as well. The vast contributions to the industrial schools of the type of Tuskegee and Hampton should by this time have opened the eyes of the American workman, to the fact, that the entrance of negro labor into industrial life of the country is a question of time only and cannot be resisted. A priori, the Socialist could have predicted that. Or was it assumed for the moment that 10,000,000 good strong pairs of arms would be left forever ununionized in the process of extracting surplus value?

And thus here and there, in the North and even in the South, labor unions are forced to organize the negro workers or to admit them into their own unions on certain terms of equality. Either this movement must grow, or the number of negro scabs must grow, and destroy the white man's union. For nothing would be more dangerous, not to say detrimental, to the entire cause of organized labor, than the systematic breeding of a large body of embittered "scabs," scabs out of choice, necessity and principle, scabs who are now taught by their own negro leaders, that their only chance to succeed is to underbid the organized white workman.

And what is true of the economic struggle must sooner or later be true of the political struggle as well.

It is not necessary for me to go into extended discussions concerning the importance of the political struggle for the betterment and final emancipation of the working class. But in this field the negro may at present appear to be absolutely powerless and therefore useless as an ally. Nevertheless, arbitrary as have been curtailments of the negro's political rights, his political influence has not altogether been destroyed. And if this country is ever to see a powerful, influential political labor movement, it will be forced to take the negro into account.

The developments we are discussing will not take place in the immediate future, but in analysing as large and broad a problem as this, it is not wise to hedge one self within narrow time limits. We are dealing here with broad historical tendencies and these point toward certain directions. The diffusion of negroes throughout the country must proceed at an accelerated rate. The breaking up of the solid democratic South will, though slowly, reestablish in some degree the political rights of some negroes in the South. The repeated failures of the disenfranchisement amendments in Maryland, even the failure of Vardaman's senatorial campaign in Mississippi point in that direction. And with the quiet balancing of powers in the bitter political struggles between capital and labor which this country must go through in some more or less distant future, the actual balance may be formed in the hands of isolated minorities. Will the fear of amalgamation, will the objection to "parlor" equality always be strong enough to prevent the American white workman from joining hands with his natural economic ally, and thus force him to remain the political as well as economic scab in employ of the moneyed minority?

Thus in the very struggle for emancipation, and not only after achieving the victory, will the American white working class be forced to join hands with the negro, and in return help him obtain his final goal—the economic and legal equality, not out of humanitarian considerations or because of an abstract desire to solve an interesting sociological problem.

Is an ideal and a prophecy sufficient? The poet is satisfied with the dream of the golden age in the future, the calm student and philosopher studies things as they were, as they are and as they will be. But we are not all poets or philosophers, and a sorry world it would be if we were. The ordinary man, the man of action, when confronted with a difficult problem, asks: What shall I do? And only through the collective action of all these men is the prophecy and ideal realized. Whence the popularity of remedies, whether scientific or otherwise. It will be utterly futile, for me, therefore to avoid prescribing for the social disease I have described and analysed at such length.

Of remedies for the solution of the negro problem there are many more, even than there are ideals concerning the nature of the inevitable solution—for even when agreeing concerning the ideal, people may and do disagree about best, quickest and easiest way of reaching it. Supposing we agreed that the only way to solve the negro problem was to get rid of the negro. Still there would be many different opinions about the best way to get rid of him: whether to forcibly ship him back to Africa, or to let him die off gradually by refusing him all knowledge of the laws of life and health, or to kill them off, which manifestly would be the quickest way.

But obviously it is unnecessary to subject to a minute and careful scrutiny all the different remedies proposed, as for instance the very elaborate plan of Rickett, to ship them to Africa, developed in a book of 600 pages. Nor need we spend too much time on whether Vardaman's plan of denying all schooling to the negro, or the industrial institutes and schools for servants are the best method to teach the negro, "his proper station in life." Speaking as I do, to American workingmen and socialists, and assuming the ideal and the prophecy, which I have developed above—I want to consider one question only: What can the radical American workingman and the American Socialist do to help along the negro's struggle for emancipation, and to make him an ally, rather than an obstruction and an enemy to the American working class in its struggle for emancipation?

In Socialist literature the problem is not a new one. In the *International Socialist Review* alone, before this series of articles began, I counted as many as ten articles on the negro problem. Such authoritative thinkers and leaders as Debs, Darrow, Meily and Vail have participated in these discussions, in addition to Southern comrades, qualified to speak because of their local interest in and first hand knowledge of the problem.

It is a sad fact nevertheless that there is very little interest concerning the negro problem among the Socialists outside of the narrow circles of Southern locals. Perhaps the first advice that must be given to the American Socialists is to pay a good deal more attention to this as to other practical problems of American life.

In so far as the Socialists have paid attention to this problem, however, it is somewhat difficult to define their attitude on the problem, or least on its practical aspects of it. If one wants to limit himself to the official expressions of opinions such as are contained in the platform and formal party resolutions, one may get a fairly definite point of view. But I cannot help feeling that, with all due deference to official party resolutions, that they do not often reflect the true opinion of the body of the party members; and in any case there is never the unanimity of opinion which the consideration of official documents alone might lead us to assume.

Moreover, one fails to find very many expressions of official opinion. The "negro resolutions" adopted at the national convention in 1900 are specific: "Resolved that we, the American Socialist Party, invite the negro to membership and fellowship with us in the world movement for economic emancipation by which equal liberty and opportunity shall be secured to every man and fraternity become the order of the world."

But one fails to find similar expressions of opinion in the labor platforms of either 1904 or 1908. As far as I was able to discover, the word "negro" fails to appear in either platform, and even in the demands enumerated in the platform of 1904 and much more thoroughly in the platform of 1908, there is none that even by construction can be made to apply to the peculiar grievances of the negro. Even the model state and municipal platforms presented to the National Convention of 1909 by a special committee avoid this matter. And yet discriminations against the negro are frequent in municipal, state and national life.

About the only demand, that by implication may be said to favor the negro, is the immediate demand: "Unrestricted and equal suffrage for men and women."

But if in framing these demands the negro was actually kept in mind,—why were the Socialists, "in convention assembled" afraid to say so plainly? Was it because they were afraid to step on the toes of a few Southern delegates?

Is this fair? Is it wise? Is it practical?

Don't tell me that the Socialist's justice towards the negro is self-understood! Why should the radical negro make such an assumption? Have the American labor unions inspired him with such faith in the fairness and justice of the American white workingman? Haven't some of the most radical of the American politicians, such as Bryan and Watson, remained thoroughly reactionary as far as the negro is concerned? How does the radical negro, how does a Du Bois or a Trotter know that the Socialists will treat him any better?

Socialist philosophy is incompatible with negro repression, you say? How is the negro to know it? And are you so very sure that the cooperative commonwealth is unthinkable with Jim Crow cars, and other characteristic virtues of modern Southern life?

I know, that in thus pleading for a "clear cut, uncompromising, revolutionary" negro plank in our national platform I go contrary to the opinions of the highest authorities on the Socialist movement.

Says Eugene V. Debs, (or at least, he did say some 6 or 7 years ago):

> [P]ermit me to express the hope that the next convention may repeal the resolutions on the Negro question. The Negro does not need them and they serve to increase rather than diminish the necessity for explanation.
>
> We have nothing special to offer the negro, and we cannot make separate appeals to all the races.
>
> The Socialist party is the party of the whole working class, regardless of color—the whole working class of the whole world.

Nevertheless, such is the irony of circumstances, that only two months later Debs himself was forced to quote this long resolution verbatim, because "it constitutes a vital part of the national platform of the Socialist party and clearly defines its attitude towards the negro."

The negro resolution thus proved useful sooner than expected, and would prove useful again.

Far be it from me to question even for a moment the sincerity and humanity of as broadhearted a man as Debs. But wasn't the attitude quoted in the lengthy extract above, really begging the entire question?

The Socialist party in this country "in convention assembled" does not make the platform for the Socialist movement of the world, but for the United States only, and in these United States there is a negro problem, and there is no Swedish or Irish problem. For this reason no "separate appeals to all the races" are necessary, but a special appeal to the negro is necessary, for the special grievances which he suffers from are to him no less real than the general grievances of each and every wage-earner. And when Comrade Debs says: "Properly speaking, there is no negro question outside of the labor question" he voices an opinion, sincerely held by many Socialists, but unfortunately contradicted by facts of every day experience.

In the last analysis our attitude upon this one special problem of modern economic and social life will depend upon our general point of view upon the proper aims and objects of the Socialist movement. And here I feel full well, that I may come in conflict with the views of Comrade Kerr and those of the *International Socialist Review*, but the reader surely understands that no one but myself is to be held responsible for anything I may here state. Is the Socialist movement a movement exclusively shaped for the purpose of accomplishing the establishment of the cooperative commonwealth without further regard for anything that happens before that final goal is achieved, or is it the expression of all the economic and political aspirations of the working class in the immediate present as well as in the more or less distant future when the final revolution will become an immediate issue?

Until very recently, the former opinion was held by a vast majority of American Socialists. It is evidently this conception that prompts Debs to say,

[W]ith the "nigger" question, the "race war" from a capitalist view point we have nothing to do. In capitalism the negro question is a grave one and will grow more threatening as the contradictions and complications of capitalist society multiply, but this need not worry us. Let them settle the negro question in their way, if they can. We have nothing to do with it, for that is their fight.

But if, as the evolution of the Socialist movement in this country during the last five years has unmistakably demonstrated, anything that concerns the working class in the present is also a concern of the Socialist party, if in 1908 it was thought necessary to present eighteen specific industrial, political and social demands, including such as the abolition of the senate, woman suffrage, conservation of health, a creation of a department of health and what not, can we still consistently hold that the race friction is "their fight"? When the engineers and the firemen of the Georgia Railroad insisted upon the discharge of the negro firemen, because they were negroes, and the latter were supported by the Railroad managers, who ostensibly demonstrated a greater humanitarian feeling than the white fellow wage-earner, was the fight between white and black wage-earners their fight or was it our fight? No, comrades, it will not do to avoid the issue. Every struggle of this nature (and they are rapidly multiplying) is an indication that the situation is becoming graver, and every struggle of this kind that the Socialists disregard is an opportunity lost.

And supposing it were understood by the negroes that the Socialists (under socialism) expect to grant the negro his right to work and the "full enjoyment of the product of his labor?" Is that enough? Will that convince the negro that the Socialist movement is his movement?

"Socialism," says a Southern writer, "is primarily an economic and industrial movement, the object of which is to secure to every man, white and black alike, economic justice and equality in the full enjoyment of the product of his labor."

Only economic and industrial? Does it not also strive for political and social justice in its broadest sense?

Shouldn't we at least explain to the negro, that having no interest in his economic exploitation, we shall for the same reason not undertake to keep up his political and social repression, and will not hold to the psychological superstructure after the economic basis is gone?

And thus I am ready to offer my first prescription: the Socialist party must take a definite attitude on the negro problem, and must not be afraid to proclaim. And this attitude must include something a good deal more tangible than the promise of "full products of one's labor in the cooperative commonwealth." It must include, if it's to be logical and honest—a clear, unmistakable demand for the entire abolition of all legal restriction of the rights of the negro. Only on this ground will it ever succeed in proving to the negro, that the Socialist party is his party, not only in the future but in the present.

Including "social equality?" shall many a southern socialist exclaim, horrified.

I beg your pardon, but do you mean "social" equality—equality of social rights, or parlor equality in the individual home? If the former, by all means. And as to the latter, that is one thing the Socialist movement has no concern with. Whether you will insist upon receiving at your home only white persons, or only bleached blonds, or only Presbyterians, or only musical people—is no concern to the Socialist—But mind you, this is true only as far as your home is concerned.

And it was undoubtedly this loose and confused thinking that permitted the use of the term "social equality" when the question of mixed locals arose in Louisiana some five years ago. What has the Socialist local to do with your home? And when the Southern Socialists pleaded with the prejudices of the "comrades of the gentler sex," one might ask how many Socialist comrades there are among the "gentler sex" in the South?

Of course the national organization may permit, as Comrade Eraste Vidrine suggested, the negroes of any locality to organize negro branches, as it permits the organization of Polish, Italian, Jewish and other branches. But the problem is, shall the Socialist organization permit any local to discharge an Italian because he is an Italian, or a Jew because he is a Jew, or a Catholic because he is a Catholic, or . . . a Negro, because he is a Negro?

The "social" life, concomitant upon Socialist organizations, (i.e., entertainments and festivals) has often been urged as an unsurmountable difficulty against admitting negroes to Socialist locals. Here again there is a hopeless mixture of civic rights and "parlor" privileges. The difficulty is exaggerated, for the more intelligent negro (and he is the only possible candidate for membership) has no desire to invade himself upon a society in which he is not welcome. Besides, it is no secret, that in cities with a mixed population the festivities and entertainments of the Socialists are conducted on national (and for all I know may be conducted even on religious) lines.

But in thus committing himself in the most flatfooted fashion against any discrimination against the negro, within the limits of his own organization, the Socialist will not have done his entire duty by the negro, nor by the rest of the American working class.

The attitude of the Socialist movement on this all important problem must not only be passively correct and decent, but actively aggressive. Armed with the true Marxian explanation of the negro's economic, political and legal status, and thorough understanding of the only satisfactory, inevitable and necessary solution, the Socialist party has a sacred duty before it:

1. It must make an earnest effort to convince the growing negro radical element, that as economic exploitation was the cause of the dismal fate of the negroes in the past, their only hope in the future lies in joining hands with the movement towards the curtailment and final abolition of economic exploitation.

And it must make a still more earnest and energetic effort to convince the American labor movement, as expressed in labor and trade unions, that in resisting the economic and civic growth of the negro it is simply building obstructions in its way.

In other words, the Socialist movement, viewing the labor problem in its entirety, not in any utopian or phantastic way, but practically, and yet seeing much further than the immediate narrow interests of this or that little group for higher wages or a privileged position—the Socialist movement must make the one practical effort necessary to direct the negro problem in the narrow channel towards its true solution.

Will we be wise enough to do it?

Kate Richards O'Hare

Introduction

The first lady of American Socialism, Kate Richards O'Hare (1876–1948) was one of the most important figures in the Socialist Party. An editor, speaker, international representative, and organizer, she was by far the most prominent woman socialist during the party's heyday of 1902–1917. Though not known primarily for her work on the race question, her pamphlet "Nigger Equality" remains one of the most infamous examples of the party's accommodation to American racism.

Richards was born on a farm in Kansas in 1876. Her childhood was interrupted, however, by the depression of the 1870s, which forced her father to sell his farm and move to Kansas City, Missouri. There, she was quickly acquainted with the realities of frontier capitalism, living in a poor neighborhood and forced to begin working at an early age. Encouraged by her father, a socialist and populist activist, she joined the International Association of Machinists as an apprentice, enduring sexist opposition from other union members to become a machinist herself.

Richards became a socialist after hearing a Mother Jones speech at a union event in Kansas City. She briefly joined Daniel De Leon's Socialist Labor Party, but left quickly, eventually affiliating to Eugene Debs and Victor Berger's Social Democracy of America, which would become the Socialist Party of America in 1901. As an SP member, Richards plunged into socialist pedagogy, becoming a student at the International School for Social Economy in Girard, Kansas, and training to be a socialist lecturer. There, she met the man who would become her husband, Frank O'Hare. The two spent their honeymoon on the socialist lecture circuit in Kansas and Missouri.

From this point on, Kate Richards O'Hare became a full-time socialist agitator. She lectured across the Southwest, traveled to New York to report on industrial conditions there, and organized union workers in Kansas. In 1909, she and her husband became editors of the *National Rip-Saw*, transforming the regional socialist paper into a juggernaut with a circulation of 150,000, second only to the *Appeal to Reason* among socialist periodicals.

As an SP agitator, O'Hare accomplished an impressive number of firsts. She was the first American woman to run for the Senate, running for a seat in Missouri in 1916. Back in Kansas, she had been the first woman to run for the House of Representatives in that state. In the SP, she was elected International Secretary of the party in 1912, becoming the first and only woman to serve in that position. These accomplishments are only more impressive in light of the fact that O'Hare was hardly a feminist. She preferred domestic life, but felt that duty required her to embrace her political career.

Inside the party, O'Hare tended to align herself with the right wing led by Victor Berger and Morris Hillquit, against the left wing, which supported the IWW. She looked favorably on Berger's socialist political machine in Milwaukee and held that the goal of socialist politics was to elect a government to enact reforms. Impatient with abstract socialist theory, O'Hare felt strongly that local socialists should do whatever would best allow them to recruit more members, regardless of what was decided by the national party or Second International.

It was through this conviction that O'Hare approached her writing on the race question. She was not, it is important to note, a dyed-in-the-wool racist herself. As an agitator in Kansas and Missouri, she was known to oppose institutions like the poll tax and segregated housing, and to support Black movements against them. Earlier in her career, she had written in opposition to land theft against Native Americans. However, when it came to popularizing socialism, O'Hare saw no point in combating the racism of her audience, instead accommodating it at every opportunity.

"Nigger Equality" is the result of this accommodation. While at points throughout the pamphlet O'Hare argues for an identity of interest between Black and white workers, arguing that both are chained by capitalism, this impulse toward solidarity is undercut throughout by an endorsement of the most vile racist tropes. The problem with capitalism, she argues, is that it doesn't provide enough segregation. Black men work alongside white men (and even worse, white women) in factories and fields, "until there is not a shred of race distinction left."

Clearly making a pitch to white Democratic Party voters, O'Hare repeats the myth of Reconstruction as a time of "Negro Domination" over innocent whites. Because of this history, whites are perfectly justified in opposing Black equality. The appeal of socialism, O'Hare avers, is that it promises not Black equality, but a more rigorous separation than obtained under capitalism. White Democrats should thus ignore the Democrats' cries of "Nigger Equality" and vote socialist.

O'Hare's pamphlet hardly represented the main thrust of socialist thinking on the subject of race. However, in its viciousness, it stands out, alongside many of the party's contributions on the subject of Chinese immigration, as an uncomfortable reminder of just how thoroughly elements of the party accommodated themselves to American racism. Constantly decried as a foreign influence on American soil, documents like this illustrate just how "American" the party really was.

Further Reading

Basen, Neil K. "Kate Richards O'Hare: The 'First Lady' of American Socialism, 1901–1917." *Labor History* 21, no. 2 (Spring 1980): 165–99.

Miller, Sally M. *From Prairie to Prison: The Life of Social Activist Kate Richards O'Hare*. Vol. 1. Columbia: University of Missouri Press, 1993.

Foner, Philip S. and Sally M. Miller, eds., *Kate Richards O'Hare: Selected Writings and Speeches*. Baton Rouge, LA: Louisiana State University Press, 1982.

Nigger Equality (1912)

There is a reason why the cry of "Negro Domination" strikes terror to the hearts of the Southerner and is such an effective weapon in the hands of the capitalist class and their tools, the politicians. My father was a Federal soldier and I was born and reared in Kansas, the abolition state of all states, *but my heart has bled and my blood boiled as I have listened to the frightful stories of those accursed days when the "Carpet Bagger" ruled the southland and added his damnable wrongs to a country already cursed by war's devastation. To the man or woman who lived through those miserable days when the vile politicians from the north by their arrogant power forced the defeated Southerners not only to face the bitterness of war's reverses, but the stinging disgrace of having ignorant blacks placed in positions of power and authority over them, "Negro Domination" means something more than words.* Naturally they revolt at any political movement which they can be induced to believe sanctions such a thing.

In the South the great bugbear used by the Democratic politicians to keep the voters in line behind the Democratic Party is the cry that Socialism would mean "Nigger Equality." At every Socialist meeting some earnest seeker after the light gently whispers the question or some politician sneeringly hurls it at me, *"Don't you Socialists believe in nigger equality?"*

Now listen, you white voters of the South, let us settle this question fairly and definitely and forever. It is absolutely true that the very basic principle of Socialism is EQUALITY and the very goal of the whole Socialist movement of the world is EQUALITY. "There, I told you so, I knew you wanted nigger equality," every Democratic politician in the South shouts.

Sure! But just wait a moment until we decide what kind of equality we want.

There are several kinds of Equality:
Social Equality.
Physical Equality.

Originally published as a pamphlet by the *National Rip-Saw*, March 25, 1912.

Mental Equality.

Equality of opportunity, or economic equality.

"Do we want Social Equality?"

Certainly not; there will never be such a thing. Men and women always form social groups according to their various tastes and differences in social tastes and preferences will always remain and Social Equality is impossible and would be undesirable.

"Do we want Physical Equality?"

No. Socialists would like to see a condition that would enable every human being to be the best physical specimen possible, but there will always be tall men and short men, fat men and lean men, plain women and beautiful women, and such a thing as physical equality can never exist.

"Do we want Mental Equality?"

No. We want every man and woman to have the opportunity to develop their mentality to the highest point compatible with their personal wishes in the matter, but inequalities will always remain. Law can never make a bright man dull or a dull man brainy.

"Well, what kind of Equality do you Socialists want?" you ask.

"Why, just one kind, EQUALITY OF OPPORTUNITY."

SOCIALISTS WANT TO PUT THE NEGRO WHERE HE CAN'T COMPETE WITH THE WHITE MAN.

The whole aim of Socialism is that every human being, white, black, red, or yellow, shall have equal opportunity to have access to the natural resources which nature has supplied and to the machinery which man has created and then to have the full social product of his labor. "And do you want the 'nigger' to have equal opportunity to use natural resources, and machinery of production and to let him have all the wealth he creates by his labor?" you ask. Certainly—not because we love the "nigger," but because we know that every chain of economic servitude that is shackled on the ankle of the "nigger" is riveted on the wrists of the white workers. Just as long as a "nigger" can be robbed of the product of his labor by the capitalist class by being shut out from access to the means of life, just that long he can be made the club and chain that will drag and beat the white workers down into the mire of poverty. As long as the "nigger" can be forced to be a wage slave, so can the white man; as long as the "nigger" is a tenant farmer, so long will the white man be; as long as an idle capitalist can live off a "nigger's" labor, so can he live off a white man's labor.

No, we Socialists don't love the "nigger" any better than he loves us; we don't admire the shape of his nose or the color of his skin any more than he likes our insolence and intolerant attitude, but we have sense enough to know that capitalism chains us to the negro with iron chains of economic servitude and we would rather have the negro free from the chains. Because if the black man is chained it spells slavery for the white man and woman and girl—we must share it.

Wake up, you Southern voters. You have let the scarecrow of "Nigger Equality" keep you ignorant of the Socialist movement and what it means to you without understanding that you endure the very thing you dread. You have Jim Crow laws that keep the negroes out of your railroad coaches, but where is the Jim Crow law for the factory, workshop, mine, or cotton-field? A negro can't ride in a white streetcar in Memphis, but I saw a hundred men digging in a sewer ditch. Half of them were blacks and half white Democrats; there was no Jim Crow law there; it was a "nigger" and a white man, a "nigger" and a white man, as nicely placed as the stripes in a calico apron. When the water boy came along with the water pail and one dipper a "nigger" took a drink and then a white man, another "nigger" and another white man, and not a politician shouted "nigger equality." In the laundries of that aristocratic Southern city the daughters of white Democrats work side by side with big, black negro men; in the cotton mills, the white children compete with negro children. In the cotton fields the white daughters of white voters drag the cotton sacks down the cotton row next to "nigger bucks" and the *Democratic politician of the chivalrous South where womanhood is placed on a pedestal and worshipped, where it would degrade women to have a vote, raise no voice in protest.*

No, we Socialists don't want that kind of "Nigger Equality" in the North or South. God knows we have had enough of it. Negro and white alike have the equality of white slavery, tenant servitude, capitalist exploitation, illiteracy, and bitter poverty. Socialism would replace that "equality" with equality of opportunity for black and white to have access to the means of life and the opportunity to develop the best there is in both races instead of the worst.

"Nigger Equality!" Good Heavens; If the tenant farmers of the South had equality with the niggers they would be lots better off than they are. *All over the South wherever I have traveled I find the good land, down in the bottoms where cotton grows shoulder high and the soil is rich and fertile, is rented*

to the blacks. Every landlord in the South rents every acre of land he can to negroes
and the poor land up in the hills, the worn out land, the land that produces least,
he allows the Great American Sovereign Voting King, the white Democrat of the
South, to till; and then those same white Democrats shy at Socialism like a
frisky colt because Socialism would mean "Nigger equality." Well, nigger
equality would be better than the Democratic "equality" which you have
now, with the nigger getting the best of it all around, which best, God
knows is bad enough.

The "Negro Equality" which Capitalism forces on us today is not
peculiar to the South alone; we have it in the north as well. In Kansas
City black men have replaced white men in the packinghouses wherever
possible, and the white daughters of both Republican and Democratic
voters are forced to associate with them in terms of shocking intimacy.
In the coal mines of the whole United States black men have been used to
replace white miners until there is not a shred of race distinction left.

Remember there is a vast distinction between the economic equality of
opportunity for the black man along with his white neighbor to have access
to the means of production and the product of his labor and the revolting
equality of degradation which capitalism forces on us. We Socialists simply
want the negro to have his opportunity to have access to the means of life,
so he can quit competing with the white man, not because we love or hate
him, but in order that he may not be used to keep down our wages. I neither
love nor hate a negro. I am no more anxious to associate with him than he
is to associate with me. I don't want to associate on terms of social equality
with him and I know he is just as willing to dispense with my society as I
am with his, but capitalism forces us into a social, economic, and physical
relation which is just as revolting to the negro as it is to me, and as both
the negro and I want to escape, the only way we can do so is by Socialism
giving us both an equal opportunity to have access to the means of life and
the product of our labor; then we can dump the capitalists off our back and
work out our own problems, freed from the curse of race antagonism.

But you ask what is the solution of the race question?

There can be but one. Segregation. If you ask me what I am going to
work and speak and write and vote for on the race question, when it is to
be settled under a Socialist form of government, I can tell you very quickly.
Let us give the blacks one section in the country where every condition
is best fitted for them. Free them from capitalist exploitation; give them

access to the soil, the ownership of their machines and let them work out their own salvation. If the negro rises to such an opportunity, and develops his own civilization, well and good; if not, and he prefers to hunt and fish and live idly, no one will be injured but him and that will be his business.

Be sensible men, you white voters of the South, and refuse to be frightened by an empty scarecrow. "Nigger Equality" has served the politicians and the capitalist class for a long time to keep you in blind servitude; demolish it and think for yourself.

You are yoked up as a tenant farmer or wage slaves with the negro today. Vote for Socialism and be free.

Be wise, you black men of the South. While Abe Lincoln and the boys in blue were smashing your shackles of chattel slavery the capitalist class of the North was forging the shackles of economic slavery on both you and the men who fought to free you. Now you are both slaves of the same master, you are bound together by the same chains of economic servitude. Socialism is the only force on earth that can free you both, free us all, black and white, man, woman, and child. White men of the United States, black men of our country, use your ballots to sever the chain that binds you together and binds you to slavery. Black men, vote to free your wives and daughters from the despoliation of your white masters; white men, vote to free your womenkind from debasement of wage slavery yoked to Negro Equality.

Hubert Harrison

Introduction

Hubert Harrison (1883–1927) was a Black lecturer, editor, writer, and organizer who played a central role in creating the radical Harlem political culture from which figures such as A. Philip Randolph and Marcus Garvey would later emerge. Harrison, more than any other single figure, embodied the "New Negro" spirit claimed by Harlem's postwar radicals. A member of the Socialist Party in the early 1910s, Harrison eventually left the party over its accommodations to racism and its purge of its left wing. From there, Harrison wandered the ideological landscape, serving as an editor for Marcus Garvey's *Negro World*, an AFL union organizer, and a speaker for the New York City Board of Education. Throughout all of it, he distinguished himself with his own unique combination of race and class radicalism. Unfortunately, by the time of his death in 1927, Harrison had largely faded from the public eye, his death going unnoticed even in much of the Black press.

Harrison immigrated to the United States as a young man in 1900, working menial jobs for a period until he found a position at the post office. His political opinions, however, soon put an end to the relative stability afforded by public sector employment. In 1910, he wrote two letters to the *New York Sun* criticizing Booker T. Washington's accommodationist politics. These letters caught the attention of Washington himself, who used his political connections to get Harrison fired. It would not be the last time Harrison would pay for his politics.

Harrison joined the Socialist Party soon after this episode, becoming a paid lecturer for the party. As an SP member, Harrison wrote a number of pieces on the party's approach to the race question, arguing that the socialists needed to take a much more aggressive stance toward confronting American racism. Within the party, Harrison aligned himself with the left wing, who supported the IWW and called for a revolutionary confrontation with American capitalism.

Unfortunately for Harrison, the SP leadership's growing impatience with the left wing turned into a purge in 1912. When IWW leader Big Bill Haywood was removed from the party's executive council, Harrison made his allegiance clear. As a result, the leadership in New York, firmly in the camp of Haywood's nemesis, Morris Hillquit, gradually began placing constraints on Harrison. They refused his request to equalize his speakers' fee with other party lecturers, vetoed talks he planned to give, and forbade him from debating anti-socialists. By 1914, Harrison had had enough. He accused the New York leadership of racism in their treatment of him and left the party in disgust.

Over the next few years, Harrison organized a number of initiatives that sought to build a vehicle for his political vision of race and class radicalism. He founded a newspaper, the *Voice*, and an organization, the Liberty League. When World War I broke out, Harrison was at the forefront of the movement demanding black equality throughout the war and pushing for Black rights to be included in the postwar settlement.

By the early 1920s, however, Harrison had largely been displaced as the leading voice of Black radicalism. Figures like Cyril Briggs and A. Philip Randolph had moved to the forefront, while Harrison attached himself to Garvey's UNIA, which promptly went through its own crises during the same period. Though Harrison continued to write prodigiously in this period, the Harlem Renaissance brought fame to a new group of Black intellectuals. When he died of complications from an appendectomy in 1927, few remembered that a decade earlier he had been the undisputed master of Harlem street speakers.

Harrison's writings for the socialist press represent a step forward in American socialism's position on the race question. While figures like Debs had called for the party to stand against Black oppression, Harrison laid out a strategic argument for why socialists should prioritize the question, as well as some considerations on the obstacles that lay in their way. Harrison argued that the overwhelmingly working-class character of the Black population made them a natural constituency for socialism, but that Black skepticism toward white socialists would have to be actively overcome. Understanding the rifts in the SP at the time, Harrison made sure to pitch his appeal to both "political" and "industrial" socialists, arguing that both reformists and revolutionaries needed to direct their attention to building a socialist base among Black Americans. As rigorous as Harrison's case was, it would only begin to be put into action a decade later, when the Communist Party first began to turn its attention to the Black liberation struggle.

Further Reading

Foner, Philip S. *American Socialism and Black Americans: From the Age of Jackson to World War II*. Westport, CT: Greenwood Press, 1977.

James, Winston. *Holding Aloft the Banner of Ethiopia: Caribbean Radicalism in Early Twentieth-Century America*. London: Verso, 1998.

Perry, Jeffrey Babcock. *Hubert Harrison: The Voice of Harlem Radicalism, 1883–1918*. New York: Columbia University Press, 2013.

The Negro and Socialism, Part V:
Summary and Conclusion

We have seen, then, that the necessity which brought the negro here was an economic necessity. We have seen how his position at the very bottom of society was determined by that necessity. We have seen how race prejudice developed as such out of this fundamental fact of social relationship. It is conceded that the ideas, opinions and ideals dominant at any stage of human culture do not descend out of the air. They are created and shaped by the basic conditions of society. Out of an age in which social slaughter seemed necessary emerged the soldier's ideal; out of an era of large production emerged the ideals of business. And out of chattel slavery emerged the social and economic degradation of the negro, which finds its expression in race prejudice. Whenever large groups of men find profit in injustice to other men they will evolve a system of ethics to reconcile their minds to that injustice. They cannot continue to do wrong without calling that wrong right. That is why the capitalist class cannot even think justice so far as the workers are concerned. And that is why men who think that they can see a social or economic advantage for themselves in the degradation of the negro will continue to think that degradation right. If the overturning of the present system should elevate a new class into power; a class to which the negro belongs; a class which has nothing to gain by the degradation of any portion of itself; that class will remove the economic reason for the degradation of the negro. That is the promise of Socialism, the all-inclusive working class movement. In the final triumph of this movement lies the only hope of salvation from this second slavery of black men and of white.

On the other hand, this movement can succeed only by espousing the cause of all sections of down-trodden humanity. Anything short of that spells failure. The limits of such a movement, then, are determined, not by

---

Originally published in the *New York Call*, December 26, 1911, 6.

the policy of its leaders, but by the conditions of the case, and in the light of this fact the duty of the Socialist party is as clear as day. That duty it could not shirk even if it would, and I dare to believe that it would not if it could. Therefore, the Socialist propaganda must be extended in the negro people. Furthermore, I think that it will become more and more necessary for the party to take cognizance of certain definite acts of economic oppression— such as the suicidal policy of certain trades unions in excluding negroes from membership—and to condemn them. If it is expedient for us to present an old age pension bill that was not meant to be enacted into law, then surely there can be nothing against such a procedure on the ground of expediency.

But in the meanwhile the work itself confronts us. How shall we get it done. In the first place, we must raise the necessary funds. Local New York proposes to do so in two ways. First, by having each branch and language group of the local contribute a certain amount each week; and, secondly, to open subscriptions in the party press to which individual members of the party may contribute. This part of the work is of course, preparatory, because headquarters are necessary from which the work may be conducted. When negroes shall have joined the party in sufficiently large numbers there will be no further need for a special fund. The work will be self-sustaining. Then, besides, the colored Comrades can be drafted into those branches into whose territory they happen to live, thereby increasing both the finances and the working force of those branches.

If I may add, in closing, a word or two of advice. I should say that Socialists in general need to learn a great many things about the negro— not only of his racial psychology, but also of his history and of his present achievements in the various lines of human endeavor. If the white man of Europe knows nothing of the negro, the white man of America knows a great deal that isn't so. And one has to unlearn much before he can begin to learn.

Socialism and the Negro

1. Economic Status of the Negro

The ten million Negroes of America form a group that is more essentially proletarian than any other American group. In the first place the ancestors of this group were brought here with the very definite understanding that they were to be ruthlessly exploited. And they were not allowed any choice in the matter. Since they were brought here as chattels their social status was fixed by that fact. In every case that we know of where a group has lived by exploiting another group, it has despised that group which it has put under subjection. And the degree of contempt has always been in direct proportion to the degree of exploitation.

Inasmuch, then, as the Negro was at one period the most thoroughly exploited of the American proletarian, he was the most thoroughly despised. That group which exploited and despised him, being the most powerful section of the ruling class, was able to diffuse its own necessary contempt of the Negro first among the other sections of the ruling class, and afterwards among all other classes of Americans. For the ruling class has always determined what the social ideals and moral ideas of society should be; and this explains how race prejudice was disseminated until all Americans are supposed to be saturated with it. Race prejudice, then, is the fruit of economic subjection and a fixed inferior economic status. It is the reflex of a social caste system. That caste system in America today is what we roughly refer to as the Race Problem, and it is thus seen that the Negro problem is essentially an economic problem with its roots in slavery past and present.

Notwithstanding the fact that it is usually kept out of public discussion, the bread-and-butter side of this problem is easily the most important. The

Originally published in the *International Socialist Review* 13, no. 1 (July 1912): 65–68.

Negro worker gets less for his work—thanks to exclusion from the craft unions—than any other worker; he works longer hours as a rule and under worse conditions than any other worker; and his rent in any large city is much higher than that which the white worker pays for the same tenement. In short, the exploitation of the Negro worker is keener than that of any group of white workers in America. Now, the mission of the Socialist Party is to free the working class from exploitation, and since the Negro is the most ruthlessly exploited working class group in America, the duty of the party to champion his cause is as clear as day. This is the crucial test of Socialism's sincerity and therein lies the value of this point of view— Socialism and the Negro.

2. The Need of Socialist Propaganda

So far, no particular effort has been made to carry the message of Socialism to these people. All the rest of the poor have had the gospel preached to them, for the party has carried on special propaganda work among the Poles, Slovaks, Finns, Hungarians and Lithuanians. Here are ten million Americans, all proletarians, hanging on the ragged edge of the impending class conflict. Left to themselves they may become as great a menace to our advancing army as is the army of the unemployed, and for precisely the same reason: they can be used against us, as the craft unions have begun to find out. Surely we should make some effort to enlist them under our banner that they may swell our ranks and help to make us invincible. And we must do this for the same reason that is impelling organized labor to adopt an all-inclusive policy; because the other policy results in the artificial breeding of scabs. On grounds of common sense and enlightened self-interest it would be well for the Socialist party to begin to organize the Negroes of America in reference to the class struggle. You may depend on it, comrades, the capitalists of America are not waiting. Already they have subsidized Negro leaders, Negro editors, preachers and politicians to build up in the breasts of black people those sentiments which will make them subservient to their will. For they recognize the value (to them) of cheap labor power and they know that if they can succeed in keeping one section of the working class down they can use that section to keep other sections down too.

3. The Negro's Attitude Toward Socialism

If the Socialist propaganda among Negroes is to be effectively carried on, the members and leaders of the party must first understand the Negro's attitude toward Socialism. That attitude finds its first expression in ignorance. The mass of the Negro people in America are ignorant of what Socialism means. For this they are not much to blame. Behind the veil of the color line none of the great world-movements for social betterment have been able to penetrate. Since it is not yet the easiest task to get the white American worker—with all his superior intellect—to see Socialism, it is but natural to expect that these darker workers to whom America denies knowledge should still be in ignorance as to its aims and objects.

Besides, the Negroes of America—those of them who think—are suspicious of Socialism as of everything that comes from the white people of America. They have seen that every movement for the extension of democracy here has broken down as soon as it reached the color line. Political democracy declared that "all men are created equal," meant only all white men; the Christian church found that the brotherhood of man did not include God's bastard children; the public school system proclaimed that the school house was the backbone of democracy—"for white people only," and the civil service says that Negroes must keep their place—at the bottom. So they can hardly be blamed for looking askance at any new gospel of freedom. Freedom to them has been like one of "those juggling fiends . . . / That palter with us in a double sense, / That keep the word of promise to our ear, / And break it to our hope."

In this connection some explanation of the former political solidarity of those Negroes who were voters may be of service. Up to six years ago the one great obstacle to the political progress of the colored people was their sheep-like allegiance to the Republican party. They were taught to believe that God had raised up a peculiar race of men called Republicans who had loved the slaves so tenderly that they had taken guns in their hands and rushed on the ranks of the southern slaveholders to free the slaves; that this race of men was still in existence, marching under the banner of the Republican party and showing their great love for Negroes by appointing from six to sixteen near-Negroes to soft political snaps. Today that great political superstition is falling to pieces before the advance of intelligence among Negroes. They began to realize that they were sold out by the Republican party in 1876; that in the last twenty-five years lynchings have increased, disfranchisement has spread all over the south and "jim-crow" cars run even into the national capital—with the continuing consent of a Republican congress, a Republican Supreme Court and Republican president.

Ever since the Brownsville affair, but more clearly since Taft declared and put in force the policy of pushing out the few near-Negro officeholders, the rank and file have come to see that the Republican party is a great big sham. Many went over to the Democratic party because, as the *Amsterdam News* puts it, "they had nowhere else to go." Twenty years ago the colored men who joined that party were ostracized as scalawags and crooks—which they probably were. But today, the defection to the Democrats of such men as Bishop Walters, Wood, Carr and Langston—whose uncle was a colored Republican congressman from Virginia—has made the colored democracy respectable and given quite a tone to political heterodoxy.

All this loosens the bonds of their allegiance and breaks the bigotry of the last forty years. But of this change in their political view-point the white world knows nothing. The two leading Negro newspapers are subsidized by the same political pirates who own the title-deeds to the handful of hirelings holding office in the name of the Negro race. One of these papers is an organ of Mr. Washington, the other pretends to be independent— that is, it must be "bought" on the installment plan, and both of them are in New York. Despite this "conspiracy of silence" the Negroes are waking up, are beginning to think for themselves, to look with more favor on "new doctrines." And herein lies the open opportunity of the Socialist party. If the work of spreading Socialist propaganda is taken to them now, their ignorance of it can be enlightened and their suspicions removed.

The Duty of the Socialist Party

I think that we might embrace the opportunity of taking the matter up at the coming national convention. The time is ripe for taking a stand against the extensive disfranchisement of the Negro in violation of the plain provisions of the national constitution. In view of the fact that the last three amendments to the constitution contain this clause, "Congress shall have power to enforce this article by appropriate legislation," the party will not be guilty of proposing anything worse than asking the government to enforce its own "law and order." If the Negroes, or any other section of the working class in America, is to be deprived of the ballot, how can they participate with us in the class struggle? How can we pretend to be a political party if we fail to see the significance of this fact?

Besides, the recent dirty diatribes against the Negro in a Texas paper, which is still on our national list of Socialist papers, the experiences of Mrs. Therese Malkiel in Tennessee, where she was prevented by certain people from addressing a meeting of Negroes on the subject of Socialism, and certain other exhibitions of the thing called Southernism, constitute the challenge of caste. Can we ignore this challenge? I think not. We could hardly afford to have the taint of "trimming" on the garments of the Socialist party. It is dangerous—doubly dangerous now, when the temper of the times is against such "trimming." Besides it would be futile. If it is not met now it must be met later when it shall have grown stronger. Now, when we can cope with it, we have the issue squarely presented: Southernism or Socialism—which? Is it to be the white half of the working class against the black half, or all the working class? Can we hope to triumph over capitalism with one-half of the working class against us? Let us settle these questions now—for settled they must be.

The Negro and Political Socialism

The power of the voting proletarian can be made to express itself through the ballot. To do this they must have a political organization of their own to give form to their will. The direct object of such an organization is to help them to secure control of the powers of government by electing members of the working class to office and so secure legislation in the interest of the working class until such time as the workers may, by being in overwhelming control of the government, be able "to alter or abolish it, and to institute a new government, laying its foundations on such principles, and organizing its powers in such form, as to them shall seem most likely to effect their safety and happiness"—in short, to work for the abolition of capitalism, by legislation—if that be permitted. And in all this the Negro, who feels most fiercely the deep damnation of the capitalist system, can help.

The Negro and Industrial Socialism

But even the voteless proletarian can in a measure help toward the final abolition of the capitalist system. For they too have labor power—which they can be taught to withhold. They can do this by organizing themselves at the point of production. By means of such organization they can work to shorten the hours of labor, to raise wages, to secure an ever-increasing share of the product of their toil. They can enact and enforce laws for the protection of labor and they can do this at the point of production, as was done by the Western Federation of Miners in the matter of the eight-hour law, which they established without the aid of the legislatures or the courts. All this involves a progressive control of the tools of production and a progressive expropriation of the capitalist class. And in all this the Negro can help. So far, they are unorganized on the industrial field, but industrial unionism beckons to them as to others, and the consequent program of the Socialist party for the Negro in the south can be based upon this fact.

W.E.B. Du Bois

Introduction

W.E.B. Du Bois (1868–1963) was one of the most important American intellectuals of the twentieth century. Over the course of his long career, he worked as a sociologist, a historian, an editor, all the while maintaining an extraordinary level of political commitment. Du Bois also underwent considerable political evolution over the course of his life, beginning his political career with a vision of black uplift by the race's "talented tenth" (the most distinguished and accomplished members of the race) and ending it as a Communist.

Du Bois was the first black man to receive a PhD from Harvard. Soon after, he became a professor, holding jobs at Black universities like Wilberforce and Atlanta University. In 1900, he attended the First Pan-African Conference, held in London, where he played a major role in drafting statements condemning colonialism and calling on European leaders to support the struggle against racism. It was here that Du Bois issued his famous proclamation—"The problem of the twentieth century is the problem of the colour line."

Back in the United States, Du Bois played a major role in the emergence of opposition to the Black leader Booker T. Washington. Washington had risen to fame arguing that Black Americans should leave the struggle for civil rights, which was likely to provoke white opposition, and instead concentrate on making themselves an indispensable part of the economy. After proving themselves in this way, Washington argued, civil rights were sure to follow.

Du Bois quickly became Washington's most important critic, arguing that Black Americans could never develop their economic strength if they lacked the right to vote and choose a government that would protect them. Moreover, he argued that the submission to unjust segregation laws inevitably sapped Black self-respect, making the kind of steady race progress Washington counseled an impossibility. Instead, Du Bois argued that the barriers to Black advancement needed to be brought down, so that the "talented tenth" could, through their progress, lift the rest of the race up.

To advance the cause of Black civil rights, Du Bois helped found the National Association for the Advancement of Colored People (NAACP) in 1910. Du Bois came on to the staff of the new group immediately, working to edit the association's journal, the *Crisis*. From its first issue in 1910 until 1934, Du Bois served as the journal's editor, turning it into one of the premiere intellectual journals in the country, covering everything from the arts to international politics.

Shortly after the founding of the NAACP, Du Bois joined the Socialist Party. His decision to do so was no doubt influenced by SP members such as Mary White Ovington and William English Walling, who had been central figures in launching the NAACP. While a member of the party, Du Bois wrote "Socialism and the Negro Problem," a challenge to the SP's acceptance of Southern racism.

Du Bois left the party in 1912, convinced that Woodrow Wilson's presidency could be a new opportunity for Black Americans. He was bitterly disappointed on this front, as Wilson's administration worked to undo many of the small improvements in civil rights that had accumulated under the previous Republican administrations.

Du Bois's exit from the SP was hardly the end of his relationship with socialism, however. In 1926, he traveled to the Soviet Union and was impressed by the commitment to equality he heard while there. In 1935, he published his book *Black Reconstruction in America*, a work deeply informed by Du Bois's reading of Marx, which would become a classic text of American history.

In the 1940s, while Du Bois was in his seventies, he drew even closer to Marxism, working closely with Communists like Paul Robeson. As the Cold War got underway, Du Bois radicalized even further, declaring his complete opposition to American anticommunism. As a result, Du Bois found himself targeted in the McCarthyite Red Scare. In 1950, he was accused of being an agent of the Soviet Union and indicted as such. Du Bois, by then in his eighties, was hauled before a judge in chains. Though the case was dismissed, the government confiscated his passport.

In 1961, Du Bois finally joined the Communist Party after moving steadily closer to it for a decade and a half. His time as an American Communist ended quickly, however, as Du Bois moved to Ghana at the end of the year, to work as editor of a new encyclopedia of the African diaspora. Du Bois died in Ghana in 1963, at the age of 95.

Further Reading

Lewis, David L. *W.E.B. Du Bois, 1868–1919: Biography of a Race*. Vol. 1. New York: Macmillan, 1994.

Mullen, Bill V. *W.E.B. Du Bois: Revolutionary Across the Color Line*. Chicago: University of Chicago Press, 2016.

Reed, Adolph L., Jr. *W.E.B. Du Bois and American Political Thought: Fabianism and the Color Line*. Oxford: Oxford University Press, 1997.

Socialism and the Negro Problem

One might divide those interested in Socialism into two distinct camps: On the one hand, those farsighted thinkers who are seeking to determine from the facts of modern industrial organization just what the outcome is going to be; on the other hand, those who suffer from the present industrial situation and who are anxious that, whatever the broad outcome may be, at any rate the present suffering which they know so well shall be stopped.

It is this second class of social thinkers who are interested particularly in the Negro problem. They are saying that the plight of 10,000,000 human beings in the United States, predominantly of the working class, is so evil that it calls for much attention in any program of future social reform. This paper, however, is addressed not to this class, but rather to the class of theoretical Socialists; and its thesis is: In the Negro problem, as it presents itself in the United States, theoretical Socialism of the twentieth century meets a critical dilemma.

There is no doubt as to the alternative presented. On the one hand, here are 90,000,000 white people who, in their extraordinary development, present a peculiar field for the application of Socialistic principles; but on the whole, these people are demanding to-day that just as under capitalistic organization the Negro has been the excluded (i.e., exploited) class, so, too, any Socialistic program shall also exclude the 10,000,000. Many Socialists have acquiesced in this program. No recent convention of Socialists has dared to face fairly the Negro problem and make a straightforward declaration that they regard Negroes as men in the same sense that other persons are. The utmost that the party has been able to do is not to rescind the declaration of an earlier convention. The general attitude of thinking members of the party has been this: We must not turn aside from the great objects of Socialism to take up this issue of the American Negro; let the

---

Originally published in the *New Review* 1, no. 5 (February 1, 1913): 138–41.

question wait; when the objects of Socialism are achieved, this problem will be settled along with other problems.

That there is a logical flaw here, no one can deny. Can the problem of any group of 10,000,000 be properly considered as "aside" from any program of Socialism? Can the objects of Socialism be achieved so long as the Negro is neglected? Can any great human problem "wait"? If Socialism is going to settle the American problem of race prejudice without direct attack along these lines by Socialists, why is it necessary for Socialists to fight along other lines? Indeed, there is a kind of fatalistic attitude on the part of certain transcendental Socialists, which often assumes that the whole battle of Socialism is coming by a kind of evolution in which active individual effort on their part is hardly necessary.

As a matter of fact, the Socialists face in the problem of the American Negro this question: Can a minority of any group or country be left out of the Socialistic problem? It is, of course, agreed that a majority could not be left out. Socialists usually put great stress on the fact that the laboring class form a majority of all nations and, nevertheless, are unjustly treated in the distribution of wealth. Suppose, however, that this unjust distribution affected only a minority, and that only a tenth of the American nation were working under unjust economic conditions: Could a Socialistic program be carried out which acquiesced in this condition? Many American Socialists seem silently to assume that this would be possible. To put it concretely, they are going to carry on industry so far as this mass is concerned; they are going to get rid of the private control of capital and they are going to divide up the social income among these 90,000,000 in accordance with some rule of reason, rather than in the present haphazard way. But at the same time, they are going to permit the continued exploitation of these 10,000,000 workers. So far as these 10,000,000 workers are concerned, there is to be no active effort to secure for them a voice in the Social Democracy, or an adequate share in the social income. The idea is that ultimately when the 90,000,000 come to their own, they will voluntarily share with the 10,000,000 serfs.

Does the history of the world justify us in expecting any such outcome? Frankly, I do not believe it does. The program is that of industrial aristocracy which the world has always tried; the only difference being that such Socialists are trying to include in the inner circle a much larger number than have ever been included before. Socialistic as this program may be called, it is not real Social Democracy. The essence of Social Democracy is that there shall be no excluded or exploited classes in the Socialistic state; that there shall be no man or woman so poor, ignorant or black as not to count one. Is this simply a far-off ideal, or is it a possible program? I have come to believe that the test of any great movement toward social reform is the Excluded Class. Who is it that Reform does not propose to benefit? If you are saving dying babies, whose babies are you going to let die? If you are feeding the hungry, what folk are you (regretfully, perhaps, but nonetheless truly) going to let starve? If you are making a juster division of wealth, what people are you going to permit at present to remain in poverty? If you are giving all men votes (not only in the "political" but also in the economic world), what class of people are you going to allow to remain disfranchised?

More than that, assuming that if you did exclude Negroes temporarily from the growing Socialistic state, the ensuing uplift of humanity would in the end repair the temporary damage, the present question is, can you exclude the Negro and push Socialism forward? Every tenth man in the United States is of acknowledged Negro descent; if you take those in gainful occupations, one out of every seven Americans is colored; and if you take laborers and workingmen in the ordinary acceptation of the term, one out of every five is colored. The problem is then to lift four-fifths of a group on the backs of the other fifth. Even if the submerged fifth were "dull driven cattle," this program of Socialistic opportunism would not be easy. But when the program is proposed in the face of a group growing in intelligence and social power and a group made suspicious and bitter by analogous action on the part of trade unionists, what is anti-Negro Socialism doing but handing to its enemies the powerful weapon of 4,500,000 men, who will find it not simply to their interest, but a sacred duty, to underbid the labor market, vote against labor legislation, and fight to keep their fellow laborers down? Is it not significant that Negro soldiers in the army are healthier and desert less than whites? Nor is this all: What becomes of Socialism when it engages in such a fight for human downfall? Whither are gone its lofty aspiration and high resolve—its songs and comradeship?

The Negro Problem, then, is the great test of the American Socialist. Shall American Socialism strive to train for its Socialistic state 10,000,000 serfs, who will serve or be exploited by that state, or shall it strive to incorporate them immediately into that body politic? Theoretically, of course, all Socialists, with few exceptions, would wish the latter program.

But it happens that in the United States there is a strong local opinion in the South which violently opposes any program of any kind of reform that recognizes the Negro as a man. So strong is this body of opinion that you have in the South a most extraordinary development. The whole radical movement there represented by men like Blease and Vardaman and Tillman and Jefferson Davis, and attracting such demagogues as Hoke Smith, includes in its program of radical reform a most bitter and reactionary hatred of the Negro. The average modern Socialist can scarcely grasp the extent of this hatred; even murder and torture of human beings holds a prominent place in its philosophy; the defilement of colored women is its joke, and justice toward colored men will not be listened to.

The only basis on which one can even approach these people with a plea for the barest tolerance of colored folk, is that the murder and mistreatment of colored men may possibly hurt white men. Consequently, the Socialist Party finds itself in this predicament: If it acquiesces in race hatred, it has a chance to turn the tremendous power of Southern white radicalism toward its own party; if it does not do this, it becomes a "party of the Negro," with its growth South and North decidedly checked. There are signs that the Socialist leaders are going to accept the chance of getting hold of the radical South, whatever its cost. This paper is written to ask such leaders: After you have gotten the radical South and paid the price which they demand, will the result be Socialism?

The *New Review*

Introduction

The *New Review* was a journal published by Socialist Party members from 1913 through 1916. In that short time, it provided an important voice for the party after the expulsion of Big Bill Haywood in 1912. In particular, the *New Review* was host to some of the most advanced writing on the race question in those years and provided a venue in which socialists forthrightly accused the SP of insufficient attention to it.

The *New Review* was announced in 1911 by a factionally heterogeneous group of socialists, writing in the SP publication *Wilshire's Magazine*. The journal's founders proclaimed its purpose as "the dissemination of a knowledge of the theories, principles, and methods of Marxism; and the discussion and analysis of current events, and of the practical problems with which the Socialist movement is confronted, in the light of these theories, principles, and methods." The *New Review*, in other words, would be an intellectual journal and not an agitational one. The perceived need for such a publication was undoubtedly stimulated by the transformation of the *International Socialist Review* over the previous few years, after intellectual A.M. Simons was removed from editorship and the review became more focused on reporting and supporting various struggles.

Though the *New Review* began life factionally unaffiliated, it soon became home to the SP left. William English Walling, a socialist journalist who supported the IWW and the SP left, was one of its most frequent contributors in its early issues, and he was soon joined by other left-wingers, such as Henry Slobodin. By the end of 1913, Louis Fraina, who would become one of the intellectual leaders of the SP left, was also writing regularly for the journal.

From very early on, the *New Review* prioritized the race question. Its second issue contained a contribution from W.E.B. Du Bois, arguing that organizing Black workers was "A Field for Socialists." A few weeks later, it followed this up with Du Bois's much-cited essay on "Socialism and the Negro Problem." Later that same year, it ran Mary White Ovington's "The Status of the Negro in the United States," which forthrightly challenged the party to take a stronger stand on Black equality, particularly in the South. The following month, it published Marx's writings on the Civil War, bringing them at last to a mass American audience.

In mid-1916, the journal folded for lack of funds. Though its existence was short, it helped prepare the ground for the explosion of left-wing socialism after the American entry into World War I. Similarly, its propagandizing on behalf of a more committed approach to the race question helped propel the party's general radicalization on this question in the years before the war.

Further Reading

Davenport, Tim. "Introduction to the *New Review* (1913–1916)." *Marxist Internet Archive*. August 2011, www.marxists.org/history/usa/pubs /newreview/index.htm.

Lloyd, Brian. *Left Out: Pragmatism, Exceptionalism, and the Poverty of American Marxism, 1890–1922*. Baltimore: Johns Hopkins University Press, 1997.

Schneirov, Richard. "The Odyssey of William English Walling: Revisionism, Social Democracy, and Evolutionary Pragmatism." *Journal of the Gilded Age and Progressive Era* 2, no. 4 (2003): 403–30.

The Status of the Negro in the United States

by Mary White Ovington

During the controversy over the status of the Japanese in California, a wave of patriotic emotion swept through our newspapers and magazines. One heard, as an echo from the past, of the inalienable rights with which men are endowed, and one listened to the righteous wrath of those who believed that the rule of one group in the population over another spelled despotism. The sight of a race in the United States denied the franchise by the federal government, and later prohibited from acquiring property by a state, called forth a genuine expression of old-time patriotism.

But while popular periodicals have discussed their country's despotism toward the Japanese with liberty-loving hearts, they have failed to-day and for years past to mention the despotism practiced daily toward a far larger element in the population, the Negro element. With a few notable exceptions, no notice is taken in newspaper or magazine of the inalienable rights of the American colored man. And yet these rights have been denied him month by month and year by year, and are now being legally wrested from him almost as swiftly as their property rights were wrested from the California Japanese.

What civil and political rights has the Negro to-day in the United States?

Under the Constitution he is awarded the full rights of a citizen. The Fourteenth Amendment provides that all persons born or naturalized in the United States are citizens of the United States; and that no state shall make or enforce any law which shall abridge the privileges of these citizens. And the Fifteenth Amendment declares that the right to vote shall not be denied or abridged by the United States or by any state on account of race, color, or previous condition of servitude. These amendments were declared in force in 1868 and 1870, respectively, and were followed in 1875 by Charles

Originally published in the *New Review* 1, no. 20 (September 1913): 744–49.

Sumner's Civil Rights Bill which provided against discrimination against Negroes in inns, public conveyances, and theatres; and prevented Negroes from being disqualified as jurors.

Thus by legal enactment the Negro by 1875 was placed on an equality with the white; and in the northern states he has, to a considerable extent, enjoyed this equality. In the South, however, he has steadily lost the status given him by the Constitution, and has become a disfranchised alien in a democracy. In 1883, the first great legal blow was dealt him when the Supreme Court of the United States declared the Civil Rights Bill unconstitutional in the states. It did not declare it unconstitutional, however, in the territories, in the District of Columbia or on the high seas.

From the days of the Ku Klux Klans on, the white voters of the South by intimidation and by fraud prevented a great mass of Negroes from registering their votes. Nevertheless, the Negro was a power and was counted an important political factor during the eighties and early nineties—the time of the Farmers' Alliance and the Populist party. Bargains were often made with Negroes for their votes; as in Atlanta, Georgia, when in 1885, the Prohibition party secured a majority of the colored votes on the promise of a new school house for colored children (the last school to be built for Negroes in this wealthy southern city). All the bargains were not of so pleasant a complexion, but wise or foolish they represented political power. They were therefore stopped by legislative enactments which were initiated in Mississippi in 1890, and later imitated in South Carolina, Louisiana, North Carolina, Virginia, Georgia and Oklahoma.

Disfranchisement was accomplished in various ways. State constitutions were amended or new constitutions adopted which provided property tests, the payment of poll taxes and educational qualifications. Then, seeing that these qualifications, if enforced, were disfranchising nearly all the whites as well as the blacks, some of the states passed "grandfather" clauses which gave the right to vote to an old soldier or the descendant of an old soldier. As most of the soldiers in the southern states had fought against the Union, this legislation presented the delightful anomaly of authorizing men to vote for President and Congressmen because their fathers had fought to destroy the United States government. The Negro vote was soon so reduced as to be inappreciable; and the twentieth century found no Representative in the South with a Negro constituency. The white men in the state legislatures represented white men only, and were there to advance the interests of their white constituents; and when the new, liberty-loving Progressive party at its noble convention refused to seat delegates sent by Negroes from the states where disfranchisement was in force, it but proclaimed to the whole country that southern rule is the rule of the white alone.

After disfranchisement, came, as with the Japanese, the seizure of property rights.

At first this was accomplished by intimidation and violence. A man who became unpopular with his neighbors because he was worth too much, or didn't know enough to know his place, was driven out of town. The Atlanta riots seriously affected the colored property holders of that city, for the rioters, avoiding those parts of the town in which the criminal Negro resided, attacked the lives and property of industrious, often well-to-do, artisans. But again as in the case of the franchise, violence is giving way to legalized confiscation. The Negro, by ordinance, is losing control of his property.

It is done in this fashion. In Mooresville, North Carolina, a colored carpenter started to build a house on a piece of property which he had owned for four years. The residents of that section forbade his building. He continued at his work and the city then passed an ordinance prescribing the part of the city in which colored people might live, and providing a penalty if they attempted to break through the limit. The carpenter had to desist from building and his property remains unimproved.

For three years Baltimore has tried to enforce a segregation ordinance, and the question of its constitutionality is now before the Supreme Court of the state of Maryland. The ordinance defines "colored blocks" and "white blocks," and imposes a penalty for permitting a colored person to live in a white block or a white person in a colored. It affects property owners, and thus far the whites have been the chief pecuniary sufferers; but if it is declared constitutional it will have a profound effect upon the Negro's property rights, especially in those states in which he is deprived of all participation in the government. The poorest sections of the city can then be assigned to him, and these sections can be left in a state of neglect, physical and moral. And if the city may legally prescribe where he shall dwell and acquire property, why may not the country districts as well? One sees before one whole vistas of comfortable confiscation by the whites of fertile, Negro-owned lands. If anyone doubts this, let him study the history of our dealings with the Indians.

The federal Civil Rights Bill for which Charles Sumner worked so doggedly, and which was declared unconstitutional by the Supreme Court, gave the Negro the ordinary privileges of a resident in any country—the right to stop at a hotel and get a meal and a bed, to enter a theatre or concert hall and hear the entertainment provided, to ride in the street car and on the railroad. All these rights have been taken from the black man in the South except the last, and he may not ride in street or railroad car save segregated in an equally expensive, but distinctly inferior, seat. But in the District of Columbia, the territories, and on the high seas this law has been technically in force. It has not prevented discrimination, but it has modified it. Negroes have not been segregated in street cars or in many public places. This June, however, the Supreme Court of the United States has declared the law unconstitutional everywhere. This has called forth a flood of bills in Congress designed to segregate the Negro of Washington. The negro-phobist is rampant, and black men and women in the nation's capital may soon be subjected to every indignity that the ingenuity of a senator from Mississippi can devise.

But who cares whether a colored woman in Washington can sit in a vacant seat in the forward part of a street car, or must stand in the rear while a white rowdy, lolling comfortably, blows his smoke in her face? Who is troubled when the black man is ordered out of the railroad restaurant and goes hungry on his travels? Who is concerned whether the state of South Carolina gives the colored children their equal share of the school funds or allows them one-fourth of what it allows the white child? Who bothers when the police in Atlanta or Birmingham or New Orleans arrest each Negro who is out of work as a vagrant; or who troubles himself when the court sends the vagrant to the chain gang where he is vilely housed and debauched and beaten? Who, among the many that have been filled with sympathy for the fifty thousand yellow people in California, is stirred at hearing of the segregation of eight million black- and brown- and white-skinned Americans, all conveniently classed as Negroes? Who cares?

There are two organizations in this country that have shown that they do care. The first is the Association for the Advancement of Colored People. This organization is made up of white and colored men and women and is pledged to oppose the segregation of the Negro and to strive for the enforcement of the Fourteenth and Fifteenth Amendments. It appeared before the Supreme Court of Maryland on the Baltimore Segregation Act, and it expects to appear before the Supreme Court of the United States in October in a case to test the constitutionality of the "grandfather clause." It is in the anomalous position of a society espousing an amazingly unpopular cause and finding its stronghold in the United States Constitution. The Association carries on a vigorous publicity campaign through its organ, the *Crisis*, of which Dr. Burghardt Du Bois, a contributor to the *NEW REVIEW*, is the editor.

The second organization that attacks Negro segregation is the Industrial Workers of the World.

When it looked as though William D. Haywood and the organization that he represents would be recognized at the national Socialist Convention at Indianapolis, Haywood turned to the delegates and said: "Now I may go back to tell the millions of women and children and the eight million Negroes that you stand with them." The I.W.W. has stood with the Negro. The Brotherhood of Timber Workers in Louisiana has fraternized with black men and together the two races have battled against their exploiters. Only one familiar with the South can appreciate the courage of this position, and the bravery demanded of both races. Mixed locals have been organized despite the fact that there is a law in Louisiana prohibiting public gatherings of black and white. The common enemy has obliterated the color line.

I wish I might cite the Socialist party, the party I so love, as the third force to stand aggressively for the Negroes' full rights. In some Southern states, notably Oklahoma, the white Socialists have supported the blacks in their manhood struggles. In Louisiana and Texas, on the other hand, they have, at times, shown a race prejudice unexcelled by the most virulent Democrats. But it would not be just to judge the party by the action of a small group in the South. We need to note the position of the national body. This body in 1901, passed a noble resolution expressing its sympathy with the Negro in his subjection to lawlessness and oppression, and inviting him to membership and fellowship in the world movement for economic emancipation. This was in 1901, but there has been no word since. At the last national Socialist Convention, while the delegate spent hour after hour in frenzied talk over amendments to amendments of motions which no one remembered, no word, save that of Haywood's, was uttered in appreciation of the existence of this most exploited race. One Negro delegate was present, but he was not given the opportunity to speak. To this convention, the United States Negro, composing one-fifth of all the workingmen in the Union, did not exist.

And yet the color problem is not one that we can dispose of by saying, as did many at the Socialist convention, that it is economic and will be solved by the coming of Socialism. Our goal is still far off; we are on the road, and we must beware of the forces that will be used to retard us. Among these forces is race discrimination. The creation of a segregated class in our democracy, a class without a ballot, without civil rights, poorly educated, with a low standard of living, will seriously retard the coming of the Co-operative Commonwealth. So we must watch each effort that is made to prevent black men and white men from meeting on equal terms.

For decades, Negroes and whites have been working side by side in the various departments in Washington, but since the coming in of the Democratic administration they have been separated. In some rooms screens have been placed about the colored men that they might not be seen by their white co-workers. This screen is not only an outrageous insult to the black man, it is also a barrier that prevents men in the same economic class from meeting and working for the incoming of a genuinely Democratic government. The segregated black laborer will learn to believe that his cause is antagonistic to the cause of the white laborer. Increasingly he will serve the capitalist—to whom, indeed, he will alone owe any possible loyalty—and he will logically become a means for building up privilege and increasing the power of the few.

The screen that the present administration is placing between black men and white men, and between black women and white women, we are assured, is needed to preserve the integrity of the races—which simply means that under no circumstances shall the white race assume any responsibility for the consequences of its immoral acts. It is time that we tore down this screen of hypocrisy, and that we faced the awful fact: the fact that we starve our workers; and that those who are black, as they turn homeward, their long day done, we afterwards stone.

"Democracy" and Negro Segregation

by Louis C. Fraina

The American press is practically unanimous in its condemnation of the Mexican people—their alleged savagery and general all-around uncivilized habits. But the Mexicans have been fighting, are fighting against injustice and oppression, while the American people are devising new forms of injustice and new means of oppression. Just now, our oppression of the Negro has been emphasized by the adoption in St. Louis of a segregation ordinance. The question was brought before the electorate by means of the initiative, that palladium of bourgeois progressivism, and the ordinance passed by an overwhelming majority. The sentiment for Negro segregation was hitherto believed to be confined to the South; how much deeper the evil is has been proven by St. Louis. It is all disgustingly discouraging, particularly as the vote cast represented all sorts and conditions of peoples, many of whom have only recently fled oppression to come to this country of equal opportunity.

All this brings to mind American criticism of the Russian "pale." How about the American "pale" being forced upon the Negro? Our gallant defenders of all the bourgeois virtues hysterically condemn "autocracy" and "frightfulness" in Germany. How about the white oligarchy of the South disfranchising the Negro and battening upon his helplessness? How about the policy of frightfulness being practiced upon the Negro? It is all a hideous nightmare. We are a democracy, yes; but we are a democracy in the old Athenian sense, an oligarchic democracy superimposed upon a mass of slaves,—the slaves in our case being the Negro and unskilled foreign labor.

The American Socialist movement has criminally neglected the race problem. It is one of the most potent instruments of oppression in this country. It is a serious obstacle to Socialism. The interests of Socialism, of common decency, require an agitation for justice to the Negro and all subject races.

Originally published in the *New Review* 4, no. 4 (April 1916): 102–3.

The *Class Struggle*

Introduction

The *Class Struggle* was a journal of the left wing of the Socialist Party. Founded in 1917, it existed for only two years. In that time, however, it gathered together many of the leading lights of American revolutionary socialism, publishing Eugene Debs, Louis Fraina, and Sen Katayama. The journal also served as one of the primary links between the revolutionary currents in European socialist parties and the traditions of American socialism.

The *Class Struggle* emerged out of the factional struggles within the Socialist Party in early 1917. Since the beginning of World War I, the party had been divided over how to respond to the conflict. The party's left wing argued that the war signaled the beginning of a revolutionary period, and that implacable opposition to the war needed to be linked to a revolutionary program. The party's right wing, by contrast, argued against American intervention in the war but refused to commit the party to all-out opposition to the war effort, still less, a revolutionary strategy for ending it.

In early 1917, representatives of the left wing met in an apartment in Brooklyn to discuss how best to advance their cause. They were joined by a number of Russian exiles, including Leon Trotsky, Nikolai Bukharin, and Alexandra Kollontai. At the meeting they debated whether to remain within the SP or split immediately to begin a new revolutionary party. The former course was adopted, and the group decided to found a new publication to win more of the SP to its perspective. The first issue of the *Class Struggle* came out in May of 1917.

For the next two years, the magazine would be a consistent voice for the left wing in its escalating conflict with the party leadership. In addition to providing a left-wing perspective on the SP, it also republished pieces from the antiwar socialist left internationally. Figures like Lenin, Karl Radek, and Rosa Luxemburg were all brought to an American audience through the *Class Struggle*.

The journal's final issue came in November of 1919. After the expulsion of the left wing from the SP over the course of the previous year, the newly formed Communist Labor Party had taken up responsibility for its publication. When the postwar wave of anticommunist repression began late that year, it quickly drove the CLP underground and destroyed its ability to maintain the journal.

The article reprinted here gives a perspective on the race riots that swept the country in the "Red Summer" of 1919. It is noteworthy for the decidedly left perspective it advances on the riots, laying blame squarely on the segregation and oppression of Black Americans. Though the article implicitly accepts elements of racial scapegoating, referring to the "incipient thief or rapist" created by that oppression, its advocacy for raising the conditions of Black schools and neighborhoods places it firmly on the left of SP discussions of the race question. In particular, its concluding paragraph, which targets racial divisions among workers as the most important barrier to stopping race riots, echoes arguments by Hubert Harrison, and anticipates later arguments from the Communist Party.

Further Reading

Draper, Theodore. *The Roots of American Communism*. New Brunswick, NJ: Transaction Publishers, 2003 [1957].

Lloyd, Brian. *Left Out: Pragmatism, Exceptionalism, and the Poverty of American Marxism, 1890–1922*. Baltimore: Johns Hopkins University Press, 1997.

Weinstein, James. *The Decline of the American Socialist Movement, 1912–1924*. New York: Monthly Review Press, 1967.

The Negro Problem—A Labor Problem

For the moment the race riots that raged in Washington and in Chicago are quelled. But they will break out again, there and in the cities where colored people have congregated in great numbers. For decades the states of the North have looked passively on while the conflict raged in the South between Black and White, with the quiet superiority of the onlooker who refuses to interfere in affairs that are none of his business.

But the last two years have radically changed the situation. The acute labor shortage brought about by the artificial stimulation of American industries during the war and the withdrawal of hundreds of thousands of young men from the labor market led to the mass importation of Negro labor from the South. And with the Negro the North has imported his problems; without attempting, however, to find a solution for the difficulties that were sure to arise.

Among the first of these was the housing problem. Even under more favorable circumstances it has always been difficult for a Negro family to find quarters in the large cities of the North. To allow a family of colored people to live in a house in a respectable neighborhood in decent houses, among decent surroundings meant an immediate exodus of the Whites living in that vicinity. Real estate values consequently decreased and houses were bought for a song by profiteering speculators, to be rented out, at enormous rentals, to the colored population. Indeed, this method has been used on more than one occasion in real estate controversies, one party to the difficulty renting out his property to Negro tenants and then causing a depreciation of the value of the property of his neighbor litigant.

This chronic shortage became acute with the importation of thousands of Negroes into the larger cities of the North. Colored families paid fantastic prices for dwelling places and thus secured a foothold in neighborhoods that were closed to them before, to the consequent irritation of

---

Originally published in the *Class Struggle* 3, no. 3 (August 1919): 339–41.

their white neighbors. Passive prejudice against the Negro became active resentment.

That the health and morals of the colored population must suffer under such adverse conditions is obvious. They raised the money necessary to pay the high rentals by overcrowding their cramped quarters. Immorality and disease flourish under such conditions. The *Survey* reports that in Cincinnati the death rate of the colored population is double that of the Whites, that pneumonia among the colored people is three times as deadly as among their white neighbors, that their syphilis rate is five times as high. That in proportion to the population, three times as many colored children die before birth, that three times as many colored babies, born alive, die before their first birthday; that the excess in colored deaths from preventable causes alone is so great that it accounts for more than one point in the general death rate of the city. Conditions in other large cities are very similar. Nor is this due to racial weakness on the part of the colored population, for the physical examination of the male population during the draft revealed the surprising fact that the white men of the South show a far greater percentage of physically unfit than the colored population.

The returning soldiers and the subsidence of inflated war industries to their normal level have produced a situation that is little short of a calamity. The white man finds the job that used to support him in the hands of Negroes who are willing to underbid him in the labor market in order to maintain an existence. Labor unions which excluded Negroes from membership find their existence threatened by the influx of colored labor into their industries. Everywhere the colored man has become the dangerous competitor of the white. It is this fact, above all, that lies at the root of the race trouble that is brewing everywhere.

Popular discontent will remain, and will continue to culminate in horrible excesses such as occurred in Washington and Chicago, and in East St. Louis a year ago, so long as State and National authorities maintain the passive attitude of "neutrality" they have hitherto affected. Punishment of the offenders on both sides will do little good—and, indeed, we doubt whether there exists the slightest intention of calling to account those white hoodlums who precipitated the trouble. The remedy must be more fundamental, more far-reaching in its effects.

So long as the colored children of the South are allowed to grow up with practically no schooling, because state and county appropriations for education are barely sufficient to give a rudimentary education to the children of the Whites; so long as the Negro of the South can receive a high school and college education only in schools and universities maintained by colored people themselves; so long as in many sections of the South Negro communities must maintain their own public schools and yet pay school taxes for the upkeep of white schools in their districts; so long as no attempt is made to develop and improve the moral tone of the Negro boy or girl after school hours, to maintain institutions of correction for the wayward boy or girl, for the incipient thief or rapist outside the county jail or state prison— so long will the moral and mental standard of the Negro be beneath that of the White. The authorities of the North must meet this problem with a vigorous and efficient program of education and public hygiene.

But the most important factor in the permanent cessation of these race riots is the white workingman himself. So long as he insists upon Negro segregation, so long as he closes the doors of his industrial organization to the colored man, he will have in him a dangerous competitor on the industrial field. No protest, however emphatic, can drive him from the labor market, for, to the capitalist entrepreneur, Negro labor is cheap labor. Race feeling will persist until economic competition between the white and the black man will have ceased. But first the white man must understand that there is but one alternative—either competition to the utmost or a common fight of all workers, without regard to color, race or creed, against the common enemy, the capitalist class.

Part II
The Industrial Workers of the World

Ben Fletcher

Introduction

Ben Fletcher (1890–1949) was a Black IWW organizer and longshore worker in Philadelphia. From just before World War I until the early 1920s, Fletcher was a leading figure in the IWW-affiliated Philadelphia longshoremen's union, Marine Transport Workers International Union Local 8. Fletcher helped lead the union through a successful strike against the stevedore companies and through the war years. In late 1917, he was indicted as part of the state's campaign of repression against the Wobblies, as IWW members were called. Fletcher's subsequent conviction removed him from his position of centrality in Local 8, and though he attempted in various ways to advance his militant antiracist unionism on the docks, by the end of 1930s he had left Philadelphia and faded into obscurity.

Very little is known about Fletcher's early life. There are suggestions, though no proof, that he was a Socialist Party member around 1910. By 1912 he was a known IWW activist in Philadelphia, speaking at IWW rallies in the area.

His rise to prominence came along with that of the dockworkers union. In 1913, longshoremen struck for union recognition and better wages. Soon after the strike began, they voted to affiliate themselves with the IWW. Though no record of Fletcher's involvement in this decision survives, it seems likely he played a key role in it. Throughout the strike, the union maintained a militant posture of racial egalitarianism. The bargaining committee had members representing every nationality found on the docks, and though the employers brought in Black scabs, the subsequent battles between strikers and scabs acquired none of the ugly racial character that so often surfaced in strikes of this period.

Within a few weeks, the strike was won. Fletcher proceeded to try and spread the example of Local 8 around the region, traveling to other ports like Baltimore to organize workers there on a similar basis. Unfortunately, his efforts never bore fruit, and Local 8 remained an anomaly among American dockworkers.

When World War I broke out, Local 8 went along with most of the American union movement in supporting the war effort and halting their strike activity. This posture, however, was not sufficient to allay governmental suspicions of the Wobblies, and Fletcher and other Local 8 leaders were arrested along with most of the rest of the IWW's leadership in the fall of 1917. Convicted in the farce of a trial that ensued, Fletcher nonetheless won release while his appeal was being processed in 1920. That year, he returned to Philadelphia to assist Local 8 with its massive strike to make up for wartime inflation. Though 10,000 dockworkers struck for a month, the strike ended as a draw.

From here, Local 8 went through a devastating series of crises. That same year, Local 8 was suspended from the IWW twice—first, it was accused of loading munitions to be sent to the counterrevolutionary white armies in Russia; and second, the local's steep initiation fee, which it used to control entry to the workforce, disqualified it from IWW affiliation. These internal controversies sapped the union's strength, even as the employers prepared to smash it completely.

The blow came in 1922, when the employers launched a lockout. During the lockout, Fletcher finally received his pardon from the president, but, still under governmental surveillance, he stayed out of the spotlight. Missing Fletcher's leadership dearly, the local found itself internally weak and was confronted with both determined employers and AFL unions hoping to move in on its turf. The union splintered along racial lines, with black workers returning to work. Fletcher would attempt to reorganize black workers on the docks in a new union, independent of the IWW, but never succeeded in gaining recognition for it. In a few years, he would leave Philadelphia, and political activity, altogether.

His article here, published in the *Messenger*, is an attack on the AFL's acceptance of racial segregation in its unions. No doubt buoyed by what he had seen accomplished through Local 8's interracialism, Fletcher made the case that segregation and discrimination were weaknesses the union movement could not afford in its battle with employers.

Further Reading

Cole, Peter. *Ben Fletcher: The Life and Times of a Black Wobbly, Including Fellow Worker Fletcher's Writings & Speeches.* Chicago: Charles H. Kerr Publishing Company, 2007.

———. *Wobblies on the Waterfront: Interracial Unionism in Progressive-Era Philadelphia.* Champaig: University of Illinois Press, 2007.

Seraile, William. "Ben Fletcher, I.W.W. Organizer." *Pennsylvania History: A Journal of Mid-Atlantic Studies* 46, no. 3 (July 1979): 212–32.

The Negro and Organized Labor

In these United States of America, the history of the Organized Labor Movement's attitude and disposition toward the Negro Section of the world of Industry is replete with gross indifference and, excepting a few of its component parts, is a record of complete surrender before the color line. Directed, manipulated, and controlled by those bent on harmonizing the diametrically opposed interests of Labor and Capital, it is for the most part not only a "bulwark against" Industry of, by and for Labor, but in an overwhelming majority of instances is no less a bulwark against the economic, political and social betterment of Negro Labor.

The International Association of Machinists as well as several other International bodies of the A.F.L. along with the Railroad Brotherhoods, either by constitutional decree or general policy, forbid the enrollment of Negro members, while others if forced by his increasing presence in their jurisdictions, organize him into separate unions. There are but few exceptions that are not covered by these two policies and attitudes. It is needless to state that the employing class are the beneficiaries of these policies of Negro Labor exclusion and segregation. It is a fact indisputable that Negro Labor's foothold nearly everywhere in organized labor's domains has been secured by scabbing them into defeat or into terms that provided for Negro Labor inclusion in their ranks. What a sad commentary upon Organized Labor's shortsightedness and profound stupidity. In these United States of America less than 4 per cent of Negro Labor is organized. Fully 16 per cent of the Working Class in this country are Negroes. No genuine attempt by Organized Labor to wrest any worthwhile and lasting concessions from the Employing Class can succeed as long as Organized Labor for the most part is indifferent and in opposition to the fate of Negro Labor. As long as these facts are the facts, the Negro Section of the World of Industry can be safely counted upon by the Employing Class as a successful wedge to prevent any

Originally published in the *Messenger*, July 1923, 759-60.

notable organized labor triumph. The millions of dollars which they have and continue to furnish Negro Institutions will continue to yield a magnificent interest in the shape of Negro Labor loyalty to the Employing Class.

Organized Labor can bring about a different situation. One that will speed the dawn of Industrial Freedom. First, by erasing their Race exclusion clauses. Second, by enrolling ALL workers in their Industrial or Craft jurisdictions, in the same union or unions, and where custom or the statutes prohibit in some Southern states, so educate their membership and develop the power and influence of their various unions as to force the repeal of these prohibiting statutes and customs. Thirdly, by aiding and abetting his entrance into their various craft jurisdictions, unless he comes, of course, as a strike breaker. Fourth, by joining him in his fight in the South to secure political enfranchisement. Fifth, by inducting into the service of organized labor, Negro Labor Organizers and other officials in proportion to his numbers and ability.

The Organized Labor Movement has not begun to become a contender for its place in the Sun, until every man, woman and child in Industry is eligible to be identified with its Cause, regardless of Race, color or creed. The secret of the Employing Class rule and Industry's control, is the division and lack of cohesion existing in the ranks of labor. None can dispute the fact that Organized Labor's attitude of indifference and often outspoken opposition to Negro Labor, contributes a vast amount to this division and lack of cohesion.

Organized Labor Banks, Political Parties, Educational Institutions, co-operatives, nor any other of its effort to get somewhere near the goal of economic emancipation from the thraldom of the rich, will avail naught, as long as the color line lies across the pathway to their goal and before which they are doomed to halt and surrender. Until organized labor generally casts aside the bars of race exclusion and enrolls Negro Labor within its ranks on a basis of complete sincere fraternity, no general effort of steel, railroad, packing house, building trades workers or any workers for that matter, to advance from the yoke of Industrial slavery can succeed. Just as certain as day follows night, the Negro will continue to contribute readily and generously toward the elements that will make for their defeat. Personally, the writer would not have it otherwise unless organized labor, majorly speaking, right about faces on its Negro Labor attitude and policy!

Signs are not wanting that men and women of vision in the ranks of organized labor, of both the radical and conservative wing, are alive to the necessity of reformation of organized labor's attitude on the Negro, and are attempting to bring their various organizations in line with such organizations as the United Mine Workers of America, Amalgamated Clothing Workers and the Industrial Workers of the World. Negro Labor has a part to play also in changing this present day attitude of organized labor. It should organize a nation-wide movement to encourage, promote and protect its employment and general welfare. Divided into central districts and branches thereof, it would be able to not only thereby force complete and unequivocal recognition, but at the same time render yeoman service in procuring the increased employment of tens of thousands of fully capable Negro workers in such positions as are now closed to them because of the lack of sufficient organized Negro Labor pressure in the right direction and with the right instrumentality of intelligent vision.

This organization would by virtue of its being comprised of Negro Labor of all Industries and crafts be able to safeguard its every advance and prevent any successful attack against same. Collective dealing with the Employing Class is the only way by which Labor can procure any concessions from them of effect and meaning. It is the only way in which to establish industrial stability and uniformity in its administration and finally Industrial freedom. This holds good for Negro as well as white labor. There are fully 4,000,000 Negro men, women and children, eligible to participate in such a Negro Labor Federation.

The beginning of such an organization a generation ago, the attitude of organized labor to the Negro would be just the reverse today. Organized Labor for the most part, be it radical or conservative, thinks and acts, in terms of the White Race. Like the preachers, politicians, who when preaching about the "immortality of the soul" or orating about the "glourious land of the free" have in mind and so explain, white folks. So with organized labor generally. To a large extent Negro Labor is responsible for this reprehensible exclusion because of its failure to generate a force which when necessary could have rendered low the dragon head of Race prejudice, whenever and wherever it raised its head. It is not too late, however, to begin to rectify and to reap the benefits of united effort. Only by unifying our forces in such a way as to force organized labor to realize that we can do lasting good or lasting evil, will they, with the assistance of those men and women already in their ranks fighting to change their erroneous way, understand and "come over into Macedonia and help us."

IWW Documents

Introduction

The Industrial Workers of the World (IWW) was a revolutionary, industrial union founded in 1905 as an alternative to the conservative craft unionism of the American Federation of Labor (AFL). While the AFL paid little attention to unorganized, unskilled workers, the Wobblies argued that the entire working class had to be united in "One Big Union" to take on capital. In accordance with this perspective, the IWW practiced interracial unionism to an extent previously unknown in American history, organizing black and white workers together in the fight against the employers.

The IWW was founded at a small convention of radical American unionists, where Socialist Party members like Eugene Debs and Big Bill Haywood played a prominent role. At the convention, Haywood explicitly condemned the AFL for its practice of organizing segregated locals, and he declared that the IWW would tolerate no such practices. The constitution adopted at the convention made good on this promise, reading "no working man or woman shall be excluded from membership because of creed or color."

The first few years of the IWW's existence were difficult. The recession of 1908 struck particularly hard against the precarious workers who were the organization's main constituency, and internal conflict over its direction cost the Wobblies dearly. Nevertheless, by the end of its first decade, the organization could boast some major successes, particularly in its goal of breaking down the divisions of color that afflicted the American working class.

In the South, the Wobblies embraced the unionization efforts among Southern timber workers, who labored in a massive industry that employed hundreds of thousands of Black and white workers. The Brotherhood of Timber Workers (BTW) arose directly from the organizing of the workers themselves, but it soon joined the IWW. Though the BTW organized black and white workers alike, it initially organized them along Jim Crow lines, in separate units. Haywood and other IWW members argued the organization needed to drop this practice, even though it was illegal in states like Louisiana for blacks and whites to hold meetings together. The BTW was won over and proceeded to build a strong base among Black workers in the timber camps. When the union struck, and the employers attempted to use Black scabs to break the strike, black workers held the line, refusing to scab on the union and often joining the pickets. Though the union was eventually destroyed through a combination of mob violence and state repression (which were often difficult to tell apart), it nonetheless demonstrated what was possible in interracial organizing, even in the Deep South.

The other main IWW success story in confronting the color line is the Marine Transport Workers (MTW) Local 8 in Philadelphia. Led by Black Wobbly Ben Fletcher, the MTW voted to affiliate with the IWW during their 1913 strike for recognition. Representing a workforce that was roughly half Black and half Eastern European or Irish, the MTW devised a number of innovative techniques for forging interracial class unity. While across the country dockworker crews were segregated, in Philadelphia the MTW broke down segregation, bringing integrated working crews to the docks. The union itself instituted a system whereby the chair of the local rotated each month between a black and a white worker. Through these kinds of initiatives, the union succeeded in building a resilient base among the dockworkers, which would take employers a decade to finally dislodge.

As daring and accomplished as the IWW was when it came to race, it must be said that its propaganda lagged far behind its practice. While IWW texts were basically unanimous in condemning racism and exclusion, they offered little for Black workers beyond their general workplace militancy. Issues like disenfranchisement and segregation (outside of unions, at least) received virtually no discussion in IWW publications. Moreover, the organization had a troubling tendency to idealize chattel slavery in comparison with capitalist exploitation, often arguing that the Civil War was a war like any other in which the poor fought and died while winning nothing for themselves. These kinds of postures no doubt hampered the IWW's efforts to gain more support among Black workers.

These texts, however, should not be allowed to overshadow the IWW's real accomplishments on the front of interracial organizing. The Wobblies committed themselves to interracial organizing half a century before the rest of the labor movement caught up, and whatever their failures, they honored that commitment.

Further Reading

Cole, Peter, and Lucien van der Walt. "Crossing the Color Lines, Crossing the Continents: Comparing the Racial Politics of the IWW in South Africa and the United States, 1905–1925." *Safundi: The Journal of South African and American Studies* 12, no. 1 (Winter 2011): 69–96.

Dubofsky, Melvyn. *We Shall Be All: A History of the Industrial Workers of the World*. Champaign: University of Illinois Press, 2013.

Foner, Philip S. "The IWW and the Black Worker." *Journal of Negro History* 55, no. 1 (January 1970): 45–64.

"Nigger" Lovers

by H.M. Witt

Everywhere I chance to go I find that the sentiment of the "boss" toward the "nigger" grows *more* endearing.

This place Glenmora is *no* exception to the rule.

A few days ago the woods foreman of the Enterprise Lumber Company here discharged a good white man without any apparent reason, and I am *sure* without a legitimate one, because his work gave *entire* satisfaction. He put on a "nigger" in the white man's place.

Of *course*, this is done in dozens of places *every* day, in this, the land and home of the timber thieves.

As a matter of *fact*, *no* "nigger" lover can ever legitimately enter the portals leading to the home in the skies.

But, should he happen to slip by the ticket seller or gate-keeper, it would be *no* Heaven for him because his *"Right hand bower"* the "nigger" would be *missing*.

According to orthodox teaching anyone to reach that city made without hands eternal in Heavens and where the streets are paved with gold, he *must* first have a soul or rather mind.

I take the "nigger" to be *void* of that *essential* quality the soul, (mind) which is *necessary* in order to enter the Pearly Gates.

However, it is *inconsequential* what becomes of the "nigger" in the hereafter. The question *is* what is his future to be here? We *know* that he has become a factor upon the industrial field.

We *know* that he is in direct competition with the white workers and is crowding the white man into the background.

Are the white "nigger" lovers going to continue to give the "nigger" preference until the *black* supremacy reigns *supreme*?

Originally published in the *Voice of the People* 11, no. 33 (August 21, 1913): 3.

Indications *now* point that way.

In *many* of the larger saw-mills you will see *only* two or three white men in the mill. They are the sawyers or log-rippers and saw filers.

The "nigger" would *now* be filing saws and ripping up logs in the mill, but the sawyers and filers "union" which is *merely* a mutual agreement among themselves have kept the "nigger" away from the saw-lever and his hand off the file.

The filers and sawyers' "union" has also been able to keep down the supply of filers and sawyers by making the "bone-heads" believe it *requires* three or four years to learn to whet a saw or rip up a log. As a matter of *fact* he could learn it in six months if he ever could. By keeping the supply down, the filers and sawyers are yet getting from five to seven dollars per day, when otherwise they would be getting three dollars per day at *most*. So much for the law of supply and demand.

I will now return to the "nigger." Some *very poor*, but aristocratic whites have given as a reason for *not* joining the ONE BIG UNION that they did not care to belong to an organization that takes in the NEGRO. Yet many of these *very* blue-blooded whites affiliate with the "niggers" tho. They think *nothing* of working shoulder to shoulder with "niggers," they "chew the rag" with them, and visit some colored lady's house in the *small* hours of the night. But, there is *no* telling what a genuine bonehead or damphool will do.

This class of "white trash" are *very* inconsistent when they refuse to "jine" the union because it takes in NEGROES. The people who are doing the work *must* be members regardless of race or color.

As before stated, the "nigger" appears to be the coming man.

P.S. In Southern lumberjack parlance a "nigger" is a black-skinned scab or a company sucker. A NEGRO is a *man*, a *union* man, an I.W.W. "White trash" means the same thing as "nigger," only it has a white skin.

A Class, Not a Race Problem

To the I.W.W. there is no race problem. There is only a class problem. The I.W.W. does not look on the Negro, Jap or Chinaman as a menace or a problem, but as workers, men of our class.

The economic interest of all workers, be they white, black, brown or yellow, are identical, and all are included in the program of the I.W.W. It has one program for the entire working class. We demand for the Chinese worker and the Jap worker the same thing that it demands for the white worker—"the abolition of the wages system." We demand for all, the ownership of the earth and the machinery of production that we may be able, unfettered, to provide ourselves with the necessities and luxuries of life. The I.W.W. demands industrial equality for all. Social equality is not a demand of the I.W.W.

The Chinese, Japanese or Negro worker has the same right to life, liberty (whatever that means) and the pursuit of happiness as any other worker. The social life of a people will always depend on the economic and be moulded in detail by the desires of the individual.

Workers are all of one nation, no matter what their sex, or race, or color, or nationality; and have one flag—the Red Flag representing internationalism. The I.W.W. does not, however, worship any flag. Flags will give neither you nor I the full product of our labor.—DIRECT ACTION WILL!

—Alexander

Originally published in the *Industrial Worker*, February 3, 1917, 3.

Colored Workers of America: Why You Should Join the IWW

Fellow Workers—

There is one question which, more than any other, presses upon the mind of the worker today, regardless of whether he be of one race or another, of one color or another—the question of how he can improve his conditions, raise his wages, shorten his hours of labor and gain something more of freedom from his master—the owners of the industry wherein he labors.

To the black race who, but recently, with the assistance of the white men of the northern states, broke their chains of bondage and ended chattel slavery, a prospect of further freedom, of REAL FREEDOM, should be the most appealing.

For it is a fact that the Negro worker is no better off under the freedom he has gained than the slavery from which he has escaped. As chattel slaves we were the property of our masters and, as a piece of valuable property, our masters were considerate of us and careful of our health and welfare. Today, as wage workers, the boss may work us to death at the hardest and most hazardous labor, at the longest hours, at the lowest pay; we may quietly starve when out of work and the boss loses nothing by it and has no interest in us. To him the worker is but a machine for producing profits, and when you, as a slave who sells himself to the master on the installment plan, become old or broken in health or strength, or should you be killed while at work, the master merely gets another wage slave on the same terms.

We who have worked in the south know the conditions in lumber and turpentine camps, in the fields of cane, cotton and tobacco, in the mills and mines of Dixie, are such that the workers suffer a more miserable existence than ever prevailed among the chattel slaves before the great Civil War. Thousands of us have come and are coming northward, crossing the Mason

---

Published as a pamphlet, 1919.

and Dixon line, seeking better conditions. As wage slaves we have run away from the masters in the south only to become the wage slaves of the masters of the north. In the north we find that the hardest work and poorest pay is our portion. We are driven while on the job and the high cost of living offsets any higher pay we might receive.

The white worker is little, if any, better off. He is a slave the same as we are and, like us, he is regarded by the boss only as a means of making profits. The working class as a whole grows poorer and more miserable year by year, while the employing class, who do not work at all, enjoy wealth and luxury beyond the dreams of titled lords and kings.

As we are both wage workers, we have a common interest in improving conditions of the wage working class. Understanding this, the employing class seeks to engender race hatred between the two. He sets the black worker against the white worker and the white worker against the black, and keeps them divided and enslaved. Our change from chattel slaves to wage slaves has benefited no one but the masters of industry. They have used us as wage slaves to beat down the wages of the white wage slaves, and by a continual talk of "race problems," "Negro questions," "segregation," etc., make an artificial race hatred and division by poisoning the minds of both whites and blacks in an effort to stop any movement of labor that threatens the dividends of the industrial kinds. Race prejudice has no place in a labor organization. As Abraham Lincoln has said, "The strongest bond that should bind man to man in human society is that between the working people of all races and all nations."

The only problem then which the Colored worker should consider as a worker is the problem of organizing with other working men in the labor organization that best expresses the interest of the whole working class against the slavery and oppression of the whole capitalist class. Such an organization is the I.W.W., the INDUSTRIAL WORKERS OF THE WORLD, the only labor union that has never, IN THEORY OR PRACTICE since its beginning twenty years ago, barred the workers of any race or nation from membership. The following has stood as a principle of the I.W.W., embodied in its official constitution since its formation in 1905:

"By-Laws—Article 1. Section 1. No working man or woman shall be excluded from membership Unions because of creed or color."

If you are a wage worker you are welcome in the I.W.W. halls, no matter what your color. By this you may see that the I.W.W. is not a white man's union, not a black man's union, not a red or yellow man's union, but a WORKING MAN'S UNION. ALL OF THE WORKING CLASS IN ONE BIG UNION.

In the I.W.W. all wage workers meet on common ground. No matter what language you may speak, whether you were born in Europe, in Asia or in any other part of the world, you will find a welcome as a fellow worker. In the harvest fields where the I.W.W. controls, last summer saw white men, black men and Japanese working together as union men and raising the pay of all who gathered the grain. In the great strikes the I.W.W. has conducted at Lawrence, Mass., in the woolen mills, in the iron mines of Minnesota and elsewhere, the I.W.W. has brought the workers of many races, colors and tongues together in victorious battles for a better life.

Not only does the I.W.W. differ from all organizations in regard to admission of all races, but there is a fundamental difference in form of organization from all other labor unions. You have seen other labor unions organized on craft, or trade lines. Craft unionism means that any small section of an industry has a labor union separate from all other sections that cannot act in any concerted movement of labor because of this craft separation. For example, in the railroad industry there are the engineers' union, the firemen's union, the conductors' union, the brakemen's union, the switchmen's union and many others on the road and in the shops and yards.

Each unions acts for itself and usually has time agreements with companies for a term of years, each agreement ending at a different time than the others. When one craft union goes on strike at the end of the time agreement the other craft unions keep at work and by remaining on the job act as scabs and strikebreakers in defeating their fellow workers of the craft on strike.

Thus in 1911 the men in the shops of the Harriman lines went on strike and the trainmen, who belonged to different craft unions, remained at work; the train crews took cars and delivered cars to the strikebreakers in the shops because they were organized separately and had separate time agreements with the companies. That strike was lost because the railroad workers were organized wrong. The I.W.W. has INDUSTRIAL UNIONISM, which means that all crafts in any industry are organized together and act together. Had the I.W.W. been in the place of the craft unions on the Harriman lines in 1911, all workers could have gone out together, and not a wheel would have turned, not a train would have moved till the companies would come to terms with the shopmen. For the I.W.W. makes NO TIME AGREEMENTS with any employer and makes AN INJURY TO ONE AN INJURY

TO ALL. The I.W.W. always leaves its members free to strike when they see an opportunity to better themselves or support their fellow workers.

The foundation of the I.W.W. is INDUSTRIAL UNIONISM. ALL workers in any division of any industry are organized into an INDUSTRIAL UNION OF ALL the workers in the ENTIRE INDUSTRY; these INDUSTRIAL UNIONS in turn are organized into INDUSTRIAL DEPARTMENTS of connecting, or kindred, industries, while all are brought together in THE GENERAL ORGANIZATION OF THE INDUSTRIAL WORKERS OF THE WORLD—ONE BIG UNION OF ALL THE WORKING CLASS OF THE WORLD. No one but actual wage workers may join. The working class cannot depend upon anyone but itself to free it from wage slavery. "He would be free, himself must strike the blow."

When the I.W.W. through this form of INDUSTRIAL UNIONISM has become powerful enough, it will institute an INDUSTRIAL COMMONWEALTH; it will end slavery and oppression forever and in its place will be a world of the workers, by the workers and for the workers; a world where there will be no poverty and want among those who feed and clothe and house the world; a world where the words "master" and "slave" shall be forgotten; a world where peace and happiness shall reign and where the children of men shall live as brothers in a worldwide INDUSTRIAL DEMOCRACY.

The following is the preamble of the I.W.W. constitution, showing the reason and form of its organization, the aims and purposes of its membership:

> The working class and the employing class have nothing in common. There can be no peace so long as hunger and want are found among millions of working people and the few, who make up the employing class, have all the good things of life.
>
> Between these two classes a struggle must go on until the workers of the world organize as a class, take possession of the means of production, abolish the wage system, and live in harmony with the Earth.
>
> We find that the centering of the management of industries into fewer and fewer hands makes the trade unions unable to cope with the ever growing power of the employing class. The trade unions foster a state of affairs which allows one set of workers to be pitted against another set of workers in the same industry, thereby helping defeat one another in wage wars. Moreover, the trade unions aid the employing class to mislead the workers into the belief that the working class have interests in common with their employers.

These conditions can be changed and the interest of the working class upheld only by an organization formed in such a way that all its members in any one industry, or in all industries if necessary, cease work whenever a strike or lockout is on in any department thereof, thus making an injury to one an injury to all.

Instead of the conservative motto, "A fair day's wage for a fair day's work," we must inscribe on our banner the revolutionary watchword, "Abolition of the wage system."

It is the historic mission of the working class to do away with capitalism. The army of production must be organized, not only for everyday struggle with capitalists, but also to carry on production when capitalism shall have been overthrown. By organizing industrially we are forming the structure of the new society within the shell of the old.

The I.W.W. welcomes you as a member, no matter in what industry you may work. The initiation fee is $2, the dues are 50 cents a month. After you once join you have the right of free transfer into any industry. All that is necessary to continue membership is the payment of dues, regardless of where you go or what your work may be.

For further information write to
GENERAL SECRETARY
1001 W. Madison Street. Chicago, Illinois.

Justice for the Negro—How He Can Get It

Two lynchings a week—one every three or four days—that is the rate at which people in this "land of the free and home of the brave" have been killing coloured men and women for the past thirty years—3,224 Negroes known to have been put to death by mobs in this country since 1889, and put to death with every kind of torture that human fiends could invent.

Even during the war, while coloured soldiers were being obliged to "fight for democracy" abroad, ninety-one of their race were lynched at home.

The wrongs of the Negro in the United States are not confined to lynchings, however. When allowed to live and work for the community, he is subjected to constant humiliation, injustice and discrimination. In the cities he is forced to live in the meanest districts, where his rent is doubled and tripled, while conditions of health and safety are neglected in favor of the white sections.* In many states he is obliged to ride in special "Jim Crow" cars, hardly fit for cattle. Almost everywhere all semblance of political rights is denied him.

The Colored Worker Everywhere Unfairly Treated

When the Negro goes to look for work he meets with the same systematic discrimination. Thousands of jobs are closed to him solely on account of his color. He is considered only fit for the most menial occupations. In many cases, he has to accept a lower wage than is paid to white men for the same work.† *Everywhere the odds are against him in the struggle for existence.*

Throughout this land of liberty, so-called, the Negro worker is treated as an inferior; he is underpaid in his work and overcharged in his rent;

Originally published as a pamphlet, date unknown.

*   "The normal average death rate of males in a city is about 147.10 per 1,000; for negroes, 287.10 per 1,000"—*New York Times*, Feb. 22, 1919.

†   The wages of colored kitchen workers in New York City average $20 a month lower than white employees.

he is kicked about, cursed and spat upon; in short, he is treated, not as a human being, but as an animal, a beast of burden for the ruling class. When he tries to improve his condition, he is shoved back into the mire of degradation and poverty and told to "keep his place."

How can the Negro combat this widespread injustice? How can he not only put a stop to lynchings, but force the white race to grant him equal treatment? *How can he get his rights as a human being?*

Protests, petitions and resolutions will never accomplish anything. It is useless to waste time and money on them. The government is in the hands of the ruling class of white men and will do as they wish. No appeal to the political powers will ever secure justice for the Negro.

The Master Class Fears the Organized Worker

He has, however, one weapon that the master class fears—the power to fold his arms and refuse to work for the community until he is guaranteed fair treatment. Remember how alarmed the South became over the emigration of colored workers two years ago, what desperate means were used to try to keep them from leaving the mills and cotton fields? **The only power of the Negro is his power as a worker;** his one weapon is the strike. Only by organizing and refusing to work for those who abuse him can he put an end to the injustice and oppression he now endures.

The colored working men and women of the United States must organize in defense of their rights. They must join together in labor unions so as to be able to enforce their demand for an equal share of "life, liberty and the pursuit of happiness." When they are in a position to say to any community, "If you do not stop discrimination against the colored race, we will stop working for you," the hidden forces behind the government will see to it that lynchings cease and discrimination comes to an end. Only by threatening to withdraw their labor power and thereby cripple industry and agriculture can the Negroes secure equal treatment with other workers.

The Workers of Every Race Must Join Together

But the Negroes cannot accomplish this alone; they must unite with the other workers in order to make their industrial power count to the utmost. If they form separate racial organizing they will only encourage race prejudice and help the master class in their effort to divide the workers along false lines of color and set one race against the other, in order to use both for their own selfish ends.

The workers of every race and nationality must join in one common group against their one common enemy—the employers—so as to be able to defend themselves and one another. Protection for the working class lies in complete solidarity of the workers, without regard to race, creed, sex or color. "One Enemy—One Union!" must be their watchword.

Trade Unions Do Not Want the Negro

Most American labor organizations, however, shut their doors to the colored worker. The American Federation of Labor excludes him from many of its unions.* In those to which he is admitted, he is treated as an inferior. **The Negro has no chance in the old-line trade unions.** They do not want him. They admit him only under compulsion and treat him with contempt. Their officials, who discourage strikes for higher wages or shorter hours, are always ready, as in the case of the Switchmen's Union, to permit a strike aimed to prevent the employment of colored men.

This narrow-minded policy of excluding the Negro from the trade unions often forces him to become a strike-breaker against his will by closing legitimate occupations to him. The consequence is racial conflicts such as the frightful tragedy in East St. Louis in 1917.

The I.W.W. Admits Negro to Full Membership

There is one international labor organization in this country that admits the colored worker on a footing of absolute equality with the white—The Industrial Workers of the World. The first section of its By-Laws provides that "no working man or woman shall be excluded from membership because of creed or color." This principle has been scrupulously lived up to since the organization was founded. In the I.W.W. the colored worker, man or woman, is on an equal footing with every other worker. He has the same voice in determining the policies of the organization, and his interests are protected as zealously as those of any other member.

---

*   The constitution of the International Association of Machinists, for example, requires each member to agree to introduce no one into the union but a sober, industrious WHITE man.

Not only does the I.W.W. offer to the Negro worker union membership free from any taint or suggestion of racial inferiority, but in its form of organization it is far superior to the old-fashioned trade unions.

Industrial Unionism the Strongest Form of Organization

The I.W.W. organizes the workers by industries, not trades. Instead of the American Federation of Labor plan of dividing the workers in any plant into ten or twenty separate craft unions, with separate meetings and separate sets of officials, the I.W.W. unites **all the workers in each industry,** whatever their particular line of work may be, into One Big Industrial Union. In this way, the industrial power of the workers is combined and, when any of them have a disagreement with their employer, they are backed by the united support of ALL the workers in that industry.

But the I.W.W. does not limit its aim, as do the trade unions, to "less work and more pay." Its greatest object is **the complete emancipation of the working class.** As long as the workers hold their jobs only by permission of some employer, they are not free. As long as there is one class that lives in ease and idleness off their labor, they are industrial slaves. Freedom for the workers will come only when everybody does his share of the work of the world and when the workers take control of the industries and operate them, not as at present, for the benefit of the leisure class, but for the welfare of society as a whole.

Servants of Capitalism Lie About the I.W.W.

Do not believe the lies being told about the I.W.W. by the hired agents of the capitalists—the press, preachers and politicians. They are paid to deceive the workers and lead them astray. They are hired to throw dust in their eyes because the master class **does not dare to let them know the truth.**

Investigate the I.W.W. for yourself and get the facts. We are confident that, when you learn the truth about it, you will realize that it is to your interest to join and help build up the organization.

Fellow workers of the colored race, do not expect justice or fair treatment as a gift from the ruling class. **You will get from them nothing but what you are strong enough to take.** "In union there is strength." The only power that workers of any race or nationality have is their power to act together as workers. We, therefore, urge you to join with your fellow workers of every race in the

ONE BIG UNION of the INDUSTRIAL WORKERS OF THE WORLD

1001 West Madison Street, Chicago, Illinois Workers' Halls, with Reading Rooms, at 119 S. Throop St. and 951 W. Madison St.

NOTE – The I.W.W. admits to membership every wage worker, man or woman, young or old, skilled or unskilled. Its plan of organization includes all workers. No matter what your occupation, if you work for wages, you can get a union card in the I.W.W.

To Colored Workers: Attention!

by Waub Lee

It is just 310 years since the first Negro Chattel Slaves were imported to the U. S. coming from the savage jungles of Africa direct. Throughout the ages they had been in correspondence with the natural environment only; they knew little or nothing [. . .] Consequently they were easy victims to the treacherous tyranny of the white slave holders of the South.

And so in the U. S., for 252 years the ruling class decided that the status of Chattel Slavery was right and correct, and for no other reason than the simple reason that Chattel Slavery was at that time and place the most profitable form of slavery.

And here on the estates of the Southern Feudal Land Barons labored the black slaves of the South. They did all the necessary labor on a plantation, and in return for their labor they were permitted the use of a tiny tract of land, from which they needs must further labor to produce their own subsistence. This latter subsistence is always imperative and necessary.

Labor is a commodity exactly the same as wagons, apples, lumber or pins are commodities, something made for society for social exchange. The value of a commodity is the amount of labor socially necessary to produce that commodity. Then it necessarily follows that the value of the commodity "Labor Power," is the necessary food, shelter and clothing to sustain the laboring class, is what we recognize today as "wages." Wages have never at any time amounted to more than a bare means of subsistence for the wage earning class.

It takes less than two hours to produce what we consume, even under this most wasteful profit system. It is clearly evident then that whatever time we labor beyond this said two hours, is a voluntary gift to the employing class.

Originally published in the *Industrial Worker*, July 9, 1919, 3.

And so it was with the Chattel Slave of the South prior to the Civil War. He worked a fractional part of the day to earn his own means of subsistence, and the remaining larger portion of his total laboring time was a free-will offering to the master class.

The Civil War like all other wars, was an economic war. It was a war in which each of the two contending capitalistic factions strove to maintain its own economic system of working-class exploitation.

The Northern capitalist class found it more profitable to have wage slavery, because it forced the workers to shift for themselves and to compete against each other in times of unemployment. The North was a country almost entirely devoted to manufacturing industry, and the machine was the impelling factor in production. As machine production increased on the one hand, so as a direct result did unemployment increase on the other. Machine production is at all times dependent upon the ever increasing army of unemployment. It is at once clear that the factories of the North with their machine production, with their fluctuating and seasonable markets, must under private ownership retain wage-slavery. Here all responsibility on the part of the employing class ceases with the attendant and frequent state of unemployment.

The South with its old Feudal Land Policy, and the necessity of constant employment, could profit better with Chattel Slavery. The Southern capitalist class, because of the ready adaptability and profitableness of the Negro to the prevailing Southern environment found Chattel Slavery the more profitable system of exploitation, in direct contrast to the North with its manufacturing or economic environment. Further, the climatic conditions of the South furnish a nearly exact parallel to those the Negroes had been accustomed in Africa.

And so in the case of all wars the worker whom it seems should be the most concerned, did nothing in the critical time for his own good, but instead marched away to the slaughter, on whichever side his own ignorance forced him to ally himself. The Northern capitalist class said, "If we win, we will free the slaves." After the workers had slaughtered and gored one other to the satisfaction of the master class, after all that was said and done, I ask you in all fairness: Are the Negroes free today? If you have been and studied their condition, you must truthfully say they are not! [*sic*] They are for reasons stated above even deeper in the mire of slavery than [illegible] before.

And to make their condition more worse, little or no educational advantages are offered the Negroes. Scarcely any Negro in the South can even read or write. Their standard of living is deplorable, beyond description, their necessities are reduced to a minimum.

The haughty, vain and brutal Southern Land Barons have not forgotten how to carry out every known method of savagery from vile language to "burning at the stake," directly to the job where they may play upon the ignorance and fears of these black workers, thereby increasing their profits. The Southern employer, like his Northern brother in robbery, always emphasizes his right to be lazy, for he too never performs any useful service to society. He is a parasite, nothing more and often less.

Ignorant workers are always humble, meek, servile and contented workers. They never seek to improve conditions, they fear to revolt against tyranny and autocratic control because they are ignorant. The employing class know this, and thus you see them the world over, fighting every attempt of the workers to organize with intelligent action, whether they be black or white. They never oppose the worker who would join such an organization as the church of the 4L's. Why? Because such institutions foster and play upon the worker's ignorance, diverting his untrained mind from the real issues, such as for example shorter hours, more food, and better conditions. Thus you find many of the Negroes in the South are church-goers.

And is there no hope that the Negro race may be truly free? Decidedly there is a way out of their degradation and poverty, and but one way. By educating and organizing on the job in the One Big Union of the workers— the "Industrial Workers of the World." Alongside of their Fellow Workers of all colors and all nations, on every job they must organize themselves into One Big Union of the industry in which they as individuals work— each of these big industrial organized units to be an integral part of the great General Organization [...].

And in conclusion let me say to you colored workers; your troubles are not black troubles, neither are the white man's troubles white, but the troubles of both are economic or industrial troubles. On the job is where you are fleeced. The man who owns your job owns you, so it is obvious that if you would be free, you must own your job. If you are a satisfied slave stay as you are; but if you would rise up out of the generations of your own slavery and be a man—investigate the I. W. W. When you have done this we know you will join the I. W. W.; and when you have joined we know you will go out and help fight the battles of your class and our class. You will then have a clear enough head to see that this is a struggle between two classes, and a large enough heart to place yourself on the proper side of the struggle. The individual worker is helpless alone, but impregnable when organized. An injury to one is an injury to all. When you, Mr. Colored Worker, see these things, you have achieved the emancipation of your race, and you will have ennobled all mankind.

Part III
The *Messenger*

Editorials

Introduction

T he *Messenger* was founded in 1917 by A. Philip Randolph (1889–1979) and Chandler Owen (1889–1967), two Black southerners who had recently arrived in Harlem and joined the Socialist Party. It quickly became a major publication, gaining a circulation of 26,000 in the immediate postwar years, with each issue often shared around among numerous readers. Randolph and Owen knew how to make a splash and were often deliberately provocative in their writing, going out of their way to tweak the nose of their enemies, whether they were white racists, capitalists, or agents of the state. As the radicalism of the postwar years faded, however, the journal became more conservative, abandoning most of its radical commitments by the mid-1920s.

The *Messenger* grew out of Randolph and Owen's editorship of a magazine for the hotel waiters union. When the two uncovered corruption in the union and published it in the magazine, they were promptly fired. Undeterred, they began their own publication, calling it "the only magazine of scientific radicalism in the world, published by Negroes."

The new magazine took an uncompromising stance on capitalism and American racism. Though some scholars have branded the *Messenger* as "class-first" radicalism, as a result of their allegiance to the SP and opposition to black nationalism, such a description dramatically distorts the magazine's political content. This was a magazine that, in reference to World War I, declared, "No intelligent Negro is willing to lay down his life for the United States as it now exists." Similarly, Randolph and Owen were merciless in their attacks on the AFL for excluding Black workers, encouraging their readers to support the IWW instead. While their

169

theoretical pronouncements on the relationship between class and race were often mechanistic and crude, politically they were uncompromising in their opposition to white supremacy.

The *Messenger* also distinguished itself through its close attention to the international situation. From the very first issue, the magazine covered the unfolding revolution in Russia. It closely tracked the Bolsheviks' early diplomacy to end their involvement in the war, reported on the progress of the Russian civil war, and, when famine broke out, helped organize a labor relief effort. Throughout this, Randolph and Owen were insistent that American radicals had a great deal to learn from the Russian example. In particular, they argued that the Soviet struggle against anti-Semitism in Russia proved that socialism in the United States had the potential to strike a decisive blow against racism.

By the early 1920s, it was clear that such a blow would not be forthcoming any time soon. The postwar radical surge had faded, and as it did, Randolph and Owen turned to the right. They reconciled themselves with the AFL and its leadership, and began arguing that the Russian example was not repeatable in the United States.

Both Randolph and Owen would go on to long careers in politics. Owen moved to Chicago, becoming a Republican political operative who was active into the 1960s. Randolph became a union leader, emerging in the 1930s as the leading Black unionist in the country, a position he would occupy for the following three decades. Neither of them, however, would ever return to the radicalism that characterized the *Messenger's* early years.

Further Reading

Anderson, Jervis. *A. Philip Randolph: A Biographical Portrait*. Berkeley: University of California Press, 1973.

Arnesen, Eric. "A. Philip Randolph: Emerging Socialist Radical." In *Reframing Randolph: Labor, Black Freedom, and the Legacies of A. Philip Randolph*. Edited by Andrew E. Kersten and Clarence Lang. New York: New York University Press, 2015.

Kornweibel, Theodore. *No Crystal Stair: Black Life and the Messenger, 1917–1928*. Westport: Greenwood Publishing Group, 1975.

Bolshevism and World Democracy (1918)

Bolshevism is the Banquo's ghost to the Macbeth capitalists of the world whether they inhabit Germany, England, America or Japan. It is a foreword of a true world democracy. The Soviets represent the needs and aims of the masses.

Bolshevism has already defied the imperialist vultures to lay their cards of secret diplomacy on the table of justice before the High Court of World Opinion. It has led the world in making a concrete application of the principle of self-determination of smaller nationalities.

Ukrania, Finland and Persia have been permitted to achieve their own destiny.

A sound and just economic, political and social programme of reconstruction is gradually being adopted.

Bolshevism is not yet one year old in Russia. Russia is still at war with a great nation and is virtually without help from her former allies. One hundred and eighty-seven million people have been delivered from the autocracy of the Czar—a people 85 per cent of whom are illiterate.

Bolshevism has given these peoples a new hope, a new promise, a new ideal—economic and political freedom!

Will Bolshevism succeed? The Tories of England and America asked the same question about the American people after the revolution of 1776. The Bourbons of France doubted the power of the French people to exist without the aristocracy—after the revolution of 1789. Governments are living organisms which have structure and function and are governed by the laws of growth. Hence, the Russian people must be helped; not hindered, they are still young.

Originally published in the *Messenger*, July 1918, 9.

The Right and Left Wing Interpreted (1919)

In all parties there are radical and conservative elements, keeping in mind, of course, that both terms are relative. The phenomena are monistic for we find the same or similar evidences in all countries, among all nations and all races. In Germany formerly we had our Fatherland party, which represented the landed interests, and a National Liberal party, which represented the industrial classes. In England today we have the Unionist and Liberal parties, which represent landed estates and industrial interests, respectively. In America we have our National Democratic Party representing landed Bourbonism and a Republican Party which represents big business and the industrial classes. As to all of these groups the Socialist Party represents a left wing. The Socialist Party regards them as hypo-conservative, and they in turn regard the Socialists as extremely radical.

Now all the time a change is going on in all these parties. Men from the extremely conservative parties become quasi-liberal and go into the liberal party, while men from the liberal parties gradually drift into the Socialist parties. To illustrate: Watch the present trend of the Republican party. We have a so-called progressive, independent wing led by La Follette, Hiram Johnson, Borah and Cummins, while the standpatters like Lodge, Penrose, Smoot, Wadsworth and Nelson call them radical Socialists or Bolsheviks. In the Democratic party we have a so-called liberal or left wing led by President Wilson (?), J. Hamilton Lewis, Walsh of Massachusetts, Frank P. Walsh, Brandeis, Villard, Frederick C. Howe and Amos Pinchot. At the same time we have a reactionary wing led by the Southern South with its John Sharp Williams, Hoke Smith and Col. E.M. House, also such standpatters as Senators King of Utah and Reed of Missouri.

To continue the illustration, we find the same thing taking place in our own party—the Socialist party. In Russia we have our more conservative Social-Revolutionary party and our Bolsheviki party. We have our Kerenski

---

Originally published in the *Messenger*, May 1919, 20–21.

and our Lenine, Trotsky, Radek and Tchitcherin. In Germany we have our Ebert and Scheidemann leading the right wing of Socialism and, at the same time, we have our Liebknecht, Rosa Luxemburg, Franz Mehring and George Lebedour. In France we have a conservative "social patriotic" leadership of the right wing Socialists in Albert Thomas and Renaudel. At the same time we have our more splendid leaders of the left wing in Jean Longuet and Loriot. In England we see such conservative leaders of the right wing as George Barnes, J.H. Thomas, Adams and even Henderson. We see a more courageous left wing led by Robert Smilie [*sic*.], Philip Snowden, Ramsay MacDonald and McLean. We could trace all the countries at length to show that the law of evolution is moving with the same inexorableness and absoluteness in social as in physical life. In America, then, it could not be different. The forces of conservatism and radicalism are clashing here, too. The Socialist party is in the midst of a keen and sharp discussion as to tactics and policies. The Left Wing has issued a manifesto with ten planks, points—or whatever you wish to call them—in its program. Let us examine them critically and fairly, giving them full credit where such is due and withholding such credit where the planks are without merit.

Program of the Left Wing

1. "We stand for a uniform declaration of principles in all party platforms both local and national, and the abolition of all social reform planks now contained in them."

First, a uniform declaration of principles in all party platforms— both local and national—is illogical. In the South in some states, we have disfranchisement and Jim-Crow laws. In Northern, Western and Eastern States we do not have them. It would not be worth while for New York and Ohio in their state platforms to declare against Jim-Crow and Grandfather laws.

Second, with respect to social reform planks, we cannot dispose of that matter with platitudes. The opposition to social reform is based upon a wide-spread fallacy and a great deal of misinformation on social evolution. As Lester F. Ward says: "Discontent increases with social improvement." The more concessions granted, the more concessions will be demanded. The best cared for workers, the highest paid, are usually the least contented. Bismarck attempted to hold back socialism in Germany by adopting social reform legislation, but here thereby increased it. Wisconsin has more social reform legislation than any State in the Union, but Wisconsin also has proportionately more socialism. The legislators feel that unless they grant certain concessions, they will be supplanted, and they do what we call "stealing socialist thunder." But the truth is, that the more they grant the more they must grant, and social reform legislation has not hindered, but has accelerated, socialist and radical growth.

2. "The party must teach, propagate, and agitate exclusively for the overthrow of Capitalism and the establishment of Socialism, through a Proletarian Dictatorship."

Here again amateur enthusiasm is not keeping pace with scientific method. The mere uttering of the words, "overthrow of capitalism" and "proletarian dictatorship" are not so material. It is method that counts. Every time we can pull a brick out of the capitalist wall we are hastening its overthrow, speeding the day when it will topple over. Get woman suffrage today. Strike to increase wages and shorten hours. Abolish child labor. Take over your railroads. Take over your telephones and telegraphs. Don't refuse to strike these blows, because all cannot be gotten at once.

Remember, Comrades, that we are in a war, and several battles are generally fought in order to win. But each battle won gives aid and comfort to the winner and weakens the morale of the loser. Every triumph creates fresh hope and new faith in the victor. So with the proletariat. Each strike won means much more toward creating the *industrial proletarian militarism* which is necessary to fight the organized capitalists and employers.

3. "The Socialist candidates elected to office shall adhere strictly to the above provisions."

Of course, unless the first two provisions are sound, there is no reason why the Socialist candidates should adhere to the provisions.

Plank number 4 calls upon the Socialist party to assist industrial organization by a propaganda of revolutionary industrial unionism as part of its general activities. This plank is absolutely sound, but, so far as I know, this is just what the party has been doing. It supports the workers' strikes, criticizes constructively and destructively their labor organizations, attempts to stir labor into newer and more revolutionary modes of action. That is why the Gompers American Federation of Labor machine opposes the Socialist party so bitterly.

5. "We demand that the official party press be party owned and controlled."

This is in harmony with the constitutional requirements at present and the party is not supposed to donate funds to any other press. There are, however, certain Socialist organs owned by private parties who were able and willing to organize and float them when the party was not. Whether the Left Wing would purchase these organs, start new ones, or destroy them, we have no intimation.

6. "We demand that officially recognized educational institutions be party owned and controlled."

This is a sound demand for newly created institutions, but should not affect certain existing institutions, which are efficiently organized and manned like the Rand School.

Article 7 demands that the party discard its obsolete literature and publish new literature. Such literature as is obsolete should unquestionably be discarded and literature in keeping with the times should take its place.

Article 8 demands that the National Executive Committee call an immediate national convention for the purpose of formulating party policies and tactics to meet the present crisis. We recognize that such conventions cost much money, but we believe there are a number of problems necessitating such a convention. There is the New Labor Party. What position does the Socialist party take on it? There is the Non-Partisan League. What is the party's position on that? There is the march of Soviet government with the cosmic tread of revolution. What is the real position of the party on Soviets? It is time that the leaders stopped proclaiming in the party press and out of the party press that they are not Bolsheviks. Are the Bolsheviki something to be shunned, despised and disclaimed? If we oppose them, why? If the soviet system is sound, then let the party say so. If it is not adapted to conditions generally, then let us discuss the facts and interpret them. What about real propaganda among Negroes? Does the party believe in that? If so, let us get on the job. We believe the Left Wing demand for an emergency convention is sound. We believe that such a convention should be called by the National Executive Committee.

Article 9 demands the repudiation of the Berne Congress as engineered by "Moderate Socialists" and social patriots. The March issue of the *Messenger* sharply took that Congress to task for such trite things as appointing commissions to fix the blame of the war—or the "bad nation" theory, which is about as fallacious as the "bad man" or "good man" theory. Repudiation of that nationalistic Berne Congress would do credit to the party.

Article 10 calls for the American Socialist Party to elect delegates to the International Congress proposed by the Communist Party of Russia (Bolshevik) and that our party shall participate only in a new International formed of Left Wing parties or groups.

We think that the party should send delegates to the International Congress proposed by the Bolsheviki. We do not agree, however, that we should determine the representation from other countries. If the majority party of France were under the leadership of Albert Thomas, we would receive the delegates and exchange opinions with them just as readily as with the Left Wing, now in the majority and led by Jean Longuet.

So much for the program of the Left Wing. What else must we admonish?

First, we believe that there is a sincere difference of opinion in the party, that there is an honest difference between men of high purpose and loyal devotion to the socialist movement. The solution cannot be helped by calling names, whether it be the Right Wing calling the Left Wing Anarchists, lunatics and traitors, or the Left Wing calling the Right Wing reactionaries, standpatters and Scheidemanns. There are men also in the party like Nearing, Lochner, Berenberg, Glassberg, and ourselves who do not desire an unnecessary split. Fight the difference out on its merits if there is a deep conviction with you! Then take a clean, straight vote. If the Left Wing wins, let us yield to the majority. If the Right Wing wins, let us do likewise. Don't have a split. Stay in the party and fight for the change within!

The tendency is world-wide just now. The fight grows intense and bitter. But in the words of Lester F. Ward, "We need more light than heat." We need clear, intelligent thinking. It is not action but the direction of our action that counts. Let us submerge any personal feeling for the best interests of the Socialist movement. The Left Wing of today will be the Right Wing of tomorrow! Let us remember this, too.

The Cause of and Remedy for Race Riots

Race riots are miniature wars. Like wars, they are injurious to the masses who fight them. Like wars, a few profit from them. Like wars, they also have causes—ultimate and contributory causes. It is the purpose of the writers to ascertain those causes in order that the remedy may be prescribed.

History of the Problem

In order to understand any social phenomenon of the present, it is essential to inquire into the history of the conditions out of which it grew.

The race problem of America is a relic of chattel slavery. It is more acute in the United States than in any other country, because slavery was abolished here, after it had been abolished in every other country. Besides, every American document has recognized and sanctioned the institution of slavery.

The Declaration of Independence was signed by men, 50% of whom were slave-holders. The Constitutional Convention endorsed slavery, while recognizing its viciousness.

George Washington, "the father of the country," and first President of the United States, and one of the largest slave-holders in the world, asked that the term "bound persons" be used in the records of the Constitutional Convention instead of the term *slaves*, because he recognized that history would repudiate and condemn their hypocritical professions in the Declaration of Independence. Even Thomas Jefferson was a big slave-holder, and attempted to salve his conscience with this celebrated soliloquy: "I tremble for my country when I reflect that God is just!" The statement in the Declaration of Independence that "all men are created free and equal" meant "all white men."

The Constitution also recognized and upheld the institution of slavery, for slavery continued 73 years after its adoption. The Supreme Court of the

Originally published in the *Messenger*, September 1919, 14–21.

United States re-entrenched the institution in the "Dred Scott Decision" of 1847. It gave political power and sanction to slavery. It permitted five slaves to be counted as three white citizens, and upon this basis representation in Congress was increased for the South.

This brings us to the Civil War, the inevitable consequence of slavery. The length and bitterness of the Civil War in which the problem of slavery was uppermost, fanned the fires of race hatred. The South hated the slave because it feared his revolt. The rebellions of Gabriel, Denmark Vesey and Nat Turner justified their fears, while John Brown's raid intensified their apprehensions. Hatred against the Negro grew in the North, because it was felt that white soldiers were giving their lives for Negro slaves. The feeling was manifested by the New York riots, and the dragging of William Lloyd Garrison through the streets of Boston.

Reconstruction

Reconstruction still further fanned the flames of race prejudice. The 13th, 14th and 15th Amendments to the Constitution were resented by the South. The Freedmen's Bureau, the Force Bill, the Sumner Civil Rights Bill and the Military Bill—measures adopted in the interest of the Negroes—were indignantly repelled by the Southern white sympathizers. The South retaliated with the Black Code and Vagrancy laws, the Ku Klux Klan, the Tissue Ballot and the Bloody Shirt. It rejected the 13th, 14th and 15th Amendments. Finally, however, when these amendments were ratified by the necessary votes of other states, the white South, reluctantly and sullenly, submitted along with its Northern supporters which were very large, as shown by the States of New York, New Jersey, and Ohio (great abolition states) withdrawing their ratification of the 14th Amendment.

Wage Slavery

The industrial revolution had prepared the way for the abolition of slavery by the introduction of labor saving machinery. The abolition of chattel slavery paved the way for the next step—wage slavery. It marked the passing of Feudalism and the introduction of capitalism in the United States. Coming fast upon the heels of slavery, however, there were relics of the old order, which manifested themselves in the transition period. These were peonage, tenant-farming, the crop-lien system, the Black code and the vagrancy laws. These bring us to the consideration of the economic causes of mob violence and race wars.

First, what are economic causes? By economic causes, we mean material gains which are the motor-forces of individual and social actions. For instance: A Jewish and an Irish lad were fighting and they were calling each other all kinds of humiliating names. Presently, along came two passersby who speculated as to the cause of the fight, giving various religious and sentimental reasons. But upon inquiry they were informed by the Irish lad that the D— Jew had his foot on his nickel. Thus you see, not race nor religion, but the crass, materialistic, economic factor—the nickel—was the sound reason for the scrap.

As to our first proposition, the economic cause, we maintain that the capitalist system is the fundamental cause of riots. By the term capitalist system, we mean, in short, the exploitation of human labor-power and the natural resources of the country, for private profits.

This is a system under which the tools with which the laborer works are owned by private individuals. Now our capitalist system expresses itself in different forms in different sections of the country. For instance, in the East, factories, railroads and steamships are the paramount economic factors; in the West, mining, railroads and steamships; and in the South, cotton plantations, lumber mills, turpentine and railroads. The banking institutions of the South, which extend loans to the poor black and white farmers, are the channels through which the commodities of the industries find their way to their local, national and world markets. out of these industrial arrangements have grown certain socio-economic conditions, namely, peonage, the crop-lien system, tenant-farming and peasantry, which are the more immediate causes of lynching.

First, what is peonage? Peonage is a system of serfdom, the principle of which is, that if an employee owes his master he must continue to serve him until the debt is paid, the only escape being that if another employer is willing to come forward and assume the debt, the employee is allowed to transfer his obligation to the new master. In practice the system amounts to vassalage, inasmuch as the debt is usually allowed to reach a figure which there is no hope of paying off.

Now how is this system maintained? During the Reconstruction Period the Negro tasted and became intoxicated with the new wine of freedom and was loath to return to the farm, under conditions, in many instances, worse than slavery. Unsophisticated Negroes looked wistfully for the promised "mule and forty acres." But lumber must be cut, cotton must be picked and turpentine must be dipped. In short, profits must be made. Negroes must work or be made to work, besides they must work cheaply.

Thus the "black code" and vagrancy laws of the South. These laws provided for imprisonment of all Negroes who had no visible means of support. The result is that, hordes of unemployed Negroes are hustled off to jail and the convict camps. Their fines are paid by the lumber, cotton and turpentine operators; they are assigned into their custody; put to work at starvation wages, besides being compelled to trade at the company's store, which prevents their ever getting out of debt. They are also compelled to sign certain labor contracts, the non-performance of which the state laws make a crime. And as a white planter himself tells the story: A planter can arrest a man upon the criminal charge of receiving money under false pretenses, which is equivalent to the charge of stealing; you can get him convicted; he is fined, and being penniless, in lieu of the money to pay the fine, he goes to jail; then you pay the fine and costs and the judge assigns him to you to work out the fine and you have him back on your plantation, backed by the authority of the state. This is peonage. It is an economic system. It is maintained for profit.

We pass next to the crop-lien system. The crop-lien system is the method of mortgaging the planted and unplanted crops of the poor farmers. It operates in this way: The poor farmers are in need of provisions until harvesting time; the white merchants supply them for a part of their crops—the share usually being so large as to keep a perpetual lien on the farmers' crops. Under this system the Negroes are fastened to the farms.

The Negro farmer being in debt, cannot leave. To escape is to violate a contract; to violate a contract is to commit a crime which might result in being remanded to the convict camps or lynched. Next we shall consider tenant-farming, which is explained by its title.

Usually, however, the tenant-farmer has been a farm-owner, who, due to the crop-lien system, has lost control of the staid farm. The next stage of the tenant-farmer is the farm laborer, which is the final goal of the poor white or black in the South. Thus an economic system which makes peasants out of Negroes and poor whites. In the South the peasants are objects of reproach, the scum—the flotsam and jetsam of society. They are illiterate, morally depraved and physically broken. The fruits of this system are prejudice, jim-crowism, segregation and lynching. Banking institutions and loan agencies supply the money for their maintenance at rates of interest as high as 60 and 100 per cent on the dollar.

Negroes don't protest or resist because they are intimidated and cowed by lynching bees. Negroes and poor whites don't unite against a common exploiter—because race prejudice exists and is artfully cultivated to keep them apart. The weapons of capital in other parts of the country are the state militias, secret-detective-strike-breaking agencies, religion or nationality. So that in the East and West we have our Bayonne, West Virginia and Ludlow, and in the South we have our Waco and Memphis horrors. Of more recent date we have the East St. Louis massacre, the cause of which is fundamentally economic. Negro laborers were imported into the above named place to work. They were either imported to take the jobs of white workers or to increase the supply of labor, and thereby force down wages. This was the real cause of the conflict.

This is similar to the principle of picketing by labor unions. White laborers will not only shoot down Negro laborers, but also white laborers who are imported by capitalists to take their jobs or lower their wages. Such is the history of the labor movement in this country. Negro laborers would do the same thing, if they were in the white laborers' places.

We might as well meet the big, bald fact that Self-Interest is the supreme ruler of the actions of men. The reason does not lie in race prejudice, but in the class struggle. Blame your capitalist system. Of course, this does not justify or expiate the crime; it simply explains it. Certainly the culprits should be brought to justice. We also have had a race riot in London, the roots of which go back to our capitalist system. The association with white women was but the occasion of the London race riot.

Proximate Economic Causes

During the last half of the nineteenth century, and until a very late date, the Negro has been largely a scab. This, of course, was due chiefly to the short-sighted position of organized white labor. Nevertheless, his scabbing created great hostility between the races. Within the last decade, however, there has been a movement from the competition of black and white workers to the unionism of black and white workers.

The IWW prohibit discrimination on account of race or color in the first clause of their constitution, and they carry it out in practice. The recent convention of the American Federation of Labor held in Atlantic City went on record as favoring the organization of all Negro workers. In addition to this, the Negroes have shown a marked tendency toward unionizing among themselves. They have formed the National Brotherhood Association of America, which is an organization on the order of the United Hebrew Trades. (Just as the Hebrew Trades were organized to protect Jewish workers, so the National Brotherhood Association was organized to protect Negro workers.) At the convention of the Virginia State Federation of Labor in Alexandria, Va., June of this year, 30 Negroes were seated and took an active part in the proceedings. Everywhere the white and black workers show signs of co-operation in combining against the common enemy— Capitalism. This, naturally, breeds its counter-irritant—the attempt, on the part of capital, represented in the banks, railroads, manufacturers, packers and mine owners, to *divide* the workers—to get the black and white working dogs fighting over the bone of race prejudice in order that they, the yellow capitalist dogs, may get away with the *meat*. And this illustration carries with it more than the figure. It is very apt, for it is literally true.

In Chicago, the riots grew out of the fight between the packers and the workers. There are about 60,000 workers in the packing industry. Of these workers, it is estimated that about 15,000 or 18,000 are colored. They were just on the verge of organizing to get more wages, shorter hours and decent working conditions. About 6,000 Negroes had already joined the union. For all of them to join the union would enable the workers, by calling a general strike, to paralyze the entire industry and to secure their demands. If the workers secured their demands, it would greatly lessen the $120,000,000 profits made by the "Big Five" packers in 1918. The more wages for the workers the less profits for the packers. This would never do. Hence, something must be done to prevent this combination of black and white workers. The race riot was the most convenient and effective instrument at hand. Besides, the riots in Washington and Chicago were the best places for calling them. Washington is the capital and what happens there would be heralded throughout the country and world. This would inflame the feeling between colored and white persons in all other sections of the country. Chicago, on the other hand, is the second largest city in the United States. And particularly, it is home of the packing industry, and what happens there is second only to what happens in the capital. While what happens in the packing industry ramifies throughout the United States, since the "Big Five" packers, according to the latest reports of the Federal Trade Commission, control the manufacture of 775 commodities in the United States, and Negroes are employed in very nearly every one of those industries. The Chicago riot, therefore, struck a blow at the unionism of black and white workers in nearly every industry in the United States. So much for the economic causes of race riots.

Now the question arises: what other method shall be brought into play? What other weapons may be used? This brings us to the psychological or contributory causes.

Race Prejudice

The red embers of race prejudice are always smouldering in America. To fan them for a moment is sufficient to start the fire. Consequently, this vestige from slavery was a good starting point for the combined capitalists and manufacturers in America to ignite race wars. Again, there are Southern agents provocateurs in the United States who are carrying on a tireless and systematic campaign, to poison public opinion against the Negroes. They have Southern clubs in every big college of the North, East and West, and Southern societies in the big cities. No one would know the significance of a Northern, Eastern or Western club, but everyone immediately understands the purpose of a Southern Club. The average Southerner still sullenly broods over the lost cause. The progress of the Negro rankles in his breast and he would secede tomorrow to maintain his reactionary and bourbon traditions. They carried their propaganda to France, and disseminated the falsehood that Negroes, like monkeys, had tails.

Newspapers carry inflammatory headlines about alleged crimes of Negroes. The rape of white women is invariably played upon. Approbrious [sic] terms are used such as "nigger," "darky," "coon," "black burly brute," etc. Papers like the *Washington Post* even announced mobilization almost at the doors of the "White House." The *Chicago Tribune* becomes more inflammatory than the *Atlanta Constitution*. The *New York Times* writes viciously about the inferiority of the Negro.

The schools in the United States are largely segregated, which reduces the contact between colored and white children to the minimum. Biased and mischievous histories are written—histories which distort the facts about Negroes in every phase of American life. In Virginia, the history used in the schools is written by General Robert E. Lee's grand-daughter. Alleged scholars like Professor John Burgess of Columbia College in his *Reconstruction and the Constitution* and Albert Bushnell Hart in the *Southern South* show lamentable ignorance of the problems they are discussing, while the former is as violent and rabid as Vardaman and Hoke Smith might be. Franklin H. Giddings, Professor of Sociology in Columbia, on Friday, August 1st, makes frequent use of the term "darky" in a class composed of colored and white teachers. Dr. Miller of Bellevue Hospital, in 1914, used the term "darky" in the class room of the New York School of Philanthropy. *The Spectator*, the official organ of Columbia, in a leading editorial endorses and defends the use of the term "darky." Numbers of colleges like Princeton, Johns Hopkins, West Point, Annapolis, the latter two of which are government schools, refuse admission to colored students. In nearly all of the large white universities, Negroes are excluded from the dormitories. Again school equipment is inadequate for both whites and blacks in the south. John R. Commons of Wisconsin University points out that in 1910, $2.22 and $4.92 were spent on the Negro and white child respectively in the South. In Washington, D.C., in 1913, despite the fact that Negroes comprised 30 per cent of the school population, they received only 10 percent of the school appropriation for equipment. And a member of the Chicago City Council in 1918, introduced a bill for segregated schools.

The church is usually reactionary. The Presbyterian Church invested $93,000 in the slave trade. In 1830, all the white churches met in conference in Charleston, S. C., and issued a manifesto stating that the Negro had no soul. The Church was a bulwark of slavery. It taught them "servants obey your masters." It preaches a doctrine of humility. It is seldom that a white minister preaches a sermon against lynching. In the Negro church, the ministers are largely ignorant, venal or controlled. (There are certain marked exceptions, of course.) The disgraceful "Mitchell Slush Fund" in the campaign of 1917, stained the character of every Negro minister in New York, with the exception of one or two.

The screen and stage also arouse race prejudice. "The Birth of a Nation," based on Thomas Dixon's *Clansman*, did much to prepare the American mind for race riots and lynchings, *"Pride of Race"* (which ignorant Negroes knew no better than to produce themselves), was propaganda against race equality. *"The Nigger"* was a play of similar type. Previous to this, the

Clansman had been presented throughout the United States. The black face comedian is another menace to harmonious race relations. The Negro is always shown in the capacity of an inferior. He is making fun—the lowest form of pleasure. Those who see comedians like Bert Williams, Al Jolson, Lew Dockstadter, Al G. Fields, and other black faced comedians, acting the part of buffoons and clowns do not generally see Negroes in their best light. They regard the presentation on the stage as typical. And one who is constantly shown as a clown, thief, gambler, or crapshooter, gets eventually the stigma of an inferior. This so-called American Negro music, such as plantation songs and old spirituals, sung by the Fisk Jubilee Singers, the Hampton and Tuskegee Quartettes, has been more funny than musical. Besides it has served to instill the spirit of servility into Negro youths. Capitalists contribute large sums of money to these institutions, because they know that if they can get the black and white workers to singing slave songs, they can more successfully rob them, for they cannot think about their own interests. The stage and screen, then, have done a big part to create and crystalize race prejudice. Part of the race prejudice is vicious and grows out of the contempt in which an inferior is held.

To sum up: First, how has the press caused riots? The Southern press has been controlled by the regnant economic forces in the South. Their editorial and news policies have been so adjusted as to suit the Southern plutocracy. Here, again, it is apparent that he who controls the bread and butter will also control and shape the ideas. Newspapers like the *Atlanta Georgian* have carried such headlines: "A Subject for the Stake," "Lynch the Brute," "Lynch the Wretch." During the Atlanta Race Riot, September 22, 1916, the *Atlanta Evening News* carried inflammatory headlines which fanned the fires of race prejudice.

Second, the church is the recipient of large contributions from the financial rulers of the South and naturally preaches the Christianity of profits.

In very truth the beneficiaries of a system cannot be expected to destroy it. Hence, the Methodist Church split over the issue of slavery (which was an economic question pure and simple) into North and South, in 1860. The Church of the South prayed and preached for the victory of the cotton kings. The Church of the North blessed and anointed the industrial capitalists.

Third, the most important social institution of the South is controlled by legislators who are controlled by political parties which are, in turn, controlled by financial lords who regard it safer and more profitable to keep the common people, white and black, in virtual ignorance and superstition, because ignorant people don't strike for higher wages and better working conditions. So that the school terms, in some parts of the South, last only three months. The educational appropriation of the Southern states is the lowest paid in any section of the country. The slave states appropriate $2.22 for each Negro pupil per year and $4.92 for each white.

This but indicates the low social state of both races in the South.

Fourth, the propinquity of the races in the South has, undoubtedly, operated to accentuate the feeling of race prejudice.

This doubtless is due to the extreme oppositeness of physical characteristics. Of course, the racial differences are not a cause, but an occasion, for race strife. The social mind of the South is the product of a peculiar environment. For instance, the social heritage of slavery and the Reconstruction Period still rankles the bosom of Southern society. And the attack of a Negro on a white person, the doctrine that the Negro is a hewer of wood and a drawer of water; the Bible citation of Canaan in proof; the doctrine of the white man's superiority preached by political, religious and journalistic demagogues to the poor, ignorant whites; the doctrine of the sacredness of the Southern white woman shown by the Southern white man's chivalry toward her in public conveyances, combined with the ignorance and superstition of the common whites and blacks, has a tremendous psychological and emotional power in occasioning lynching. We say occasioning because the cause lies deeper. They are the fuse. The magazine is the capitalist system. Most anything in the South may be the occasion of lynching. It may be a "well-dressed" Negro in country districts, the use of the word "yes" by a Negro to a white man, asking a white woman for the name of a street, the fighting of a colored and white boy, and the use of good English to white folks. A very conspicuous characteristic of the South is its hyper-sensitiveness. There still persists the duel. Homicides are more numerous than in any other part of the country. When the sister of a young white man or daughter of a father is fooled by another white man, seldom is recourse made to courts, but the accused is generally shot down like a dog in the open streets.

Political Causes

Political causes are back of the riots also. Negroes are largely disfranchised. They cannot take political revenge upon those who make and administer the law. Consequently, police are careless and indifferent about giving them protection. The police system is controlled, as a rule, by the mayor, and the mayor is elected by the party, and the party is controlled by those who make up the campaign funds. And the Negro comes nowhere in this chain. The fact that he votes in Chicago, does not alter the case, because of his relative numbers. (There are about 30 white persons to every Negro.) Another political reason for the riots was the desire on the part of the passing Democratic administration to get some anti-Negro legislation enacted. Immediately the race-riot in Washington, D.C. began. Senator Harrison of Mississippi, introduced a bill for jim-crow cars in Washington. A representative from Arkansas introduced a bill against the inter-marriage of the races. Moreover, the Northern and Western states are threatening to penalize the South for forcing prohibition on the country, by reducing her representation in the coming apportionment, by enforcing the 14th and 15th Amendment. So the South feels that if sufficient race prejudice can be stirred up in the North, it will act toward changing opinion for the enfranchisement of the Negro.

Social Causes

Social causes are always present where there are social diseases. Race riots are symptoms of social diseases. Segregation is a long standing American social disease. It lessens the contact between the races. It prohibits harmony between the races through such methods as the jim-crow car, discrimination in public accommodations, residential segregation and laws against inter-marriage. The prohibition of an act creates the desire to perform that act. A striking example of the proof of this principle is the relation between the races in the South. There the races are segregated in every way as they are in no other part of the world, and yet the feeling is worse. In the North, there is more contact, despite considerable discrimination, and the feeling is much better than in the South. In countries like France, where there is absolutely no discrimination, the feeling is as harmonious, cordial, and kindly between white and black persons as among white persons themselves.

The housing problem has also been productive of friction. Negro migration created a fertile field for real estate speculators. With its many advantages there were certain concomitant evils. It enabled the real estate speculators to exploit both whites and Negroes. The whites had to pay higher rents and they had to go into worse quarters. The Negroes, too, had to pay higher rent and were forced to convert their quarters into lodging houses in order to pay the rents. The deprivation of one's home is irritating and engenders strife and ill will against those who replace them. This gave rise to bombing of Negro homes purchased in former white sections of Chicago.

Military Causes

Lastly, military causes have not been without their effect in the production of race riots. For four and one-half years the religion of violence had been taught to both white and black people of America. War has engendered the spirit of violence. The transition from shooting a white German is not very far from shooting a white American. Besides, Negroes hate American whites, but they almost uniformly report that the Germans were among the fairest and best people they have ever met. They like the Germans as well as the French. Everybody overseas was better to the Negro soldier than the white American. Hence the Negro returned with vengeance and hatred for the white American in his breast. He noted the difference in the treatment abroad from that he got at home The white American also noted this difference. The Negro favored it: the white American disapproved of the French fraternal spirit. Hence, the clash. Upon returning home, the Negro found conditions worse than when he left, despite his fight to "make the world safe for democracy." He is dissatisfied with his reward for his participation in the war. Not knowing President Wilson, he took him at his word. He wants to make the world safe for democracy, and therefore determined to make America safe for himself. He secured the knowledge of the art and value of organization. And he is determined to use this knowledge and art in the interest of himself.

Effects

The spirit of independence of Negroes has increased, because with their inferior numbers they feel that they have gotten the better of the contest. The prejudice of the whites has increased because they are not accustomed to Negroes striking back. The result is a social magazine which may explode at any moment upon lighting the fuse. Almost anything might serve as the fuse, such as, the use of the word "nigger," "a fight between a black and white boy." Negroes owning fine automobiles, purchasing fine houses in so-called white neighborhoods, accidentally stepping on a white woman's foot—ad infinitum.

The Remedy

What it is not. It is not segregation. As pointed out above, the South is segregated to the (nth) power, yet there, feeling is worse, mob violence, lynching, and race riots most frequent. Upon the advent of white Americans in Europe with their segregation measures between the races, riots in London and Liverpool followed.

The solution will not follow the meeting of white and Negro leaders in love feasts, who pretend like the African ostrich, that nothing is wrong because their heads are buried in the sand.

On the economic field, industry must be socialized, and land must be nationalized, which will thereby remove the motive for creating strife between the races. Black and white workers must unite in the same unions, ask for the same wages, same hours and the same working conditions. Identity of conditions between the workers will do more to produce equality of citizenship than any other force. Jevons the logician, aptly says: "Nothing happens without a reason why it is so rather than otherwise." This is true of large scale industry in the United States. It does nothing without a motive or a reason. It would not be interested in the production of race riots if not profits were realized therefrom. The beneficiary of a system cannot be relied upon to overthrow that system. The workers only can be relied upon consciously to destroy the industrial autocracy in the United States.

Politically, all peoples must be enfranchised without regard to race, creed, sex or color.

Educationally, schools must be revolutionized. Equal pay must be granted to teachers with equal equipment for school children. This can be made secure by abolishing segregation in the schools, for when all children sit in the same classrooms, it is not possible to discriminate in teachers' equipment. Besides, it produces the spirit of fraternity. The curriculum needs to be changed. More economics, history and sociology and the physical sciences need to be taught and less Latin, Greek and Bible.

The people must organize, own and control their press.

The church must be converted into an educational forum.

The stage and screen must be controlled by the people.

Immediate Program

We recognize that the preceding remedy is a comprehensive and fundamental remedy which may take years for attainment. In the meantime, an immediate program must be adopted to meet the demands of the transition period. Hence, we offer this immediate program.

1. *Physical force in self-defense.* While force is to be deplored and used only as a last resort, it is indispensable at times. The lesson of force can be taught when no other will be heeded. A bullet is sometimes more convincing than a hundred prayers, editorials, sermons, protests and petitions. (The resistance of Negroes in the race riots just passed has been helpful to the white and colored people throughout the country.) It has saved us in other cities from riots. Negroes have shown that riots hereafter will be costly and unprofitable, and when you make a thing unprofitable you make it impossible.

2. *Larger Negro police force.* A larger Negro police force in Negro districts will help to keep down riots. The behavior of the police in all the race riots in the United States has justified Negroes in believing that the police, so far from being impartial, were in collusion with the white rioters. A prompt and impartial arrest of the aggressors in Washington and Chicago could have nipped the riots in the bud. Moreover, Negroes understand the psychology of Negroes better than the Irishmen and Southern white men who very largely compose the police forces of the cities. Negroes even receive no protection from the militia or army which is called out in order to suppress the riots. In East St. Louis the soldiers are reported to have given their rifles to the white rioters. And it is obvious that you cannot expect prejudiced white soldiers and policemen impartially to adjust the relations between the races, when they are a part of the race doing the mobbing.

Finally, the courts of law must indict both white and colored without fear or favor, according to their culpability. Besides, the jury should be made up of both white and colored persons. How can Negroes expect to get justice from an all-white jury? In Chicago, the jury has returned indictments against 57 Negroes and only 4 whites. Think of it! Negroes are justified in regarding the so-called Department of Justice as a department of injustice, where they are concerned. In Washington, 200 Negroes have been arrested, and only 20 whites, despite the fact that the whites in Washington, as in Chicago, are known to have begun the riots.

Lastly, revolution must come. By that we mean a complete change in the organization of society. Just as absence of industrial democracy is productive of riots and race clashes, so the introduction of industrial democracy will be the longest stop toward removing that cause. When no profits are to be made from race friction, no one will longer be interested in stirring up race prejudice. The quickest way to stop a thing or to destroy an institution is to destroy the profitableness of that institution. The capitalist system must go and its going must be hastened by the workers themselves. The capitalists are the beneficiaries of race riots. The workers are the losers by race riots. The same is true of war. The workers entail huge burdens of expense and lose their life and limb. Make wars unprofitable and you make them impossible. This is the task of the workers, white and black, and especially the imperative duty of the white workers by virtue of their numbers, their opportunity and their intelligent class consciousness.

The International Debacle

The world is not only not settled, but it is becoming more unsettled. War is not only not over, but new wars are looming upon the international horizon. The League of Nations has not only failed to function, but new miniature leagues or secret compacts are being formed that bid fair to overshadow the "League of Versailles." Great Britain has negotiated a secret compact with Persia, and is seeking to effect one with Japan, America, France and Great Britain, and here the League of Nations has shuffled off its swaddling clothes, formed a secret triple alliance for their mutual benefit.

In short, the League of Nations is not trusted by even those who made it to resettle the world.

So the world keeps lumbering on distressingly unwitting of its way.

Germany has been strangled by the bloody fingers of a ruthless crowd of desperate and willful diplomats at Versailles. Wilson, Makino, Orlando, Clemenceau and Lloyd George, in their efforts to save the crumbling edifice of capitalism for the bankers of New York, Paris, London, Rome and Tokyo, have pulled down the house on their masters' heads. What they sought to conserve, they have destroyed; what they sought to destroy, they have preserved.

The working people of Russia simply would not stay put, and one fine day, they discharged Czar Nicholas of all the Russians, brought peace to the people, and gave the land to the peasants and the factories to the workers. This was, indeed, passingly strange. The capitalist world was aghast, a picture of consternation and despair. For what an example the workers of Russia have set for the workers of England and America, France, Italy and Japan! What the workers of one country have done, the workers of other countries can do, and, what is worse, they are likely to think of following the example of their Russian cousins. This contemplation is not the occasion of pleasant dreams of the masters of the coal mines,

---

Originally published in the *Messenger*, November 1920, 134–35.

railroads, the bankers and landlords of the civilized countries of the world. Hence, Soviet Russia is blockaded, Generals Korniloff, Kolchak, Denikin, Yudenich and Wrangel—the "White Hopes" of bankrupt Capitalism, have been unleashed to do their darndest. They went to Soviet Russia, they saw; but they did not conquer.

Finally, Poland, under the leadership of the music master, Paderewski, was recruited and annointed to start a holy crusade against the impious band of violators of Capitalism's code of Righteousness: the right of the capitalists to say to the workers, "You make bread, and we will eat it; you fight wars, and we will make them and profit from them."

But the upturn of Russia would not have forebode such dreadful omens, were it not for the unimaginable sympathetic attitude of the workers of England, France, Germany, Italy, Japan and America toward the Soviet Republic of Russia.

The workers of England organized the Labor Council of Action, a new invention in labor structures, for the purpose of preventing Lloyd George from sending munitions and soldiers to Poland to fight the workers of Russia. This struck such terror into the hearts of the lords, earls, dukes, marquises, oil, coal, and transportation kings of England, that the question was immediately raised: Who shall rule Great Britain, the Labor Council of Action or Parliament? Nor are the British workers contented with prices of wages. The coal miners and transport workers may yet produce an impasse for Lloyd George, and wreck his ministry. At least, the present government is not sure of the extent of its life, so long as British labor is recalcitrant, and presumes to say to the King "ne plus ultra."

Again, Ireland is not the calmest spot on the British map. Sinn Feinism will not back down, the British Empire is loath to accord independence to the "emerald isle." Hence, civil war proceeds apace, thirty thousand British bayonets are pointing at the hearts of determined Irishmen and women, while the Lord Mayor of Cork mocks the British crown with a hunger strike in Brixton prison.

And the flames of nationalism continue to burn at the base of the empire of "perfidious Albion" in India. Amritzar, like Banquo's ghost, rises ever and anon to haunt His Majesty's Highness. Meantime the Gadar party prepares for the final overthrow of British rule in India.

And according to the trend of events, England may yet clash with her erstwhile ally, America. The American capitalists need oil, and England has gobbled up the available oil resources of the world. Oil bids, in the near future, to become King. It is the chief motive power on land and sea. It is reported that, in the next five years, if America is not able to rob some weaker peoples of their oil, she will be paying five billion a year to England for the precious fluid. This explains the reason for America's itching palm for Mexico.

Italy, too, is in the throes of a revolution. The metallurgical workers have seized the factories, raised the red flag, barricaded themselves with machine guns, and announced to the world that: no longer will they be robbed and exploited by the pious thieves of Italy. Even the Pope may yet be forced to abdicate his throne to calm an enraged and outraged populace. Signor Gioletti is struggling to effect a rapprochement between the workers and owners of the factories. He has demanded the confiscation of war profits. His policy is: This is done to pacify the workers. But the workers still cry: long live the Soviets! All power to the workers! and proceed to vote their allegiance to the Moscow Third International.

No man dares predict the next step of the workers of the Mediterranean.

At the same time, France, England and America sit taut, ready to blockade a Soviet Italy.

Also, the wily capitalists of Nippon manifest their fears of an awakened and aroused working class Japan. A panic has already shaken the financial and industrial fabric of the country. The lot of the workers is becoming worse, while they threaten to challenge the sacred tenure in power of the Elder Statesmen.

Recent dispatches from Germany indicate a change in the political complexion of the country. In the industrial centers, the Independent Socialist party is being captured for the Third International. The spirits of Liebknecht and Rosa Luxemburg seem to be guiding the Sparticides to victory. *Will Germany go Bolshevik?* is the question that haunts the diplomats in Downing Street, the Quai d'Orsay, and the Hotel Crillon, and our own Wall Street. Each day will witness new changes in Germany. The German worker may yet revise the peace of Versailles. The Fates may have reserved the German workers the task of striking the final blow to European capitalism, and finally to world capitalism.

Now will American capitalists believe that the flood of the proletarian revolution, begun at the shrine of the Czar of Russia, will not leap the dikes of three thousand miles of distance and engulf the land of the free (?) and the home of the brave?

Besides, the workers of America are not in love with their own prices and wages. Houses are scarce and becoming scarcer. They, too, show signs of unrest. They threaten to vote for Debs; they are opposed to war over in Soviet Russia; they announce sympathy for a free Ireland, and even indicate a change of heart on the Negro question.

Then, too, 15,000,000 Negroes declare they have grievances to redress; and the young, intelligent Negro is looking askance at Socialism. In fact, five Negroes have been nominated on the Socialist Party ticket, and it is rumored that the Negroes are thinking strongly as to whether or not Socialism will solve their problem.

Yes, the times are pregnant with change. Nothing escapes the God of Metamorphosis. Even empires rise and fall. Kings are deposed, Kaisers exiled and Czars banished. Presidential candidates speak from prison, and elected representatives are expelled from legislatures. Men and women are deported from countries for the opinions they hold, and a working-class government has actually been established in the world.

And the end is not yet. The mills of the Gods grind slowly, but exceedingly fine. The workers appear to be at the mills this time, grinding out a new world as a workers' world; at least the high priests of capitalism, Woodrow Wilson, Lloyd George and their ilk are not impressed with their present control of world affairs. This international debacle, indeed, passeth their (the capitalists') understanding. Only the workers hold the key to its solution.

The General Strike and Lawlessness (1922)

DUBLIN, April 24—"The movement for enforcing a suppression of the terrorism which has been raging in Ireland for weeks was materially aided by the general protest strike today of the Labor party and the trade unions it represents.

"For 15 hours, Southern Ireland scarcely turned a wheel. One hundred thousand workers participated in the strike here, completely tying up every kind of activity.

"Huge mass meetings were held throughout this city where speakers protested against militarism and threatened to stop the munitions industry by a walkout, if necessary, to bring the gunmen to their senses."

Such is the way by which labor in Ireland proposes to stamp out lawlessness, and restore peace, law and order. Not a bad weapon this! When properly and courageously wielded, it is the Nemesis of the ruling class. Even a threat sends pandemonium through the ranks of the silk-gloved fraternity. A mere threat of a strike by the British Labor Council of Action forced the British government to abandon its project of sending aid to Poland when she was trying to overthrow the workers' republic, Soviet Russia. If, at the time it was fairly certain that the war cloud would burst over Europe in July, 1914, the workers of Germany, France, Great Britain, Austria-Hungary and Russia had had sufficient international solidarity to call a general strike, there would have been no Great War. Of course, there is that "if" which never downs. The fact is the workers talked about the general strike, passed resolutions in their congresses against war, pledging themselves to a general strike in the event of war, but that was all. However, their failure then is no proof that it can not or will not be employed by labor. Labor moves slowly but surely. Witness Soviet Russia, a workers' government actually functioning in the interest of labor. Also witness the general strike in Germany which put down the Kapp revolution. Strange things are happening today.

Originally published in the *Messenger*, June 1922, 427.

It is not impossible either for the Negro workers to stage a *general strike demonstration* against the lawlessness, murder and crime of the Ku Klux Klan, and the burnings and lynchings of Negroes in the South, North and West.

This, of course, is based upon the assumption that Negroes join the unions, or organize themselves where they are denied entrance into the unions. A general strike could not have been called in Ireland, if the Irish workers had not been organized.

A general strike against lynching and the Ku Klux Klan by Negro workers would dramatize the issue of a federal law against lynching as nothing else possibly could. It would awaken the entire world to the Negro problem. The Workers in all of the European, South and Central American countries would seize the opportunity to condemn American democracy. It would be effective not so much for what it did but chiefly for what it portended.

Lenin (1924)

At last Lenin is dead. The foreign news agencies have had him dead or dying many a time before. His, doubtless, was the most difficult task of any of the rulers of the war or after-war periods, for his regime was opposed by the combined world from without and determined counter-revolutionary groups from within. Still, he was always serene, rigidly logical, surveying the most difficult and baffling problems, foreign and domestic, with a calm and dispassionate sureness, which both startled and overmastered his friend and foe. While he was the strong man of the Communist Party, he persistently opposed with his great power of dialectics and biting satire the infantile irrational leftism which impregnated the Third Internationale, that more than any other force won for Russia the hostility of both labor and capital in Europe and America. His statesmanship was grounded upon a universal vision and a broad scholarship in economics and social, scientific history which stamped him as the intellectual colossus of the statesmen of his period. As the premier of the first great workers' republic, he will be accounted by thinkers of the future as one of the truly great figures of human history.

Originally published in the *Messenger*, March 1924, 59.

W. A. Domingo

Introduction

Wilfred Adolphus Domingo (1889–1968) was a Jamaican-born socialist who was, for a time, an important bridge between Harlem socialists and Marcus Garvey's Universal Negro Improvement Association. Little known today, contemporaries such as Claude McKay judged him as one of the most impressive of the young New Negro radicals.

Domingo was born in Jamaica and active with Garvey in the National Club there, Jamaica's first nationalist political group. Domingo moved to the United States in 1910, first to Boston, before settling in New York in 1912. When Garvey arrived in New York in early 1916, Domingo made several introductions for him, helping Garvey to establish himself in the city. One of the most important of these was introducing Garvey to Henry Rogowski, the printer who put out the Socialist Party's New York newspaper, the *Call*. Through Rogowski, Garvey began publishing his own paper, the *Negro World*, which Domingo edited until 1919.

In Harlem, Domingo became close with the group of Black socialists around the *Messenger*, edited by A. Philip Randolph and Chandler Owen. Along with other Black socialists, he participated in the SP's 21st Assembly District and was also active in the party school, the Rand School of Social Science.

Domingo's associations with the socialists eventually got him into trouble with Garvey. Garvey was unhappy with Domingo's use of the *Negro World* to spread socialism, and when Garvey came under government repression in 1919, he quickly judged Domingo more of a liability than an asset. Garvey used the excuse of a government raid on the Rand School, which turned up a pamphlet of Domingo's on the race question, *Socialism*

Imperilled, as an excuse to launch a "trial" of Domingo, and force him to resign his editorship.

After this, Domingo continued writing for the Black socialist press, often on the question of what the Russian Revolution meant for Black radicals. In 1920, he and Richard B. Moore, another Black socialist, started their own journal, the *Emancipator*, though only ten issues came out before it folded. By this time, Domingo, along with most of the other New Negro socialists, had become convinced that Garvey was guilty of significant misleadership, and needed to be opposed. Around this time, Domingo joined African Blood Brotherhood founded by Cyril Briggs, who had come to similar conclusions about Garvey.

From about mid-1920 on, the campaign against Garvey ran throughout the Black socialist press, even extending to W.E.B. Du Bois and the *Crisis*. Yet though Domingo agreed that politically, Garvey was a fantasist, he became uncomfortable with the tenor of the campaign against him, particular as it came from the *Messenger* and the *Crisis*. In these periodicals, writers heaped scorn on Garvey as much for his Caribbean background as for his failed business ventures. Domingo wrote privately to Du Bois to complain about this and publicly broke with the *Messenger* over a particularly abusive piece from Chandler Owen in 1923.

Unlike most of the ABB leadership, Domingo never joined the Communist Party, and little is known about his political activity after 1923. In the mid-1930s, he surfaced again in New York as a presence in Jamaican nationalist circles. In 1941, he returned to Jamaica, only to be arrested by the colonial government along with other labor leaders. Eventually freed, he returned to New York in 1947, remaining active in Jamaican diaspora politics until a stroke in 1964.

Further Reading

Floyd-Thomas, J.M. "Domingo, Wilfred Adolphus." In *Encyclopedia of the Harlem Renaissance,* Vol. 1, edited by Cary D. Wintz and Paul Finkleman, 304–305. New York: Routledge, 2004.

Hill, Robert A. *The Marcus Garvey and Universal Negro Improvement Association Papers*, Vol I. Los Angeles: University of California Press, 1983.

James, Winston. *Holding Aloft the Banner of Ethiopia: Caribbean Radicalism in Early Twentieth-Century America.* London: Verso, 1998.

Socialism Imperilled, or the Negro— A Potential Menace to American Radicalism

At this time, when a considerable portion of Europe is reorganizing itself; when for the first time in history millions of working people have begun to think in terms of their class; when the old form of political State is in danger of dissolution, and when sparks of proletarian unrest have passed from Russia, to Germany, Argentina, Italy, and the Pacific Coast of the United States, it is well for those who are agitating along radical lines in this country to comprehend all the dangers which beset them. Failure on the part of those who are immediately interested to recognize danger is sure to result in disaster—disaster which may set back economic radicalism in America for an indefinite period. On the other hand, the old adage, "Forewarned is forearmed" takes on significant importance to those who by failure to properly gauge a situation may precipitate their own destruction. Avoidance of such an eventuality should be the controlling influence in framing the tactics and strategy of American radicals. No element of the population should be despised nor any reliance be placed upon a purely theoretical and dogmatic assumption that groups of the population can be depended upon, because of their sufferings and oppression, to arrive at an instinctive understanding of where their support should be cast when the crucial moment arrives.

Tactics based upon such a fallacious premise must, and will result in, a catastrophe to those who so calculate, for at the bottom it rests upon no firmer basis than that the wish the father of the thought.

Since the Russian revolution of 1917, when the revolutionists, Lenin and Trotsky, came into power, radical propagandists of all shades of belief have been encouraged to extend and intensify their propaganda in the United

---

Originally an SP pamphlet, it was published as part of a report conducted by New York State's Joint Legislative Committee Investigating Seditious Activities, with the title *Revolutionary Radicalism: Its History, Purpose and Tactics, With an Exposition and Discussion of the Steps Being Taken and Required to Curb It*, 1489.

States. Every social theorist, every genuine social revolutionist is today fired with the determination to institute industrial freedom in America. "The home of the brave and the land of the free."

All of these movements are maliciously labelled Bolshevism by the press, and ignorantly regarded as something dangerous by the majority of American newspaper readers and churchgoers.

No section of the American people can claim to be immune from being influenced by this wicked characterization which is being made of Socialism and other species of economic radicalism by the press, the pulpit and the platform.

While during the war everything un-American (which means not profitable to Wall Street) was stigmatized as German propaganda, today it is Bolshevik. As a consequence, Socialist propaganda, although more intense and efficient than in the past, is being met by an equally efficient, less scrupulous and more intensive and extensive capitalistic counter-propaganda. That this counter-propaganda is at present very powerful will not be denied by anyone who is familiar with the political ignorance and national egotism of the average, so-called free American citizen. Abundant evidence of this is extant, notwithstanding the Seattle trouble, the Lawrence strike and the existence of the National Non-Partisan League.

For proof we have only to note the stolid acquiescence of the masses to the fate of the Industrial Workers of the World, the persecution of conscientious objectors and Socialists, and the complacent willingness with which "Best Citizens" lead, presumably, the worst citizens to lynch or tar and feather a fellow citizen in the name of patriotism. This attitude is national, permeating the country from the Atlantic to the Pacific coast, and from Maine to Texas, but perhaps, its zenith is reached in the Southern states where Americanism is most rampant and least contaminated by contact with tolerant foreigners.

Revolutionary Socialists in the Socialist Party are agitating for a restatement of the party platform and tactics in terms of Bolshevik tactics which, with the class struggle as its basis, maneuver to establish a proletarian dictatorship in order to accomplish the transition from a capitalist to a Socialist state.

Already Massachusetts, Michigan and several other States have gone "Left" and New York is in the throes of an internal struggle for party control, waged between the Right and Left Wings. This, in itself, is nothing strange as nearly every Socialist movement in Europe has had similar disputes all of which center on the question of tactics. The objective sought is the same, but how to attain it is the bone of contention. In France there are all kinds of factional splits in the movement; in Germany there are Majority Socialists, Independent Socialists and Spartacides; in Norway, Denmark and Sweden there are Left and Right Wings; in Great Britain there are British Socialists, Independent Laborites, Industrial Workers of the World and members of the Socialist Labor Party, and in the United States there are the Socialist Party and the Socialist Labor Party. There are some who bitterly denounce those who agitate for a restatement of Socialist tactics in terms of the present-day revolutionary Socialism; but perhaps, this party shake-up is not altogether undesirable if it results in a clarifying of tactics and a readjustment of propaganda so as to reach every working-class element that is a potential danger to the establishment of the Socialist State whether achieved through a proletarian dictatorship or a majority vote. So long as there is a numerically considerable group that is a danger to the establishment of the co-operative commonwealth, every ounce of propaganda should be directed at that group. A potential danger should be recognized and steps taken to render it harmless or if possible into a source of strength.

In the past the officials of the Socialist Party have been doctrinaires so far as their propaganda was concerned. Acting purely upon theory, and in some cases displaying an opportunism that played fast and loose with principles, they have confined most of their efforts to the industrial centers of the West, North and Middle West. Little, if any, attention was paid to farmers as a class (unless the maudlin and unscientific agrarian arguments that the *Appeal to Reason* used to send out can be regarded as such), and still less was paid to that unexplored continent of labor reaction—the South. On a few occasions speakers were sent to tour the South but with little success, for some, like Eugene V. Debs, refused to sacrifice their Socialistic principles upon the altar of race-prejudice. In general, the Socialist Party might be said to have consciously or unconsciously adopted the tactics of the American Federation of Labor and neglected the white Southerner while leaving the negro severely alone.

The Industrial Workers of the World, avowedly non-political, on the other hand, did not confine their activities to any particular section of the country, nor did they excuse their failure to face facts and consider the circumstances surrounding any particular national element by making general statements that their appeals were made to all, and not to particular groups of the working class. Instead, these intrepid evangels of industrial unionism made special appeals to the migratory farm workers of the West, the ignorant white man of Louisiana, and the despised negro, with the result that they brought all these workers to realize the truth of the Marxian injunction: "Workers of the World, unite; you have nothing to lose but your chains. You have a world to gain!"

So powerful is the unity achieved by the I.W.W. that at their trial in Chicago were men of all races as defendants, among them being Ben Fletcher, a negro, and among the witnesses for the defense were four negroes who gave their testimony despite military and secret service intimidation.

In recognizing the importance of reaching negroes with their gospel the I.W.W. are showing statesmanlike farsightedness. They are facing facts squarely and by so doing are removing potential dangers from their path. If the Socialist Party comes under the control of the "Left" or the "Right" let those who will be responsible for its success profit from the mistakes of the A.F.L. which has shown such deplorable inaptitude as has resulted in making the negro an enemy of that organization and the scab of America.

If they follow the methods of the I.W.W. they will secure to themselves the adherence of over 12,000,000 people, and active support, without whose help no radical movement in America can hope to succeed.

There are (?) [*sic.*] over negroes in the United States. The majority live in the South and form the bulk of its laboring population. All the hard work which the white man, the traditions of slavery as a millstone around his neck refuses to do, is performed by negroes.

As a portion of the working class, negroes are industrially unorganized and in most cases bitterly antagonistic to organized labor. This is due to racial discrimination against them, the wages they receive and the kind of work usually reserved for them. They are given low wages and are told to be grateful to those who gave them a chance to earn a living, hence, although hating their employers, still they regard them as friends, in that they are given work to the exclusion of members of their employer's own race. In addition to this is the subtle control exercised over negro opinion through negro schools, colleges, churches and newspapers by Northern capitalists.

The South, that is, the dominant Bourbon South that needs ignorant docile labor to exploit, is frankly hostile to negro education on the theory founded in economic grounds, that "education spoils a negro for work." What is really meant is that education protects negroes from being mercilessly exploited. Due to Southern opposition to education, negro leaders naturally turn to the North for financial assistance in founding schools and colleges. By endowing Southern negro institutions of learning, Northern capitalists like Julius Rosenwald of Chicago and Andrew Carnegie of Pittsburg, control the various boards of trustees of these schools, and shape their policies. Thus the curricula are usually framed in such a manner as to train potential industrial scabs, and the students very naturally regard those who endowed the schools as their real friends and benefactors.

The same thing is true of negro newspapers. For the most part they exist upon the bounty of the Republican Party and, it is alleged, receive subsidies from big corporations for advising their readers to be hostile to organized labor and radicalism in general. Their policy is usually to denounce the white working class, while extolling the virtues of Mr. Rosenwald, Mr. Carnegie, and their ilk. They usually condemn every form of political and economic radicalism and laud patriotism.

Negro churches are the real source of negro opinion. These churches are usually presided over by the graduates of schools endowed by Northern philanthropists, and true to their training they praise the rich while inveighing against the laboring class. Then there is the question of material interests. Many negro churches have had mortgages lifted, organs presented or stained glass windows installed by philanthropically inclined millionaires.

Thus every medium of negro thought functions in the interests of capital.

The individual negro is also subjected to influences that tend to make him defy those who profit from his oppression. For the most part negroes are a distinct caste in American life. They are mostly cooks, waiters, porters and body servants who because of their inferior social and economic status, place an exaggerated value upon opportunities common to others, but denied them. On the trains, in hotels and other places where they work as menials, they come in contact with people who can indulge in luxuries, and whose opinions are necessarily of a kind to extol conservatism and condemn radicalism. With the exception of the few who work in the garment industry in New York and come in contact with wholesome radicalism of Russian Jews, the majority of negro men and women are deprived of the stimulating influence of advanced political thought.

Servants unconsciously imbibe their masters' psychology and so do negroes. Nobody is more intolerant against foreigners than negroes, despite the fact that their lives are safer in the North where so many foreigners reside than in the South where there are so few. Occupational traits are also developed to a marked degree. Being of slave origin and depending on tips doled out to a large degree, the tipper or those in a position to dole out tips take on magnified importance in the eyes of the tip receiver.

All of the foregoing influences exerted upon negroes have tended to make the race docile and full of respect for wealth and authority, while creating an immense gulf between the white and black workers which is widened by the fact that white workers on their part exhibit racial prejudice in refusing to give negroes an opportunity to work under the more favorable conditions achieved by union labor.

Smarting under the injustice of industrial discrimination and seeing the economic results upon himself and family, the average negro worker develops a not unnatural bitterness and hostility towards the white worker who, reacting to the cunning of the capitalist press that is intent on dividing the workers, reciprocates the hostility in terms of race hatred of the vilest and most unreasoning kind.

This results in a warping of the ordinary human instincts of both whites and negroes. They both become indifferent to the sufferings of each other and fail to recognize that most of what they suffer is both preventable and of common origin. So marked is this attitude that it is next to impossible to rouse a white audience of workingmen to the enormity of the crimes committed against society and the black race when the latter is denied elementary justice and fair play. Equally difficult is it to awaken in the breast of negroes any resentment against a vicious system that thrives on the labor of children, the sweating of adults and the robbery of one class by another. Any attempt in that direction among negroes is usually met by them in the same questioning spirit as they meet the tale of any great disaster. If a railroad wreck occurs, or a ship is sunk, the attitude of the average negro is to scan the death list diligently and if none of his race is among the victims, ejaculate "Thank God, they are all white people. There are no colored folks among them." In short, negroes react to prejudice and discrimination by becoming distinctly race conscious, but so far as their class consciousness is concerned, it is not even as much as scratched. It is therefore the function of whichever wing, Right or Left, that controls the Socialist Party to transmute the race consciousness of negroes into class consciousness. This will be necessary when cognizance is taken of some of the ingredients of negro ideology. Some of their ideas are contradictory and illogical but that does not rob them of their vitality and power for good or evil. While it is true that, reacting to oppression, negroes become racially conscious and think that they hate all white people, still, because of the various influences exerted upon them, they nevertheless make a distinction and feel that the better class among the whites are their friends and should be protected from being encroached upon by the working class who, because of capitalistic tutelage, and unfortunate experience, they regard as their enemy. They speak contemptuously of poor white trash and wreak vengeance upon them whenever possible. In their hearts, too, while they may hate individual State governments, yet they look to the Constitution as their Gibraltar and the Federal Government as their all-powerful protector. States may forfeit negro loyalty, but the federal Government has a firm grip upon it.

Jack London in his *Iron Heel* forecasts how mercenaries can be used to destroy Socialism if voted into power in the United States. Sixty thousand armed White Guards in Finland are holding down a population of over 3,000,000 people who voted a Socialist government into power. Then there is the classic example of a few thousands of well-armed Czecho-Slovaks being deceived and being used by counterrevolutionary elements and foreign capital to render nugatory the Russian proletarian revolution.

In Finland, through the martyrdom of 30,000 Socialists, it has been clearly demonstrated that one armed person in a population is able to cow and subdue 500 unarmed ones. The Czecho-Slovaks in Russia have shown how the just national aspirations of the oppressed people can be so successfully manipulated that they become instruments of their own ultimate enslavement.

The tragic part that the Czecho-Slovaks played in the Russian revolution is too well known to radicals to render a recital necessary. Suffice to say that, although oppressed Slavs longing for national freedom, they are being used by reactionaries as tools to restore a despotic Czaristic regime. Having these examples, and comprehending how much more dangerous the situation in the United States is for radicals it will be the quintessence of revolutionary good sense and self-interest for those who contemplate the transference of industrial and economic power from the hands of the few to the hands of the many to consider the ominous possibility of three or four million black working men being used by the plutocracy as black White Guards, or Czecho-Slovaks in America.

Let it be supposed that the Right Wing predominates in the Socialist Party; that it continues in the past policy of the party, concentrates its efforts upon vote getting in the North, flirts with the white South and ignores negroes except in Northern urban centers where their votes are needed to elect a municipal official.

Let it be further supposed that a majority of senators and congressmen are elected along with a Socialist president. The moment such a result had been flashed over the wires, the bourgeoisie would realize that their days were numbered and would immediately begin to formulate plans for the prevention of their own social and economic extinction. This would be done as a measure of supreme self-preservation. Secret meetings would be held and the situation carefully gone over. Orders would be issued to the prostitute press, time-serving ministers of religion, lecturers and the myriads of parasitical instruments that exist for the corruption of public opinion, to begin a campaign for the purpose of proving that the election was irregular, illegal, and consequently void; that the Socialists be not permitted to take control of the government as their program was un-American, atheistic and anarchistic; that it would be the duty of all loyal citizens to save the country from a new form of slavery. In the meantime (and there would be five months between the election in November and induction of the Socialist administration into office in April of the following year) a careful survey would be made of the various sections of the country and groups of the population that were least affected by the virus of Socialism, and having the facts at their finger tips they would quickly turn to the white south and the negroes of the nation as the most likely defenders of the old order. They would play upon the ignorance of both and seek to use them against the class-conscious Northern proletariat. Soon all kinds of propaganda would flood negro sections. Negro ministers, past masters in the art of hypnotic emotional appeal and crude declamatory oratory, would preach diatribes against Socialism and warn their congregations, Cato-like, that the Bolsheviks, Socialists and Anarchists who seek to re-enslave the race and rob them of Jesus must be destroyed. In this the ministers would be actuated by their own material interest, as colored ministers are, perhaps, the most parasitic of celestial navigators. Evidence of their venality is easily supplied by the fact that most of them are quasi-politicians, and that after the Hylan-Hillquit-Mitchel mayoral campaign of 1917, the majority of colored preachers in New York City were proven to have participated in the notorious Mitchell Slush Fund.

Leaflets and pamphlets condemning Socialism supposedly written by prominent negroes, but really written by skilled agents of capitalism would be distributed broadcast among negroes. This form of propaganda was resorted to by a colored newspaper in New York in 1918 with the result that nearly all the negro votes, which in a previous election had gone 20 per cent Socialist as a protest against Mitchel, went to the Republican candidates. Speakers who were secretly paid by the master class would appear on the street corners of negro sections, where from ladders and soapboxes they would exhort their race-conscious but politically ignorant and gullible fellow-negroes to die rather than submit to re-enslavement. From ministers, teachers, upstart military officers, newspapers and a diversified tribe of race "leaders" would come arguments whose gravamen would be to recount the friendship of the capitalists and the enmity of the workers in the past. Eloquent and grateful references would be made to those whose generosity had furnished the beginnings of negro education; those who had out of their magnificent altruism endowed Fisk, Meharry, Talladega, Hampton, Atlanta, Lincoln, Livingston, Tuskegee and other institutions of learning for the negro race; those who had from the fullness of their hearts done acts of charity and philanthropy to uplift the downtrodden race. References would be made to the fact that the race was just getting a grip upon the material things of life and that the white masses, jealous of negro improvement, were determined to confiscate what they had acquired after much personal privations and labor. By tongue, pen and picture negroes would be reminded of the terrible things they had suffered at the hands of the white masses. The horrors of East St. Louis would be painted and retold in harrowing language in order to excite the bitterest feelings of revenge in the breast of those who were of the same race as the victims of that terrible massacre that put the United States to shame when compared with Turkey. The old hostility of the average American workingman to permitting negroes to earn an honest livelihood in the industrial field among the classes of best paid workers would be trotted out with telling effect. Then, to cap the climax, the pathetic and morbid desire on the part of negroes to gain prominence which was denied them in almost every walk of life except where it was criminal or it was military would be catered to by making a few spectacular military promotions and by giving negroes a little more meritorious publicity in the various organs of public information. These negro officers for the most part sharing the common status of their race in industries are not as far removed from the majority of their people as white officers are from theirs. On the contrary, when mustered out it is the dire fate of the black lieutenant or captain to find himself a competitor with his erstwhile private for the same menial job in a hotel or on the train as waiter or porter. This, apart from racial consciousness, more firmly cements the solidarity of the race which on the whole takes place when any of its members can make even a temporary rise out of the common contempt to which they are all more or less condemned. All of this is already known to the plutocracy, but, unfortunately, it is not known to those for whom it constitutes a portentous peril. Already it has been suggested in the press that a sure preventative against Bolshevism (Socialism) in America would be to enfranchise the negro vote which would mean a permanent increase of the Republican vote in the country.

Analysis of the recent municipal elections in Chicago proves that the election of Mayor Thompson was due to the solidly Republican negro votes which had been increased in number by large accretions of enfranchised negro emigrants from the South!

Charles Schwab, the ironmaster of Bethlehem fame, is reported to have made a speech in New York in which he said that negroes can be relied upon to stay radicalism in this country. Col. Watterson of Kentucky said some years ago that the South and the negro will be the firmest bulwarks of conservatism against which the waves of American radicalism will be dashed in vain. After such testimony can anyone doubt that driven to desperation by a Socialist victory at the polls, the plutocracy would not hesitate to use force or fraud to prevent the establishment of a Socialist regime in the United States?

Let the hypothetical election of Socialism into office be further indulged in, and the fact that capitalism, beaten at the polls, has four months of grace before surrendering the sceptre of power be kept in mind; let it be remembered that until the April when it is supposed to abdicate, that reaction still controls the army, navy, railroads, press, steamships and all the various things that make for power in the modern world. Confident that there are 12,000,000 of racially conscious people friendly to it, that it can mobilize the petit bourgeoisie and the various classes of the priest-ridden South, what is there to deter Capitalism from boldly declaring the election null and void and its intention to retain power? To accomplish this, pretexts will have been found to declare martial law several weeks before April arrived; also specially trained armed mercenaries whose loyalty was unquestioned would be secretly mobilized and placed in charge of arsenals, railroad terminals and all places of strategic or economic value. At the same time negro White Guards would be organized and held in readiness for any emergency. Perhaps Northern workers goaded to desperation by seeing their hard earned political victory stolen from them might rise in revolt, but what measure of success could they hope to achieve without arms and without control of the means of communication? Finland gives the answer. And if one armed person can hold down fifty unarmed ones, how much easier will it not be for one armed negro to hold down less than ten unarmed white proletarians? Thus can the negro be the black White Guards of America: Thus can they be as effectively useful to American Junkers as the Czecho-Slovaks are to the Kolchaks and Denekins of Siberia!

Let it be supposed the alternative happens, that the Left Wing succeeds in gaining control of the party, that it adheres to a strictly theoretical position and shapes the party propaganda on the purely theoretical syllogism, viz., the negro is a worker, he is part of the lowest stratum of the American proletariat, hence when mass action is galvanized into mass movement, he will be swept along with the rest of his class. Such reasoning has the appearance of logic but fails to recognize the existence of such a thing as group psychology and is out of harmony with the practical experiences of the Russian Bolshevik Party from which the extreme groups of American Socialists profess to have copied their tactics. Be it remembered that the program of that party is fundamentally sound although it had a suggestion of opportunism when it adjusted itself to the immediate needs of the Russian proletariat composed of peasants and workers. Land to the peasants and bread and peace to the people are the ultimate aims of Socialism, but in order to gain power Lenin had to give it an immediate application regardless of all else and thus secure the adhesion of the masses to his policies. In order to accomplish world revolution the Bolsheviki have not hesitated to encouch in their platform statements that are calculated to attract and gain for them the support of all the oppressed peoples of the world. They have made the declaration that they are wiling to extend the principle of self-determination to even the toiling "masses of Africa, Asia and all the colonies"; they have gone further and encouraged the nationalistic ambitions of Ireland, India, and Egypt. Afghan emissaries are reported to have secured aid from Lenin for the purposes of recovering from England territory stolen in former years. Lenin, himself, has justified his employment of highly paid capitalistic experts, the signing of the Brest-Litovsk treaty with imperial Germany and his treating with French monarchist officers on the ground that the international social revolution is a species of warfare and temporary alliances must be made in order to secure ultimate victory for the proletariat. All of this proves the willingness of Lenin to adjust his tactics to existing conditions provided there is no sacrifice of principle involved. He is perfectly willing to use one enemy for the weakening of another with deliberate intention of subsequently destroying this present ally, if capitalistic. In this respect Lenin reveals himself as a master strategist who is willing to adopt the tactics of the capitalists who do not scruple to use one race against another for the purpose of breaking a strike or suppressing incipient revolts. He uses realities, not theories to cope with the facts of a given situation. He, however, does not make the mistake of alienating from or failing to secure to his cause the friendship of those who by virtue of class affiliations are his logical adherents. To this end he stresses the needs of the poorest peasants and the industrial workers, and cements their loyalty by placing them in the first class in the scheme of rationing. Since it is the avowed object of the Left Wing to establish Socialism through the medium of the dictatorship of the proletariat, how can they expect to accomplish it with a large portion of the American proletariat untouched by revolutionary propaganda?

Let the hypothesis of the Left Wing domination of the Socialist party be further pursued. Having captured the party machinery the Left Wing discards all old literature and prepares new and more revolutionary material. It is spread over the country broadcast. Negroes and white people receive it alike. The former, because of radical discrimination, against them, attend no revolutionary mass meetings, do not come in contact with class-conscious workers, and are emotionally religious and intensely race conscious. They attend Lyceums and Forums connected with their churches, read their weekly racial newspapers and listen to lectures, besides reading the usual capitalistic daily, weekly and monthly trash. From all of these sources directly and indirectly controlled by the plutocracy they are poisoned against radicalism and abjured to fight it as the enemy of their most valuable possessions—the Constitution which secures them the modicum of freedom they enjoy; their churches which are their social centers and the source of their spiritual exaltation and the other things that are to them sacred. Every subtle device would be exhausted to counteract radical propaganda, and will success.

On the other hand, let it be supposed that the propaganda among whites makes headway and the workers of the great Northern, Eastern and Western industrial centers reinforced by a few converts in the South, including agricultural workers, prepare for the day when the expropriators are to be expropriated. All radical groups submerge their difference and unite. A working arrangement is effected between the American Federation of Labor and the Industrial Workers of the World, and with the Left Wing in control, a general strike is planned. Of course, it must not be forgotten that among the whites considerable numbers of the working class would be unaffected and would join the ranks of the bourgeoisie out of a perverted sense of patriotism. This would be particularly true of the South where the doctrine of State rights is a fetish even among the most ignorant and where new ideas on social and economic questions are resisted with intolerant fanaticisms. It must also be remembered that the masters, unlike the working class, are very practical and ignore no factor that can be converted into a source of strength by making minor concessions. Being in control, the plutocracy would be in a position to make concessions to distinct radical or other groups so as to seduce them from working-class ranks. Informed by their spies in the ranks of militant labor of what is brewing, the capitalists would begin beforehand to mobilize their strength. And this is now being done with the negro. Witness the calling of a National Conference on Lynching immediately after the Union League Club discovered Bolshevist propaganda was making headway among New York negroes, and Charles Evans Hughes, ex-Republican candidate for the presidency, a member of this club, making a radical speech against a practice which by silence he condoned for years before! Witness the plea of certain big capitalists to the dominant interests in New York to be a little more considerate to the negro in matters of employment and their rights. Witness the attitude of Samuel Gompers, member of the Civic Federation and president of the American Federation of Labor, the little brother of Big Business and in close touch with President Wilson and other political leaders, at the last convention of his organization held at Buffalo, for the first time openly inviting negroes into the ranks of organized labor, although, no doubt, fully cognizant of the racially discriminatory constitutions of many labor bodies. These concessions and many others are straws that show the direction of the wind.

The scene for the general strike is set. Enthusiastic leaders fondly believe that this mass action will be transformed into mass movement and lay their plans accordingly. The strike is declared, but the plutocracy already anticipating every move on the party of the proletariat declares martial law, quickly mobilizes thousands of negroes and uses them as slave drivers to compel unwilling white working men to return to the shops, mines and farms.

In Germany Noske pays his soldiers $2.50 a day. What is to prevent any other government from doing likewise? Chaos reigns for a while but the plutocracy soon lets loose its unknown trump cards. Negro aspirations are played upon and their just human grievances are diverted so as to make them play the part that the Czecho-Slovaks played in Russia. Working men armed with nothing more formidable than propaganda, promises and revolutionary zeal are beaten to their knees and their leaders seized and quickly executed. With their leaders dead or in jail the workers become panic stricken as the White Terror employs black workers who are not class conscious to render the mass movement one of mass murder. Thus would perish some of earth's noblest in an abortive attempt to institute a dictatorship of the proletariat. Thus because of a tactical error, one set of workers will have brought defeat to their fellow-workers.

The point stressed in the foregoing imaginative pictures is that failure to make negroes class conscious is the greatest potential menace to the establishment of Socialism in America whether by means of the ballot or through a dictatorship of the proletariat, and in this must all Socialists and radicals, whether Right or Left Wingers, see their danger. For the sake of their cause, if not for the sake of negro workers, must they confront this problem squarely and firmly. How can the disaster portrayed be escaped, is the task of this booklet to point out. In the first place danger must not be ignored by a gesture or met by a theory. It must be removed. To do this it is necessary for American radicals to do the following:

First.— They must unequivocally condemn all forms of injustice practiced against negroes and encouch same in their declarations of principles and platforms, and Socialist officials and legislators must embrace every opportunity to make public denouncements of lynching, etc.

Second.— They must give the negro more prominence in their discussions whether by speech or in their publications relative to injustices done in America.

Third.— They must seek to attract negroes to their meetings and induce them to become members of their organizations.

Fourth.— Those who are members of labor unions must work for the repeal of all racially discriminatory practices in their organizations and endeavor to gain the admission of negroes into them on terms of equality.

Fifth.— They must have specially prepared propaganda showing negroes how they as a group are likely to benefit and improve their social and economic status by any radical change in the present economic system.

Sixth.— Radical negro publications must be supported financially even if subventions are to be made to them.

Seventh.— Radical white speakers must be instructed to try and reach negro audiences while competently paid negro speakers must be kept touring the country spreading radical propaganda. So far, the Socialist Party has taken a definite position on the 14th and 15th amendments, but this fact is not known to the majority of negroes. It is only known to a few Northern negroes in districts where their votes were catered for. This, and even stronger pronouncements on the negro, should be distributed among the race in the South, because it is the Southern negroes who are most likely to be used as mercenary White Guards. Giving the negro more publicity would induce them to read more radical literature. Already many negroes read the *Call*, the *Liberator* and *Pearson's* for that reason. The same will, no doubt, be true of radical lectures. Induce intelligent negroes to attend radical meetings and to become members of radical organizations and radical propaganda will spread among them. Most negroes avoid these meetings at present because they fear social discrimination. More social contact carries great potential propaganda value. It has healing in its wings. If it becomes known among negroes that Socialists are fighting discrimination in labor unions they will soon learn that Socialists are their friends. At present, as a result of persistent capitalistic misrepresentation negroes identify Socialists with the discriminatory practices of the American Federation of Labor.

Specially prepared propaganda is absolutely essential. This propaganda should frankly discuss the economics of so-called race prejudice. It should avoid stressing the question of race and should be designed to wean negroes from their belief that all white people hate them. It should paint the advantages of the co-operative commonwealth and point out its inevitable destruction, if any of its component groups is exploited and discriminated against. It should expose the sham democracy today existing in America, with special references to negroes. It should explain why Metropolitan newspapers abuse negroes, labor, Socialism and similar other exploited groups. It should explain how capitalists who control the Church, press, platform and stage use these agencies for the purpose of dividing white and black workers, playing one against the other in order to make their exploitation all the more easy. It should point out that Christ, William Lloyd Garrison, Horace Greeley, John Brown and Abraham Lincoln were abused as radicals in their day and that today they are esteemed as among the world's great benefactors. In short, it should aim to change the race-conscious negro into a class-conscious worker. In supporting radical negro publications financially, white radicals will be making their best investments. Already a few such journals exist but they are woefully handicapped by lack of funds. The easiest avenues to approach negroes though are those used by the master class. Let negro ministers and newspapers preach Socialism and the negro race will be converted to it. At present many white speakers address negro audiences, but they are usually social patriots like Walling and Russell, anti-socialists like John Wesley Hill, and patriots of the Roosevelt kind. All make time-worn rhetorical allusions to negro loyalty, military records, etc. Socialist speakers should try and avoid the patronizing style and speak Socialism and its relation to the negro as a portion of the working class. As it would be difficult for radical white speakers to get immediate access into negro churches as at present controlled, it will be necessary to maintain a few subsidized negro speakers to prepare the minds of their people and to hold mass meetings at which prominent radicals be invited to speak and deliver the message of class unity.

On their party radical negroes are doing a little, but it is indeed little. The 21st A.D. branch of the Socialist Party, Local New York, is almost entirely composed of negroes. They are doing their best to enlighten their brothers and sisters to the doctrine of Socialism, but they are terribly handicapped by lack of funds.

A Peoples' Forum is maintained and prominent radical speakers address it every Sunday afternoon, but the result while encouraging is entirely out of proportion to the enormity of the task. It may be argued that since negroes have so much at stake they must help to encompass their own salvation. Granted, but upon white radicals devolves the duty, out of consideration for their own self-preservation and the success of their cause, to aid to the limit of their greater ability to enlighten the most benighted section of the American proletariat.

It may also be argued that negroes are no more race conscious than Jews and since the latter have become intensely class conscious by reason of economic pressure and oppression negroes must of themselves realize that their racial salvation is ultimately wrapped up with the struggles and victories of labor. This argument is plausible but not true. In the first place, the founder of Scientific Socialism, Marx, and its most active early propagandist, Lassalle, were Jews, hence it would have been absurd to think of carrying to Jews a doctrine formulated by members of their own race. Next, there is no analogy between negroes and Jews, so far as propaganda is concerned. Jews have a distinctive language press which acts as a kind of screen against strictly "National" ideas; they are inter-racially arrayed against each other as capitalists and workers; they are essentially industrial proletarians—factory workers; and they have an almost unbroken tradition of resistance to oppression without scrupulous regard as to the methods employed. On the other hand these things are not true of negroes, who are most pathetically "Americans." They speak the same language, have the same ideals and have traditions which teach them to place reliance upon prayer to God, gratitude and "constitutional" means for their liberation. Added to this is constant pressure exerted upon them to convince them that they are inherently inferior to their fellow Americans. Then their circumspection tends to narrow their outlook which rarely reaches beyond their own racial concern. The few negroes who have become radicals have been in many cases foreigners and, if natives have been led to their way of thinking through mental curiosity stimulated by contact with white radicals. In New York, Jews, as ever great propagandists, have been instrumental in making more radicals among negroes than perhaps all the non-Jewish radicals put together. And this small success should be the most convincing sign to Socialists and other radicals that negroes constitute at present the most fertile field for their propaganda. Do not the enemies of radicalism poison and control the wells of public information from which negroes like other Americans freely imbibe? Are they not reached by the subtle propaganda of reaction? If so, are not white radicals justified by self-interest in making every possible effort and sacrifice to win over to themselves the support of over one-tenth of the population that is overwhelmingly of the working class? Was it not necessary to convert the majority of class-conscious workers to their present frame of mind by means of a Socialist tract, book or pamphlet? Look at the Christians! Do they not dispatch missionaries all over the world to convert the most benighted "heathens," and are not American negroes heathens so far as Socialism and economic radicalism are concerned? It is true that the "heathens" need salvation, but in order to keep them "saved" and avoid their destruction, it is for them to see that the heathens are converted. Just as Christians follow the biblical injunction, "Go yet into all the world and preach the gospel to every creature," so must radicals preach their gospel to every member of the working class who is not a "convert."

Experience has taught the workers that Socialism will not be permitted to flourish in isolated spots. Russia like the Paris Commune realizes that international capitalism will ruthlessly destroy any government not built upon the pillars of rent, profit and interest, hence no effort should be spared to hasten world revolution.

Russian emissaries are sent everywhere and communist propaganda reaches from South Africa to England, Argentina to India, Cuba to Canada. Propaganda is not localized, but goes everywhere. In like manner must propaganda inside a nation reach every element. If America with her boundless resources remains non-Socialist, she will be a menace to world Socialism and America can remain non-Socialist if 12,000,000 negroes so will it. That some Socialists are getting to realize how serious a menace negroes are likely to be to the movement, is proved by the willingness of the Rand School to institute lectures by giving out the necessary facts relating to race in America; but it is clear that the national leaders and the rank and file of the party do not comprehend their peril. Instead, they sentimentally flirt with the far distance problems of India and China in blissful disregard of the material fact that they will never be in a position to render tangible aid to these oppressed peoples until they succeed in making allies out of American negroes. But perhaps this attitude on the part of American radicals is because of the fact that that they are Americans and share the typical white American psychology towards negroes. If this is so, then their radicalism is not genuine and is deservedly doomed to failure. For anyone to think the negro unworthy of consideration is for that one to fly in the face of history. Mere acquiescence in a conventional national belittling of negroes will not make them race-conscious or remove their potentiality for being black White Guards or Czecho-Slovaks. Perhaps a few ominous and startling facts from history may disabuse the minds of those in doubt and sober the blind enthusiasm of the fanatical theorists. These facts contain lessons that even white radicals who are still under the influence of the American psychology which thinks in terms of races, not class, may well heed.

During the Civil War in which the freedom of negroes from the bonds of chattel slavery was incidentally involved, thousands of negroes were employed by the confederates as soldiers and in other capacities for the express purpose of perpetuating human slavery.

Negroes, although an oppressed race, volunteered for service and were employed as soldiers to crush the uprising of the Filipinos under Aguinaldo for national freedom.

In the present war, although denied a voice in the national government, lynched and prescribed against, negroes volunteered for military service in such numbers as to call for limits being placed upon their further acceptance.

When the interests of capital are endangered, governments do not hesitate to employ soldiers of any race to destroy those who menace it. This is proved by England and France scouring the universe for black, brown and yellow soldiers to protect their interests against the enemy. At first the German capitalist government was the "enemy," now it is the Hungarian and Russian Soviet government and negroes who are being used against them. At Archangel, West Indian negro soldiers were attached to Canadian regiments, while American negro soldiers were alleged to have been rushed from the Philippines to participate in the taking of Vladivostok from the Bolshevik. Official dispatches tell of 60,000 French Colonials under General Mangin marching to capture Budapest and an official Bolshevik document states that negroes were being employed against them at Odessa.

Colored West Indian troops, until recently demobilized, were stationed in England and Ireland and some of them have said that they were told by their officers that in case of "trouble" (it was during the strikes in England and the intense Sinn Fein agitation in Ireland early in 1919) they would be called upon to do their "duty." In England some of them were given fifty rounds of ammunition while those in Ireland marched to church with fixed bayonets.

These are but a few examples showing that capitalists, or rather governments, do not discriminate as to the weapons they employ to achieve their ends; they also show that unless instructed, negroes, in their present state of ignorance of the real aims of Socialism, are liable to be willing tools of the plutocracy. History has a curious way of repeating itself and it is quite possible that interested capitalists may help it to repeat itself on the American continent.

Having regard to the fact already outlined, to the future of mankind; amicable relations between races; the destruction of capitalism and the successful operation of Socialist principles, it devolves upon white radicals to concentrate their efforts and propaganda upon the negro race. Let white radicals remember and be guided by the fate of the Czecho-Slovaks in Russia.

White Socialists, radicals and liberals, remember that self-preservation is the first law of nature and safeguard yourselves.

Socialism The Negroes' Hope

It is a regrettable and discontenting anomaly that, despite their situation as the economic, political and social door mat of the world, negroes do not embrace the philosophy of socialism, and in greater numbers than they now do. It is an anomaly because it is reasonable to expect those who are lowest down to be the ones who would most quickly comprehend the need for a change in their status and welcome any doctrine which holds forth any hope of human elevation. In matters of religion they respond and react logically and naturally enough, for to them, the religion of Christ, the lowly Nazarene, brings definite assurance of surcease from earthly pains and the hope of celestial readjustment of mundane equalities. Their acceptance of the Christian religion with its present day emphasis upon an after-life enjoyment of the good things denied them on the earth is conclusive proof of their dissatisfaction with their present lot, and is an earnest [missing word] of their susceptibility to Socialism, which intends to do for human beings what Christianity promises to do for them in less material regions.

That they and all oppressed dark peoples will be the greatest beneficiaries in a socialist world has not been sufficiently emphasized by Socialist propaganda among Negroes.

Perhaps this is not clearly understood, but a little more examination of the facts will prove this to be the case.

Throughout the world Negroes occupy a position of absolute inferiority to the white race. This is true whether they are black Frenchmen, black Englishmen, black Belgians or black Americans.

As between themselves and the mass of white proletarians their lives are more circumscribed, their ambitions more limited and their opportunities for the enjoyment of liberty and happiness more restricted. White workingmen of England who are socialists are immeasurably the political and social

---

Originally published in the *Messenger*, July 1919, 22.

superiors of the average Negroes in the West Indies or Africa; white workingmen of France, who are Socialists are unquestionably the political and social superiors of the Senegalese and Madagascaran Negroes; white workingmen of the United States who are Socialists are indisputably the social and political superiors of the millions of Negroes below the Mason and Dixon line; yet despite their relative and absolute superiority these white workers are fighting for a world freed from oppression and exploitation, whilst Negroes who are oppressed cling to past and present economic ideals with the desperation of a drowning man.

Socialism as an economic doctrine is merely the pure Christianity preached by Jesus, and practiced by the early Christians adapted to the more complex conditions of modern life. It makes no distinction as to race, nationality or creed, but like Jesus it says "Come unto me all ye who are weary and heavy laden and I will give you rest." It is to procure that rest that millions of oppressed peoples are flocking to the scarlet banner of International Socialism.

So far, although having greater need for its equalizing principles than white workingmen, Negroes have been slow to realize what has already dawned upon nearly every other oppressed people: That Socialism is their only hope.

The 384,000,000 natives of India groaning under the exploitation of the handful of English manufacturers, merchants and officials who profit out of their labor are turning from Lloyd George and the capitalistic Liberal Party to Robert Smillie, the Socialist and the Independent Labor Party. The 4,000,000 Irish who suffer national strangulation at the hands of British industrialists and militarists have turned to the Socialists of England for relief besides becoming Socialists themselves. The Egyptians who are of Negro admixture being convinced that their only hope for freedom from British exploitation is in international Socialism are uniting forces with British Socialists and organized labor. In fact, every oppressed group of the world is today turning from Clemenceau, Lloyd George and Wilson to the citadel of Socialism, Moscow. In this they are all in advance of Western Negroes with the exception of little groups in the United States and a relatively well-organized group in the Island of Trinidad, British West Indies.

Because of ignorant and unscrupulous leadership, Negroes are influenced to give their support to those institutions which oppress them, but if they would only do a little independent thinking without the aid of preacher, politician or press they would quickly realize that the very men like Thomas Dixon, author of "The Clansman," Senators Hoke Smith of George and Overman of North Carolina, who are fighting Socialism or as they maliciously call it Bolshevism, are the same men who exhaust every unfair means to vilify, oppress and oppose Negroes. If anything should commend Socialism to Negroes, nothing can do so more eloquently than the attitude and opinions of its most influential opponents toward people who are not white.

On the other hand, the foremost exponents of Socialism in Europe and America are characterized by the broadness of their vision towards all oppressed humanity. It was the Socialist Vendervelde of Belgium, who protested against the Congo atrocities practiced upon Negroes; it was the late Keir Hardie and Philip Snowdon [sic.] of England, who condemned British rule in Egypt; and in the United States it was the Socialist, Eugene V. Debs, who refused to speak in Southern halls from which Negroes were excluded. Today, it is the revolutionary Socialist, Lenin, who analyzed the infamous League of Nations and exposed its true character; it is he as leader of the Communist Congress at Moscow who sent out the proclamation: "Slaves of the colonies in Africa and Asia! The hour of proletarian dictatorship in Europe will be the hour of your release!"

Did Bolshevism Stop Race Riots in Russia?

But for the fact that Pushkin, Russia's greatest poet, was of Negro descent and further fact that his descendants are a part of the now deposed royalty of that great country, the majority of Negroes have little knowledge of and still less interest in Russia. Because of its rigorous climate and its removal from close and easy contact with the rest of the world, particularly the tropics, few Negroes have emigrated to or travelled in Russia. Those who have gone there, went as sailors, body servants or theatrical performers.

The great war did more to familiarize the minds of the outside world with Russian affairs than all the lectures, histories and geographies had ever accomplished. This is also true of Negroes. They, like the rest of mankind, viewed with astonishment the bewildering military successes and reverses of Russia in the war which finally terminated in the destruction of the mightiest autocracy in the world and the rise of the proletariat—the common working people—into power. To the average Negro these various historical events have no greater significance than as passing phases of human conduct. Few of them are able to discover any connection between themselves—their futures—and the new society that is slowly but surely emerging from the alleged chaotic social and industrial conditions of Russia. To them, and naturally so, it is a very far cry from Alabama to Turkestan, from the West Indies to Archangel and from Sierra Leone to Moscow.

The distances are too great and the connections seemingly nebulous. But despite this there is a great connection between the future of the Negro race the world over and the success of the theories—now under trial in Russia—which are collectively known as Bolshevism.

Comparing Old Russia with the countries bent on the destruction of Soviet Russia it will be noticed that they stood for many things in common—things that benefitted those countries whilst doing harm to "backward peoples" and subject races.

Originally published in the *Messenger*, September 1919, 26–27.

England, France, Portugal, Belgium and the United States are countries with large Negro and other subject races under their control who are varyingly exploited economically, ostracized socially, and powerless politically. Czarist Russia resembled those countries in that the Empire was a congeries of various subject races, such as Jews, Tartars, Kalmuks, Poles, Armenians and Lithuanians, who were disfranchised, oppressed and murdered. When Czardom was overthrown and Bolshevism was established the first thing done by the new government was to proclaim the absolute equality of all the races that occupied that vast territory. This equality was not theoretical, but was made practical from the very start. As a result Trotsky, a Jew, became Minister of War, and Karl Peters, a Lett, was made a Commissar.

So completely devoted to their ideals of human equality and justice were the Bolsheviki that they immediately renounced sovereignty over the portion of Persia, a dark-skinned country, that had been occupied by Russia in agreement with Great Britain in 1906. Be it noted that Great Britain, although ostensibly fighting for democracy and the rights of small nations, continued to occupy its portion of Persia and vigorously protested against the noble act of national restitution done by Soviet Russia.

As if to show to the Negro race that justice and equality are only possible under Bolshevism, an American Negro named Gordon, who had gone to Russia with the American Ambassador to occupy the dignified position of doorkeeper, became converted to Bolshevism and was elected to a high official position in one of the Russian Communes. This was reported in the *World's Work* Magazine for October, 1918, and later confirmed by testimony given by the Rev. George Simons of Petrograd before the Overman Congressional committee investigating Bolshevism in America. A cynic has said that perhaps the deposition of Gordon from his exalted position is the real reason why President Wilson, a Southerner, is waging war on Russia without a formal declaration of war by Congress.

Perhaps the greatest analogy between Russia and the United States can be found in the former's treatment of Jews and in the latter's treatment of Negroes. Under the autocratic Czar Jews were treated in very much the same manner as Negroes are treated in the democratic United States. They had no political rights, they were segregated in the Pale, and the avenues of opportunity were closed to them. Life to them was merely a cycle of sorrow, oppression and despair. Just as American Negroes have had their

Atlanta, East St. Louis, Washington and Chicago, so had the Jews of
Russia their Kishineff and other pogroms. Just as Negro loyalty in wars has
proven futile as a deterrent or preventative of lynch law and oppression, so
did Jewish fealty to Russia prove non-effective in abating their persecution
and suffering.

However, the great revolution came and the Czar and the newspapers
that lied about the Jews, priests who condoned the persecution of a weaker
race and military officers who inflamed the blood-lust of the common
soldiers, were swept out of office.

In their place was established a government led by men who had
suffered the scorn of the high and the abuse of the lowly, men who could
understand and appreciate the real causes of Jewish oppression. One of
the first things that the new government did was sternly to suppress and
punish those of the old regime who retained the old psychology of race
hatred if caught inciting the people to start pogroms—race riots—against
Jews. After a few executions of lynchers and race-rioters the Bolshevik
government succeeded in making Soviet Russia unsafe for the mobocrats,
but safe for Jews and other oppressed racial minorities.

According to latest, reliable reports, such as those of Isaac Don
Levine of the New York *Evening Globe*, Moscow and Petrograd are safer
for all their population—Jew, Gentile and Infidel—than Chicago and
Washington have presently been for their black inhabitants. On the other
hand, in Poland, where Bolshevism does not hold sway, an American
Commission is at present investigating the recent massacre of Jews in that
recently reconstructed and freed country. In Siberia, under Kolchak, the
Jewish population see their daughters raped and men slain by brutal soldiers
who are egged on by corrupt and fanatical priests and anti-Bolshevists. In
Southern Russia the soldiers of General Gregorieff, who, with the support
of the Allies, is redeeming Holy Russia (?) from "barbarism," have treated
Odessa to a saturnalia of Jewish blood while the following clipping speaks
for itself as to conditions in the Ukraine:

The anti-Bolshevik Yiddish *Day*, of New York, has the following
cablegram from its European correspondent, N. Shifrin, under date
of July 11th: "Persons who have arrived in Copenhagen tell about the
cruelty of Petlura's soldiers of which they have been eye-witnesses.
At the station Tchudnovolinsk, 36 Jews were killed in one car. In
Dubno, they saw 18 Jews executed in the marketplace. In Rovno and

Lutnik they find daily two or three Jews murdered in their houses. Under the Ukrainian Soviet government no pogroms have ever occurred anywhere."

The lesson to be gained from these numerous examples is that racial oppression in its various forms of disfranchisement, lynching and mob murder prevails in non-Bolshevik Russia but has been abolished in the territory dominated by Lenine and his followers. The Allies who are today fighting Soviet Russia in the name of freedom, have colonies which they exploit, and sections of their own countries in which they at times permit the restrained passions of the white majorities to run riot upon Negro minorities. In contrast to this racial failure on the part of the self-righteous Allies and non-Bolshevik governments to protect small racial groups it is noticeable that all minorities are successfully protected in Soviet Russia.

The question naturally arises: Will Bolshevism accomplish the full freedom of Africa, colonies in which Negroes are in the majority, and promote human tolerance and happiness in the United States by the eradication of the causes of such disgraceful occurrences as the Washington and Chicago race riots? The answer is deducible from the analogy of Soviet Russia, a country in which dozens of racial and lingual types have settled their many differences and found a common meeting ground, a country which no longer oppresses colonies, a country from which the lynch rope is banished and in which racial tolerance and peace now exist.

Will Bolshevism Free America?

Without doubt the most important happenings in international affairs, from the standpoint of the Negro and all oppressed nations and races, are the defeat of imperialist Poland, the legitimate offspring of French militarism and British finance, by the Soviet troops, and the spread throughout eastern and southwestern Asia of the liberating doctrines of Bolshevism. Poland which contests with the United States for primacy in mob law and racial arrogance, was designed to be an outpost of "civilization" against Muscovite "barbarism" and so as to make the security of "noble" France, "liberty-loving" England and "democratic" Germany more secure, this little country ruled by the fake Socialist Pilsudski, embarked upon a war of conquest. Lacking factories for the adequate supplying of their armies of deluded Jew-murdering conscripts, the Polish junkers had their needs supplied by the products of English, French and—American factories. Even the officers of high rank were furnished by the two first named countries, while the aviators were mainly Americans.

Apart from other "ties that bind," apart from the international interests of all capitalist nations, apart from the benevolent instigation of that synthetic harlot, the "Plague of Dam-Nations," there was one great purpose influencing the conduct of Polish aggression upon Socialist Russia. And that purpose grew out of the circumstances that Poland was in one particular a replica of Great Britain, France and the United States. While these countries differed upon religion and language there was one question upon which they agreed thoroughly: the oppression of weaker peoples.

A thief will invariably help another thief to escape. It is part of an unwritten but none the less observed code of conduct that where interests are similar alliances are advantageous.

The strengthening of Poland by France, England and America meant to those countries the increase in the total power possessed by the

Originally published in the *Messenger*, September 1920, 85–86.

race-persecuting nations. A strong Poland would mean a strong nation that would look with benign indifference upon another Amritsar, another expropriation of the ancestral territories of native Africans, another Congo, another Ireland drenched in blood, another Haiti, Nicaragua and Santo Domingo, another Morocco, another Tripoli, another Shantung and another East St. Louis. But thanks to the Communist arms, brains and valor, Poland is no more, and out of the debacle just ended, oppressed peoples should take hope and pray that what was recently a catspaw of wily Lloyd George, the Socialist renegade Millerand and the unblushing and clumsy diplomatic prestidigitator Churchill will become a corridor into Germany for the forces of civilization and of humanity represented by Lenin and Trotsky.

May the pianist Paderewski play a fitting requiem to his country's evil ambitions!

While Bolshevist arms are winning in Western Europe and undermining the great imperialist nations France and England, Bolshevist propagandists, men and women who count life cheap when compared to their ideals, are destroying the foundations of British and French power and wealth in the East. Bullets are to be respected and feared, but ideas are the bête noire of those who prey upon ignorance.

Having accomplished what all the weasel words of Wilson in his now infamous 14 points could not do—break the morale of the German troops; having influenced British and Italian workers to oppose the foul conduct of the masters of their own countries, Bolshevist doctrines—Socialist propaganda—are now being carried to the victims of imperialism. Persia, India and Armenia are infected and combined with a nationalism that is coterminous with self-determination. These people are girding up their loins to do battle with alien and native exploiters alike.

Nor is Bolshevist help a negative one: it is highly positive. It includes the furnishing of arms and technically trained minds to the Armenians and Persians. Sooner or later British rule in the East, which is frankly based upon force exercised by a minority of aliens, must go.

Another phase of Franco-British financial imperialism supported by the silent acquiescence of the United States is the campaign to dismember and emasculate Turkey. To achieve this appeals are being made to the lowest passions and the basest emotions. The Turk is not a genuine European! The Turk is a Mohammedan! These are the cries that are being bellowed to the world by a bigoted and self-righteous Caucasian press, European and American.

The Turk must leave Europe, his crimes against Christian Armenia must be punished and the only adequate penalty is for him to abandon the great mineral and agricultural wealth of lands that have been occupied by him for centuries. But expulsion is not easy; hence a recourse to force of arms which can be most effective when backed by the peals of church bells and the chants and prayers of hypocritical clergymen. From India, Algeria and Senegal as well as from England and France mercenaries are despatched whose holy mission is to drive the crescent from its only foothold on sacred European soil. Desperately in need of a friend the Turk like other oppressed peoples, turned their eyes to Moscow and found a friend in non-imperialistic Russia. Emissaries are despatched and now the Near East, from Armenia to Arabia, is ablaze with Bolshevism. And from Arabia to Egypt—Africa—is but a short distance. Soon the light-giving current of Bolshevism will pass over the conducting wires of Turkish, Syrian and Arabian nationalism until it reaches the better conductor of Mohammedanism which will challenge British, French and Belgian imperialism in the heart of tropical Africa. Soon, perhaps, will the stately Mandingo and the industrious Kroo, the despoiled Masai and the progressive Vais realize their essential political kinship with the humble peasants of Turkestan, Samarkand and Ukrainia.

This threat of Bolshevism into Egypt and into the heart of Africa via Arabia constitutes the greatest danger to imperialism and the greatest hope to the Negro race everywhere. For opposition to imperialism makes allies of all oppressed races and those who support Socialism in Russia and the rest of Europe must, sooner or later, support Socialism in Asia and Africa. The world cannot be half socialist and half capitalist, and not all the straddling moderate Socialists, liberals and laborites of England, France and American can overcome this fact.

Verily, the forces of freedom, represented by Soviet Russia, and guided by impersonal economic laws are on the side of the Negro. It is, therefore, for the New Negro, whose newness represents intelligence and clear vision, who has no excess baggage of emotion to discard and who carries no deadweight of prejudice and ignorance, to support the political and industrial groups of his country which are today supporting Soviet Russia.

And in America the Socialist Party is the only recognized political organization that has longest and consistently supported the Moscow government. Bolshevism—Socialism—is the only weapon that can be used by Negroes effectively to clip the claws of the British lion and the talons of the American eagle in Africa, the British West Indies, Haiti, the Southern states and at the same time reach the monsters' heart (they have a common one) in London, Paris, New York, Tokyo and Warsaw.

A vote for Socialism is a vote against imperialism—a vote to strengthen the forces that are now engaged in destroying the foul and merciless monster.

Part IV
The *Crusader*

Cyril V. Briggs

Introduction

The *Crusader* was primarily a project of one man: Cyril Valentine Briggs (1888–1966). Born on the Caribbean island of Nevis, Briggs immigrated to the United States in the early twentieth century, eventually becoming an editor at New York's premier Black newspaper, the *Amsterdam News*. However, his opposition to American involvement in World War I brought him into conflict with the paper's publisher, leading him to found the *Crusader* in late 1918.

The *Crusader* quickly established itself as a militant voice in Black politics. It took an uncompromising stand for Black independence, in the United States and abroad. Denouncing colonialism, domestic racism, and political repression against radicals, the magazine carved out a political space for itself as the exponent of a radical, left-wing Black nationalism. Particularly in its early days, this nationalism was an important component of the journal's ideology, as Briggs and his co-writers repeatedly insisted that history proved there could be no peace between the races. The only solution, they argued, was for the Black race to assert itself and forcefully overthrow white domination.

Briggs combined this nationalist commitment with socialist politics. From early on, the *Crusader* recognized that capitalism was an oppressive social system and that capitalists eagerly used racism to divide workers against one another. Briggs looked with favor on the Socialist Party, supporting its candidates (particularly when it ran Black socialists, such as A. Philip Randolph) and recommending them to his readers.

In 1919, Briggs founded a secret society to advance the politics he advocated at the *Crusader*. The African Blood Brotherhood was announced discreetly in a small advertisement in the magazine, inviting to join only those "who are willing to go the limit." The organization advocated armed self-defense against white violence, and though its membership never exceeded a few thousand, it achieved some notoriety during the race riots of 1919, as members organized the defense of black neighborhoods against white mobs. Among its leadership were future black communist luminaries like Richard B. Moore and Claude McKay.

Dedicated as he was to his race, Briggs was not afraid to call out Black leaders whom he judged guilty of failing to advance the interests of Black people. Chief among the misleaders was Marcus Garvey, head of the Universal Negro Improvement Association (UNIA). Garvey was a Jamaican immigrant who espoused a more traditional Black nationalism, which at times flirted with left politics, but by about 1920 had moved away from any kind of direct confrontation with American racism, and toward a more quiet separatism. Briggs assailed Garvey and the UNIA for their conservative nationalism, accusing them of diverting the race's energy into useless schemes like Black-owned shipping companies. He also directly targeted Garvey's politics, juxtaposing his own support for African self-determination with Garvey's vision of diasporic Blacks colonizing and "civilizing" the continent.

Briggs's embrace of class struggle socialism and Black nationalism brought him into the orbit of the Workers Party in 1921. Impressed with the Communist International's support for black self-determination, Briggs and most of the leadership of the ABB joined the party that year. The ABB and the *Crusader* continued to function as independent ventures until 1923, when a lack of funds led Briggs to effectively merge his journal and organization with the Communist Party. Briggs would play an important role in the CP for the next decade and a half, heading up the American Negro Labor Congress, which replaced the ABB, and joining the party's Central Committee in 1929. In the late 1930s, however, he would be expelled among the party's violent twists and turns in policy in response to changing orders from Moscow.

Important as Briggs's role was in the early CP, however, he never attained the same level of prominence inside the party that he did while editor of the *Crusader*. In part, this is a testament to his success in his earlier endeavor. By the time Briggs was settled into the party, a whole host of Black communist cadres were beginning to make their mark, including some, such as Richard B. Moore, whom Briggs himself had brought into the party. If Briggs was eclipsed in the 1930s by other prominent Black Marxists, it is in no small part because of his success in staking out a radical Black communism earlier and making a place for it in the party.

Further Reading

James, Winston. *Holding Aloft the Banner of Ethiopia: Caribbean Radicalism in Early Twentieth-Century America*. London: Verso, 1998.

Makalani, Minkah. *In the Cause of Freedom: Radical Black Internationalism from Harlem to London, 1917–1939*. Chapel Hill: University of North Carolina Press, 2014.

Zumoff, J.A. "The African Blood Brotherhood: From Caribbean Nationalism to Communism." *Journal of Caribbean History* 41, no. 1/2 (2007): 201–26.

Deporting Aliens and Negroes

It has recently been announced that the Federal authorities would deport all alien radicals in this country. Unannounced the local authorities of Coatsville, Pa., HAVE deported Negro steel workers who have been induced to come North during a crisis in the Labor Market. On the face of it the two deportations would appear to be unrelated, but those who scan below the surface of things can see the same hand in both. The capitalists who would bring the Negro North during a crisis and then shuffle him back willy-nilly to the old hateful conditions and Lynch Law—all of which were cited in the argument to make him leave the South—are the same capitalists who would send out of the country all workers who dare to talk against the system.

The lesson should be plain to anyone. In both cases the mailed fists of capitalism were aimed at the worker. To capitalism it makes no difference whether it was a colored or a white worker that was to be exploited and then deported. Yet in both cases it found the Negro uninterested in what was being done to the whites and the whites ignoring the blow struck at the colored. Thus labor suffers by its race prejudice! Capitalism, on the other hand, knows neither prejudice nor nationality save the brands it seeks to foster, for its own benefit, among the workers.

Originally published in the *Crusader*, April 1919, 10.

Out for Negro Tools

The Plutes,* daily becoming more and more afraid of the influence of Bolshevism in America, are showing signs of turning to the Negro for protection of their ill-gotten loot in case of a conflict between capitalism and labor. Schwab and others are now engaged in soft-soaping the Negro. And the servile "weakly" Negro press is giving its support—as usual—to the white capitalists' schemes to hoodwink and use the Negro.

But the Plutes—and the "weakly" press are forgetting one little detail: the fact that the Negro race in America is almost wholly of the proletariat and that Negroes more than any others have reason to be dissatisfied with the present system by which the white capitalists exploit the black and white masses and spread imperialism throughout the world at the expense of both their own and "the weaker peoples" in which the latter class is at present included the oppressed and exploited millions of Africa and Asia.

Mr. Schwab and his tribe will have more to give out—and this time permanently—more than a paltry dollar a man to change the Negro's conditions and thus his frame of mind. At present having nothing he is in no frame of mind to concern himself with the protection of the Schwab and Rockefeller millions. Let those who have the looted millions protect them. For our part we believe in the doctrine that a man should eat by the sweat of his brow, or by some other equivalent sign of physical or mental endeavor more than the mere twiddling of one's thumbs. We do not see why one should have millions he can never spend while others should have stomachs they can never feed. We fail to see why some should be unable to earn a dollar, while others should have the privilege of stealing millions.

Originally published in the *Crusader*, May 1919, 5
* Plutocrats.

Make Their Cause Your Own

The Soviet Government of Russia is the only government outside our own Africa and democratic South America in which a Negro occupies a high and respectable position. And Soviet Russia has neither Negro population nor Negro "colonies."

The *New York Call*, a Socialist newspaper, is the only paper in New York City which is perpetually and honestly concerned about the Negro and which nearly every day comments upon his wrongs and calls the nation to task for their existence.

The Socialist Party is the only party in the United States that dared to place an anti-lynching plank in its national platform; the only party that demanded honest self-determination for the African peoples and the end of disfranchisement in the southern states of the United States.

No race has less of the idle non-producing rich than the Negro race.

No race would be more greatly benefited proletariat [*sic.*] than the Negro race, which is essentially a race of workers and producers.

With no race are the interests of Labor so clearly identified with racial interests as in the case of the Negro race.

No race would be more greatly benefited by the triumph of Labor and the destruction of parasitic Capital Civilization with its Imperialism incubus that is squeezing the life-blood out of millions of our race in Africa and the islands of the sea, than the Negro race.

Is the lesson clear?

We need not fight alone if we breast the sea upon the irresistible tide of liberalism that is at present sweeping the world.

Originally published in the *Crusader*, July 1919, 6

Bolshevism and Race Prejudice

Many of our editors and cartoonists are showing an inclination to couple Bolshevism with race prejudice.

On a basis of hard, cold facts nothing could be further from the truth. The only pogroms against the Jewish race being committed in Russia today are occurring outside of Soviet Russia, in the territories jointly controlled by Denikine and Holy Allies and by Kolchak and the Holy Allies and by the said Holy Allies and their minor tools. In Soviet Russia pogroms are no more because, for one thing, there are no reactionary capitalist influences at work to pit worker against worker and race against race. In America where these influences are still in operation, race riots and pogroms are the rule rather than the exception. In Soviet Russia all men are equal, of whatever race, and nearly all races are represented in high offices, the principle of merit ruling rather than color of skin or racial origin, and the Negro race, too, though almost nil in point of population, comes in for such representation as was related by a disgusted citizen of these *truly y'know* democratic United States, who threw up his hands in holy terror at the spectacle of a Negro in high office and rushed back to this land of the *truly y'know* brave and the free to relate with hot resentment to his almost as hotly resenting white fellow citizens the shocking heresy on the part of Russia in that she recognized the Negro as a man.

That Negro editors and cartoonists should fall for the lies about Soviet Russia put out by the white capitalist press is all the more surprising when it is considered that these same Negro cartoonists and editors are members of a race even more viciously lied about by the same white capitalist press. Surely with our own experience with the lie factories in mind, we should be wary about swallowing, hook, sinker and all, all they say about others to whom they are also opposed.

Originally published in the *Crusader*, December 1919, 9–10.

Bolshevism's Menace:
To Whom and to What?

Of a truth, Bolshevism is a menace. That much is conceded alike by friend, foe and neutral. That is the chief motif of the tune that is constantly dinned into the ears of the Negro and the world in general.

But just who and what does Bolshevism menace? Is it not vital that we should know exactly against whom and what is directed this alleged threat of Bolshevism? Against the Negro and the rest of the workers, or against those who are exploiting the workers of the world and robbing the Negro group both of its labor and its fatherland? If against us, should we not fight it, and if against the imperialist thieves of Europe, who are our foes, should we not be glad of its spread?

England and France and the rest of the piratical crew claim that Bolshevism is a menace to "democracy." What "democracy"? The "democracy" in which an autocratic minority living in France and England rule and oppress "subject peoples" against their known wishes and legitimate aspirations and solely for the benefit of home industries and manufacturers? The "democracy" which imposes its will upon weaker peoples by force and murders them when this alien superimposed will is questioned, as "democratic" England is to-day in Egypt, India, Persia, Mesopotamia, the West Indies and many other unfortunate countries, as "democratic" France is now doing in Morocco, West Africa, and Indo-China? The "democracy" which exploits, under the murderous capitalist system, its own people, its weak women and young children? Is this the "democracy" to which the spread of Bolshevism is a menace? Then may God advance the spread of Bolshevism throughout Europe, Asia and Africa, and in every country where oppression stalks!

On the other hand, what is Bolshevism? Regarding it there are myriad lies, tales and rumors, but from what one can deduct from the testimony

---

Originally published in the *Crusader*, February 1920, 5–6.

of impartial witnesses like Col. Robins and Mr. Bullitt it appears to be a system of government of the people, by the people and for the people, and under which the resources of the country, like the mines, the coal fields and water power, are owned and operated, as they ought to be, by the State. Under Bolshevism all persons are producers. There are no classes. All are workers. We are told that Bolshevism's success in forcing the parasites to work lies in the fact that preference in rationing is given, and rightly, to those who produce, after, of course, the wants of the mothers, children and sick have been attended to. But this is the domestic side of Bolshevism and while a study of this side will do much to explain the phenomenon now taking place in Russia, it is in the international side in which we are especially interested. What is Russian Bolshevism's attitude toward the people of other countries, especially oppressed people like the Africans, Indians, and the Irish?

Bolshevism in its international phase is feared by the capitalist-imperialist powers even more than they fear Bolshevism in its domestic operations.

Bolshevism, from the international standpoint, is totally different from, and wholly opposed to imperialism. In fact, one of the first acts of Soviet Russia was the renunciation of the imperialistic claims of Czarist Russia on the territory and destiny of the people of Persia, thus repudiating the part played by old Russia with Great Britain in the strangling of Persia. Soviet Russia has gladly and promptly recognized the right of self-determination of the peoples of Finland, Poland, the Ukraine and other parts of the former Russian Empire. The right to self-determination of even certain weak and so-called "backward" peoples in Asiatic Russia has been recognized by the Bolshevists.

Bolshevism so far, then, is in direct opposition and contradiction of the "principles" of "democracy" as those principles are applied by England in India, Africa, Ireland, and elsewhere, and by France in Africa and Indo-China. And it is to these "principles," to this "democracy" that Bolshevism is a menace. Like Wilson's mistake in talking about the rights of "peoples great and small," Bolshevism is setting a bad example to the enslaved populations under British and French rule. It is putting ideas extremely injurious to the masters in the heads of the African, Indian and Irish peoples. That Bolshevism is a direct menace (and is seen as such) to the lying wickedness of *European eminent domain* under guise of carrying "the white man's burden," is demonstrated by the following statement from a capitalist source: "And now the triumph of Russian Bolshevism, as now constituted, means the victory of the doctrine of their allies, the I.W.W. in America, and the destruction of Great Britain's power in India, in all other parts of Asia and in the Dark Continent."

If Bolshevism will free the "subject races," what should be the attitude of these races towards Bolshevism?

The *New York Sun*, in an editorial comment on the overwhelming defeat of Kolchak, Denikine and other anti-Bolshevists, also lets the cat out of the bag in these two paragraphs:

> And so now Lenine and his disciples are turning their faces eastward as to the land of promise. Mohammedan hostility against the European rulers that hold so much of Islam in bondage is to be the great means of spreading Bolshevism throughout Asia.
>
> Already Great Britain becomes anxious. She realizes that the new Russia offers a menace to her power in the East not less than that of the former Czar. But what means she will take to prevent the threatened overflow of radicalism from the north into Persia and India remains to be seen. That she must act at once, however, is becoming evident to all.

And in these confessions and indiscreet comments of the capitalist press, in this anxiety of the chief enslaving powers, we have the answer and the truth as to who and what Bolshevism menaces.

At the Crossroads (Part I)

That the Negro is at the crossroads is generally recognized by thinking people of both radical and conservative tendencies.

What is not generally recognized is that many other races have preceded the Negro to the crossroads of destiny and there hesitated awhile and finally made their choice and gone on to fame, power and respect, or to ignominy, impotence and race extinction.

The Israelites of old faced practically the same problems that the Negro faces today. So did many other people whose flight from "the land of bondage" was not honored by record in the Bible. The Negro in this country (America) is not oppressed merely because he is a Negro, but because he is weak. If there were no Negroes in America there would still be oppressed and oppressor. In all epochs of history the story is the same—of the strong oppressing the weak, of the weak being subjugated, repressed or exterminated. There is no Negro problem in Ireland, Poland and other lands of Europe, but there is, nevertheless, the problem of the strong and the weak, of the oppressor and the oppressed, of the subjugated Irish and the subjugating English, of the down-trodden Jews and the tyrannous Poles, of Czech and Magyar and many other combinations of oppressed and oppressor.

It appears to be a part of human nature—as we know it, read of it and have experienced it—to want to "boss it over the other fellow." And questions of socialism and Christianity enter very little into the problem. True Socialism, like True Christianity, is a promise of the distant future, rather than an achievement of the present. The ethics of Jesus Christ, the first and greatest of known Socialists, preached and disseminated around the world for nearly 2,000 years, have changed human nature very little, but have been greatly changed, camouflaged or diverted into strange channels by this perverse human nature. (As, not the reactionary tendencies of the church, its

---

Originally published in the *Crusader*, June 1920, 12–13.

championship of the capitalist system, etc.) Yet human nature, or rather the human outlook, can be greatly changed, in our belief, by a careful process of education. But such a process of education to effect the changes required would have to extend over a period of hundreds—perhaps thousands—of years. And who wants to wait one or two thousand years for an alms of right that should be ours without begging and with the possibility that Socialism at the end of that period may be as degraded as Christianity is after the lapse of not nearly two thousand years, when experience teaches that the strong never voluntarily relinquish their oppressive hold over the weak?

The writer is a Socialist. Any intelligent Negro who gave thought to the matter would be a Socialist. Most intelligent people—white and colored—are Socialists at heart, even if not at the polls. The writer looks upon political Socialism more as a stepping stone by which (by virtue of inter-racial alliances) can be achieved the political liberation of oppressed peoples rather than a "cure-all" for the ills of the world. He believes that the vicious principle of "European eminent domain" could as easily flourish under a perverted form of Socialism as it now does under a perverted form of Christianity. And there are even now signs of perversion of the Socialist doctrines, both at home and abroad.

The Negro is at the crossroads and his predicament calls for serious thought and fearless, intelligent discussion. The tendency to abuse those with whom we do not agree, as well as the slavish fear to stand in the right "with two or three" must both be eliminated. Sentiment, too, and emotionalism must be thrown out of court. The destiny of a race is at stake, and the occasion calls for the most serious and comprehensive consideration of the factors governing the problem and the possibilities of a way out to safety, honor and power, rather than the downward slide of the road of least resistance to ignominy, impotence and extinction.

We have already seen that the chief factor in race problems is the existence side by side of widely differentiated racial groups and the resultant clash of ideals and interests. In the Negro's case the problem is only *accentuated*, but not *created*, by reason of the great differences in the color of black and white peoples. The economic factor enters into the race problem only to the same extent that it enters into the relations of members of a single group, save that the existence of two opposing groups gives the capitalists (of both groups) unusual opportunities at economic exploitation. But white capitalists would as soon use (and have often used) white scabs as they would use Negro scabs. They would as soon (and do) exploit the weak bodies of little white children as the weak bodies of little black children, and vice versa with the black capitalists should these ever attain full development. It is not, therefore, by overstressing the economic factor and ignoring the other factors that we can best serve our race in particular and humanity in general.

While other factors enter into the problem they are all of satellitic relations to the chief factor: the existence side by side of widely differentiated racial groups, and the very human instinct which sets on the stronger group to tyrannize it over the weak group. This instinct also fosters the imperialistic tendency and inspires the strong to extend their dominion over the weak of distant lands. But alien domination does not alone constitute a race problem. Moreover, alien domination, if unaccompanied by colonization, is comparatively easy of solution as against the solution of a problem created by the existence side by side of two opposing groups. If these two groups are of equal or nearly equal strength and numbers, then what is known as a "balance of power"—based upon the mutual respect for the force possessed by each—is established, and clashes will be few and far between, but all the more bloody and terrible when they do occur because of the mutual preparedness and the equality of strength.

And now, as to the possibilities of solution or adjustment: These may be grouped under two main headings, thus:

(1) *The probability of an ultimate, peaceful, just and honorable solution between the white and Negro peoples in residence side by side in America; and*

(2)*The alternative if such a probability does not exist or is not sufficiently strong to warrant our staking the future of our race and children upon it.*

As to number one, we do not say that it is not possible. But we do say, and most emphatically, that it is highly improbable. Neither in the ample records of history nor in the light of contemporary experience is there aught that would give to the logical, honest, truth-seeking mind the slightest hope of probability of solution along the lines of number one. Stronger has never yet voluntarily relinquished his strangle hold upon weaker. As in the days of Pharaoh and the Children of Israel so through the numerous pages of history to the present day. Our experience has been as harsh as that of other weak groups. No more, no less. And what is there to guide our faltering feet if not "the lamp of experience"?

Under number one may come all such suggestions towards solution or adjustment here as the "acquirement of education," "the ownership of property," "alliance with white labor," the "exercise of the franchise," "industrial and commercial development," the shifting North of the Negro population of the South (a policy latterly advocated by Dr. Du Bois among others).

Of these the exercise of the franchise—the political factor—is the only one promising of results. In fact, without the franchise the others are not attainable or cannot be protected when obtained. Mere ownership of property and possession of education do not in themselves protect the Negro. On the contrary, the education and propertied Negro invites the envy, hate, spite and persecution of the whites. It is a recognized fact that the "white South" would rather have ignorant, illiterate, self-debasing and ne'er do well Negroes than educated, ambitious and prosperous Negroes whose self-respect will force them to demand the rights of men. In industry and commerce the Negro cannot attain his fullest development so long as there are so many handicaps of laws and sentiment against him. And these handicaps will remain so long as his is the weaker group. Nor would shifting the Negro population from the South solve the problem evoked by the existence side by side of two widely differentiated racial groups. It would merely shift the problem.

The exercise—fearlessly and industriously—of the franchise by the Negro would undoubtedly secure many beneficial results, but would just as surely bring about a reaction upon the part of the stronger group to prevent the attainment of "too much power" by the despised weaker group. This reaction may take the form of intimidation at the polls (as is now the case in some parts of the South where the Negro is not completely disfranchised by law) or it may take the form of a revision (where convenient) of political districts to the end of breaking up Negro majorities that might make trouble for the bosses (as has been done several times in the case of the Harlem Negro population) or the reaction might take the form of complete and nation-wide disfranchisement of the weaker group. The form of the reaction will depend chiefly upon the determination and energy evinced by the weaker group. That such a reaction—in one form or another—would be inevitable should not, of course, influence us to any abject surrender of our franchise rights, but its inevitability constitutes one of the many important reasons why an open and intelligent discussion of our situation is absolutely imperative. We know that the white man would not hesitate to use any means within his power to maintain the unchallenged supremacy of the stronger, usually referred to in this country as "white supremacy." Therefore, the reaction against the determined use of the ballot by the Negro may well be the use of the bullet by the white man, or some attempt at scientific, but quite as murderous, annihilation.

Thus we may safely assume that any benefits and advantages achieved by the weaker group through exercise of the franchise will be of a temporary nature, and not permanent.

As to the proposed "alliance with white labor," when it is considered that white labor has only latterly and that most reluctantly, begun to admit Negroes to their unions, and that this reluctant recognition of Negro labor on the part of white labor was caused solely by the extremities to which white labor had been forced by the use of Negroes as scabs by the capitalists, what Negro in his sense can expect a continuance of the "alliance" when there is no capitalist system to menace white labor and consequently no necessity to fear the Negro as a club in the hands of the capitalist group?

At the Crossroads (Part II)

Last month we confined our efforts to arrive at a plan or solution to the first of the two main headings under which we have grouped the existing possibilities of solution or readjustment, namely:

(1) *The probability of an ultimate peaceful, just and honorable solution between the white and Negro people in residence side by side in America.*

The method used was that of elimination. The possibilities discussed included "education," "acquirement of property," "alliance with white labor," "exercise of franchise," "industrial and commercial development," and "shifting North of the Negro population."

Our opinion of the various possibilities grouped under this heading was summed up in the following paragraph:

As to number one, we do not say that it is not possible. But we do say, and most emphatically, that it is highly improbable. Neither in the ample records of history nor in the light of contemporary experience is there aught that would give to the logical, honest, truth-seeking mind the slightest hope of probability of solution along the lines of number one. Stronger has never yet voluntarily relinquished his strangle hold upon weaker. As in the days of Pharaoh and the Children of Israel so through the numerous pages of history to the present day. Our experience has been as harsh as that of other weak groups. No more, no less. And what is there to guide our faltering feet if not "the lamp of experience"?

This month we propose to discuss the second of the two main headings, namely:

(2) *The alternative if such a probability (see No. 1) does not exist or is not sufficiently strong to warrant our staking the future of our race and children upon it.*

The method of elimination will also be used here. Under this second heading may come such suggestions as (a) the turning over to the Negro

Originally published in the *Crusader*, July 1920, 5–6.

of one of the 48 states in which he may enjoy local autonomy, (b) a free Negro State out of the territory now included in the United States, (c) the erection of a Negro buffer State between Mexico and the United States from territory from both countries, (d) Negro migration for the purpose of State building, to Haiti, South America, Mexico or Africa.

Now, while these suggestions are all based upon the vital racial necessity for autonomy ("government of the Negro, by the Negro, and for the Negro") we can very quickly eliminate *a* and *b* as unsatisfactory to both the Negro and the white man. From the Negro standpoint *a* would give rise to too many serious complications and would encourage and facilitate discrimination against him on the part of the other States and their white populations who would have an overwhelming preponderance in the House of Representatives. Nor is *b* any more promising. A free Negro State anywhere between Mexico and Canada, unless it be in California, would be far too vulnerable for permanent independent existence. The topography of North America, unlike that of Europe, does not favor the existence of many independent states.

Our consideration of *a* and *b* has been so far solely from the Negro viewpoint and interests. From the white viewpoint and interests, both would be unsound and of potential menace, for the white man already sees the trend of the darker races towards alliance in determined opposition to white domination. Furthermore, even were an American Government to sponsor either *a* or *b*, it would find it a difficult, if not impossible, task to pre-empt the white population from any State which may be chosen for the purpose. Even in Mississippi the white minority would protest and would be supported in their objections by all the whites of the other Southern States and by most of the Northern whites.

In *c* the difficulties would be even greater, since to the domestic problem of how to pre-empt the white population would be added the international problem of getting Mexico to consent to the arrangement. Furthermore, from the Negro viewpoint and interests a Negro State must have fairly safe, natural boundaries and be of a size sufficient not only to support the present Negro population of the United States, but its natural and immigrant increases as well.

To us it would seem that only solution lies in *d*: Negro migration for the purpose of State building. But even this question is complex, for to what country shall we migrate? Not that there are not several countries to which we could migrate, but rather that we must decide which of these countries can best meet the needs of the situation. The island of Haiti, while near and capable of supporting a population of over twenty million (present population about three million) does not offer us the potential reinforcements of man-power held out by the motherland, Africa, and to a lesser degree by South America. Mexico, nearer yet, is too turbulent a state for consideration.

Between South America and Africa, the choice would undoubtedly be Africa on the basis of both sentimental attachment and strategic requirements and vastness of resources. But most of the gates of Africa are at present in the hands of the European robbers. Only Liberia is still open to the New World Negro. And Liberia is not sufficiently developed industrially to be able to take care of any large influx of immigrants. Her position, too, is somewhat unfortunate. While she has an interior plateau that is as healthy as any other part of the world, the low coastlands, being so near to the Equator and cursed with disease-breeding mangrove swamps (which, however, could be drained) are unhealthy and require a trying and often fatal process of acclimatization. In the East, Abyssinia, with its Negro government and fine cool climate, is cut off from the sea by the surrounding holdings of France, Britain and Italy. Migration to Abyssinia is, however, not impossible, but certainly mass migration would arouse the suspicions of the Powers surrounding her and then it would become a question of whether those Powers considered themselves strongly enough entrenched in East Africa to imitate the Italian attempt that ended with such disaster to Italian arms at Adowa. Or would Abyssinia be sufficiently organized to effectively resent any action that these Powers may take to prevent Negro migrants from reaching her territory?

Of course, with money to back the project and a vanguard of expert artisans to precede the first wave of migration, most of the handicaps of Liberia could be removed and that country put upon an industrial basis that would enable it to absorb and accommodate any number of Negro migrants from America. And, as these migrants the industrial prosperity they would create would very soon make of Liberia a powerful nation in the sense of organized and potential force, European tenure would likely soon become impossible in the face of the rising tide which Liberian precept and example would inspire. Certainly European tenure could not survive Liberian military opposition should Liberia find it possible to train and equip an army of one hundred thousand and to keep pace with aerial development for her protection from enemy planes and warships. But these are merely hopes, wishes and surmises and we are endeavoring to deal with existent realities.

Upon the basis of existent realities, then, it is obviously South America which offers us the best field for the purpose of state-building.

This continent duplicates all of the advantages of Africa save that of immense man-power reserve. It is immensely rich in ratio to its size, being the next smallest continent to Australia, while Africa is the second largest. It is well served by navigable rivers, and in a high state of industrial development. It possesses a healthy climate throughout, and has a highly strategic commercial situation, lying between the Pacific and Atlantic oceans. The colored races are in the majority in the population of South America, which fact accounts for the absence of race prejudice. The known Negro population is over ten million, and Negro blood has been indiscriminately mixed with white and Indian, and the latter with white until now there is a large mixed population.

The industrial development of South America enables it to absorb large numbers of migrants each year. Agriculturists would find an El Dorado in the Brazilian portion, as in Brazil so great has been the rubber fever that agriculture has been badly neglected and the price of foodstuffs as a result is extremely high.

Naturally, a strong Negro state, covering all or most of the South American continent, would exert a mighty influence upon the future of Africa, as the racial inspiration which Africa would derive from the existence of a free and powerful Negro State in the New World would be incalculable, and certain to influence them to unite and offer most determined opposition to European domination. Now would the help be negligible which such a State could give to Africans fighting for their liberty. And with African liberty effected and Africa returned to the Africans, two rich continents would be dominated by African races, as well as various islands of the sea necessary to the adequate defence of these continents, among which would be the West Indian islands, in themselves a rich possession, and by virtue of Negro population and Negro suffering, a heritage of the race.

It is thus seen that migration would lead not only to an escape from galling and degrading serfdom, but to a glorious and proud future as well.

Trend of World Events
in Their Relation to the Negro

The most important of world events which may be adjudged favorable to the aspirations of the Negro Universal are the failure of the imperialistic League of Nations and the successes of Soviet Russia in the numerous wars engineered against her by the Entente nations, especially Britain and France. Both of these events, with the train of minor events which they have started, are pregnant with gigantic possibilities that may soon be opportunities for the Negro.

In the Near East there is rising upon the horizon the flaming dawn of a terrible *Jehad*, or Holy War, which is rapidly eliminating or forcing to the background the various differences between Turk and Arab Mohammedans and bringing into line the Persian and Egyptian Nationalists. For this rejuvenating union of Islam the grabbing and selfish policies of the Entente nations are largely responsible. During the war, Arab fought against Turk, and the Persian was willing to do the same upon condition of Persian independence. The Entente refused the proffered aid of Persia because Britain would not consider releasing her stranglehold on Persia. The Entente double-crossed the Arab because both Britain and France wanted to control the rich lands and oil fields of Mesopotamia and Syria.

Further East there is India chafing under "British" rule, and near-by ready Afghanistan as a link between Asia Minor and southern Asia and again between those two sections of Asia and Soviet Russia.

In Farther Asia China is undergoing a metamorphosis from the most pacific of nations to the most militaristic. In the Celestial Empire the fervor of Nationalism, fired by European aggression, is so great that the volunteers for military service cannot be accommodated in the Chinese armies, and, as a result, many are taking service with the Russian Bolsheviki. Every

---

Originally published in the *Crusader*, September 1920, 9–10.

town of importance is engaged in the manufacture of arms and munitions. Every square resounds to the martial tread of drilling soldiers.

All of these conditions, with the spread of Bolshevism, whether by force of arms or by the effective propaganda of Lenine, are favorable to the aspirations of the Negro. The disposal of Poland (and should the Russo-Polish war continue she will be disposed of in spite of recent Polish-French successes around Warsaw) and the diversion of Bolshevik forces southward to crush Wrangel and cross over into Asia Minor to join hands with the Turkish and Arab Nationalists would be the signal for a general uprising and *Jehad* against the infidel from the straits of Malacca to the Straits of Gibraltar, and possibly enlisting even China and Central and Southern Africa in the onset against the Europeans.

In the past there have been rebellions against European domination in both Asia and Africa. But these were separate, sporadic and far apart, having none of the co-ordination and vastness that the coming uprisings have. Furthermore, Europe is in a greatly weakened condition as the result of the late world war and the present series of minor but destructive wars. She has neither the vitality nor the man-power to withstand the coming onslaught. Too, aligned with Asia and Africa is Soviet Russia. Moreover, Asia, or a great part of Asia, is now possessed of all the engines of modern warfare. And, in the background, Japan mayhap awaits her opportunity. All in all, an interesting situation and one promising of genuine world democracy.

"Africa for the Africans"

"Africa for the Africans" is synonymous in meaning to those older and better known racial slogans of "Europe for the Europeans" and "Asia for the Asiatics."

"Africa for the Africans" no more means that all Africans and people of African descent must be confined to the African continent than "Europe for the Europeans" means that all Europeans must be kept in Europe. Negroes in other parts of the world will not necessarily have to pull up stakes and go to Africa, though there is ample room and vast opportunities on the wide and healthy African plateaus for many times their numbers. *But Negroes everywhere would derive colossal and immediate benefits from the successful application of the slogan "Africa for the Africans."* Masters of their ancestral home, they could demand respect in the lands of the other great races. Even weak Liberia and Haiti, handicapped as they have been by foreign political interference and financial discrimination, have helped to increase Negro prestige. With powerful Negro states in the motherland to back us up bars not raised against us would automatically collapse overnight. Nations have little respect for the weak and unorganized, but are mighty diplomatic where organized force is concerned. Japan, with her 70,000,000, gets more respect from her sister nations than the Negro race with its unorganized 250,000,000.

"Africa for the Africans" means government of the people of Africa by the people of Africa and *for* themselves and the glory, advancement and protection of the entire Negro race, as opposed to the present system of government of Africa by and in the interests of European capitalists. With strong and stable Negro states in Africa (or elsewhere, for that matter; South America, for instance), the reproach so often thrown at the Negro that he is not fit for self-government would no longer have force, nor would its accompanying corollary that, not capable of governing himself, he is

Originally published in the *Crusader*, October 1920, 8–9.

necessarily not fit for participation in the political systems of other peoples among who he may be thrown.

"Africa for the Africans" does not necessarily mean a single empire or republic of the huge continent, the second largest of the great land masses on earth. Europe and Asia both harbor scores of independent nations. Even the comparatively new Americas are divided up into many separate entities.

"Africa for the Africans" is not offered as a panacea for all the ills of the Negro race, but specifically for those political and economic ills which are the outgrowth of the white domination of the Negro race and exploitation of the vast mineral, forest and agricultural wealth of the Negro motherland. Too, it can hardly be questioned that independent, unhampered evolution for the Negro in Africa must greatly influence for the better the position of Negroes throughout the world, thus tending to a solution of *most*, if not all, of the ills of even the Negro resident in other lands and freeing the majority of the Negro race for progress along the lines of its own race-genius.

"Africa for the Africans" does not necessarily mean that African development thereafter would be along capitalistic lines. Those who nave studied the Negro peoples of Africa are aware that wherever these peoples have had opportunity for independent development their particular race-genius has led them into the sphere of what in the European world are today known as Socialism and Communism, both having been in practical application in Africa for centuries before they were even advanced as theories in the European world.

The fight for a free Africa now being taken up by large numbers of New World Negroes in support of the "Ethiopian Movement" in South Africa and the Mohammedan renaissance in the North and East does not mean that these New World Negroes are losing interest in the fight against injustices at home. It merely means that they have at least recognized the lessons of history. And history teaches nothing more clearly than that national independence, bolstered up and protected by powerful force, is the only way of escaping alien domination and oppression.

The Salvation of the Negro

As the Negro's position, even in America, is not utterly hopeless there must be at least several *possibilities* of achieving his salvation.

The important thing, then, would be to sift these *possibilities* with a view to picking out the fairest *probabilities*. One may argue that it is possible for black and white men to live together in peace and equality without fear of refutation on the point of *possibility*. But history has shown that it is highly *improbable* that they would so live together. At least, history shows that they would not so live together *under the Capitalist System*. Replace the Capitalist System with the Socialist Co-operative Commonwealth and they *might* live together in peace and equality. Anyway there is this much to say in favor of the Socialist Co-operative Commonwealth, i.e.: while the oppression of one group by another is a necessary and ever present feature of Capitalism, such a thing in the Socialist Co-operative Commonwealth would be impossible, since were one group to exert even the mildest form of oppression toward another group that would be the signal for the disintegration of the Socialist Co-operative Commonwealth, and for the return of Capitalism. Just as today the democratic state can be destroyed as such and its citizens' rights annulled by imperialistic tendencies outward, so in the Socialist Cooperative Commonwealth freedom from exploitation would be lost for all the moment it were lost for one.

It is clear then that it is *possible* to achieve the Negro's salvation through the destruction of the present system and the substitution for it of the Socialist Co-operative Commonwealth. This, always a *possibility*, has become, since the destruction of Czarist Capitalism in Russia and the Establishment of a Communist Co-operative Commonwealth, a *probability*. The Russian Jews have found their salvation—of course, that salvation can be no more permanent than the communist state through which it was achieved—in the destruction of Capitalism in Russia. Along with Capitalism went Jew-baiting.

Originally published in the *Crusader*, April 1921, 8–9.

That the Negro can *possibly*—even *probably*—achieve his salvation though the Socialist Co-operative Commonwealth, does not mean, however, that he can achieve it *only through that means*. Other groups have saved themselves in the past without engaging in a death struggle with Capitalism. World-wide substitution of the Socialist Co-operative Commonwealth for the vicious Capitalist System is only one way whereby opposing *races* may save themselves from the oppression engendered by the functioning of imperialist capitalism. Of course, it has the virtues of offering the most complete salvation since saving not only from alien political oppression but from capitalistic exploitation by members of its own group as well. It has the advantage for the Negro race of being along the lines of our own race genius as evidenced by the existence of Communist States in Central Africa and our leaning towards Communism wherever the race genius has had free play. It is supposed to have the advantage, too, of making unnecessary a general Exodus. But it has not that advantage exclusively. That advantage is also held by the proposition of a strong, stable and independent Negro state, whether in Africa, South America, the Island of Hispaniola or elsewhere. The establishment of such a state would not necessarily require a wholesale exodus of American Negroes, though it is not altogether inconceivable that American Negroes would rather build up a state of their own for themselves, under governments of the Negro, by the Negro and for the Negro, in preference to helping build up a state in which the vast majority are white and in which the rights of minorities would always be dependent upon *the state of mind* of the majority.

From the point of view of "humanity" it would be much more preferable to gain our rights through the Socialist Co-operative Commonwealth. But the Negro has been treated so brutally in the past by the rest of humanity that he may be pardoned for now looking at the matter more from the viewpoint of the Negro than from that of a humanity that is not humane. And again, he may prefer that his rights and immunity from oppression be based upon his own power rather than upon the problematical continued existence of the Socialist Co-operative Commonwealth. To the writer it is inconceivable that the Socialist Cooperative Commonwealth once established would ever be abolished, but then the oppressive Capitalist System was also inconceivable to our Communist African forefathers, as was also the European dictum latterly flung in the face of Asiatics and Africans that "might makes right."

The surest and quickest way, then, in our opinion, to achieve the salvation of the Negro is to combine the two most likely and feasible propositions, viz: salvation for all Negroes through the establishment of a strong, stable, independent Negro State (along lines of our own race genius) in Africa or elsewhere; and salvation for all Negroes (as well as other oppressed peoples) through the establishment of a Universal Socialist Co-operative Commonwealth. To us it seems that one working for the first proposition would also be working for the second proposition, and offer the free use of our columns for the purpose.

Africa and the White Proletariat

The real "Horror on the Rhine" was the use, against their will, of Black troops forcibly recruited and violently torn away from their homes and transported to Europe to be engaged like so many chess men in the imperialistic gambles of a Capitalist State. And for that horror, Africa holds France and Germany equally guilty.

In one way or another, Africa always repays. The use of African troops by the capitalist French state against the capitalist German state is but a prelude to the use of African troops against the revolutionary proletariat of Europe! Today it is German capitalist and proletarian who alike may repay the debt to Africa. Tomorrow may see the French proletariat called to account for its acquiescence in the despoliation of Africa by the bourgeois governments of France and other European states. Nor is the time remote when British Labor, at last convinced that only revolutionary tactics can overthrow the capitalistic regime and its crushing exploitation of the proletariat, shall feel the impact of African bayonets recruited by the bourgeoisie to uphold its sway.

In the bourgeoisie's extension of control over Africa the white proletariat has been a not unwilling factor. Helping to make new slaves for the bourgeoisie's machine, the proletariat has blindly helped to establish the means for the prolongation (at the least) of its own slavery. Not only that, but hotly denouncing the dastardly efforts of capitalism through its tools Kolchak, Denikin, Wrangel, etc, to destroy the Russian Communist Co-operative Commonwealth the white proletariat has yet—now as in the past—acquiesced in the destruction of many an African Communist state. The white proletariat was in ignorance of the existence of such states? It was not necessary to be in such ignorance! That white radicals (the leaders of the proletariat movement) have failed in the past to familiarize themselves with

Originally published in the *Crusader*, April 1921, 10–11

the real facts as to Africa and its cultures is one of the greatest reflections of an otherwise apparently alert and generally well-informed body. We would advise that they begin at once to remove this reflection on their ability and earnestness by reading "The Black Man's Burden," by E.D. Morel. There were always other sources during the last fifty years through which they could have gleaned valuable information about the culture of the Africans. We recommend Morel's book because it covers several phases of the relations between white and black, as well as giving some excellent comparisons between African Communist States and Soviet Russia, as for instance, the following:

> Curiously enough there is a type of European Socialist mind that unconsciously reinforces these capitalist tendencies, of course, from an entirely different standpoint. This type of mind visualizes the mass of African humanity in terms of a dogmatic economic theory. It would stand aside from any effort to preserve the native races from capitalistic exploitation, which it regards as a necessary and inevitable episode in human development. It would do nothing to safeguard native institutions, which it looks upon as archaic and reactionary. It would apply the same processes to all races (it refuses, apparently to admit any form of civilization than the European socialized State) at whatever stage of cultural development. It would cheerfully, and with the purest of motives, assist at the destruction of African institutions, and assent to the conversion of African cultivators and farmers into wage-slaves, sublimely indifferent to the social havoc and misery thereby inflicted upon millions of living Africans and Africans yet unborn, content with the thought that in the fullness of time the wage-slaves would themselves evolve the Socialist African State. The only comment that I would venture to make up the contentions of this school, is that the form of Socialism which Russia has evolved, and which, I suppose, is the most advanced form of European Socialism now available to study, approximates closely to the social conditions of an advanced tropical African community. The spinal column of both is a system of land tenure which ensures to the population a larger measure of economic independence—in tropical Africa the degree of economic independence is necessarily greater; while the corporate character which the Soviet system imparts to all economic activities is substantially identical with the African social systems. It seems a strange anomaly to laud advanced Socialism in Europe, and to assent to its destruction in tropical Africa.

The Acid Test of White Friendship

Are all white people enemies of the Negro? And if not, are all white people who call themselves friends of the Negro really such?

It would be idle to argue that all, or most, white Americans are friendly toward the Negro, for such argument would be diametrically opposed to the facts. But it would be just as idle to argue that all white people are enemies of the Negro, since, from the time of John Brown, Wendell Philips, Garrison, etc., to the present-day, the facts in the case would overwhelmingly controvert such an argument.

Those who sponsor the first argument are blind to realities, while the sponsors of the second are reacting in a childish manner to the faults of the gullibility of their own natures. Having been grievously deceived in the past, along with the mass of Negroes, by the false protestations of friendship of white opportunists who projected themselves into the Negro's fight for one of two purposes—personal gain or the curbing of Negro "radicalism"—and subsequently betrayed the misplaced faith of the Negro, the exponents of the second argument have been soured by the experience of and have lost their perspective. Refusing to recognize that the fault lies principally with their inexcusable gullibility they have formed the erroneous opinion that *all* white people must be enemies of the Negro, forgetting that self interest plays a greater part in this world than does race and that consequently the Negro must have many friends among those groups whose interests are identical with his own and whose aims are unattainable without the aid and co-operation of the Negro. Already the most radical white labor organizations have thrown themselves open to the Negro. Already white men have fought together with Negroes in defence of their common interests, and have staunchly refused to accept divisions in their ranks and betray their Negro comrades, although white employers have offered to concede to the workers' demands in the case of the white workers if

Originally published in the *Crusader*, July 1921, 8–9.

the latter would betray their Negro comrades. And increasingly with the spread of radical thought, the white workers are coming to the recognition that the interests of all workers are identical and that the workers of all race have but one enemy—*Capitalism.*

At the present time it is still true that every white person is a *potential* enemy of the Negro. This does not mean, however, that every white person is an *actual* enemy. Whether he becomes an *actual* enemy depends to a large extent upon ourselves. There are schisms in the white race which, by encouraging, we can ultimately benefit ourselves.

However, there is also the danger of unwise statements and policies on our part acting to solidify anew the white race. Plainly, it is to our interest to encourage the schisms in the white race, while at the same time discouraging any division in our own race except such as absolutely necessary for progress as, for example, the class division which is rapidly taking form among the Negroes of America.

We need to repel the advances of white groups, nor need we accept as genuine every protestation of friendship from a white group or individual. It is always possible to apply the acid test of friendship, and that test in the case of the white person professing friendship for the Negro is simply whether that person is willing to see the Negro defend himself with arms against aggression, and willing even to see Negroes killing his own (white) people in defence of Negro rights.

Program of the A.B.B.—Offered for the Guidance of the Negro Race in the Great Liberation Struggle

A race without a program is like a ship at sea without a rudder. It is absolutely at the mercy of the elements. It is buffeted hither and thither and in a storm is bound to flounder. It is in such a plight as this that the Negro race has drifted for the past fifty years and more. Rarely ever did it know exactly what it was seeking and never once did it formulate any intelligent and workable plan of getting what it was seeking, even in the rare instances when it did know what it wanted. It is to meet this unfortunate condition and supply a rudder for the Negro Ship of State—a definite directive force—that the following program adopted by the African Blood Brotherhood is herewith offered for the consideration of other Negro organizations and of the race in general.

There is nothing illusory or impractical about this program. Every point is based upon the historic experience of some section or other of the great human family. Those who formulated the program recognized (1) the economic nature of the Struggle (not wholly economic, but nearly so); (2) that it is essential to know from whom our oppression comes: that is, who are our enemies; and to make common cause with all forces and movements that are working against our enemies; (3) that it is not necessary for Negroes to be able to endorse the program of these other movements before they can make common cause with them against the common enemy; (4) that the important thing about Soviet Russia, for example, is not the merits or demerits of the Soviet form of government, but the outstanding fact that Soviet Russia is opposing the imperialist robbers who have partitioned our motherland and subjugated our kindred, and that Soviet Russia is feared

---

Originally published in the *Crusader*, October 1921, 15–18.

by those imperialist nations and by all the capitalist plunder-bunds of the earth from whose covetousness and murderous inhumanity we at present suffer in many lands.

Africa

Our Motherland, Africa, is divided by the Big Capitalist Powers into so-called "colonies."

The colonies in turn are parcelled out to white planters and capitalists, some of them colonists, others absentee landlords. To this end the free life of the African peoples have been broken up and the natives deprived of their lands in order to force them to work, at starvation wages, on the lands of these white capitalists. These planter-capitalists have settled down in our country to exploit the riches of the land as well as the labor of our people.

But our people were not tamely submissive and had to be subjugated. They refused to be exploited and rebelled and fought the invader in an unequal struggle. The invaders, armed with weapons of modern technique and precision as against the primitive and old weapons of our forefathers, were finally able to subdue our people. But not until many a "British square" had been broken and many a sudden disaster suffered by the forces of all the invading capitalist Powers.

How We Were Enslaved

And the fight is not yet over. A people living in oppression may be compared to a volcano. At any moment it may rise like a giant and run its enemies into the sea. To prevent this eventuality the capitalist planters, with the aid of their home governments, have organized "Colonial Armies," formed and equipped according to methods of modern technique. And to conquer our militant spirit and win us to slavish acceptance of their dominance they brought in the white man's religion, Christianity, and with it whiskey. By the white man's religion our people's militant spirit was drugged; with his whiskey they were debauched. The white man's treachery, the white man's religion and whiskey had as great a part in bringing about our enslavement as the white man's guns.

But in order to more intensively exploit our rich motherland and the cheap labor power of an enslaved people it was necessary to bring into our land certain machine industries and certain material improvements, like railroads, etc., and today we may witness, especially in the coast cities of Africa, the steady growth of modern enterprise. With the introduction of modern equipment the African has learned to wield the white man's machines, his guns, his methods, and with the possession of this knowledge has grown a new hope and determination to achieve his freedom and become the master of his own motherland.

Hope Never More Justified

Indeed, the hope of the Negro people to free themselves from the imperialist enslavers was never more justified than at present. The home governments of the planter capitalists are weakening day by day, and are trembling under the menace of the Proletarian Revolution. The oppressed colonies and small nations are in constant rebellion, as witness the Irish, Turks, Persians, Indians, Arabs, Egyptians, etc.

While the interior of Africa is as yet barely touched by predatory Capitalism the tribes fully realized the danger they would be subjected to should the enslavers penetrate more into the interior. Under the leadership of the more able and developed Negroes in the coast districts, the tremendous power of the Negro race in Africa could be organized. Towards this end we propose that every effort shall be bent to organize the Negroes in the coast districts and bring all Negro organizations in each of the Africa countries into a world-wide Negro Federation. The various sections of the federation to have their own Executive committees, etc., and to get in touch with the tribes in the interior with a view to common action. The Supreme Executive Committee to get in touch with all other peoples on the African continents, the Arabs, Egyptians, etc., as well as the revolutionists of Europe and America for the purpose of effecting co-ordination of action.

Must Organize Pan-African Army

Labor organizations should be formed in the industrial sections in order to protect and improve the conditions of the Negro workers.

No opportunity should be lost for propagandizing the native soldiers in the "colonial armies" and for organizing secretly a great Pan-African army in the same way the Sinn Fein built up the Irish Republican Army under the very nose of England.

Modern arms must be smuggled into Africa. Men sent into Africa in the guise of missionaries, etc., to establish relations with the Senussi, the various tribes of the interior, and to study the topography of the country. The Senussi already have an "army in existence," a fact that is keeping European capitalist-statesmen awake at night.

Every effort and every dollar should be spent to effect the organization of a pan-African army, whose very existence would drive respect and terror into the hearts of the white capitalist-planters, and protect our people against their abuses. Remember: MIGHT MAKES RIGHT—ALWAYS DID AND ALWAYS WILL.

America

Whatever interest the Capitalists displayed in the Negro was always motivated by considerations of cheap labor power.

It was early recognized that the Negro people were the most endurant in the world, and when the New World was discovered the rich exploiters organized expeditions to enslave our people and forcibly carry them into New World lands, to build empires and create wealth where otherwise none would have been possible. This is the history of most of the Negro populations in foreign lands.

The Cause of the Civil War

In the United States, as is well known, the Negroes but a few decades ago were exploited according to the most crude and primitive system of exploitation: chattel slavery. This chattel slavery prevailed in the South, while in the North the modern Capitalist method of exploitation (wage slavery) prevailed. The two systems could not exist side by side and therefore the so-called war of liberation in which Northern Capitalists and their retinue, in a smoke of idealistic camouflage, went to war against feudal Capitalists in the South in order to decide supremacy between the two systems in the Americas. Northern Capitalists won and chattel slavery in the South was abolished with lurid speeches and glamor about Liberty, Democracy, etc.

But the Negroes were not to have even the comparative liberty which the great Capitalist Czars tolerate under the wage-slavery system. They were scrupulously disarmed, while their former owners with their henchmen remained armed. To repress all Negro aspirations for real freedom and suppress all desires to better their condition, secret murder societies like the Ku Klux Klan were organized by the former owner class who tortured and murdered secretly and in cold blood thousands of defenceless Negroes and many whites everywhere the humanitarian instincts prompted them to champion the Negro's cause. And the victorious Capitalist "Liberators" of the North not only did not move a finger to enforce justice but suppressed the facts of this terrible persecution of the Negro and his few white friends. Through the years of terror exercised by these white cracker societies the Negro again became totally subjugated, and Peonage is the lot of many today in the Southern States, while many are lynched or massacred each year. Lately the New Negro has come upon the scene and in response to his rebellious spirit and that of the exploited in general we see the resurrection of the Ku Klux Klan.

Negro Migration

As a result of continued oppression and maltreatment in the South, many thousands of Negroes have managed to escape to the North, and today every big Northern city has a large Negro population.

The comparative freedom of the North is propitious for great organizations and cultural activities, and it is here that the vanguard and general staff of the Negro race must be developed.

A Great Negro Federation

In order to build a strong and effective Movement on the platform of Liberation for the Negro People and protection of their rights to "life, liberty and the pursuit of happiness," etc., all Negro organizations should get together on a Federation basis, thus creating a united, centralized Movement. Such a Movement could be carried on openly in the North, but would have to be built up secretly in the South in order to protect those members living in the South and to safeguard the organization from premature attack. Within the Federation a secret protective organization should be developed—the real Power—to the membership of which should be admitted only the best and most courageous of the race. The Protective organization would have to function under strict military discipline, ready to act at a moment's notice whenever defence and protection are necessary.

Labor and Economic Organizations

Millions of Negroes have come North and are employed as laborers and mechanics, etc., in the various industries and Capitalist enterprises of the North. Being unorganized they are compelled to work at the meanest jobs and under the worst conditions. When depression in industry appears they are the first to suffer. The white workers, through their labor organizations, have not only compelled the capitalist to give them more money and a shorter work day, but also partial employment during slack times. And when better times arrive the white workers, through their organization, are ready to take full advantage of the situation. Negro workers, wherever organized in labor unions, have improved their living conditions, won shorter hours, more money and steadier employment, as witness the sleeping car conductors, the Negro Longshoremen of Philadelphia, etc. And since the strength of a people depends upon the degree of well-living by that people we must by all means strive to substantially improve the standard of living, etc. All worthwhile Negro organizations and all New Negroes must therefore interest themselves in the organizing of Negro workers into labor unions for the betterment of their economic condition and to act in close co-operation with the class-conscious white workers for the benefit of both.

Negro Farmer Organization

The same principle applies to the small Negro farmers and farm laborers. They must get together to resist exploitation as well as to protect themselves against peonage and other injustices. Wherever cooperation with white farmers is possible it is of course desirable.

Co-operative Organizing

There has developed among our people the naive belief that permanent employment, better conditions and our salvation as a race can be accomplished through the medium of Negro factories, steamship lines and similar enterprise. We wish to warn against putting too great a dependence along this line as sudden financial collapse of such enterprises may break the whole morale of the Liberation Movement. Until the Negro controls the rich natural resources of some country of his own he cannot hope to compete in industry with the great financial magnates of the capitalist nations on a scale large enough to supply jobs for any number of Negro workers, or substantial dividends for Negro investors. Let those who have invested in such propositions tell you whether they have obtained either jobs or dividends by such investment.

The only effective way to secure better conditions and steady employment in America is to organize the Negro's Labor Power as indicated before into labor organizations. Every big organization develops certain property in the shape of buildings, vacation farms, etc. In prosperous times they may even develop co-operative enterprises such as stores, etc., but such enterprises must be co-operative property of all members of the organization and administered by members elected for the purpose. Under no circumstances should such property be operated under corporation titles written over to a few individuals to be disposed of at their pleasure. But experience has proven that such enterprises can only exist when the oppressed class is well organized. Without adequate organization an industrial crisis like the present would sweep them off their feet. But where backed by adequate organization the cooperative idea can be worked to advantage. Unlike the corporation, which lifts a few men on the shoulders and life-savings of the many, the co-operative is of equal benefit to all.

Alliances

There can be only one sort of alliance with other peoples and that is an alliance to fight our enemies, in which case our allies must have the same purpose as we have. Our allies may be actual or potential. The small oppressed nations who are struggling against the capitalist exploiters and oppressors must be considered as actual allies. The class-conscious white workers who have spoken out in favor of African liberation and have shown a willingness to back with action their expressed sentiments must also be considered as actual allies and their friendship further cultivated. The non-class-conscious white workers who have not yet realized that all workers, regardless of race or color, have a common interest, must be considered as only potential allies at present and everything possible done to awaken their class-consciousness toward the end of obtaining their co-operation in our struggle. The revolutionary element which is undermining the imperialist powers that oppress us must be given every encouragement by Negroes who really seek liberation. This element is led and represented by the Third Internationale which has its sections in all countries. We should immediately establish contact with the Third Internationale and its millions of followers in all countries of the world. To pledge loyalty to the flags of our murderers and oppressors, to speak about alliances with the servants and representatives of our enemies, to prate about first hearing our proven enemies before endorsing our proven friends is nothing less than cowardice and the blackest treason to the Negro race and our sacred cause of liberation.

It is the Negroes resident in America—whether native or foreign born—who are destined to assume the leadership of our people in a powerful world movement for Negro liberation. The American Negro by virtue of being a part of the population of a great empire has acquired certain knowledge in the waging of modern warfare, the operation of industries, etc. This country is the base for easy contact with the whole world, and the United States is destined, until the Negro race is liberated, to become the center of the Negro World Movement. It is in this country, especially, that the Negro must be strong. It is from here that most of the leaders and pioneers who will carry the message across the world will go forth. But out strength cannot be organized by vain indulgence in mock-heroics, empty phrases, unlearned decorations and titles, and other tomfoolery. It can only be done by the use of proper tactics, by determination and sacrifice upon the part of our leaders and by intelligent preparatory organization and education.

To be kidded along with the idea that because a few hundreds of us assemble once in a while in a convention that therefore we are free to legislate for ourselves; to fall for the bunk that before having made any serious effort to free our country, before having crossed swords on the field of battle with the oppressors, we can have a government of our own, with presidents, potentates, royalties and other queer mixtures; to speak about wasting our energies and money in propositions like Bureaus of Passports and Identifications, diplomatic representatives, etc., is to indulge in pure moonshine and supply free amusement for our enemies. Surely, intelligent, grown-up individuals will not stand for such childish nonsense at all if they are serious about fighting for Negro liberation! We must come down to earth, to actual practical facts and realities and build our strength upon solid foundations—and not upon titled and decorated tomfoolery.

The Caribbean section of the program dealing with the West Indies, South and Central America will be published in the November *Crusader*.

Part V
The Communist Party

Official Documents

Introduction

The Communist Party of the United States was the American affiliate of the Communist International. From the late 1920s through the mid-1950s, it was the largest and most important organization on the American far left. Beginning as a fractious alliance of forces expelled from the Socialist Party in 1919, it grew to nearly a hundred thousand members during the Great Depression. While for the period of this book the CP remained mostly small and relatively lacking in influence, the discussions and debates it hosted over the proper approach to the race question set the stage for its dramatic successes in antiracist organizing during the Depression.

The Communist Party first emerged as two separate organizations, both splits from the Socialist Party. When the SP's leadership decided to expel the left in 1919, it created a large, ready-made constituency for a new communist party. However, the expelled promptly fell out among themselves. Most of the foreign-born radicals established the Communist Party of America, which emphasized underground revolutionary action, a strategy whose advocates had imported directly from their experiences in Europe. The native-born radicals set up the Communist Labor Party of America, which argued for an orientation to the union movement, particularly the IWW. These two groups existed as parallel formations until May of 1921, when Comintern prodding finally compelled unity between them.

For the rest of the decade, the CP would remain divided by factionalism. At the same time, however, it began its first steps toward real participation in struggle in the United States. Its associated publications, like the *Liberator* and its successor, *Workers Monthly*, were high-quality journals, containing international news, poetry, and theoretical discussions side by side. As much of the socialist press had been destroyed in wartime repression, the new communist publications found themselves with little political competition. Much of the party's debate over the race question would play out in these venues.

The party also launched new initiatives in organizing. The International Labor Defense, which would become a prominent part of the party's Depression-era success, was launched in this period. William Z. Foster headed the Trade Union Education League, the party's intervention into the union movement. In 1925, it launched the American Negro Labor Congress, an attempt to organize militant Black workers that internal bungling prevented from ever taking off.

The factional struggles that wracked the party only came to an end in 1929. In 1928, James P. Cannon and his supporters were purged from the party for supporting Leon Trotsky's criticisms of Stalin and the Russian Communist leadership. The following year, Jay Lovestone, who had carried out the purge of the Trotskyists, was himself expelled for supporting the Russian Communist Nikolai Bukharin, who had fallen out of favor with Stalin. William Z. Foster emerged as the party's leader with Comintern blessing, and for the next few decades, the policies and leadership of the Communist Party would largely be determined in Russia.

The two documents here were both drafted at congresses of the Comintern. The first emerged from the Fourth Congress in 1922, while the second came from the Sixth Congress in 1928. Both attest to the importance the Comintern and its American adherents placed on the struggle for black liberation. While the Black Belt Thesis is the more famous, both for its idiosyncratic analysis and its proximity to party success in organizing Black workers during the 1930s, the theses of the Fourth Congress are equally significant. They recognize how important the struggle against racism is to the class struggle, and they commit the CP to complete equality between Black and white. Together, the two texts form the theoretical basis for the CP's interventions in Black liberation struggles for the first two decades of its existence.

Further Reading

Draper, Theodore. *The Roots of American Communism.* New Brunswick, NJ: Transaction Publishers, 2003 [1957].

Palmer, Bryan D. *James P. Cannon and the Origins of the American Revolutionary Left, 1890–1928.* Urbana: University of Illinois Press, 2007.

Solomon, Mark. *The Cry Was Unity: Communists and African Americans, 1917–1936.* Jackson: University Press of Mississippi, 1998.

Theses of the Fourth Comintern
Congress on the Negro Question

During and after the war a movement of revolt against the power of world capital developed among the colonial and semi-colonial peoples which is still making headway. The penetration and intensive colonization of the areas inhabited by the black races is the last great problem on the solution of which the further development of capitalism itself depends. French capitalism has clearly recognized that the power of French postwar imperialism can be maintained only by the creation of a French African empire connected with the motherland by a railway across the Sahara. America's finance magnates (who already exploit 12 million Negroes in the United States) have now begun on the peaceful penetration of Africa. England's fear of the threat to its position in Africa is shown clearly in the extreme methods used to suppress the Rand strike. Just as the danger of a new world war has become acute in the Pacific, as a result of the competition between the imperialist Powers there, so there are menacing signs that Africa is becoming the object of their rival aspirations. Moreover, the war, the Russian revolution, and the powerful movements of revolt among the Asiatic and Moslem peoples against imperialism, have awakened the race consciousness of millions of Negroes, who have for centuries been oppressed and humiliated by capitalism not only in Africa, but also, and perhaps to a greater degree, in America.

The history of the Negroes in America qualifies them to play an important part in the liberation struggle of the entire African race. Three hundred years ago the American Negro was dragged from his homeland, brought in indescribably horrible conditions on board ship, and sold into slavery. For 250 years he worked as a slave under the lash of American overseers. His labour cleared the forests, built the roads, planted the cotton,

Originally published in the *Worker* 4, no. 265 (March 10, 1923): 1, 4.

laid the railways, and kept the aristocracy of the south. His wages were poverty, ignorance, humiliation, and wretchedness. The Negro was not a docile slave; his history is rich in revolts, disturbances, and subterranean methods of gaining freedom. But all his struggles were savagely suppressed. He was forced into subjection by torture, and the bourgeois press and religion justified his enslavement. Slavery then became an obstacle to American development on a capitalist basis; personal slavery came into conflict with wage slavery, and personal slavery was bound to go under. The civil war, which was not a war to free the Negroes, but a war to maintain the industrial predominance of capital in the northern states, confronted the Negro with the choice between slavery in the south and wage slavery in the north. The longings, the blood, and the tears of the "emancipated" negroes were a part of the fabric of American capitalism. As America, which had meanwhile risen to the position of a world Power, was inevitably dragged into the maelstrom of the world war, the Negro was declared to be equal in rank to the whites. He had to kill and be killed for "democracy." Four hundred thousand coloured workers were enrolled in the army and organized in Negro regiments. Immediately after the terrible sacrifices of the world war the returning Negro was met with racial persecution, lynching, murder, deprivation of franchise, inequalities between him and the whites. He defended himself and had to pay dearly for it. Negro persecution became more intense and widespread than before the war, until he learned to forget his "presumption." The postwar industrialization of the Negro in the north, and the spirit of rebellion provoked by persecution and brutality after the war (which, although suppressed, still flared up in protest against such atrocities as the events in Tulsa), give the American Negro, particularly in the north, a place in the vanguard of the fight against oppression in Africa.

The Communist International notes with satisfaction the resistance of the exploited Negro to the exploiters' attack, for the enemy of his race and the enemy of the white workers are one and the same—capitalism and imperialism. The world struggle of the Negro race is a struggle against capitalism and imperialism. The Negro movement throughout the world must be organized on this basis; in America, the centre of Negro culture around which the Negro protest crystallizes; in Africa, the reservoir of human labour power for the further development of capitalism; in Central America (Costa Rica, Guatemala, Colombia, Nicaragua, and the other "independent" Republics) where American imperialism rules; in Porto Rico, Haiti, San Domingo, and the other islands of the Caribbean, where the brutal treatment of our black fellow beings by the American occupation troops has aroused a protest from the conscious Negro and the revolutionary white workers throughout the world; in South Africa and the Congo, where increasing industrialization of the Negro population has led to various outbreaks; in East Africa, where the penetration of world capital is driving the native population to active resistance against imperialism.

It is the task of the Communist International to bring home to the Negroes that they are not the only people suffering from the oppression of imperialism and capitalism, that the workers and peasants of Europe, Asia, and America are also victims of the imperialist exploiter, that in India and China, in Persia and Turkey, in Egypt and Morocco the oppressed coloured workers are defending themselves heroically against the imperialist exploiters, that these peoples are revolting against the same intolerable conditions which drive the Negroes themselves to desperation—racial oppression, social and economic inequality, intense industrial exploitation; that these peoples are fighting for the same objects as the Negroes—political, economic, and social emancipation and equality. The Communist International, which embodies the world-embracing struggle of the revolutionary workers and peasants against the power of imperialism, which is not only the organization of the enslaved white workers of Europe and America, but also the organization of the oppressed coloured peoples of the world, regards it as its duty to support and promote the international organization of Negroes in their struggle against the common enemy.

The Negro problem has become a vital question of the world revolution; the Communist International, which has already realized what valuable help the Asiatic coloured peoples in the semi-colonial countries can give to the proletarian world revolution, considers the collaboration of our oppressed black fellow beings absolutely essential for the proletarian revolution and the destruction of capitalist power. For these reasons the fourth congress declares it the special duty of communists to apply the "Theses on the colonial question" to the Negro problem also.

1. The fourth congress recognizes the necessity of supporting every form of the Negro movement which undermines or weakens capitalism, or hampers its further penetration.

2. The Communist International will fight for the equality of the white and black races, for equal wages and equal political and social rights.

3. The Communist International will use every means at its disposal to force the trade unions to admit black workers, or, where this right already exists on paper, to conduct special propaganda for the entry of Negroes into the unions. If this should prove impossible, the Communist International will organize the Negroes in trade unions of their own and use united front tactics to compel their admission.

4. The Communist International will take steps immediately to convene a world Negro congress or conference.

Black Belt Thesis

1. The industrialization of the South, the concentration of a new Negro working class population in the big cities of the East and North and the entrance of the Negroes into the basic industries on a mass scale, create the possibility for the Negro workers, under the leadership of the Communist Party, to assume the hegemony of all Negro liberation movements, and to increase their importance and role in the revolutionary struggle of the American proletariat. The Negro working class has reached a stage of development which enables it, if properly organized and well led, to fulfill successfully its double historical mission: (a) To play a considerable role in the class struggle against American imperialism as an important part of the American working class; and (b) To lead the movement of the oppressed masses of the Negro population.

2. The bulk of the Negro population (86%) live in the southern states; of this number 74 per cent live in the rural districts and are dependent almost exclusively upon agriculture for a livelihood. Approximately one-half of these rural dwellers live in the so-called Black Belt, in which area they constitute more than 50 per cent of the entire population. The great mass of the Negro agrarian population are subject to the most ruthless exploitation and persecution of a semi-slave character. In addition to the ordinary forms of capitalist exploitation, American imperialism utilizes every possible form of slave exploitation (peonage, share-cropping, landlord supervision of crops and marketing, etc.) for the purpose of extracting super-profits. On the basis of these slave remnants, there has grown up a super-structure of social and political inequality that expresses itself in lynching, segregation, Jim Crowism, etc.

Originally published in the *Daily Worker*, February 12, 1929, 3.

Necessary Conditions for National Revolutionary Movement

3. The various forms of oppression of the Negro masses, who are concentrated mainly in the socalled Black Belt, provide the necessary conditions for a national revolutionary movement among the Negroes. The Negro agricultural laborers and the tenant farmers feel most the pressure of white persecution and exploitation. Thus, the agrarian problem lies at the root of the Negro national movement. The great majority of Negroes in the rural districts of the south are not "reserves of capitalist reaction," but potential allies of the revolutionary proletariat. Their objective position facilitates their transformation into a revolutionary force, which, under the leadership of the proletariat, will be able to participate in the joint struggle with all other workers against capitalist exploitation.

4. It is the duty of the Negro workers to organize through the mobilization of the broad masses of the Negro population the struggle of the agricultural laborers and tenant farmers against all forms of semi-feudal oppression. On the other hand, it is the duty of the Communist Party of the U.S.A. to mobilize and rally the broad masses of the white workers for active participation in this struggle. For that reason the Party must consider the beginning of systematic work in the south as one of its main tasks, having regard for the fact that the bringing together of the workers and toiling masses of all nationalities for a joint struggle against the landowners and the bourgeoisie is one of the most important aims of the Communist International, as laid down in the resolutions on the national and colonial question of the Second and Sixth Congresses of the Comintern.

For Complete Emancipation of Oppressed Negro Race

5. To accomplish this task, the Communist Party must come out as the champion of the right of the oppressed Negro race for full emancipation. While continuing and intensifying the struggle under the slogan of full social and political equality for the Negroes, which must remain the central slogan of our Party for work among the masses, the Party must come out openly and unreservedly for the right of the Negroes to national self-determination in the southern states, where the Negroes form a majority of the population. The struggle for equal rights and the propaganda for the slogan of self-determination must be linked up with the economic demands

of the Negro masses, especially those directed against the slave remnants and all forms of national and racial oppression. Special stress must be laid upon organizing active resistance against lynching, Jim Crowism, segregation and all other forms of oppression of the Negro population.

6. All work among the Negroes, as well as the struggle for the Negro cause among the whites, must be used, based upon the changes which have taken place in the relationship of classes among the Negro population. The existence of a Negro industrial proletariat of almost two million workers makes it imperative that the main emphasis should be placed on these new proletarian forces. The Negro workers must be organized under the leadership of the Communist Party, and thrown into joint struggle together with the white workers. The Party must learn to combine all demands of the Negroes with the economic and political struggle of the workers and the poor farmers.

American Negro Question Part of World Problem

7. The Negro question in the United States must be treated in its relation to the Negro questions and struggles in other parts of the world. The Negro race everywhere is an oppressed race. Whether it is a minority (U.S.A., etc.), majority (South Africa) or inhabits a so-called independent state (Liberia, etc.), the Negroes are oppressed by imperialism. Thus, a common tie of interest is established for the revolutionary struggle of race and national liberation from imperialist domination of the Negroes in various parts of the world. A strong Negro revolutionary movement in the U.S.A. will be able to influence and direct the revolutionary movement in all those parts of the world where the Negroes are oppressed by imperialism.

8. The proletarianization of the Negro masses makes the trade unions the principal form of mass organization. It is the primary task of the Party to play an active part and lead in the work of organizing the Negro workers and agricultural laborers in trade unions. Owing to the refusal of the majority of the white unions in the U.S.A., led by the reactionary leaders, to admit Negroes to membership, steps must be immediately taken to set up special unions for those Negro workers who are not allowed to join the white unions. At the same time, however, the struggles for the inclusion of Negro workers in the existing unions must be intensified and concentrated upon, special attention must be given to those unions in which the statutes

and rules set up special limitations against the admission of Negro workers. Primary duty of the Communist Party in this connection is to wage a merciless struggle against the A. F. of L. bureaucracy, which prevents the Negro workers from joining the white workers' unions. The organization of special trade unions for the Negro masses must be carried out as part and parcel of the struggle against the restrictions imposed upon the Negro workers and for their admission to the white workers' unions. The creation of separate Negro unions should in no way weaken the struggle in the old unions for the admission of Negroes on equal terms. Every effort must be made to see that all the new unions organized by the Left wing and by the Communist Party should embrace the workers of all nationalities and of all races. The principle of one union for all workers in each industry, white and black, should cease to be a mere slogan of propaganda, and must become a slogan of action.

Party Trade Union Work Among Negroes

9. While organizing the Negroes into unions and conducting an aggressive struggle against the anti-Negro trade union policy of the A. F. of L., the Party must pay more attention than it has hitherto done to the work in the Negro workers' organizations; such as the Brotherhood of Sleeping Car Porters, Chicago Asphalt Workers' Union, and so on. The existence of two million Negro workers and the further industrialization of the Negroes demand a radical change in the work of the Party among the Negroes. The creation of working class organizations and the extension of our influence in the existing working class Negro organizations, are of much greater importance than the work in bourgeois and petty-bourgeois organizations, such as the National Association for the Advancement of Colored People, the Pan-African Congress, etc.

10. The American Negro Labor Congress continues to exist only nominally. Every effort should be made to strengthen this organization as a medium through which we can extend the work of the Party among the Negro masses and mobilize the Negro workers under our leadership. After careful preparatory work, which must be started at once, another convention of the American Negro Labor Congress should be held. A concrete plan must also be presented to the Congress for an intensified struggle for the economic, social, political and national demands of the Negro masses. The

program of the American Negro Labor Congress must deal specially with the agrarian demands of the Negro farmers and tenants in the south.

11. The importance of trade union work imposes special tasks upon the Trade Union Educational League. The T.U.E.L. has completely neglected the work among the Negro workers, notwithstanding the fact that these workers are objectively in a position to play a very great part in carrying through the program of organizing the unorganized. The closest contact must be established between the T.U.E.L. and the Negro masses. The T.U.E.L. must become the champion in the struggle for the rights of the Negroes in the old unions, and in the organizing of new unions for both Negroes and whites, as well as separate Negro unions.

White Chauvinism Evidenced in the American Party

The C.E.C. of the American Communist Party itself stated in its resolution of April 30, 1928, that "the Party as a whole has not sufficiently realized the significance of work among the Negroes." Such an attitude toward the Party work among the Negroes is, however, not satisfactory. The time is ripe to begin within the Party a courageous campaign of self-criticism concerning the work among the Negroes. Penetrating self-criticism is the necessary preliminary condition for directing the Negro work along new lines.

12. The Party must bear in mind that white chauvinism, which is the expression of the ideological influence of American imperialism among the workers, not only prevails among different strata of the white workers in the U.S.A., but is even reflected in various forms in the Party itself. White chauvinism has manifested itself even in open antagonism of some comrades to the Negro comrades. In some instances where Communists were called upon to champion and to lead in the most vigorous manner the fight against white chauvinism, they instead yielded to it. In Gary, white members of the Workers Party protested against Negroes eating in the restaurant controlled by the Party. In Detroit, Party members, yielding to pressure, drove out Negro comrades from a social given in aid of the miners on strike. Whilst the Party has taken certain measures against these manifestations of white chauvinism, nevertheless those manifestations must be regarded as indications of race prejudice even in the ranks of the Party, which must be fought with the utmost energy.

13. An aggressive fight against all forms of white chauvinism must be accompanied by a widespread and thorough educational campaign in the spirit of internationalism within the Party, utilizing for this purpose to the fullest possible extent the Party schools, the Party press and the public platform, to stamp out all forms of antagonism, or even indifference among our white comrades toward the Negro work. This educational work should be conducted simultaneously with a campaign to draw the white workers and the poor farmers into the struggle for the support of the demands of the Negro workers.

Tasks of Party in Relation to Negro Work

14. The Communist Party of the U.S.A. in its treatment of the Negro question must all the time bear in mind this twofold task: (a) To fight for the full rights of the oppressed Negroes and for their right to self-determination and against all forms of chauvinism, especially among the workers of the oppressing nationality. (b) The propaganda and the day-to-day practice of international class solidarity must be considered as one of the basic tasks of the American Communist Party. The fight—by propaganda and by deeds—should be directed first and foremost against the chauvinism of the workers of the oppressing nationality as well as against bourgeois segregation tendencies of the oppressed nationality. The propaganda of international class solidarity is the necessary prerequisite for the unity of the working class in the struggle.

"The center of gravity in educating the workers of the oppressing countries in the principles of internationalism must inevitably consist in the propaganda and defense by these workers of the right of segregation by the oppressed countries. We have the right and duty to treat every socialist of an oppressing nation, who does not conduct such propaganda, as an imperialist and as a scoundrel." (Lenin, selected articles on the national question.)

15. The Party must seriously take up the task of training a cadre of Negro comrades as leaders, bring them into the Party schools in the U.S.A. and abroad, and make every effort to draw Negro proletarians into active and leading work in the Party, not confining the activities of the Negro comrades exclusively to the work among Negroes. Simultaneously, white workers must specially be trained for work among the Negroes.

16. Efforts must be made to transform the "Negro Champion" into a weekly mass organ of the Negro proletariat and tenant farmers. Every encouragement and inducement must be given to the Negro comrades to utilize the Party press generally.

Negro Work Part of General Work of Party

17. The Party must link up the struggle on behalf of the Negroes with the general campaigns of the Party. The Negro problem must be part and parcel of all and every campaign conducted by the Party. In the election campaigns, trade union work, the campaigns for the organization of the unorganized, anti-imperialist work, labor party campaign, International Labor Defense, etc., the Central Executive Committee must work out plans designed to draw the Negroes into active participation in all these campaigns, and at the same time to bring the white workers into the struggle on behalf of the Negroes' demands. It must be borne in mind that the Negro masses will not be won for the revolutionary struggles until such time as the most conscious section of the white workers show, by action, that they are fighting with the Negroes against all racial discrimination and persecution. Every member of the Party must bear in mind that "the age-long oppression of the colonial and weak nationalities by the imperialist powers, has given rise to a feeling of bitterness among the masses of the enslaved countries as well as a feeling of distrust toward the oppressing nations in general and toward the proletariat of those nations." (See resolution on Colonial and National Question of Second Congress.)

18. The Negro women in industry and on the farms constitute a powerful potential force in the struggle for Negro emancipation. By reason of being unorganized to an even greater extent than male Negro workers, they are the most exploited section. The A. F. of L. bureaucracy naturally exercises toward them a double hostility, by reason of both their color and sex. It therefore becomes an important task of the Party to bring the Negro women into the economic and political struggle.

19. Only by an active and strenuous fight on the part of the white workers against all forms of oppression directed against the Negroes, will the Party be able to draw into its ranks the most active and conscious Negro workers—men and women—and to increase its influence in those intermediary organizations

which are necessary for the mobilization of the Negro masses in the struggle against segregation, lynching, Jim Crowism, etc.

20. In the present struggle in the mining industry, the Negro workers participate actively and in large numbers. The leading role the Party played in this struggle has helped greatly to increase its prestige. Nevertheless, the special efforts being made by the Party in the work among the Negro strikers cannot be considered as adequate. The Party did not send enough Negro organizers into the coalfields, and it did not sufficiently attempt, in the first stages of the fight, to develop the most able Negro strikers and to place them in leading positions. The Party must be especially criticized for its failure to put Negro workers on the Presidium of the Pittsburgh Miners' Conference, doing so only after such representation was demanded by the Negroes themselves.

21. In the work among the Negroes, special attention should be paid to the role played by the churches and preachers who are acting on behalf of American imperialism. The Party must conduct a continuous and carefully worked out campaign among the Negro masses, sharpened primarily against the preachers and the churchmen, who are the agents of the oppressors of the Negro race.

Party Work Among Negro Proletariat and Peasantry

22. The Party must apply united front tactics for specific demands to the existing Negro petty bourgeois organizations. The purpose of these united front tactics should be the mobilizing of the Negro masses under the leadership of the Party, and to expose the treacherous petty bourgeois leadership of those organizations.

23. The Negro Miners Relief Committee and the Harlem Tenants League are examples of joint organizations of action which may serve as a means of drawing the Negro masses into struggle. In every case the utmost effort must be made to combine the struggle of the Negro workers with the struggle of the white workers, and to draw the white workers' organizations into such joint campaigns.

24. In order to reach the bulk of the Negro masses, special attention should be paid to the work among the Negroes in the South. For that purpose, the

Party should establish a district organization in the most suitable locality in the South. Whilst continuing trade union work among the Negro workers and the agricultural laborers, special organizations of tenant farmers must be set up. Special efforts must also be made to secure the support of the share croppers in the creation of such organizations. The Party must undertake the task of working out a definite program of immediate demands, directed against all slave remnants, which will serve as the rallying slogans for the formation of such peasant organizations. Henceforth the Workers (Communist) Party must consider the struggle on behalf of the Negro masses, the task of organizing the Negro workers and peasants and the drawing of these oppressed masses into the proletarian revolutionary struggle, as one of its major tasks, remembering, in the words of the Second Congress resolution, that "the victory over capitalism cannot be fully achieved and carried to its ultimate goal unless the proletariat and the toiling masses of all nations of the world rally of their own accord in a concordant and close union. (Political Secretariat, Communist International, Moscow, U.S.S.R., Oct. 26, 1928.)

John Reed

Introduction

John Reed (1887–1920) was a socialist journalist and agitator. Though from a privileged background, Reed identified with the leftmost currents in American socialism. He reported on labor struggles in the United States, traveled to Mexico to document the Mexican Revolution, and went to Europe to cover World War I. His most famous work was his documentation of the Russian Revolution, after which he became a determined advocate for Bolshevism in America. Reed died of typhus while in Russia in 1920.

Reed was born to a wealthy family in Portland, Oregon. An indifferent student, he nonetheless was accepted to Harvard, where he joined the Intercollegiate Socialist Society (ISS). The ISS both hosted speakers and conducted agitation; at Harvard, it led a campaign to raise the pay of serving staff. Through the ISS, Reed was exposed to the growing world of American socialism.

After graduation, Reed worked as a freelance journalist. He was arrested while covering the Paterson silk strike, supporting the IWW leadership of the strike. Reed threw himself into the struggle, fundraising for the striking workers at Madison Square Garden.

In late 1913, he left to cover the Mexican Revolution, later publishing his journalism as a book, *Insurgent Mexico*. When World War I broke out the following year, he traveled to Europe, covering the war on the Eastern front, and publishing antiwar journalism. In August of 1917, he traveled to Russia to cover the ongoing revolution, producing *10 Days That Shook the World*, his reporting on the October Revolution.

As an American socialist, Reed was welcomed as an ally of the new Bolshevik government and was able to meet figures such as Lenin and

Trotsky. When he returned to the United States in the Spring of 1918, he threw himself into radical organizing. He was arrested and charged multiple times for his antiwar agitation, and eventually fled back to the Soviet Union to escape prosecution. Before he left, however, Reed was instrumental in establishing the Communist Labor Party out of the left wing of the Socialist Party.

Back in Russia, Reed worked for the Communist International. It was in this capacity that his travels across Russia exposed him to typhus. Reed died of the disease in October 1920, and was buried at the Kremlin with state honors.

Reed's document here comes from a speech he gave at the Second Congress of the Comintern in 1920. In it, Reed both details the extent of Black oppression in the United States for his audience (who would have been almost entirely ignorant of this history) and argues for a political perspective based on the independent movement of Black Americans against racism. Reed dates this movement to the Spanish–American War at the turn of the century and the subsequent agitation by Black veterans and their allies for equal treatment. Reed's emphasis on the movement of Black Americans themselves was, at this point, still quite unusual for a white socialist. His speech thus anticipates the work of communists such as Robert Minor, who would build on Reed's perspective here a few years later. While Reed concludes his speech on a somewhat workerist note, dismissing Black nationalism even at a moment when the Garvey movement was commanding a mass following, his orientation to the liberation struggle being conducted by Black Americans themselves is an important moment in the origins of communist thinking on the race question.

Further Reading

Homberger, Eric. *John Reed*. Manchester: Manchester University Press, 1990.

Lehman, Daniel W. *John Reed and the Writing of Revolution*. Athens, OH: Ohio University Press, 2002.

Newsinger, John, ed.. *Shaking the World: John Reed's Revolutionary Journalism*. London: Bookmarks, 1998.

The Negro Question in America

In America there live 10 million Negroes who are concentrated mainly in the South. In recent years however many thousands of them have moved to the North. The Negroes in the North are employed in industry while in the South the majority are farm laborers or small farmers. The position of the Negroes is terrible, particularly in the Southern states. Paragraph 16 of the Constitution of the United States grants the Negroes full civil rights. Nevertheless most Southern states deny the Negroes these rights. In other states, where by law the Negroes possess the right to vote, they are killed if they dare to exercise this right.

Negroes are not allowed to travel in the same railway carriages as whites, visit the same saloons and restaurants, or live in the same districts. There exist special, and worse, schools for Negroes and similarly special churches. This separation of the Negroes is called the "Jim Crow system," and the clergy in the Southern churches preach about paradise on the "Jim Crow system." Negroes are used as unskilled workers in industry. Until recently they were excluded from most of the unions that belong to the American Federation of Labor. The IWW of course organized the Negroes, the old Socialist Party however undertook no serious attempt to organize them. In some states the Negroes were not accepted into the party at all, in others they were separated off into special sections and in general the party statutes banned the use of Party resources for propaganda among Negroes.

In the South the Negro has no rights at all and does not even enjoy the protection of the law. Usually one can kill Negroes without being punished. One terrible white institution is the lynching of Negroes. This happens in the following manner. The Negro is covered with oil and strung up on a telegraph pole. The whole of the town, men, women and children, run up

Originally published in *The Second Congress of the Communist International, as Reported and Interpreted by the Official Newspapers of Soviet Russia*, Washington, DC: Government Printing Office, 1920, 151–54.

to watch the show and take home a piece of the clothing or the skin of the Negro they have tortured to death "as a souvenir."

I have too little time to explain the historical background to the Negro question in the United States. The descendants of the slave population, who were liberated during the Civil War, when politically and economically they were still completely underdeveloped, were later given full political rights in order to unleash a bitter class struggle in the South which was intended to hold up Southern capitalism until the capitalists in the North were able to bring together all the country's resources into their own possession.

Until recently the Negroes did not show any aggressive class consciousness at all. The first awakening of the Negroes took place after the Spanish-American War, in which the black troops had fought with extraordinary courage and from which they returned with the feeling that as men they were equal to the white troops. Until then the only movement that existed among the Negroes was a semi-philanthropic educational association led by Booker T. Washington and supported by the white capitalists. This movement found its expression in the organization of schools in which the Negroes were brought up to be good servants of industry. As intellectual nourishment they were presented with the good advice to resign themselves to the fate of an oppressed people. During the Spanish War an aggressive reform movement arose among the Negroes which demanded social and political equality with the whites. With the beginning of the European war half a million Negroes who had joined the US Army were sent to France, where they were billeted with French troop detachments and suddenly made the discovery that they were treated as equals socially and in every other respect. The American General Staff approached the French High Command and asked them to forbid Negroes to visit places used by whites and to treat them as second-class people. After the war the Negroes, many of whom had received medals for bravery from the English and French governments, returned to their Southern villages where they were subjected to lynch law because they dared to wear their uniforms and their decorations on the street.

At the same time a strong movement arose among the Negroes who had stayed behind. Thousands of them moved to the North, began to work in the war industries and came into contact with the surging current of the labor movement. High as they were, their wage rates trailed behind the incredible increases in the prices of the most important necessities.

Moreover the Negroes were outraged by the way all their strength was sucked out and the terrible exertions demanded by the work much more than were the white workers who had grown used to the terrible exploitation in the course of many years.

The Negroes went on strike alongside the white workers and quickly joined the industrial proletariat. They proved very ready to accept revolutionary propaganda. At that time the newspaper *Messenger* was founded, published by a young Negro, the Socialist [A. Phillip] Randolph, and pursuing revolutionary propagandist aims. This paper united socialist propaganda with an appeal to the racial consciousness of the Negroes and with the call to organize self-defence against the brutal attacks of the whites. At the same time the paper insisted on the closest links with the white workers, regardless of the fact that the latter often took part in Negro-baiting, and emphasized that the enmity between the white and black races was supported by the capitalists in their own interests.

The return of the army from the front threw many millions of white workers on to the labor market all at once. The result was unemployment, and the demobilized soldiers' impatience took such threatening proportions that the employers were forced to tell the soldiers that their jobs had been taken by Negroes in order thus to incite the whites to massacre the Negroes. The first of these outbreaks took place in Washington, where civil servants from the administration returning from the war found their jobs occupied by Negroes. The civil servants were in the main Southerners. They organized a night attack on the Negro district in order to terrorize the Negroes into giving up their jobs. To everybody's amazement the Negroes came on to the streets fully armed. A fight developed and the Negroes fought so well that for every dead Negro there were three dead whites. Another revolt which lasted several days and left many dead on both sides broke out a few months later in Chicago. Later still a massacre took place in Omaha. In all these fights the Negroes showed for the first time in history that they are armed and splendidly organized and are not at all afraid of the whites. The results of the Negroes' resistance were first of all a belated intervention by the government and secondly the acceptance of Negroes into the unions of the American Federation of Labor.

Racial consciousness grew among the Negroes themselves. At present there is among the Negroes a section which preaches the armed uprising of the Negroes against the whites. The Negroes who returned home from the war have set up associations everywhere for self-defence and to fight against the white supporters of lynch law. The circulation of *The Messenger* is growing constantly. At present it sells 180,000 copies monthly. At the same time, socialist ideas have taken root and are spreading rapidly among the Negroes employed in industry.

If we consider the Negroes as an enslaved and oppressed people, then they pose us with two tasks: on the one hand a strong racial movement and on the other a strong proletarian workers' movement, whose class consciousness is quickly growing. The Negroes do not pose the demand of national independence. A movement that aims for a separate national existence, like for instance the "Back to Africa" movement that could be observed a few years ago, is never successful among the Negroes. They hold themselves above all to be Americans, they feel at home in the United States. That simplifies the tasks of the communists considerably.

The only correct policy for the American Communists towards the Negroes is to regard them above all as workers. The agricultural workers and the small farmers of the South pose, despite the backwardness of the Negroes, the same tasks as those we have in respect to the white rural proletariat. Communist propaganda can be carried out among the Negroes who are employed as industrial workers in the North. In both parts of the country we must strive to organize Negroes in the same unions as the whites. This is the best and quickest way to root out racial prejudice and awaken class solidarity.

The Communists must not stand aloof from the Negro movement which demands their social and political equality and at the moment, at a time of the rapid growth of racial consciousness, is spreading rapidly among Negroes. The Communists must use this movement to expose the lie of bourgeois equality and emphasize the necessity of the social revolution which will not only liberate all workers from servitude but is also the only way to free the enslaved Negro people.

Claude McKay

Introduction

C laude McKay (1889–1948) was a Jamaican-born poet, novelist, and essayist who became a prominent figure in postwar radicalism in both Britain and the United States. Better known as a Harlem Renaissance figure, McKay was deeply committed to radical politics in the postwar years, writing for Communist journals like the *Liberator* and traveling to the Soviet Union to speak at the Fourth Congress of the Communist International. While he eventually distanced himself from the communist movement after Stalin's consolidation of power in the USSR, he remained a socialist, continuing to publish in the left press until his health declined in the mid-1940s.

McKay was born to a prosperous farming family in Jamaica, emigrating to the United States in 1912 to study at the Tuskegee Institute. When he arrived in the United States, McKay was shocked to confront American racism for the first time. While Jamaica had color prejudice, nothing on the island had prepared McKay for the intensity of Jim Crow racism. McKay's rage at the injustice he encountered in the United States would shape much of his subsequent writing.

After traveling around the country for a time, McKay arrived in New York in 1914. While working menial jobs, he began publishing some of his poetry. His talent caught the eye of Max Eastman, a Greenwich Village editor and nodal figure in New York's radical political culture. Eastman became a champion of McKay's poetry, and the two men would shape each other's political evolutions over the next decade.

McKay's relationship with Eastman brought him on to the editorial staff of the *Liberator*, a left cultural journal that would soon become closely associated with the Communist Party. Here, McKay published his most famous poem, "If We Must Die," a defiant response to the race riots that swept the country in 1919. Shortly thereafter, McKay left for England, becoming involved in socialist circles there. He became an editor of the *Workers' Dreadnought*, a journal associated with the left communism of Sylvia Pankhurst.

In 1922, McKay traveled to the Soviet Union as part of the American delegation to the Fourth Congress of the Communist International. Though not a member of the American CP, McKay was welcomed as a fraternal delegate. Feted by the Russians as an authentic black revolutionary, McKay was deeply impressed by the egalitarianism of soviet society. At the congress, he gave a speech on the race question in the United States that influenced the drafting of the "Theses on the Negro Question" the congress released. While in Russia, he also wrote a book, *Negroes in America*, giving an analysis of the history of racism in America.

For the next few years, McKay moved frequently, spending time in Morocco and Western Europe. He returned to the United States in 1934. While continuing to write throughout this period, including several novels, McKay never regained the prominence he had in the postwar years. In 1944 he moved to Chicago to work with the Catholic Youth Organization, and he died there in 1948.

Further Reading

Cooper, Wayne. *Claude McKay: Rebel Sojourner in the Harlem Renaissance.* Baton Rouge: Louisiana State University Press, 1996.

Holcomb, Gary Edward. *Claude McKay, Code Name Sasha: Queer Black Marxism in the Harlem Renaissance.* Gainesville: University Press of Florida, 2007.

Maxwell, William J. *New Negro, Old Left: African American Writing and Communism Between the Wars.* New York: Columbia University Press, 1999.

Socialism and the Negro

Chiefly through the efforts of Dr. Du Bois, author of *The Souls of Black Folk*, there came into being in the United States, some ten years ago, the National Association for the Advancement of Colored People. In the main, the organization strove to combat the wide and insidious influence of Booker Washington who, making light of the social and political status of his race, had put into practice, for its material benefit, the principle of work advocated by the latter-day Carlyle. A group of wealthy and socially and politically influential bourgeois of the North, helped to launch the movement and became its directing spirit.

In it were men and women representative of the old conservative and Quaker aristocracy of New England and Pennsylvania, and the liberal capitalists. It comprised intellectual and commercial Jews, and its finest spirit was Oswald Garrison Villard, editor of the American *Nation* and grandson of the great Abolitionist, who, vilified and denounced by the hide-bound capitalist press, stands out as the solitary and only consistent representative of the American bourgeoisie, counseling peace and moderation between aggressive Capitalism and its government, and Militant Labor and Socialism, and all the forces of passion struggling in America today. This group, palpably ignorant of the fact that the Negro question is primarily an economic problem, evidently thought it might be solved by admitting Negroes who have won to wealth and intellectual and other attainments into white society on equal terms, and by protesting and pleading to the political and aristocratic South to remove the notorious laws limiting the political and social status of colored folk. So far as I am able to judge, it has done good work on the technically legal and educational side. It developed race-consciousness in the Negro and made him restive; but on the political side it has flirted with different parties and its work is quite ineffective.

Further, it has taken a firm stand against segregation, which is a moot

---

Originally published in *Workers' Dreadnought*, January 31, 1920, 1–2.

and delicate question. While all Negroes are agreed that the social barriers must be removed, there is much difference in regard to education and some institutions like hospitals and churches. The growing numbers of cultured Negro men and women find it extremely difficult to obtain employment that is in keeping with their education under the capitalist system of government. For one instance, had a scholar like Dr. Du Bois been white he would certainly have secured a chair at Harvard, Yale or Columbia University, for which he is eminently fitted. Many Negroes have obtained a sound education at great sacrifice, only to be forced, upon completion of their studies, into menial or uncongenial toil. In the black belt of New York City, where there is an estimated population of 100,000 Negroes, the Police Force, hospital, library, and elementary schools—patronized chiefly by colored people—are entirely manned by white staffs. It would be impossible for such conditions to exist under a soviet system of Government.

Just about the beginning of the late War the Socialists and the I.W.W., realizing that the Negro population offered a fertile field for propaganda, began working in earnest among them. With the aid of the *Messenger* magazine, edited by two ardent, young Negro university men, and the *Liberator*, they have done real constructive work that is now bearing fine fruit. The rank-and-file Negroes of America have been very responsive to the new truths. Some of them have been lured away by the siren call of the American Federation of Labor to enter its ranks. For years this reactionary association held out against Negro membership, but recently the capitalist class, alarmed over the growth of revolutionary thought among the blacks, used its creature, Gompers, to put through a resolution admitting Negroes to membership at the last conference. It has, however, had no effect on the lily-white and inconsequential trade unions of the South.

A splendid result of the revolutionary propaganda work among the blacks was the Conference of the National Brotherhood of Workers in America (entirely Negro) which was held at Washington, D.C., in September of last year. Its platform is as revolutionary in principle as that of the I.W.W. Over a hundred delegates were in attendance and the majority came from the South. As always, the colored workers are ready and willing to meet the white workers halfway in order that they might unite in the fight against capitalism; but, owing to the seeds of hatred that have been sown for long years by the master class among both sections, the whites are still reluctant to take the step that would win the South over to Socialism. The black workers hold the key to the situation, but while they and the white workers remain divided the reactionary South need not fear. The great task is to get both groups together. Colored men from the North cannot be sent into the South for propaganda purposes, for they will be lynched. White men from the North will be beaten and, if they don't leave, they will also be lynched. A like fate awaits colored women. But the South is boastful of its spirit of chivalry. It believes that it is the divinely appointed guardian of sacred white womanhood, and it professes to disfranchise, outrage and lynch Negro men and women solely for the protection of white women.

It seems then that the only solution to the problem is to get lovely and refined white women volunteers to carry the message of Socialism to both white and black workers. There are many of them in the movement who should be eager to go. During the period of Reconstruction a goodly number went from New England to educate the freedmen, and, although they were socially ostracized by the Southerners, they stood to their guns. Today they are needed more than ever. The call is louder and the cause is greater. Among the blacks they will be safe, respected and honored. Will they rise to their duty?

Strangely, it is the professional class of Negroes that is chiefly opposed to Socialism, although it is the class that suffers and complains most bitterly. Dr. Du Bois has flirted with the Socialist idea from a narrow, opportunist-racial standpoint, but he is in spirit opposed to it. If our Negro professionals are not blindly ignorant they should realize that there will never be any hope—no sound material place in the economic life of the world—for them until the Negro masses are industrially independent. Many colored doctors, lawyers, journalists, teachers and preachers literally starve and are driven to the wall because the black working class does not earn enough to give the adequate support. Naturally, the white workers will hardly turn from their kind to colored aspirants to the professions, even though the latter should possess exceptional ability. And even when they are capable they are often up against the prejudice of their own people who have been subtly taught by the white ruling class to despise the talented of their race and sneer at their accomplishments.

During the War, Marcus Garvey, a West Indian Negro, went to New York and formed the Universal Negro Improvement Association, and African Communities' League for the redemption of Negro Africa, and the return thither of Negroes in exile. The movement has had an astonishing success. Negroes from all parts of the world, oppressed by the capitalists, despised and denied a fighting chance under the present economic system by white workingmen, have hailed it as the star of hope, the ultimate solution of their history-old troubles. It numbers now over two million active members. The capitalist press which ridiculed it at first now mentions the Association in flattering terms, especially since it successfully floated the Black Star Line Steamship Company. At the beginning the company had much trouble with the local authorities, but it has never been persecuted by the State or Federal Government, for it is non-Socialistic, of course. Although an international Socialist, I am supporting the movement, for I believe that, for subject peoples, at least, Nationalism is the open door to Communism. Furthermore, I will try to bring this great army of awakened workers over to the finer system of Socialism. Some English Communists have remarked to me that they have no real sympathy for the Irish and Indian movement because it is nationalistic. But, today, the British Empire is the greatest obstacle to International Socialism, and any of its subjugated parts succeeding in breaking away from it would be helping the cause of World Communism. In these pregnant times no people who are strong enough to throw off an imperial yoke will tamely submit to system of local capitalism. The breaking up of the British Empire must either begin at home or abroad; the sooner the strong blow is struck the better it will be for all Communists. Hence the English revolutionary workers should not be unduly concerned over the manner in which the attack should begin. Unless, like some British intellectuals, they are enamored of the idea of a Socialist (?) British Empire! Unless they are willing to be provided with cheap raw materials by the slaves of Asia and Africa for the industries of their overcrowded cities, while the broad, fertile acres of Great Britain are held for hunting and other questionable pleasures.

How Black Sees Green and Red

Last summer I went to a big Sinn Fein demonstration in Trafalgar Square. The place was densely packed, the huge crowd spreading out into the Strand and up to the steps of the National Gallery. I was there selling the *Workers' Dreadnought*, Sylvia Pankhurst's pamphlet, *Rebel Ireland*, and Herman Gorter's *Ireland: The Achilles Heel of England*; I sold out completely. All Ireland was there. As I passed round eagerly in friendly rivalry with other sellers of my group, I remarked aged men and women in frayed, old fashioned clothes, middle aged couples, young stalwarts, beautiful girls and little children, all wearing the shamrock or some green symbol. I also wore a green necktie and was greeted from different quarters as "Black Murphy" or "Black Irish." With both hands and my bag full of literature I had to find time and a way for hearty handshakes and brief chats with Sinn Fein Communists and regular Sinn Feiners. I caught glimpses also of proud representatives of the Sinn Fein bourgeoisie. For that day at least I was filled with the spirit of Irish nationalism—although I am black!

Members of the bourgeoisie among the Sinn Feiners, like Constance Markievicz and Erskine Childers, always stress the fact that Ireland is the only "white" nation left under the yoke of foreign imperialism. There are other nations in bondage, but they are not of the breed; they are colored, some are even Negro. It is comforting to think that bourgeois nationalists and patriots of whatever race or nation are all alike in outlook. They chafe under the foreign bit because it prevents them from using to the full their native talent for exploiting their own people. However, a black worker may be sensitive to every injustice felt by a white person. And I, for one, cannot but feel a certain sympathy with these Irish rebels of the bourgeoisie.

But it is with the proletarian revolutionists of the world that my whole spirit revolts. It matters not that I am pitied, even by my white fellow-workers who are conscious of the fact that besides being an

Originally published in the *Liberator*, June 1921, 17, 20.

economic slave as they, I am what they are not—a social leper, of a race outcast from an outcast class. Theirs is a class, which though circumscribed in its sphere, yet has a freedom of movement—a right to satisfy the simple cravings of the body—which is denied to me. Yet I see no other way of upward struggle for colored peoples, but by way of the working-class movement, ugly and harsh though some of its phases may be. None can be uglier and harsher than the routine existence of the average modern worker. The yearning of the American Negro especially, can only find expression and realization in the class struggle. Therein lies his hope. For the Negro is in a peculiar position in America. In spite of a professional here and a business man there, the maintenance of an all-white supremacy in the industrial and social life, as well as the governing bodies of the nation, places the entire Negro race alongside the lowest section of the white working class. They are struggling for identical things. They fight along different lines simply because they are not as class-conscious and intelligent as the ruling classes they are fighting. Both need to be awakened. When a Negro is proscribed on account of his color, when the lynching fever seizes the South and begins to break out even in the North, the black race feels and thinks as a unit. But it has no sense of its unity as a class—or as a part, rather, of the American working-class, and so it is powerless. The Negro must acquire class-consciousness. And the white workers must accept him and work with him, whether they object to his color and morals or not. For his presence is to them a menacing reality.

American Negroes hold some sort of a grudge against the Irish. They have asserted that Irishmen have been their bitterest enemies, that the social and economic boycott against Negroes was begun by the Irish in the North during the Civil War and has, in the main, been fostered by them ever since. The Irish groups in America are, indeed, like the Anglo-Saxons, quite lacking in all the qualities that make living among the Latins tolerable for one of a conspicuously alien race. However I react more to the emotions of the Irish than to those of any other whites; they are so passionately primitive in their loves and hates. They are quite free of the disease which is known in bourgeois phraseology as Anglo-Saxon hypocrisy. I suffer with the Irish. I think I understand the Irish. My belonging to a subject race entitles me to some understanding of them. And then I was born and reared a peasant; the peasant's passion for the soil possesses me, and it is one of the strongest passions in the Irish revolution.

The English, naturally, do not understand the Irish, and the English will not understand unless they are forced to. Their imperialists will use the military in Ireland to shoot, destroy and loot. Their bourgeoisie will religiously try to make this harmonize with British morality. And their revolutionists—I would almost say that the English revolutionists, anarchists, socialists and communists, understand Ireland less than any other political group. It appears that they would like to link up with Irish national revolution to the English class struggle with the general headquarters in England. And as Sinn Fein does not give lip-service to communism, the English revolutionists are apparently satisfied in thinking that their sympathy lies with the Irish workers, but that they must back the red flag against the green.

And the Irish workers hate the English. It may not sound nice in the ears of an "infantile left" communist to hear that the workers of one country hate the workers of another. It isn't beautiful propaganda. Nevertheless, such a hatred does exist. In the past the Irish revolutionists always regarded the Royal Irish Constabulary as their greatest enemy. Until quite recently its members were recruited chiefly from the Irish workers themselves; but the soldiers of the Irish Republican Army shot down these uniformed men like dogs, and when at last thousands of them deserted to Sinn Fein, either from fear of their fighting countrymen, or by their finer instinct asserting itself, they were received as comrades—hid, fed, clothed and provided with jobs. I saw one of the official Sinn Fein bulletins which called upon the population to give succor to the deserting policemen. They were enemies only while they wore the uniform and carried out the orders of Dublin Castle. Now they are friends, and the British have turned to England and Scotland for recruits. And so all the hatred of Irish workers is turned against the English. They think, as do all subject peoples with foreign soldiers and their officers lording it over them, that even the exploited English proletariat are their oppressors.

And it is true at least that the English organized workers merrily ship munitions and men across the channel for the shooting of their Irish brothers. Last Spring, following on a little propaganda and agitation, some London railmen refused to haul munitions that were going to Ireland. They had acted on the orders of Cramp, the strong man of their union. But the railroad directors made threats and appealed to Lloyd George, who grew truculent. J.H. Thomas, the secretary of the Railwaymen's union, intervened and the order was gracefully rescinded. As usual, Thomas found the way out that was satisfactory to the moral conscience of the nation. It was not so much the hauling of munitions, he said, but the making of them that was wrong. The railroad workers should not be asked to shoulder the greatest burden of the workers' fight merely because they hold the key to the situation!

It is not the English alone, but also the Anglicized Irish who persist in misunderstanding Ireland. Liberals and reactionary socialists vie with each other in quoting Bernard Shaw's famous "Ireland Has a Grievance." Shaw was nice enough to let me visit him during my stay in London. He talked lovingly and eloquently of the beauty of medieval cathedrals. I was charmed by his clear, fine language, and his genial manner. Between remarking that Hyndman was typical of the popular idea of God, and asking me why I did not go in for pugilism instead of poetry—the only light thought that he indulged in—he told of a cultured Chinaman who came all the way from China to pay homage to him as the patriarch of English letters. And just imagine what the Chinaman wanted to talk about? Ireland! It was amusingly puzzling to Shaw! Yet it was easy for me to understand why a Chinaman whose country had been exploited, whose culture had been belittled and degraded by aggressive imperial nations, should want to speak to a representative Irishman about Ireland.

Whilst the eyes of the subject peoples of the world are fixed on Ireland, and Sinn Fein stands in embattled defiance against the government of the British Empire; whilst England proclaims martial law in Ireland, letting her Black and Tans run wild through the country, and Irish men and women are giving their lives daily for the ideal of freedom, Bernard Shaw dismisses the revolutionary phenomenon as a "grievance." Yet the Irish revolutionists love Shaw. An Irish rebel will say that Shaw is a British socialist who does not understand Ireland. But like Wilde he is an individual Irishman who has conquered England with his plays. There the fierce Irish pride asserts itself. Shaw belongs to Ireland.

I marvel that Shaw's attitude towards his native land should be similar to that of any English bourgeois reformist, but I suppose that anyone who has no faith, no real vision of International Communism, will agree with him. To the internationalist, it seems evident that the dissolution of the British Empire and the ushering in of an era of proletarian states, will give England her proper proportional place in the political affairs of the world.

The greatest tradition of England's glory flourishes, however, in quite unexpected places. Some English communists play with the idea of England becoming the center of International Communism just as she is the center of International Capitalism. I read recently an article by a prominent English communist on city soviets. It contained a glowing picture of the great slums transformed into beautiful dwellings and splendid suburbs. When one talks to a Welsh revolutionist, a Scottish communist, or an Irish rebel, one hears the yearning hunger of the people for the land in his voice. One sees it in his eyes. When one listens to an earnest Welsh miner, one gets the impression that he is sometimes seized with a desire to destroy the mine in which his life is buried. The English proletarian strikes one as being more matter-of-fact. He likes his factories and cities of convenient makeshifts. And when he talks of controlling and operating the workers for the workers, there burns no poetry in his eyes, no passion in his voice. English landlordism and capitalism have effectively and efficiently killed the natural hunger of the proletariat for the land. In England the land issue is raised only by the liberal-radicals, and finds no response in the heart of the proletariat. That is a further reason why England cannot understand the Irish revolution. For my part I love to think of communism liberating millions of city folk to go back to the land.

The English will not let go of Ireland. The militarists are hoping that the Irish people, persecuted beyond endurance, will rise protesting and demonstrating in a helpless and defenceless mass. Then they can be shot down as were the natives of Amritsar in India. But against a big background of experience the generals of the Irish Army are cautious. The population is kept under strict discipline. The systematic destruction of native industries by the English army of occupation forces them to adopt some communist measures for self-preservation. They are imbibing the atmosphere and learning the art of revolution. I heard from an Irish communist in London that some Indian students had been in Dublin to study that art where it is in practical preparation. It is impossible not to feel the Irish revolution—nationalistic though it is—is entering a wedge directed straight to the heart of British capitalism.

Letter to the Editor of the *Crisis*

I am surprised and sorry that in your editorial, "The Drive," published in the *Crisis* for May, you should leap out of your sphere to sneer at the Russian Revolution, the greatest event in the history of humanity; much greater than the French Revolution, which is held up as a wonderful achievement to Negro children and students in white and black schools. For American Negroes the indisputable and outstanding fact of the Russian Revolution is that a mere handful of Jews, much less in ratio to the number of Negroes in the American population, have attained, through the Revolution, all the political and social rights that were denied to them under the regime of the Czar.

Although no thinking Negro can deny the great work that the NAACP is doing, it must yet be admitted that from its platform and personnel the Association cannot function as a revolutionary working class organization. And the overwhelming majority of American Negroes belong by birth, condition and repression to the working class. Your aim is to get for the American Negro the political and social rights that are his by virtue of the Constitution, the rights which are denied him by the Southern oligarchy with the active cooperation of the state governments and the tacit support of northern business interests. And your aim is a noble one, which deserves the support of all progressive Negroes.

But the Negro in politics and social life is ostracized only technically by the distinction of color; in reality the Negro is discriminated against because he is of the lowest type of worker.

Obviously, this economic difference between the white and black workers manifests itself in various forms, in color of prejudice, race hatred, political and social boycotting and lynching if Negroes. And all the entrenched institutions of white America—law courts, churches, schools, the fighting forces and the Press—condone these iniquities perpetrated upon black men; iniquities that are dismissed indifferently as the inevitable

---

Originally published in the *Crisis* 22, No. 3 (July 1921): 102.

result of the social system. Still, whenever it suits the business interests controlling these institutions to mitigate the persecutions against Negroes, they do so with impunity. When organized white workers quit their jobs, Negroes, who are discouraged by the whites to organize, are sought to take their places. And these strike-breaking Negroes work under the protection of the military and the police. But as ordinary citizens and workers, Negroes are not protected by the military and the police from the mob. The ruling classes will not grant Negroes those rights which, on a lesser scale and more plausibly, are withheld from the white proletariat. The concession of these rights would immediately cause a Revolution in the economic life of this country.

Robert Minor

Introduction

Robert Minor (1884–1952) was an American communist writer and cartoonist. Originally an anarchist, Minor converted to Bolshevism after traveling to revolutionary Russia, and he remained a loyal Communist Party member for the rest of his life. During the party's early years, he was the party's leading intellectual on the race question, and one of the first white members to devote significant attention to the issue.

Minor was born to a distinguished but poor Texan family. Unable to attend school for most of his childhood, he entered the workforce early, using his natural artistic talents to labor as a sign-painter. This talent eventually enabled him to find work as a newspaper cartoonist, and by 1911 he was the highest-paid cartoonist in the country.

Along the way, Minor had also turned to anarchism. Originally an SP member, around 1912 he sided with Big Bill Haywood and the other IWW supporters against the SP leadership. When World War I broke out, his employers tried to force him to draw pro-war cartoons, but Minor refused, moving to New York instead to begin drawing for the radical press. He found employment with the New York *Call*, the SP's New York paper, and also wrote for Max Eastman's *Masses*, a magazine of the radical Greenwich Village bohemians.

In 1918, he was sent to cover the war in Europe. After some adventures there, including being arrested for advising French workers to go on strike, he found himself in Russia in mid-1918. There, he interviewed Lenin and observed the new Soviet society. While generally skeptical, on anarchist grounds, within a few months he was won over to Bolshevism. When he returned to the United States, he joined the Communist Party.

In the party, Minor distinguished himself by his knowledge of and devotion to the struggle against racism. Early on, Minor had rebelled against the racism of his southern origins; while working in New York, he had become fast friends with Lovett Fort-Whiteman and accompanied him on his ill-fated attempt to organize the South. When the Comintern passed its theses on the Negro question in 1922, it created a new organizational niche in the CP that Minor was well suited to fill. He became responsible for reporting on party work on the race question to the Central Executive Committee.

In the party's factional battles of this period, Minor was firmly allied with Ruthenberg and Lovestone's wing of the party. Partly as a result of Minor's presence in this faction, race work in general became associated with the Ruthenberg faction. Indeed, William Z. Foster's faction was often attacked on the grounds that it accommodated itself to racism—an unfair accusation that Minor was often at the forefront of spreading.

When Ruthenberg died in 1927, and Jay Lovestone began his short-lived reign in the party, Minor continued as a supporter of his leadership. However, when Lovestone fell out of favor with Joseph Stalin, Minor quickly realigned his loyalties, throwing his support behind Stalin's new favorite, Foster.

Over the next two decades, Minor would continue to be a prominent leader of the party in New York, running for state office multiple times. In the mid-1930s, he went to Spain to help organize the Abraham Lincoln Brigades. Minor would continue to be a prominent party figure until 1948, when he suffered a heart attack that removed him from political activity.

Further Reading

Draper, Theodore. *The Roots of American Communism*. New Brunswick, NJ: Transaction Publishers, 2003 [1957].

North, Joseph. *Robert Minor, Artist and Crusader: An Informal Biography*. New York: International Publishers, 1956.

Solomon, Mark. *The Cry Was Unity: Communists and African Americans, 1917–1936*. Jackson: University Press of Mississippi, 1998.

The Black Ten Millions

Within the great white city of New York is another city of one-quarter of a million Negroes. Five other great American cities have within each of them a Black City of more than 100,000 inhabitants.

The separateness of the Black Cities within the white is fairly complete. The Negro may freely visit the white town, and may work there the day through, but, come the end of his labor, must return, be it to sleep, to eat or to amuse himself, to his own pale.

The Black Man has a culture of his own: his musicians, his poets, novelists, actors, students, his bourgeoisie, his scientific men and—his apostles of liberty. The Black Man of the city is a restless man; he wants to break down all the humiliating restrictions that confine him as a lower race, the "white supremacy" that loads his life down with limitations and holds him to a "black belt" as a prostitute is segregated.

The city Negro is the articulate Negro. It is he who forms the many organizations which have the purpose of completing the emancipation of his race. And among the city Negroes it is the Negro "inteligentzia" which at present has the lead. Thus it is characteristic that Professor Kelley Miller, Dean of Howard University, Washington, D. C., and a noted scholar, has sent out the call which brings together in Chicago on February 11, 1924, a national conference of organizations especially concerned with Negro emancipation. It is called the "Sandhedrin Conference," in memory of the ancient Jewish racial council at Jerusalem. The conference is sponsored by the National Association for the Advancement of Colored People, the Equal Rights League and the African Blood Brotherhood.

The "Negro Sandhedrin" will be a bold attempt to gather all Negro and mixed pro-Negro organizations into a "united Negro front" on a common program for race emancipation. If it were merely a matter of a few hundred Negro intellectuals gathering decorously to discuss ways and means of

---

Originally published in the *Liberator*, February 1924, 7–9.

smoothing their professional careers, one need pay little attention. But back of these intellectual leaders are the Black Ten Millions that stir in unhappy slavery on plantations from Florida to Texas and in ill-paid labor in factory, mine, mill and lumber-camp the country over. The unrest of these is pressing the intellectuals forward to perhaps greater lengths than they as yet dream of going. No matter what mild speaking may be heard from the black prophets of today, the Negro in the vast heart of his race wants, and cannot stop with less than, complete and unqualified equality both in law and in social custom. Leaders may promise to take less, but the black race will ultimately walk over the faces of any such leaders.

Slave Revolts

It is a mistake to assume that the Negro was a submissive slave. Even before the American revolution there were twenty-five insurrections of Negroes against slavery in the American colonies. One of the reasons given in favor of the adoption of the American Constitution in 1787 was that it made possible the formation of a national army with which to suppress the then threatened slave rebellions of Georgia and other southern states, which it was feared that no single Southern state with its own army would be able to suppress.

And the fears were justified. A dozen slave rebellions, large and small, occurred in the United States after the American revolution and before the Civil War of 1861. The nineteenth century began with one thousand armed slaves marching against Richmond, Virginia, led by two Negro slaves, Gabriel and Jack Bowler. Two years later an area covering ten counties in North Carolina was the scene of an armed insurrection of Negroes, and this was followed three years later by another. In the year 1811 a little army of five hundred armed slaves marched against the city of New Orleans, recruiting the adult male Negro population of each plantation as it passed. The insurrection was crushed by the garrison of Fort Charles after a military engagement. Five years later a planned slave insurrection at Fredericksburg, Virginia, was prematurely disclosed and its leaders hanged. A similar disturbance occurred in Camden, South Carolina, in that year, followed two years later by another at Charleston, South Carolina. In the next year, 1819, a Negro slave insurrection was attempted in Augusta, Georgia.

In 1822 a wide-spread conspiracy for a slave insurrection was organized by that strange Negro genius, Denmark Vesey. Throughout an area of forty or fifty miles around Charleston, South Carolina, the best of the Negroes were carefully and secretly organized by a recruiting committee. One organizer, Peter Poyas, is said to have sworn in six hundred persons. The mistake was made of trusting a meek household servant, who betrayed the plot. Thirty five leaders of the plot were hanged, including Denmark Vesey—to whom, I swear, a monument will some day be raised in Charleston, South Carolina.

Nine years later, 1831, the Negro preacher, Nat Turner, led an armed insurrection in Southampton County, Virginia, which was put down by United States troops and state militia with the loss of the lives of one hundred Negroes and sixty white persons. Twenty Negroes were afterward hanged. Before the year ended another rebellion began in three counties of North Carolina, but was betrayed by a free Negro and crushed. In Maryland there was an uprising of slaves in 1845, followed by disturbances in 1853 and in 1857. John Brown's raid on Harper's Ferry in 1859 was an attempt at Negro uprising incited and led by a white man. Because it occurred at a tense political moment it has been made in our histories to overshadow the greater uprisings which were inspired, organized and led by Negroes alone. The John Brown insurrection was comparatively and actually very small.

The outstanding fact is that the American Negro has found within his own race both the genius and the daring to fight for his freedom. That the desperate and unsuccessful insurrections of the slavery days were inadequate in method and pitifully ineffective is beside the point: The Negro possesses the initiative and the courage to make his a free race.

After Emancipation

For fifty years after the Civil War the Negro wandered in a fog of republican "emancipation." He was "free" to starve or to sell himself back to the white landlord. The white ruling class considered merely that they had been deprived of certain property, but not in the least that the Negro had attained "social and political equality with white persons," as a South Carolina statute of 1865 put it. Lincoln's "Emancipation Proclamation" of 1863 had, according to its own wording, not the purpose of abolishing slavery, but the purpose of breaking the economic backbone of a rival war-power. The aim was not to free the Negro but to destroy $1,500,000,000 worth of property in "black ivory" of a belligerent enemy. The "Preliminary Proclamation" directly offered to leave slavery intact in any part of the South that would lay down its arms. The "Emancipation Proclamation" very carefully specified that slavery should not be abolished "for the present" in sections of Louisiana and Virginia not at that time in arms against the Union.

The ex-slave was legally not a citizen, but a "freedman"—quite a different thing; he was property that had been confiscated as a means of punishment of his owners. The Negro had, in Southern eyes, been changed from a domesticated animal to an undomesticated animal.

When the Fourteenth Amendment to the Constitution was ratified in 1868, giving the rights of citizenship to "all persons born or naturalized in the United States"—and when the Fifteenth Amendment was ratified in 1870, providing that "the right of the citizens of the United States to vote shall not be denied or abridged by the United States, or by any State, on account of race, color, or previous condition of servitude,"—these Constitutional provisions merely refined the skill of Southern lawyers in writing laws to disfranchise and de-citizenize the Negro.

The emancipation of the American Negro from chattel slavery has not yet been completed. The Negro "share" farmer or tenant-farmer is still to all intents and purposes the slave of his white landlord. The white landlord continues to take the product of the labor of the Negro, and gives in return, in almost the same manner as seventy-five years ago, little more than a miserable ration of food. In Turner County, Georgia, in 1913 "the average annual cash income per Negro tenant farmer—usually a family—was only $290." The Negro tenant is kept in debt to his white exploiter, sometimes for an entire lifetime, and his "running away" is often forcibly prevented as long as his white overlord owns a "debt"—interest in his body. Peonage, a close imitation of chattel slavery, is still accomplished with the device of convicting men (both black and white, nowadays!) of "vagrancy" or "idling," or sometimes for real offenses, and then leasing them out to planters, mine-owners, lumber operators or contractors for periods of months or years. The recent cases of Martin Tabor (white) who was beaten to death by a "whipping boss" in Florida, and the eleven Negroes who were murdered on a peonage-farm in Jasper County, Georgia, are examples of a "sacred institution" of our Country.

The Negro is still not a citizen in the South. Places of public resort are divided as are the buildings of farmhouses for the (white) human beings and barns for the (Negro) animals. The railroads provide cattle-cars for cattle and Negro-cars for Negroes. In many parts of the South

(Alabama, Florida) Negroes are kept out of public parks and playgrounds; sometimes "Jim Crow" parks and playgrounds are provided. Throughout the South it is taken for granted that Negroes are not to be permitted to live in houses near the residences of the well-to-do whites. Commonly Southern towns have their "red-light" districts and their "nigger-towns"— often jumbled together for the sake of real-estate convenience. Segregation is sometimes accomplished by law—as in Tulsa, Oklahoma, among many other localities—and sometimes by terrorism alone.

Occasionally there has come over the White South a panic due to a fear that the Negro parent's zeal for educating his black child is raising the literacy of the Negro child above that of the poor white. But the white man is doing his best to keep the Negro behind the white. In South Carolina, where the Negro population approaches that of the whites, ten million dollars is spent to educate white children, while one million is spent for a similar number of Negro children. It is claimed that in some parts of the South when the Negro progresses too far the Negro schoolhouses are burned.

They say that the Negro is not disfranchised in the South, and then they explain that he is permitted to vote whenever and to whatever extent that his vote won't win anything. Throughout the South wherever the Negro population outnumbers or dangerously approximates the white population in number, the Negro is frankly and openly excluded from the ballot to an extent sufficient to give the white man a guarantee of control. Then, in most cases, the real election takes place in the Democratic primaries, where the Negro is barred, and the formal election follows automatically. The disfranchisement of the Negro is considered basic in the political system. And the tendency to transform Negro disfranchisement into working-class disfranchisement is already apparent. Three years ago the editor of the *Birmingham News* made a serious proposal that "high-class" Negroes (of the new Negro bourgeoisie) should be carefully selected and given the "privilege" of voting.

The Rise of the Black Giant

The tremors of the World War that shook the world to its foundations, did not fail to reach the Negro. To be exempted from conscription was a privilege, and the "damn nigger" received no privilege. 367,710 young Negro men were drafted and given military training. About 200,000 had the amazing experience of a trip to Europe and a flickering glimpse of what is called "social equality"—yes, even between black men and white women. The American Negro who went to France did not, when he returned, fit into the scheme of the plantation and the overseer.

What is more exciting, his neck no longer fitted meekly into the lyncher's noose! The young Negroes who had had the awakening experience of the War, and associates influenced by them, began to transform the *lynching* into what is called a *riot*—that is, a *two-sided* fight.

But it really began before the men went to France. A young Negro friend has told me of the pride and newfound security that he felt on the day of his first leave after being mobilized, when, in his new uniform, accompanied by a half-dozen of his fellow Negro soldiers, he strolled in the streets of a Southern city where before then he had never been free of the uneasiness engendered by white terrorism.

In 1917 Corporal Baltimore of the 24th (Negro) Infantry, then waiting at Houston, Texas, to be shipped to France, interfered with two policemen who were beating a Negro woman on the street. The result was—not a lynching this time, but a race-battle in which many were killed. The military authorities stepped in on behalf of the whites and hanged nineteen of the Negro soldiers. Fifty-four members of the 24th Infantry are now confined in Leavenworth penitentiary. Thus, when the Negro defends himself the Law steps in to complete the thwarted lynching.

From March 1919, when a white man attempted to exercise his privilege of slapping a "nigger woman" on a Birmingham street car and was killed for it by a Negro man, there has been a long series of incidents called "race riots" in Charleston S.C., Chicago Ills., Elaine Arkansas, Knoxville Tenn., Longview Texas, Omaha Neb., Washington D.C., Duluth Minn., Independence Kansas, Ocoee Florida, Springfield Ohio and Tulsa Oklahoma. Nearly all of these incidents would a few years ago have taken the form of a simple, respectable lynching of a Negro "without disorder." But with what the Negroes call their "new attitude," practically all of these incidents now take the form of terrific two-sided fights in which the Negroes in resisting lynching take white life for black life. As reported in the *New York Age* (Negro):

> The colored people of the District of Columbia have shown what a people can do when assailed on all hands by mob fury and deserted by the police power of the District and by the Federal Government, both

of which to all intents and purposes threw their organized influence against the colored people, the victims of the fury of the mob.

Disorganized as they were, and without leadership, when the rioting was started Saturday night and continuing through Sunday and Sunday night, without any effective interference on the part of the police, colored people were prepared on Monday to defend themselves, after a fashion, and began to do so with a grim determination to exact a life for a life. They entered into the strife with more determination than the whites who started it, and they stuck to the job all week like heroes of many battles.

The Great Migration

But mobilization in the army was not the biggest means with which the World War wrought its changes in the life of the Negro. Just at the moment when the Northern manufacturers began to book huge orders for war supplies—the war shut off the customary source of American industrial labor: European immigration. Northern manufacturers began to dip into the great stagnant pool of the South for black labor-power. At first the White South was glad to see the Negro go, but soon began to change its mind and to try to stem the tide. At the end of hostilities and of war-manufacture, it is estimated a quarter of a million Southern Negroes remained in the North, charmed by the comparative freedom and better living standards into forgetfulness of "Dixie." With the first industrial slump the Cleveland Chamber of Commerce, for instance, became worried about the 20,000 new Negroes in the city, and considered ways and means to get rid of them; until business revived and made them useful. The Negro population of Detroit rose from about 5,700 in 1910 to about 53,000 in 1923.

The Black "Foreigner" (Part I)

Afraid that immigrant labor would bring the revolutionary fever of Europe to our shores, Congress passed the severely restrictive immigration law. At the same time began the after-war industrial revival demanding cheap immigrant labor.

The Southern Negro became the "immigrant laborer." The rumor of "high wages and human treatment" that had once gathered the millions of

Eastern and Southern Europe now swept the Black South of the United States. It is recorded that one Negro church at Lone Oak, Georgia, lost ninety-eight members between a Saturday evening and Sunday morning. 478,700 are said to have migrated in one year. The total of the great migration is roughly estimated at one million.

Georgian agriculture is said to have suffered $25,000, 000 of damage in 1923 through the loss of its black peons. Other Southern States had similar experiences. The result of the migration was called by many writers a "revolution." It is said that the South will be forced now to discard its primitive economic processes and to "machinize" itself. And Northern industry is also profoundly affected by the introduction of the new and dark-faced "immigrant labor."

But most of all the *Negro* is affected. James Weldon Johnson, secretary of the National Association for the Advancement of Colored People, is quoted as declaring the great migration to be the greatest single factor in the twentieth century emancipation of the race. Whatever the objective reasons, the Negro has his own subjective reasons for no longer "wishing he was in Dixie," and he states them as:

> Mob violence.
> Inferior schools.
> Low wages.
> Inequality of law enforcement.

Let no one imagine, however, that the Negro escapes discrimination when he escapes from the South. As fast as the Negro becomes a large factor in the Northern cities and industrial centers, most of the persecutions, petty and large—especially lynching and segregation—follow at his heels. American capitalism cannot accept race equality. In fact race discrimination appears to be increasing with the bourgeois development. Racial residential segregation is as rigid in the big Northern cities as in those of the South— and seems to be in process of extension to the Jews! Advertisements for apartments to let, often carry the proviso, "for Gentiles," meaning that Jews are excluded as well as Negroes, whose exclusion is taken for granted. Race discrimination is on the up-grade, not the down-grade, in these mad days of capitalist decay.

The Black Ten Millions (Part II)

What does the Negro in America require in order to escape his condition as an oppressed race? He requires:

Abolition of restrictions upon his right of residence; that is, abolition of "black-belt" segregation. Abolition of distinction between Colored and white children in the schools; which distinction, with segregation, results not only in perpetuating race hatred, but also in the starvation of Negro schools.

Equal right to vote in the South. The organization of millions of unorganized Negro wage-laborers in industry, in the same unions with white workers.

The organization of the Negro tenant farmers and share-farmers of the South to fight against peonage and other terrible hardships.

Abolition of laws in the Southern states which put the Negro on a sub-human plane, such as the laws against inter-marriage.

Abolition of the Jim Crow system on the railroads, in the parks, theatres, hotels, restaurants, and other public conveniences.

Drastic measures against lynching.

Drastic measures against the Ku Klux Klan.

Organized solidarity with the other groups of his oppressed race in other countries for common relief.

The Negro Sanhedrin

How did the Negro fare in the supposedly great gathering of all Negro organizations, the Negro Sanhedrin Conference just closed in Chicago?

Originally published in the *Liberator*, March 1924, 15–17.

All of the above questions were placed before the conference. The outcome of each was as follows:

When it came to the question of housing, it became evident that the Sanhedrin conference was heavily dominated by Negro business men. These men are theoretically in favor of the emancipation of their race. And they talk eloquently to this effect. But when Negro working people among the delegates, through a delegate representing the Workers Party, offered a resolution calling for legislation by which the black-belt residence district could be broken up and landlords compelled to rent living quarters at a fixed rental to the first comer regardless of color and independently of the landlord's will, this measure was killed because the Negro real-estate men make enormous profits by confining the Negro tenant to a given district and charging him from twenty per cent more to twice as much as is paid for similar residence by white persons. The Negro had to give up that demand in deference to the Negro real-estate men.

When approximately the same working-class elements supported a measure demanding the abolition of separate schools for white and Colored children, on the ground that such separation is but the preparation for a future life of segregation, a Negro school-teacher from Virginia arose and protested excitedly against committing the Sanhedrin to such a measure. The very evident and scarcely concealed reason was that he was doing very well in a good job; since he profited by segregation of the Negro race in schools the Negro must remain segregated. The Sanhedrin conference was slightly besprinkled with Negro employment agents connected with the white chambers of commerce. So the Sanhedrin flatly and cold-bloodedly rejected the proposal to organize the millions of Negro industrial workers and confined their expression to a mild and meaningless phrase about equality in the labor unions for such negro wage-workers as are *already* organized.

When it came to the question of treating the Negro as a human being before the law in the most intimate phase of life, the phase of marriage— of course, everyone agreed that the black and the white race have always mixed and are now mixing, and that laws against intermarriage are merely laws protecting the Southern white man in illicit sexual practices. But when the working-class delegates, through the Workers Party delegation, offered a motion demanding the abolition of the laws against intermarriage—it turned out that so many of the gentlemen and ladies present had to cater to the good-will of white philanthropists that the

Sanhedrin conference had to give up any idea of demanding equality in law respecting marriage.

Every suggestion of organizing the millions of black tenant-farmers and share-farmers who live in virtual peonage in the South was too offensive to the well-dressed business-men and women, so the plan to organize the Negro tenant and share-farmers had to be dropped in favor of a meaningless phrase.

A vigorous resolution for organized protection against the Ku Klux Klan, introduced by the (working class) African Blood Brotherhood, was coldly rejected.

In short, nearly every measure that the Black Ten Millions require ran headlong into one vested interest or another of the Negro bourgeoisie, and expired, leaving this "All-Race" conference of American Negroes on record practically for the preservation of the present condition of the Negro.

Why? Because in this conference the Negro business man and society lady undertook to be the spokesmen of their people. And the Black Ten Millions have, to a certain extent, consented to let them be the spokesmen. The Negro in America is more or less proud of his bourgeoisie, or thinks he is; he has been trained to think, and he is now being propagandized to think that to have a class of prosperous, well-dressed, limousine-riding members of his race, is somehow to get out of the wilderness of oppression. The outcome of this conference ought to be a flash of light to the toiling, suffering black millions: the Negro bourgeoisie is allied, hopelessly tied up with the white bourgeoisie; the white bourgeoisie ruled the Sanhedrin conference through its allies, the Negro bourgeoisie.

In referring to the "Negro bourgeoisie," however, it must be remembered that it is, correctly speaking, a petty bourgeoisie, subject to wavering between the capitalist and working classes, as was shown by the strong response to speeches of the African Blood Brotherhood and Workers Party delegates.

Mass Organization

But there is much more to the Negro movement than appeared at this gathering. The great, silent millions who had so few champions there, have not been left untouched by the World War. The stirring of the Black Waters in 1917 started a new spring to flowing—the spring of mass-organization. Many important Negro organizations exist and have existed for a long time. But none of them were mass-organizations.

The close of the war-period brought a new phenomenon—hundreds of thousands closely organized on a program of militant activity for race emancipation. The new phenomenon took place under the fantastic leadership of Marcus Garvey.

The biggest and most remarkable of all Negro organizations, the followers of Marcus Garvey, refused to be represented in the Sanhedrin. This is much to be regretted. One may laugh at this self-styled "Emperor of Africa" and point out the hollowness of his program to "redeem the Ancient Kingdom of Ethiopia" by reconquering Africa for the Negro. Garvey may be what his critics call him: a windbag and self-seeker. But that does not close the question, for this writer. For the fact remains that *Garvey organized four hundred thousand Negroes*—the first compact mass organization of the race ever formed in the world.

Seven years ago this lone Negro landed in the United States from Jamaica, to proselytize for the "Universal Negro Improvement Association," which he had formed in Jamaica in 1914. There is a curious prejudice between Jamaica Negroes and American Negroes. Yet Garvey in five years destroyed the tradition that the American Negro masses cannot be organized. He organized nearly half a million active, dues-paying members (he claimed four million members) on a basis of militant race-consciousness. Race-consciousness in a dominant race takes the form of race arrogance, and we are accustomed to despise it as reactionary (which it is). But race-consciousness in a people just emerged from slavery and still spurned as an inferior people may be, and in this case is, *revolutionary*. True, Garvey is a Bolshevik-baiter. True, he might be called a "monarchist" since he set himself up as the "Negro King." He may yet be an instrument of the worst reaction and of ruin to his people, as indicated by his advice to them not to oppose the Ku Klux Klan, and by his recent concession to "white supremacy."

But Garvey's Universal Negro Improvement Association is a mass organization of four hundred thousand race-conscious Negroes, brought together on the basis of determination to throw off the remaining traces of slavery. *Such a phenomenon cannot occur without revolutionary effect*, no matter what its declaration of aims may be. Garvey's organization fiercely proclaims itself to be a submissive, docile, anti-Bolshevik, reactionary organization. It tries to be. But look over the spontaneous, classic cry of the Black Spartacus that rings through its fifty-four articles of faith adopted in its 1920 convention:

. . . 2. That we believe in the supreme authority of our race in all things racial; that all things are created and given to man as a common possession; that there should be an equitable distribution and apportionment of all such things, and in consideration of the fact that as a race we are now deprived of those things that are morally and legally ours, we believed it right that all such things should be acquired and held by whatsoever means possible. . . .

7. We believe that any law or practice that tends to deprive any African of his land or the privileges of free citizenship within his country is unjust and immoral, and no native should respect any such law or practice.

8. . . . there should be no obligation on the part of the Negro to obey the levy of a tax by any law-making body from which he is excluded and denied representation on account of his race and color.

9. We believe that any law especially directed against the Negro to his detriment and singling him out because of his race or color is unfair and immoral, and should not be respected. . . .

12. We believe that the Negro should adopt every means to protect himself against barbarous practices inflicted upon him because of color. . . .

16. We believe all men should live in peace one with the other, but when races and nations provoke the ire of other races and nations by attempting to infringe upon their rights, war becomes inevitable, and the attempt in any way to free one's self or protect one's rights or heritage becomes justifiable.

17. Whereas, the lynching, by burning, hanging or any other means, of human beings is a barbarous practice, and a shame and disgrace to civilization, we therefore declare any country guilty of such atrocities outside the pale of civilization. . . .

38. We demand complete control of our social institutions without interference by any alien race or races. . . .

45. Be it further resolved that we as a race of people declare the League of Nations null and void as far as the Negro is concerned, in that it seeks to deprive Negroes of their liberty. . . .

47. We declare that no Negro shall engage himself in battle for any alien race without first obtaining the consent of the leader of the Negro people of the world, except in a matter of national self-defense.

Which Way?

On what road lies the Negro's way to freedom? Can the Negro obtain free admission into the white bourgeois class, while a society of class superiority and class inferiority continues to exist?

Of course it is "theoretically" possible that with the retention of an upper and a lower class, the more prosperous Negro might be admitted to the upper class. But in hard reality:

1. Those Negroes who in spite of all handicaps accumulate property, are not admitted to terms of equality with the white bourgeoisie.

2. In the struggle (inevitable and now going on) between the capitalist class and the working class, the capitalist class never fails to stimulate and use every possible race prejudice—one of its chief means of dividing the adversary—class. Never a strike occurs in a big industry employing several nationalities of labor, but the employers strain every device for awakening jealousies and suspicions between the nationalities. The basic industries of America habitually and systematically choose several nationalities for employment in each plant, thus to prevent cohesion. The flames of race-hatred between the blacks and the whites can be made to burn to ashes any labor-solidarity when the employer's provocateur sets the match. This has been proven again and again with wearying repetition, in the great steel strike, the packing-house strikes, railroad shopmen's strike and countless others.

The capitalist class cannot forego the powerful weapon of race-division in its sharp struggle to divide and conquer labor. Those who would retain the division of society into an upper and a lower class, must and will retain race prejudice and the present "white supremacy" as sacred American institutions. Taking the facts as they are: In a class society the Negro will inevitably be used as bait for race hatred in the waters of class conflict.

The Republican Party Goes Over to "White Supremacy"

The old, sentimental tradition to the effect that the Republican party seeks the freedom of the Negro is being exploded. Since 1875 the tradition has been a lie. Since the World War it has become a farce.

Capitalist interests have depended upon using alternately the Republican and Democratic parties. In those seasons when circumstances compelled their backing the Republican party, they found it embarrassing that the Solid White South voted always and automatically the Democratic ticket. With the Republican party black, there was no two-party system in the South. Yet the South is fixed in "white supremacy." To be able to swing the South at will either to the Republican party or to the Democratic party, the capitalist interests had to make the Republican party acceptable to the southern white man. To get the white vote, the semi-disfranchised and therefore half-useless Negro has to be disowned. So we see the Republican Party in a "Lily-White" movement in Virginia, Georgia and Maryland, notably, and in other southern states to a less degree. In Virginia the leading Republican politicians have declared in principle against the holding of office by Negroes, but generously granting that the Negro should still have the right to vote for white candidates. In Louisville, Kentucky, the Republican political leaders adopted the practice of excluding Negroes from republican nomination; and the Negroes retaliated by putting up an all-Negro ticket for municipal offices.

In October, 1921, President Harding tried to draw the "white supremacy" vote toward the Republican party. He made a speech attuned to "white supremacy." With a little carefully applied salve for the Negroes along the conventional lines of ambiguity, Harding committed himself and his party as "uncompromisingly against every suggestion of social equality"—which, as far as it means anything, means every form of right that anyone may want to deprive the Negro of. To rid the Republican party of the black stigma to Southern white eyes, he even suggested that the (voteless) Alabama Negro ought sometimes to "vote for Democratic candidates"! And Mr. Coolidge in his turn appointed Slemp—whom the Negroes call "Lily-White Slemp"— to be his secretary-for-Southern-vote-catching.

The Negro started his American career in the class of "hewers of wood and drawers of water." He is there now. It is to the interest of the ruling class to keep him there, and at the same time to keep him divided from the other "hewers of wood and drawers of water"—the white working class— by fanning the flames of race prejudice. It is to the interest of all hewers of wood and drawers of water—white and black—to overcome race prejudice and to come together.

The Negro's fate in America lies in the labor movement, and there it is bound up with the exponents of the new order—the "radicals"—those who are fighting against the skilled labor caste system and broadening the labor movement out to the vast millions equally.

But the Negro's fate is a political question. Again we say the Negro cannot free himself from lower-class status, nor from the race-hatreds utilized to preserve the class system, until he helps to overthrow the class system. To get out of the exploited class, the Negro must abolish the exploited class.

Where Are the Negro's Allies?

To discover the forces that are ready to join hands with the Negro for his emancipation, for his equality without reservation or evasion, it would be well to compare the utterances of the American Negro bourgeoisie and intellectuals with the utterances of the Communist International. The last Congress of the Communist International adopted a drastic program for the solution of the Negro's problem, both in America and internationally, and the following are extracts from its decisions:

> (3) It is with intense pride that the Communist International sees the exploited Negro workers resist the attacks of the exploiter, for the enemy of his race and the enemy of the white workers is one and the same—Capitalism and Imperialism. The international struggle of the Negro race is a struggle against Capitalism and Imperialism. It is on the basis of this struggle that the world Negro movement must be organized. In America, as the center of Negro culture and the crystallization of Negro protest; in Africa, the reservoir of human labor for the further development of capitalism; in Central America (Costa Rica, Guatemala, Colombia, Nicaragua and other "independent" republics), where American imperialism dominates in Porto Rico, Haiti, Santo Domingo and other islands washed by the waters of the Caribbean, where the brutal treatment of our black fellow-men by the American occupation has aroused the protest of the conscious Negro and the revolutionary white workers everywhere; in South Africa and the Congo, where the growing industrialization of the Negro population has resulted in various forms of uprisings; in East Africa, where the recent penetration of world capital is stirring the native populations into an active opposition to imperialism, in all these centers the Negro movement must be organized. . . .

> (6) 1. The Fourth Congress recognizes the necessity of supporting every form of Negro movement which tends to undermine or weaken capitalism or imperialism or to impede its further penetration.

2. The Communist International will fight for race equality of the Negro with the white people, as well as for equal wages and political and social rights.

3. The Communist International will use every instrument within its control to compel the trade-unions to admit Negro workers to membership or, where the nominal right to join exists, to agitate for a special campaign to draw them into the unions. Failing in this, it will organize the Negroes into unions of their own and specially apply the United Front tactic to compel admission to the unions of the white men.

4. The Communist International will take immediate steps to hold a general Negro Conference or Congress in Moscow.

Lovett Fort-Whiteman

Introduction

L ovett Fort-Whiteman (1894–1939) was one of the most important early
black American Communists. Fort-Whiteman joined the Communist
Party soon after its founding, rapidly becoming the chief organizer
of its work among African Americans. After spending time in the USSR
at Comintern schools, Fort-Whiteman returned to the United States to
launch a new communist organization dedicated to Black struggle. In 1930,
having fallen out of favor with the CP leadership, Fort-Whiteman moved
back to Moscow, working as a Comintern functionary. In the late 1930s,
he fell victim to Stalin's purges and died in a labor camp at age forty-four.

Fort-Whiteman was born in Dallas, Texas, to a family on its way into
the middle class. Both Lovett and his sister attended the Tuskegee Institute,
and Lovett entered medical school soon after. The profession wasn't for him,
however, and he soon moved to New York to become an actor. When the
stage didn't provide a remunerative career, Fort-Whiteman left for Mexico.

Soon after he arrived in Southern Mexico, the Mexican Revolution
began. This would prove the impetus to Fort-Whiteman's radicalization,
and he was quickly swept up in the struggles that accompanied the
revolution's progress. Fort-Whiteman joined a Mexican syndicalist union,
and became a socialist.

In 1917 he moved back to New York, and joined the Socialist Party. He
began writing for the *Messenger* and took classes at the SP's Rand School
of Social Science. When, in 1919, the Left Wing of the SP formed to push
the party to affiliate with the Comintern, he joined it immediately. As the
party fractured along factional lines, Fort-Whiteman headed South to
organize Black workers in Dixie. His sojourn South was abruptly ended,

however, when he was arrested in St. Louis for giving an agitational speech authorities claimed violated the Espionage Act. Fort-Whiteman spent the next several months in jail.

While little is known of the years immediately following his arrest, by 1924 Fort-Whiteman had emerged as a leading member of the Communist Party. He wrote on the race question in the *Daily Worker* and in June, traveled to Moscow as a delegate to the Fifth Congress of the Comintern. After the Congress, he stayed in the USSR, attending the University of Toilers of the East, a special training school for Communists from oppressed countries.

By 1925, he was back in the United States, this time operating out of Chicago. There, he became known for his habit of strolling through the streets of a Chicago winter wearing knee-high boots and a long belted shirt from Russia. Fort-Whiteman's work for the party now centered on two objectives: recruiting more Black students for the University of Toilers of the East, and building a new party organization for Black workers, the American Negro Labor Congress (ANLC). In the first capacity, he was quite successful. Future prominent Black Communists, such as Otto Hall and Harry Haywood, were recruited to study in Moscow by Fort-Whiteman. The latter enterprise would prove more difficult.

As head of the ANLC, Fort-Whiteman was in charge of the CP's main initiative in organizing Black workers. The ANLC, however, faced stiff opposition from multiple fronts. The AFL denounced it as a Communist plot, declaring Black workers had a home in its unions, even as the vast majority of those unions discriminated against Black workers in any number of ways. The *Messenger*, which had accommodated itself to the AFL's racist practices as it moved to the right in the early 1920s, was similarly hostile to the new body. Despite this, Black newspapers were cautiously optimistic about the new labor body, forthright as it was in its commitment to racial equality.

Ultimately, however, Fort-Whiteman failed in what was probably an impossible task—building a revolutionary labor organization of Black workers in the 1920s. In particular, the ANLC never established any presence in the South. This fact in particular would prove Fort-Whiteman's undoing, as in 1927 he was fired from his position at the ANLC for failing to organize the South. Disheartened and demoralized, Fort-Whiteman moved back to Moscow to enroll at Moscow University to study anthropology and work as a Comintern functionary.

Unfortunately, in the mid-1930s, Fort-Whiteman became caught up in the Stalinist purges then sweeping the USSR. Increasingly disillusioned with the world communist movement's commitment to Black liberation, he became vocally critical of how the Comintern was handling Black American guests. A fellow Black American communist, William Patterson, overheard Fort-Whiteman's complaints and pronounced them "counter-revolutionary." Fort-Whiteman was accused of Trotskyism (a death sentence in the USSR at that time) and sent to a labor camp, where he would die in 1939.

Further Reading

Gilmore, Glena E. *Defying Dixie: The Radical Roots of Civil Rights, 1919–1950*. New York: W.W. Norton & Company, 2008.

McLellan, Woodford. "Africans and Black Americans in the Comintern Schools, 1925–1934." *The International Journal of African Historical Studies* 26, no. 2 (1993): 371–90.

Solomon, Mark. *The Cry Was Unity: Communists and African Americans, 1917–1936*. Jackson: University Press of Mississippi, 1998.

The Negro in Politics

Today the Negro masses are yet in the clutches of the unscrupulous politician of both Races. From year to year he votes on the simple faith that the goodness in character of the candidate is sufficient force to improve his social conditions. There is something pathetic in the childlike way the Negro voter looks at politics. The entire Race is without any political ideals. Its professional politicians are solely interested in politics only in so far as they may derive graft and lucrative jobs. The platform or program of a candidate is never considered, but for the extent of his power to purchase votes.

Nevertheless, there are manifest here and there among the younger men and women against this condition. They make up as yet the few who are able to understand that politics is but a reflection of economic conditions, that government today is but an instrument in the hands of the rich or capitalist class, and that its laws and policies are evolved primarily in the interest of its class.

The Negro who advocates among his people the necessity of breaking away from the oldline parties faces much opposition from the present set of Negro leaders. A simple explanation of this opposition is that the majority of recognized Negro leaders in some way or other live on the bounty of the white capitalist class. Most Negro higher schools and colleges are supported by the contributions of white philanthropists; also his Y.M.C.A.'s and a number of other institutions of an ethical or non-descript character. The Negro heads of these institutions are the accepted leaders of the Race. They dare not support labor unionism among Negroes, they dare not advocate other than a capitalist ticket in politics. The Negro leader has sold out the man-hood of the Race.

Yet slowly but surely we of the working class are coming to see that the Negro cannot be a man and a beggar at the same time.

Originally published in the *Daily Worker*, January 13, 1924 (Saturday Supplement).

The Negro and American Race Prejudice

The student of social problems may easily discover, after but little investigation, that race prejudice, almost all cases, has its roots in some form
of economic or industrial competition. Race prejudice is not something
inherited—transmitted thru the blood from one individual to another.
Thus, despite the fact that probably most persons believe such to be the
case. One may see in any place in the South, black and white children
playing together, even in sections where the greatest degree of animosity
exists between the races. Nor is the Negro regarded in any of the European countries as a peculiar object of hatred or prejudice such as in the
United States.

No social bitterness greeted the Negro at his advent on American
shores from Africa. His enslavement was a matter simply of meeting the
need of a labor supply in the colonies. Further, it is a well-known fact that
there was much intermixing of white women and male Negro slaves before
slavery became a definite and recognized institution in the country; that is
before the greater value of the Negro as a slave was appreciated.

With the growth of the tobacco and cotton interests, there was an
ever-increasing legislation restricting and defining the social status of the
Negro. And the ruling or slave-owning class, in order to gives it position
some sort of moral justification, claimed that slavery brought the Negro in
touch with civilization a higher plane of existence. This slave-owning class,
controlling the and [sic] christianity and elevated him to the agencies of
public opinion, preached the inherent inferiority of the Negro.

It should be easy to understand that a public opinion wholly shaped by
a slave-owning class, the belief of the inherent inferiority of the Negro and
his social unfitness, after a time, became thoroughly established, and part
and parcel of the American social consciousness.

Originally published in the *Daily Worker*, February 9, 1924 (Saturday
Supplement).

Even after the emancipation of the Negro from chattel slavery, it has remained to the interest of an exploiting class, to maintain a popular opinion of the social inferiority of the Negro. Today, the Lords of Industry, thru a servile press, the school, the church, and other agencies of public opinion, are able to keep the ranks of the working class divided on sentiment of race differences. Some of the unions bar Negroes from membership. And this is greatly to the interest of the capitalist class. This permits of a sort of a reserve army of Negro workers that may be employed to break strikes. And to enumerate the most out-standing manifestations of this sickly sentiment of American race prejudice as it effects the Negro, as follows: in the South, the latter is compelled to ride in rear seats in street cars, he is politically disfranchised, lynched and burned at the stake and in the North as well suffers industrial discrimination, residential segregation, and often denial of public accommodation. There may be such a thing as one race having a natural antipathy for another, but this does not imply hostility. Strife between races is based on some economic condition. And a struggle for economic and industrial advantages reflects itself in mutual hatred and groundless prejudice.

The Negro worker is unorganized and everything possible is done to keep him thus. We even find such organizations among Negroes as the Urban League, which is maintained by the capitalist class, and which functions as a nation-wide labor agency, supplying the Northern industries with raw cheap Negro labor from the South. And this has been a leading circumstance in the development of race riots in our Northern cities. When unionized white labor finds itself confronted in the labor market with the Negro who is willing to do the same work for much less money, the natural reaction is one of hostility toward the Negro. And the willingness of the Negro to work for less money than the white man is rather a necessity—as has been shown.

Bitterness between the Negro and the white man in America, is stimulated and promoted by the capitalist class who necessarily resort to such a method in order to split the ranks of the working class as a whole and to thus better affect its exploitation. It is simply a case of "divide and rule." But the practice having become deep-seated in our social organism, it has colored the social mind and the unthinking person regards prejudice against the Negro as a natural inheritable mental condition.

Yet this principle in the art of subjecting one race or class to another is a world-wide practice and as old as the institution of private property.

When England entered India, she found the caste system which had been created by a previous conquering race, yet at the time was in a state of rapid dissolution. It has been of paramount advantage to England to keep this social system alive. Thus rendering joint action against her rule impossible. In the British West Indies, she establishes a social cleavage between the mulatto and the pure-blooded Negro. But in Ireland, where there is but one race, she resorts to the religious sentiment. Protestants and Catholics are inspired to hate one another and even abetted to a state of civil war.

The working-class in America, shall succeed only after the workers have laid aside all racial bitterness and shall have recognized the fact that class interest far transcends race interest; that as long as the workers fight among themselves and remain disunited, just so long will they be exploited, robbed and plundered by the employing class.

The Negro in America

Today there are more than twelve millions of negro people in the United States of North America. This does not include the negro people of the Virgin Islands, which islands were purchased from Denmark by the American Government during the war. The population of these islands is several hundred thousand, and almost wholly negro. Prior to the world-war, there were not quite two million negroes in the North, but a small percentage of them engaged in the basic industries. The bulk of the race was in the South, as it is to-day. But with the outbreak of the War in 1914, and the expansion of Northern industries, a tremendous wave of negro migration set in from the Southern States to the cities of the North. This unprecedented wave of Negro migration was inspired primarily by the attraction of higher wages which could be obtained in the Northern industries. But even following the close of the War, when the industries had contracted, the warmer seasons of the year have always brought an influx of negroes from the South into our Northern centres.

The coming of the negro into the Northern industries has been responsible for much friction between the white and black workers. The negro militant being wholly unorganised and finding conditions much better than in his Southern home, thought much inferior to those of the Northern white worker, at once becomes a tool in the hands of the employing class to beat back the resistance of organised white workers. The latter, clearly conscious of the tendency of a reduction of his standard of living, because of the presence of the negro, evinces his resentment through physical attacks on the negro. The series of bloody race riots which have occurred during recent years are basically the result of this conflict of the white and black worker in the labour market. But, of course, this real and fundamental cause is seldom apparent, for the masses of American white workers are so permeated with the virus of race-hatred as a result of their bourgeois ideology, that often the

---

Originally published in *Communist International*, February 1925, 50–52.

most minor provocation of a race-riot is interpreted as the real cause. This race-hatred between blacks and whites in America has its origin and growth in the political forms and methods employed by the ruling class to safeguard and promote its economic class interest.

This race-hatred on the part of the white masses extends to all classes of the negro race. A member of the negro petty bourgeois could no more get accommodation in a first class hotel, cafe, restaurant or purchase a first-class ticket in a theatre than the most ordinary negro worker. In the Southern States, there are separate schools for all negroes, separate and inferior accommodation for negroes on tramways and railways, and enforced by State laws.

The negro being of a pronouncedly different race and colour, his complexion becomes a sort of natural badge by which is at once recognised as historically of the most oppressed and exploited group in American society. All negroes of whatever class are subject to lynching, Jim Crow-ism, mob violence, segregation, political disfranchisement in the Southern States, etc. And all negroes are interested and lend support to societies and associations endeavoring to affect the eradication of these particular social evils.

Any projected Communist work among American negroes must take as a concrete basis the general social grievances of the race. The slow growth of Marxism among negroes has been wholly due to the inability of both the social democrats and the Communists to approach the negro on his own mental grounds, and to interpret his peculiar social situation in terms of the class struggle. To-day the American negro has evolved his own bourgeoisie, even though as yet but petty. And more and more the lines sharpen in the conflict between the white and black bourgeoisies. The negro petty bourgeoisie rallies the negro masses to him in his struggle against the more powerful white bourgeoisie, and the negro masses are permeated with the belief that their social degradation flows from the mere fact that they are markedly of a different race, and are not white. It is a waste of time to circulate the same Communist literature among negroes that you would among white workers, or to make the same speech before an audience of negro workers you would before that of white workers. The negro evinces no militant opposition towards Communism, but he wants to know how it can improve his social status, what bearing does it have on the common practice of lynching, political disfranchisement, segregation, industrial discrimination, etc. The negro is revolutionary enough in a racial sense, and it devolves upon the American Communist Party to manipulate this racial revolutionary sentiment to the advantage of the class struggle.

In the Southern States, the great majority of negroes are engaged in agricultural pursuits, and at present it is encouraging to note, an agrarian movement is developing for both races. Here the American communists can find a new field for action.

The overwhelming majority of the people of the Virgin Islands are negroes. The principal industries at the time of the purchase were the factories of bay-rum. Alcohol being an ingredient of bay-rum, when prohibition became established throughout the Republic of the United States, these industries were virtually destroyed. The latter being a great mainstay of the people, the standard of living has been much reduced, and among the masses there is wide-spread dissatisfaction with American rule. This coupled with the fact that the natives do not enjoy full rights of American citizenship.

In the negro republic of Haiti, with a population of two million, since 1915 the iron heel of American imperialism has been relentless. The Haitian constitution has been torn to threads, and everything possible is being done to crush the natural aspirations of the people to the right of self-determination.

The negro has always regarded his social problem as a world problem in so far as he has believed that all negroes the world over have a common cause. The most successful organisations among the race at present with direct aims of improving the political and social status of the negro are international in their outlook and programme. No organisation in the history of the American negro has stirred the masses as has the Garvey Movement. This is a negro, nationalist movement, with Africa as its objective. It has been phenomenal in growth, overwhelming in its savage steadfastness of purpose. It represents a perfect embodiment of all the pent-up hatred and rebellious discontent towards American institutions.

So far the Communist achievements among negroes are but slight, and this primarily because as above stated, the Communists have not recognised and accepted as a starting basis the peculiar social disabilities imposed upon the race. At present in the large cities of the North, the rapid influx of negroes from the South has given rise to a new and acute

housing problem. Negroes in America are subjected to residential segregation. Such being the case, there are limited numbers of houses available for negroes in which to live. This condition has been taken advantage of by the landlords and their agents of both races, and the negro tenant is compelled to pay exorbitant rent, quite out of proportion to his income. The negro housing problem to-day is a live issue, and should be seized upon as one of the factors by which to arouse the negro masses.

Everywhere there is increasing discontent within the race. And the Communist Movement cannot afford to overlook the negro in America, for he holds a large place in industrial life, and if left alone could constitute a tremendous weapon for reaction.

Jeannette Pearl

Introduction

Extremely little is known of Jeannette Pearl. An official in the early Workers Party, Pearl played a role in the development of the party's Women's Commission in 1922, and was an early advocate of the party paying more attention to issues of women's oppression. Pearl was also one of the first white party members to show substantial interest in the race question, publishing antiracist poetry in the *Liberator* magazine.

Her *Daily Worker* article on Black women workers reflects the confluence of these commitments and also stands as one of the earliest left texts on the specific oppression of Black women. A decade later, Black Marxists like Claudia Jones, Marvel Cooke, and Ella Baker would develop more sophisticated treatments of this question, pioneering an understanding of how different systems of oppression worked together to produce unique burdens for those caught between them. Though Pearl's article is quite underdeveloped compared to these later texts, it stands out as an early intervention from the Marxist left on the specific problems confronting Black working women.

Further Reading

Davies, Carol Boyce. *Left of Karl Marx: The Political Life of Black Communist Claudia Jones.* Durham, NC: Duke University Press, 2007.

McDuffie, Erik S. *Sojourning for Freedom: Black Women, American Communism, and the Making of Black Left Feminism.* Durham, NC: Duke University Press, 2011.

Harris, LaShawn D. "Running with the Reds: African American Women and the Communist Party during the Great Depression." *Journal of African American History* 94, no. 1 (Winter 2009): 21–40.

Negro Women Workers

Negro women who entered industry during the war are fast learning that their lot is still "the last to be hired and the first to be fired." According to a report just issued by the Woman's Bureau at Washington on the "Negro Women in Industry," a great number of Negro women are being eliminated from industry and those remaining are most ruthlessly exploited. Their hours of toil range all the way from eight to sixteen hours a day and sometimes longer; their pay is miserably small and the conditions under which they work are most brutal.

The report covers a survey of 150 industries employing 11,860 Negro women. The purpose of the investigation was made in order to create a better understanding and greater sympathy among employers of Negro women with the aim of thereby raising the standard of living. This humanitarian aspiration is strongly coupled with repeated emphasis upon the fact that a higher standard of living will yield increased production.

Negro women found their OPPORTUNITY in industry during the world slaughter when the need for munitions of war created a labor shortage in the labor market. The five chief industries that women entered were textiles, clothing, food, tobacco and hand and footwear. The Negro women in the main filled the gap caused by the advancement of white women into newer and more skilled occupations.

Thirty-two and five-tenths per cent of the 11,860 Negro women investigated were working ten hours a day and over; 27.4 per cent were working nine hours a day, and 20.2 per cent were working eight hours a day. These figures do not tell all of the story. Overtime can and does follow the legal work day. Overtime "is permitted as much as desired." The report tells how workers boast of their thriftiness in beginning work, "before hours, after hours, and working during lunch hour." One worker puts it, "You just

---

Originally published in the *Daily Worker*, February 16, 1924 (Saturday Supplement), 2.

can't make ends meet unless you do extra work and often you are left in a hole even at that."

A typical case is cited indicating how these Negro women live for the most part. Rise at five, cook breakfast, dress children, prepare food and attend to things about the house, report for work at 7, leave at 5:30, resume housework on returning home, frequently continuing this work until midnight, dead tired as a result.

One woman worker states "I am so tired when I reach home I can scarcely stand up. My nerves are so bad, I jump in my sleep." Another woman complains, "I'd love to go to the Y. W. C. A., but I am so tired at night, I can scarcely go to bed. If I go out at night, I go where there is lots of life and lots of fun; I'd go to sleep at a lecture or club meeting." Another case cited, "I am so worried and worn in my strength that I feel at times as if I can stand it no longer. It is not alone the need of money but the responsibility of being nurse, housekeeper and wage earner at one time."

The average pay of the Negro women in industry is about ten dollars a week. The minimum wage is calculated at $16.50. When it is taken into consideration that many of these women have dependents and are sometimes the sole supporters of their families, one wonders whether slavery days before the civil war could have been much worse.

The frightful conditions under which most of the Negro women work add to the horror of their wretched pay. They are often segregated because of race prejudice, given inferior and harder work and because of their "ignorance" they are shamelessly cheated, false computation of wages, scales wrong, count wrong, etc. At the end of the week "you never know what you are going to get; you just take what they give you and go." The report points out that there is a strong feeling among Negro women workers that they are not getting a square deal.

Since the Negro women are unorganized they accept the most outrageous conditions of employment. They are not alone discriminated against because of their color and often segregated, but they are made to work amidst conditions the United States government would not permit its hogs to live under. Herded together in terrible congestion, in filth, fetid dust-laden, poisonous air, poorly ventilated, still more poorly lighted, these women work and often have to eat in the same atmosphere.

The report points out, "Confronted with the need for food, clothing and shelter and placed in an environment which was unhealthful and sometimes even degrading, they were seen to have lost themselves in the struggle for bare existence."

The treatment accorded most of these workers is well expressed in the words of one of the managers, "They are terribly indolent, careless and stubborn, but we know HOW to handle them. We give them rough treatment and that quells them for a while." Yet another manager observes, "You never saw a group of people so responsive to kindness? In the main, these women are conscious of their industrial experience and showed timidity which was a drawback in acquiring assurance and speed so necessary in factory production. Their patient trust and belief in the better day that should come to them as workers is pathetic."

The report points out that bad working conditions and long hours are a serious menace to the state, that the prosperity of a nation is endangered when its workers are being crippled with exhaustive labor. Loss of human energy, due to excessive working hours becomes a national loss and is bound to lessen the nation's productive yield. The reporter, therefore, recommends legislation for a higher standard of living inasmuch as a higher standard of living will produce greater efficiency in production and greater profits.

The report would have self-enlightened employers and the State jointly work out an appropriate "award" as compensation for Negro women in the industries. It would be a sort of benevolent industrialism for greater efficiency and greater national progress—for the master class.

To that end is also recommended, "A more conscientious training for efficiency in public schools, thru fostering of pride in achievement, increasing personal and family thrift, and encouraging of constancy toward a given task, would ensure that 'preparation for life' which is the purpose of all education."

Against such "purposes" in education must be posed the Communist method of education, thru labor solidarity making for self-reliance and self-development. Not a "pathetic" longing for a better day, but a resolute expression in action for a better day will result from Communist education.

William F. Dunne

Introduction

William F. Dunne (1887–1953) was a leader in the Communist Party from the 1920s until the 1940s, when he was expelled for opposing the party leadership. Born in Kansas City, Missouri, Dunne was involved in the Socialist Party and the labor movement from 1910 on. After a time as a labor organizer on the west coast, Dunne ended up in Butte, Montana. Butte was a company town, run with an iron fist by the Anaconda Copper Mining Company. In 1917, Dunne became editor of the *Butte Daily Bulletin*, the newspaper of the local labor federation. In 1918, he ran for the state legislature with the slogan "All power to the workers and farmers." In the legislature, he introduced a resolution condemning Anaconda as "the gigantic bloodsucking corporation which has its fingers on the throats of practically every man, woman and child in the state of Montana [and which has] accumulated millions . . . [of] dollars while our boys tendered their lives and sacrificed their all on the blood-soaked fields of Europe." In 1920, Anaconda managed to unseat Dunne through election fraud.

Dunne was a founding member of the Communist Party in 1919. In the party, he and his three brothers allied with the faction led by William Z. Foster and James P. Cannon. While in the party, he continued working as a union organizer, working with Foster's Trade Union Education League. In the late 1920s, he helped organize solidarity with the massive Gastonia textile mill strike, and after the Great Depression began, he organized some of the early Unemployed Councils. In the early 1930s, he spent some time working in the Soviet Union.

As the CP began its Popular Front policy and began looking to an alliance with liberal politicians and union leaders, Dunne became a vocal critic of the CP leadership. During World War II, he worked as a seaman in the Caribbean. When he returned home after the war, Dunne renewed his struggle against the party leadership. He was expelled in 1946. Though he made some effort to form a new organization with other CP members similarly expelled, this project was unsuccessful, and Dunne died in 1953.

Dunne's two-part article on "Negroes in American Industry" was written while he was a member of the Foster-Cannon faction in the Communist Party. Though the Foster-Cannon faction had the bulk of the party's union leaders, it was quite weak on the race question. Supporters of the faction led by Charles Ruthenberg and Jay Lovestone, like Robert Minor, had a far surer grasp of Black history and contemporary Black politics.

Nonetheless, the article displays considerable insight into the changing place of Black workers in the American economy, as well as a keen political understanding of the necessity of fighting racism in the union movement. To be sure, the article at times understates the extent of hostility between Black and white workers at the time, attributing white workers' racism solely to capitalist manipulation. Yet what stands out about the piece is its clear understanding of the barriers that prevented the mass organization of Black workers into unions. Dunne notes that Black suspicion of both whites in general and labor unions specifically was quite justified, and that white Communist unionists needed to prove themselves to Black workers by being the most dedicated foes of racism in the labor movement. Even before the adoption of the Black Belt Thesis, it was widely appreciated throughout the CP that a special dedication to the fight against Black oppression was necessary.

Further Reading

Dunne, William F. *The Struggle Against Opportunism in the Labor Movement—For a Socialist United States: A Contribution to the Discussion of Major Problems of Marxism-Leninism in Our Country*. New York: New York Continuations Committee, 1947.

Palmer, Bryan D. *James P. Cannon and the Origins of the American Revolutionary Left, 1890–1928*. Champaign: University of Illinois Press, 2007.

Wetzel, Kurt. "The Defeat of Bill Dunne: An Episode in the Montana Red Scare." *Pacific Northwest Quarterly* 64, no. 1 (1973): 12–20.

Negroes in American Industry (Part I)

As I look back over the years I can see that we were probably "poor white trash."

We lived on Minnesota Avenue, and Joey, a little Negro boy whose last name I do not remember ever hearing, was my first playmate while we lived in Kansas City. Certainly we were miserably poor; that we belonged to the white race has never been disputed and justification for the supposition that we were "trash" is furnished by the distinct memory of being called "nigger lover," by older children when Joey and I ventured onto the nearby vacant lot whose garbage piles furnished an inexhaustible store of treasure for the younger set of the neighborhood.

I remember the epithet held no approbrious [sic.] meaning for me, but nonetheless I resented it just as an Irishman, an Englishman or a Swede resents being classified nationally in a certain tone of voice. My attempts to revenge what was evidently, for reasons not understood by me, intended for an insult were not singularly successful. Joey was too good-natured to be much value as an ally and the conflicts were generally in the nature of rearguard actions ending in the retreat of the three of us, Joey, myself and Rover, one of the nondescript dogs with which Kansas City abounded and which Joey and I had adopted, to the fastnesses of the kitchen of one of our mothers—our houses were side by side—or to the woodshed.

Our mothers were singularly uninformed as to the reasons for our troubles and unbelievably unsympathetic—particularly towards Rover. Our fathers we saw but seldom. They worked in the Armour packinghouse and were on their way to work before Joey and I arose in the mornings. They went to bed at an early hour and so did we.

We were governed by a matriarchy.

Overshadowing all else as a source of danger to Joey, Rover and me was the city dog-catcher. He was the terror of the neighborhood children who

Originally published in the *Workers Monthly*, March 1925, 206–8, 237.

were all well supplied with unlicensed prototypes of Rover, and whatever difference existed between the races were submerged in the face of this common enemy. His advent into the district was made known by a sort of grapevine telegraph that was surprisingly efficient. Even the dogs sensed the danger and as a rule they made no protest when hurried into woodsheds and cellars.

Rover was an exception. I do not know if his mongrel heart held a sort of fearless defiance or if he was simply in rebellion against an exercise of authority but the fact remains that Rover would howl to high heaven at the most critical moments when the enemy was in earshot.

On one terrible day the grapevine failed to work and the enemy was within the gates. Joey and I adopted desperate measures. I stole a pair of mother's stockings and we lashed Rover's legs fore and aft. Joey stripped his three year old sister of her sole garment—a frock fashioned on severely simple lines—and with this emergency muffler we bound Rover's jaws while she ran screaming her protest in chocolate-colored nakedness.

Our mothers arrived as we were contemplating our work with justifiable pride. They lost no time debating the course to pursue. My mother seized Joey, Joey's mother grabbed me. With a loud smacking noise, black hand descended on white bottom and vice versa.

Joey and I left home that day with two slices of bread and three cold fried catfish to brave a world that we felt could be no more hostile than homes ruled by mothers to whom an undressed female child was of more importance than the liberty of Rover.

We were captured within four blocks of our domiciles, spanked again on already tender areas and put to bed after our commissariat had been raided.

* * *

You ask what the foregoing has to do with the Negro in industry and I reply that the Negro in industry encounters a hostility from white workers that is artificial and not instinctive, that my childhood experience is that of thousands of white children who feel no hostility toward their Negro playmates until old enough to absorb the prejudices of their elders.

Nothing is clearer than this in the report of the Chicago commission on race relations—the most exhaustive and authoritative study of the real problem yet made in the United States and which was begun after the 1919 race riots.

The problem of the Negro in industry as well as in American society as a whole, is a problem created by the background of chattel slavery and intimately connected with its traditions, the propagation of a whole series of falsehoods and fetishes, scientifically untenable, but which by repetition and a certain superficial plausibility, have become dogmas which to question means social ostracism in the former slave states—the historical home of chattel slavery whose conceptions of the Negro as a social inferior who menaces white supremacy is the obscene fountain from which flows all of the poisonous streams that carry the virus of race hatred into the ranks of the American working class and labor movement.

Slavery not Abolished

The slave south is not dead and slavery has not been abolished. It lives in song and story, it lives in every community where there are black and white human beings, it lives in the agricultural regions of the south, it exists in the industrial feudalism of the lumber and turpentine camps of the south, it lives in the southern non-union coal fields, it lives in the columns of the capitalist press of both north and south and the prejudice and strife among workers is fed and inflamed like a gangrenous wound by this filth that it exudes.

The problem of the Negro in industry—it is really the problem of the dominant white workers if a white working-class exploited as the American working class is can be termed dominant—must be approached from two viewpoints—that of the Negro and that of the white worker. Both have their prejudices. Both are victims of a constant and cunning misinformation supplied them with a deliberate aim and a diabolical cleverness hard to combat. But it must never be forgotten that those who see the danger to the workers of both races and consequently to the whole working class movement, that while the prejudices of the white workers have absolutely no foundations in fact, those of the Negro workers are, although a grave danger to working class solidarity and serious obstacles to organizing work, based upon enslavement, persecution and torture of black by white since 1619.

The Negro worker is the injured party and because he is, because the dominant white knows he is, the changes are rung on the unprovable assumptions concerning the mental and moral inferiority of the Negro as an individual and as a race in an attempt to justify the denial of political rights, denial of equal educational privileges, Jim Crowism, discrimination in unions, mass murder in race riots, hangings, burnings at the stake and the rest of the long list of Dantesque horror inflicted on the black race since its first representative was torn from his African home by white slave merchants.

Borrowed Prejudices

The opinions of the working class in all social epochs up to the immediate period preceding revolution, according to the easily demonstrable Marxian theory, are the opinions of the ruling class. This applies with the greatest force to the opinions held by whites of the Negro. The white ruling class of the south has conspired since the civil war to deprive the Negro of every economic and political right. The rise of a Negro middle class has been fought consistently and white workers, imbued with the prejudices of their rulers have been only too glad to have inferiors to whom they could transmit the kicks given their own posteriors by the feudal aristocracy and the rising industrial capitalists of Dixieland.

The final argument for the suppression of the Negro with which disagreement must be accompanied by readiness to defend one's life against both white southern workers and capitalists and the social strata lying between, takes the form of the inevitable question: "Would you want your sister to marry a black blankety blankety blank blank blank?"

This is the form into which the hatred and fear of granting equal opportunity to the Negro rationalises itself. It is the sexual motif which lies like a thick and fetid blanket over the whole south, extending into the north as well, but as a thinner fabric in which rents are appearing, rents torn by the inexorable forces of industrial, political and social development in the United States.

Into the labor movement itself has been catapulted the monstrous fallacy, promulgated by a decadent feudalism based on complete subjection of the Negroes, that the black race individually and collectively, lusts with an ungovernable passion for the bodies of white women. This false dogma has been used and is used to excuse all overt acts against the Negro on the part of whites when all other excuses fail. The white press and pulpit, the lecture platform, the moving pictures, silly but white ego-satisfying books of the Nordicmaniacs, are used to perpetuate this easy and effective means of alienating all sympathy for the Negro even when he has been made the victim of the sadistic appetites of whole communities of maddened degenerates as in Mississippi, Jan. 26, 1919, where the burning of a Negro at the stake was advertised in the press for several days, the announcement of the hour at which the officers of the law would turn him over to the mob was made and special trains were run to accommodate the curious—a desperate spectacle without parallel unless we except the holocausts of Christians in ancient Rome.

A volume could be written on this phase of the race question alone but it is enough to say here that in other countries where there are large Negro populations, the sexual question does not arise. In the British West Indies, where the Negroes outnumber the whites 50 or 60 to one, according to the statement of Lord Olivier, formerly governor-general of Jamaica, no case is on record of an attack on a white woman by a Negro.

This instance alone is enough to discredit the whole myth of white women as the basis of hostility to the Negro even if there were not available the testimony of competent and unprejudiced investigators who, without significant exception, are agreed that the opposite is true—a pronounced penchant of white southerners for Negro women—the millions of mulattoes are alone proof of the soundness of this conclusion—and that it is extremely doubtful if a dozen of cases of attack on white women could be proved as fact in the whole horrid history of the innumerable lynchings of Negroes.

So much for the justification on moral grounds of discrimination against the Negro in the labor unions and industry as a whole.

Is the Negro a "Natural" Strikebreaker?

But the discrimination of the unions against the Negro worker is justified by the white workers on other than moral grounds in the north. He is accused of being an incurable strikebreaker and therefore a willing tool of the employers.

The influx of Negro workers into industry during the last decade has brought the question of his role in the labor and revolutionary movement squarely before the American working class. The expansion of American industry during the world war and the stoppage of immigration created a great demand for labor. The drafting of thousands of southern Negroes into the army intensified the racial antagonism south of the Mason and Dixon line, tore them loose from their feudal environment and gave them an immensely broader outlook. Increasing persecution in the south and the demand for labor in the north brought hundreds of them into northern industrial centers and into contact and competition with white labor.

Chicago, Pittsburgh, New York, Boston, Gary, Minneapolis and St. Paul, Detroit, Cleveland, Buffalo and Toledo in the industrial east and middle west immensely increased their Negro working class as did cities lying halfway between north and south like St. Louis, Kansas City and Cincinnati.

Chicago is fairly typical of these industrial centers.

In sixty-two Chicago industries comprising box-making, clothing, cooperage, food products, iron and steel, tanneries and miscellaneous manufacturing, from which statistics were secured, the number of Negro workers increased from 1,346 in 1915 to 10,587 in 1920. The number of Negro workers therefore multiplied approximately eight times in the five-year period.

In forty-seven non-manufacturing industries in Chicago, employing 4,601 Negro workers in 1915, there was an increase to 8,483 in 1920, a 50 per cent increase.

In Chicago, concerns reporting the employment of five or more Negroes in 1920 and altogether employing 118,098 workers, the percentage of Negro workers classified generally by occupation was as follows:

Paper box manufacturing	14 per cent.
Clothing	14 per cent.
Cooperage	32 per cent.
Food products	22 per cent.
Iron and steel products (iron foundries)	10 per cent.
Tanneries	21 per cent.
Miscellaneous:	
Lamp shade manufacturing	27 per cent.
Auto cushion manufacturing	50 per cent.
Other industries (manufacturing)	5 per cent.

The percentage of Negro workers in non-manufacturing industries for the same year was as follows (the industries given below have always employed a larger percentage of Negroes than the industrial enterprises proper):

Hotels	53 per cent.
Laundries	44 per cent.
Mail order merchandise houses	8 per cent.
Railway sleeping and dining car service	68 per cent.
Miscellaneous (public service, warehouses, taxicabs, telegraph companies, etc.)	6 per cent.

A tabulation of the above percentages shows that in Chicago manufacturing industries in 1920 there was an average of 16 per cent of the working forces who were Negroes, with the quota rising to 23 per cent in the non-manufacturing industries.

According to the figures compiled by the Chicago Committee on Race Relations, the Negro population of Chicago increased from 44,103 in 1910 to 109,594 in 1920—an approximate increase of 250 per cent. The number of Negro workers increased from 27,000 in 1910 to about 70,000 in 1920. The increase in the percentage of Negro workers to Negro population in 1920 as compared with 1910 is undoubtedly due to the influx of Negro workers without families and consequently better able to leave the south.

Migration North

Chicago is the heart of industrial America and from these figures we can gain a good idea of the magnitude of the problem created for the Negro himself—the labor movement and the Workers (Communist) Party by a social phenomenon which is well expressed in statistics showing that already in 1920 about 20 per cent of the workers in Chicago, the greatest industrial center in America, were Negroes.

The influx of Negro workers did not cease in 1920. It continued through 1921–22–23, and figures made public by the southern state governments show that in this period more than 500,000 Negroes took their scanty belongings and left the southern exploiters to sulk in a helpless rage. The Negro has at last found a way to avenge himself on his southern prosecutors.

In 1924 the number of Negroes "goin No'th" decreased due to the demand for agricultural labor in the south, where several million acres had reverted to jungle because of the scarcity of labor.

The figures on lynching of Negroes in the south for 1924 speak volumes—they show a decrease of fifty per cent with a total of "only 19"

Negroes done to death; horrible enough, but eloquent in that they show the increased safety of life and improved treatment in the drop from the 1923 total of 38 as a result of the withdrawal by the Negroes of their labor.

Most of the Negroes are in the north to stay and it is not necessary that the migration continue in a flood to bring the problem of the Negro in industry to the attention of the American workingclass. "The iron march of historical development" has already placed it on the order of business.

The unions of the industrial north and of southern states like Tennessee, North Carolina and Georgia that are rapidly becoming industrialized, can no longer shut their eyes and presume that only in isolated instances will they be called upon to make a decision. One-fifth of the American industrial workers now have black skins. They are in industry and are going to stay.

Negroes in American Industry (Part II)

Two tendencies show themselves in the labor movement. One is the blind, dangerous and senseless hatred of the Negro workers, encouraged by the unscrupulous capitalists and carried on by the camp followers of capitalism—real estate sharks, prostitute journalists, labor misleaders and all the carrion crew that live on the offal of the system.

This is the tendency that brought white and Negro workers into conflict in the Chicago race riots in 1919, in which 23 Negroes and 15 whites were killed and 537 persons of both races injured.

The other tendency, manifested only by the Communist Party and the most intelligent and militant of the workers outside its ranks, is perhaps best illustrated by the white workers who gave their lives in an armed struggle to protect a Negro organizer of the Timber Workers' Union from the attack of gunmen of the Great Southern Lumber Company, November 22, 1919.

The heroic stand of these southern white union men shines like a golden star in the bloody history of 1919—the year in which the antagonism between white and colored workers, as a result of the advent of the Negro into industry, reached its climax, expressing itself in race wars, lynchings and dozens of cases of terror against Negroes.

The employers have taken full advantage of the racial antagonism, if this term can be used to describe a problem that has, so far as the labor movement is concerned, an almost exclusive economic basis—the competition of the black workers with the white for the means of livelihood.

That Negroes were used to break strikes in the meat packing, steel and transportation industries, that they are undoubtedly hard to organize in some of the existing unions and are in many cases prejudiced against them, complicates the situation, but it no more proves that the Negro is a natural strikebreaker than the seduction of Negro women by white men proves that the whole white male race is engaged in this pastime.

Originally published in the *Workers Monthly*, April 1925, 257–60.

There are two reasons for the Negro's distrust of the labor unions, but it is yet to be proved that a much higher percentage of Negroes than white workers remain outside of labor organizations which they have an opportunity of joining. The fact that in those occupations and industries where there are functioning labor unions and where there are any considerable number of Negro workers, but little complaint of the attitude of the Negro workers is heard, is proof that Negro workers can be organized successfully. In the United Mine Workers of America there are not only hundreds of Negro coal miners but Negro organizers as well; in the Teamsters' union, the Building Laborers' union, the Longshoremen's union—organizations that have something of a mass character, there is practically no color discrimination and none of the racial prejudice found in other unions of the purely craft type.

The inescapable conclusion from the evidence is that when the Negro acquires industrial experience, is in actual competition with the organized white workers, two things happen—the white workers swallow their prejudices in the face of the need for better organization and the Negro worker abandons his suspicion of the labor union and its objects. This brings us again to the two principal reasons for the lack of organization among the Negro workers. They are:

1. The baseless prejudice of the organized white workers caused by

(a) Artificially created racial antagonisms—sexual jealousy fanned by the constant stream of propaganda, belief in the mental inferiority of the Negro, etc.

(b) The belief that the Negro worker is a natural strikebreaker as a result of his use as such in strikes of longshoremen, packinghouse workers, steel workers and other strikes.

(c) The distrust of the organized workers of any new elements in the ranks of the working class (the Negro inherits the labor union prejudice formerly displayed against the foreign-born worker).

2. The Negro workers coming into industry are peasants with the lack of organizational experience characteristic of peasants the world over and with all the ignorant peasant's suspicion of the city worker.

(a) Under the very poorest conditions in industry they have better wages, better food and better living than they have ever experienced before;

they must acquire an entirely new standard of comparison before they are interested in unions.

It must not be forgotten in making any estimate of the importance of the first reason given, that of the whole American working class numbering approximately 28,000,000, less than 4,000,000 are organized, even though we broaden the definition of "union" to include many organizations that are not unions at all in the correct sense of the word. The weakness of the labor movement is an important contributing factor to the unorganized condition of Negro workers.

The second reason is clearly understandable and its primary importance is appreciated more fully when we find, according to a report of the United States Census Bureau entitled, "Negro population in the United States, 1790 to 1915" (1915 saw the beginnings of the Negro influx into industry) that of 5,192,535 Negroes in the United States in 1915, who were "gainfully occupied," 2,893,674 were engaged in agriculture.

In the south, in 1910, 78.8 per cent of the Negro population lived in rural communities and 62 per cent of all those employed were in agriculture. The peasant character of the Negro migrants is therefore clearly established and no one who has had any experience with American farmers and workers at the time of or soon after their transplantation into industry, will be inclined to blame the Negro peasant who is in the process of becoming an industrial worker, for his lack of interest in unions.

If in addition to the well known difficulty of organizing farmers from northern states, who in bad crop years have established quite a strikebreaking record of their own, we take into account the fact that the agricultural south is comparable to the last years of a feudal society in Europe; that in the state of Mississippi as an example, the amount until recently allotted to the public schools was but $6 per capita, we gain a larger insight into the background of the overwhelming majority of the Negroes who came into industry since 1915.

It is useless to rail at workers who are the products of such an environment as this. There must be understanding and the patience which can only come from understanding. Industry itself is the chemist that compounds the antidote for the backward Negro worker, but while the harsh hand of the exploiter is forcing him to drink again and again of the bitter cup of the working class there must be the most energetic direction of the educational and organizational methods at the disposal of the working class.

Upon the white workers rests the responsibility for bringing the Negro workers into the class struggle. When the white workers rid themselves of their ruling class-inspired prejudices, when they see the Negro worker not as an enemy but as an ally, when they realize and acknowledge in tones that can be heard by the Negro workers (and by the capitalists who profit from and foment divisions of the races), that the Negro workers are necessary for the final victory over capitalism, the task of organizing the Negro workers will be found not so difficult after all.

In every union the left wing must carry on a constant and fearless struggle against every manifestation of racial prejudice. The militants must be prepared to challenge the trade union bureaucracy on this issue just as they have on the general questions of policy and tactics of the labor movement and as always the Communists must take the lead.

The work among the Negroes in industry must parallel the work done in the unions of white workers, but for some time it will be of a more elementary character and can only progress as the Negro workers can be shown by concrete instances that the American labor movements wants them as equals because they are workers.

The Negro workers must be shown that the Workers (Communist) Party is the only party that fights their class and racial struggle uncompromisingly and without counting the cost. They must be shown by actual activity that the Communists are the foe of every enemy of the Negro worker whether he be a Negro-hating trade union official or capitalist.

Like the white workers the Negroes are victimized and misled by their middle class. There is nothing more despicable in American life than the Negro business man, the Negro preacher and the Negro journalist who teach the men and women of their race that the way to secure concessions and recognition is by servility and meekness, by trying to outdo the white man in smug respectability. It is a matter of record that some of these traitors have sold their followers into industrial slavery by means of fake unions which were nothing but scab agencies.

These two-time betrayers—betrayers of the black race and betrayers of the black working class—must be fought and discredited and this will have to be done by Negro Communists—revolutionary Negro workers who understand both the racial and class issues in the struggle.

The Workers (Communist) Party must train Negro organizers and Negro writers so that as the labor movement is forced by economic pressure to organize Negro workers, the Negro workers, acquainted by these leaders of their own race with the true role of the labor movement, can become a tower of strength to the revolutionary elements within it.

A survey of those unions that have organized Negro workers affords irrefutable proof that in the unions where black and white workers discuss the ways and means of combatting the tyrannies of the employers, the racial lines become so faint as to be almost invisible. The necessity for common struggle pushes into the background the question of color and it is soon forgotten. Quite aside from the increased economic and political power of the workers that the organization of the Negro workers brings, in the unions is where white and black workers meet in the nearest approach to complete equality.

In the labor unions is where the work of solving the problem of the Negro in industry gets the quickest results and it is there that the problem will be solved as well as it can be under capitalism, while the social-reformers and middle class liberals, "friends of the Negro," are lavishing wordy sympathy upon him and appealing to hide-bound enemies of the Negro to allow not quite so many lynchings next year.

The task that confronts the American Workers (Communist) Party in organizing the Negro workers and rallying them for the daily struggle and the final overthrow of capitalism side by side with the white workers is no light one. On the contrary it is a difficult and dangerous job.

No one who does not appreciate this fact should be allowed to come within a thousand miles of the work. It is something that cannot be expedited by undue optimism nor can the work be furthered by magnifying to Negro comrades the mistakes of the party and exaggerating its present strength and abilities.

Ill-balanced comrades who know little of the role of the Negro in American industry and less of the labor movement, comrades who appear to think that the whole problem centers around the right of the races to inter-marry, whose utterances give one the impression that they believe the labor movement, as a product as it is of the historical conditions in America, is a conscious conspiracy against the Negro workers, comrades who without thought of possible consequences would have the party begin immediately the organization of dual independent Negro unions, such comrades as these are useless in this work.

There are two things necessary before we can mobilize any great number of Negro workers for our program. The first is the development of some Communist Negro leadership. The second is a point of contact with the Negro masses.

There are excellent prospects for securing both these fundamental necessities and with the work already under way in the unions the American Communist party will be able to make steady progress in demonstrating to the Negro workers in industry and the whole American working class that it alone has a program for the working class, black and white, that strengthens it in the continual combat with the capitalists and that will bring the working class through victorious struggle, to full exercise of its power by the proletarian dictatorship under which men and women will be judged by what they do and not by the color of their skin.

Sometime this year will be held a conference of delegates from Negro working class organizations. Every effort must be made to have this conference representative of the most advanced group of Negro workers. It will be the first gathering of this kind in America and will establish a center for organizing work among the Negroes in industry.

There must be established as soon as possible a Communist Negro Press as a vital part of the party machinery. The existing Negro press is feeble when it is not actually traitorous.

The problem of the Negro in American industry has taken on an important international aspect. The colonial regions of Africa, where British, French, Belgian and Italian imperialists exploit the masses of Negro workers, are astir. As in America, the war brought the world to the masses of African Negroes. They discovered that the white tyrants had forced them to weld their own chains; that they were expected to fight and die to perpetuate their own slavery.

White supremacy is no longer accepted at the valuation placed on it by the white robber class.

Writing in a recent number of a semi-official publications of the British colonial office, a colonial bureaucrat tells of the changes taking place in the British African territories. He shows that the Negro tribes are holding tremendous semi-political gatherings at which a high degree of organizational ability is displayed. He writes of the complicated structure of Negro states destroyed by the white invader and tells of the new interest displayed by the Negro masses in the history of their states and customs before the white man came.

He cites their adaptability to modern warfare and modern machinery and warns the British ruling class that new and more subtle methods must be used if the Africans are to be kept within the confines of the empire.

From among the American Negroes in industry must come the leadership of their race in its struggle for freedom in the colonial countries. In spite of the denial of equal opportunity to the Negro under American capitalism, his advantages are so far superior to those of the subject colonial Negroes in the educational, political and industrial fields that he is alone able to furnish the agitational and organizational ability that the situation demands.

The American Communist Negroes are the historical leaders of their comrades in Africa and to fit them for dealing the most telling blows to world imperialism as allies of the world's working class is enough to justify all the time and energy that the Workers (Communist) Party must devote to the mobilization for the revolutionary struggle of the Negro workers in American industry.

The Negroes as an Oppressed People

A FEDERATED PRESS dispatch under date of June 10, says:

> Lynchings of Negroes for the first five months of 1925, show an in-
> crease over lynchings for the corresponding period last year. Eight
> persons have been lynched up to June 1, 1925, while ONLY five were
> lynched in that period last year.

The emphasis on "only" is mine.

The amount of freedom from outrages not usually perpetrated on
members of the ruling race possessed by a colonial people or a national
minority is a good measure of their social status. Judged by this standard the
10,000,000 Negroes in the United States and particularly the overwhelming
majority of the Negro population which lives in the southern states are
immeasurably lower in capitalism's social scale than the most oppressed
section of the white working class—the foreign-born workers in steel, coal
copper and textile towns where their homes are on company property.

In the north the Negroes, having acquired industrial experience in
an environment which, while far from being free from racial prejudice
and hatred, is nevertheless far superior to that of the semi-feudal south,
are demanding and forcing treatment equal at least to that of the white
workers.

Labor has been moved at last to make an organization campaign among
the Negro workers part of its program. But in the south the lynching of
Negroes as a community enterprise, and the murder of Negroes by whites
without punishment of the offenders continue unabated.

Moved by what I am willing for lack of proof to the contrary to call a
sincere desire to shame the United States into stamping out this horrible
practice and of advancing the cause of the black race, a number of Negro
and white intellectuals, publicists and middle class elements from time to

---

Originally published in the *Workers Monthly*, July 1925, 395–98.

time point out that in European countries Negroes are not discriminated against either socially, politically or economically.

They never tire of recounting the equal rights enjoyed by the Negroes in la belle France, or democratic England or fascist Italy. If they can discover a person of Negro blood upon whom some of these countries have conferred honors, they are deliriously happy in having found further proof that the attitude of the American ruling class and its dupes in America is an arbitrary one.

Such uncritical acceptance of superficial facts as evidence that the example of other capitalist nations on the Negro question is one we should follow here is proof of a monstrous ignorance of one fact:

That the Negroes are oppressed as a RACE and not as individuals.

It is not the purpose of this article to deal with the further oppression of the majority of the Negro race as workers and peasants, but to prove that whatever the Negro suffers in the United States, it differs only in degree but not in kind from the indignities inflicted on him in other spheres of capitalism—is part of the world system which decrees that certain peoples, mostly of the darker-skinned races, are the legitimate prey of the dominant white majority, wherever they are found in sufficient numbers to make suppression necessary because profitable.

What is the colonial policy of America, France, Great Britain, Spain, Portugal, Italy, Belgium and Holland but the enforcement of this decree? And what is the attitude of the white ruling class in the United States but the expression of this universal (outside of Soviet Russia) doctrine, with the changes made necessary by the historical conditions here?

Every attempt to make the struggles of the Negro masses in the United States a purely national question, to isolate it from the struggles of the Negro race in all of imperialism's colonies and spheres of influence, or even to isolate it from the struggles of ALL the darker-skinned peoples is to play into the hands of the ruling class. Equally true is it to say that any misunderstanding of the common interest in, or attempt to draw a line of separation between, the world proletarian revolutionary struggle and the liberation movements of the colonial peoples and racial minorities, leads straight to disaster.

How otherwise well-informed and intelligent persons can have been taken in by the friendly attitude of officialdom to individual members of the dark-skinned peoples residing in this attitude genuine and indicative of a desire for racial equality is a mystery unless we realize the inevitable tendency of the class mentioned to seek always an easy way of escape from problems that can be solved only by struggle.

There is a wealth of testimony at hand, of which the facts set forth are not disputed, showing that wherever white capitalism has established itself the code of ethics that governs social contacts between its members is discarded the very moment it encounters in considerable numbers any "backward" people whose subjection it desires.

The history of imperialism in India, in Africa, in China, in the Philippines, is filled with bloody incidents, in proof of this contention. The record has many gaps in it for obvious reasons, but what has been written would fill a good-sized building.

Some day (and the rising of the Chinese against imperialism shows that the day is not far distant) the black, brown and yellow-skinned races will deliver their indictment against the white race and it will be well for that race if the accumulated wrongs of centuries have been atoned for in some measure by a proletarian dictatorship acknowledging these wrongs and righting them, when that day comes.

But here I want only to show that to the Negro, whether in Africa or forcibly torn from his continent and brought to America, the white ruling class of all countries has given him as a race nothing but blows, bullets, bayonets—and chains to the accompaniment of psalms and prayers.

For every true Nordic (and even the lowlier Alpine) knows that God is white and on the side of the white race. So it was that the first successful foray on the Negro race was the occasion for profuse thanks being given to the white god of battle.

The Portuguese were the first to discover that black slaves were handy things to have. The armored knights were soon systematically descending on African settlements of naked natives and carrying away the Negroes who escaped their swords. An old Portuguese chronicle gives the following description of one of these noble exploits:

> Then you might see mothers forsaking their children and husbands their wives, each striving to escape as best they could. Some drowned themselves in the water, others sought to escape by hiding under their huts; others stowed their children among the sea-weed, where our men found them afterwards, hoping they would thus escape notice. . . . And

at last our Lord God, who giveth a reward for every good deed, willed that for the toil they had undergone in His service they should that day obtain victory over their enemies, as well as a guerdon and a payment for all their labor and expense; for they took captive of those Moors, what with men, women and children, 165, besides those that perished and were killed. And when the battle was over, all praised God for the great mercy He had shown them, in that he had willed to give them such a victory with so little damage to themselves. They were all very joyful, praising loudly the Lord God for that he had deigned to give such help to such a handful of His Christian people.

The sanctimonious slaughter of Negroes begun by the Christian Portuguese continues to this day in all the colonies of imperialism. The lynching of Negroes with the added spice of bestial tortures is only the American method of this international process which Yankee ingenuity has improved upon.

The triumphant religious note can still be heard in the southern jungles.

Let us leap four centuries and see if those altruistic upholders of democracy and the rights of small nations, the British ruling class, show in their attitude towards Negro colonials anything that would warrant the assumption that British capitalism differs from American capitalism in this respect. Speaking of the attitude of the whites towards the Africans in British colonies, Lord Grey, who can hardly be accused of partiality, said in 1880:

Throughout this part of the British dominions the colored people are generally looked upon by the whites as an inferior race, whose interests ought to be systematically disregarded when they come into competition with their own, and who ought to be governed mainly with a view to the advantage of the superior race. And for this advantage two things are considered to be especially necessary: First, that facilities should be afforded to the white colonists for obtaining possession of land heretofore occupied by the native tribes; and secondly, that the Kaffir population should be made to furnish as large and as cheap a supply of labor as possible.

Could the policy of imperialism be stated more frankly and concisely?

What is the effect of the application of this policy:

Let one, a member of the Matabele—one of the African tribes under British rule, speak for the natives. Testifying before a Royal Commission he said: "Our country is gone, our cattle have gone, our people are scattered, we have nothing to live for, our women are deserting us; the white man does as he likes with them; we are the slaves of the white man, we are nobody and have no rights or laws of any kind."

The natives were herded into "labor camps" and forced to work for the conquerors. Says E. D. Morel, the famous English liberal, in his "The Black Man's Burden": "Some hundreds of native police were raised and armed, and, as happens EVERYWHERE in Africa where the supervision is not strict, committed many brutal acts. Their principal duty appears to have been 'assisting' to procure the needed supply of labor, and hunting down deserters." (Emphasis mine).

The *Matabele Times* spoke brutally: "The theory of shooting a nigger on sight is too suggestive of the rule of Donnybrook Fair to be other than a diversion rather than a satisfactory principle. We have been doing it up to now, burning kraals simply because they were native kraals, and firing upon fleeing natives simply because they were black."

In 1920 the family of Lobengula, the former native ruler of a large section of British South Africa signed a petition to his Royal British Majesty which says:

The members of the late King Lobengula's family, your petitioners, and several members of the tribe are now scattered about on farms parcelled out to white settlers, and are practically created a nomadic people living in this scattered condition, under a veiled form of slavery; they are not allowed individually to cross from one farm to another, or from place to place except under a system of permit or pass and are practically forced to do labor on these private farms as a condition of their occupying land in Matabeleland.

Instead of getting better the conditions of the Negroes in the colonies of British imperialism become worse as the remnants of land left are taken from them. In the South African mining districts is almost an exact replica of the conditions suffered by the Negroes in the southern states.

We will deal with Germany more briefly because she is no longer a ruler of colonies. But the record established by her rulers before her empire was divided among her foes shows little difference from the incidents already cited. Speaking in the Reichstag in 1904 on the Colonial Budget, Herr Schlettwein delivered himself of the following, which I ask you to compare with the statement of white policy by Lord Grey:

The Hereros (a West African tribe) must be compelled to work, and to work without compensation and in return for their food only. Forced labor for years is only a just punishment, and at the same time it is the best method of training men. The feelings of Christianity and the philanthropy with which missionaries work, must for the present be repudiated with all energy.

The Germans killed the Hereros who refused to work. It was very simple. It was a slaughter on a wholesale scale of poorly armed natives by troops equipped with the most modern weapons of death. A German writer records a conversation between some settlers arriving after the crushing of the natives, and one of the soldiers: "Children, how could it be otherwise? They (the Hereros) were ranchmen and landowners, and we were there to make them landless workingmen."

It seems hardly necessary to mention Belgium when the record of her atrocities on the Negroes of the Congo was heralded to the world, but perhaps the world war and the flood of sympathy that went out to her because she suffered one-millionth part of what her rulers inflicted on the Negroes, may have dimmed the memory. To keep the record straight we give two quotations describing the methods by which rubber was obtained:

There is not an inhabited village left in four days steaming through a country formerly so rich; today entirely ruined. . . . The villages are compelled to furnish so many kilos of rubber every week. . . . The soldiers sent out to get rubber and ivory are depopulating the country. They find that the quickest and cheapest method is to raid villages, seize prisoners, and have them redeemed afterwards for ivory.

It is blood-curdling to see them (the soldiers) returning with the hands of the slain, and to find the hands of young children amongst the bigger ones evidencing their bravery. . . The rubber from this district has cost hundreds of lives, and the scenes I have witnessed, while unable to help the oppressed, have been almost enough to make me wish I was dead. . . The rubber traffic is steeped in blood, and if the natives were to rise and sweep every white person on the upper Congo into eternity, there would still be a fearful balance to their credit. (Letter of an American missionary named Clark, quoted by E. D. Morel in the work already cited.)

In 20 years the population of the Belgian Congo was reduced by these methods from more than 30,000,000 to less than 9,000,000.

"Bleeding Belgium," indeed, but the blood of Negroes, not her own.

And now for a glance at the colonial policy of France wherein is located that dear Paris where the Negro is allowed all the privileges accorded the whites—or was until it was filled first with American soldiers and then with American tourists who come to see the graves of those who died to save that dear France and incidentally "make the world safe for democracy."

France is the second great European colonial power. Her African holdings are immense, inferior in size only to those of Great Britain. She recruited hundreds of thousands of Negro troops during the world war and she still enforces conscription in her African colonies. These troops have Negro officers who meet French officers on equal terms and who are dined and feted when they come to Paris.

Does this mean that French policy toward "backward" peoples is a model for the world? Hardly, as we shall see.

Sending in long and detailed reports is one of the best things that the colonial bureaucrats do. Unfortunately for the admirers of France, some of these reports have seen the light of day and show—

That France conducts the same bloody, brutal and ruthless policy among the Africans that we have already seen in operation in British, German and Belgian Africa. That is to say:

> Soon, if this policy is persisted in, if the incendiarism and devastation of villages does not stop . . . if the concessionaires are always to enjoy the right of imposing such and such a "corvee" (Forced labor levy—W. F. D.) upon the inhabitants, and to place an embargo upon all the latter possesses, the banks of the Congo, the Ubanghi, and the Bangha will be completely deserted.

Another French official wrote:

> The dead, we no longer count them. The villages, horrible charnel-houses, disappear in this yawning gulf. A thousand diseases follow in our footsteps. . . . We white men must shut our eyes not to see the hideous dead, the dying who curse us, and the wounded who implore, the weeping women and starving children.

In one typical region 20,000 out of a total of 40,000 Negroes were killed off in two years.

We have now had a brief glimpse of imperialism in Belgian colonies and we find it as similar as two drops of water—or shall we say blood?

The conclusion can be drawn that when in the imperialist nations a Negro is treated as an equal by the ruling class it is for only two reasons:

First: He has betrayed or is betraying his fellows—is a tool of the imperialists.

Second: Because the imperialist nation does not wish to cause itself unnecessary trouble among the colonials by bad treatment of individuals when good treatment costs nothing.

Let the Negro in France or England or Belgium try to take the privileges in the colonies that he is accorded in the imperialist nation proper and there is a different story.

The social reformists of Europe have accepted the doctrine of racial equality and they are much concerned to see that the black man is not ill-treated in Europe. They have no wish however, to link up the struggles of the colonial peoples with those of the working class at home. They may realize the revolutionary role of the dark-skinned peoples in the world struggle against capitalism, but they are not for it any more than are the liberal intellectuals. E. D. Morel comments upon this as follows:

And curiously enough there is a type of European socialist mind that . . . reinforces these tendencies (of capitalism). This type of mind visualizes the mass of African humanity in terms of a dogmatic economic theory. It would stand aside from capitalistic exploitation, which it regards as a necessary and inevitable episode in human development. It would do nothing to safeguard native institutions which it looks upon as archaic and reactionary. It would apply the same processes to all races (it refuses, apparently, to recognize any other form of civilization other than the European socialized state) at whatever stage of cultural development. It would cheerfully assist . . . at the destruction of African institutions and assent to the conversion of African cultivators and farmers into wage-slaves. . . . The only comment I would venture to make upon the contentions of this school, is that the form of socialism which Russia has evolved, and which, I suppose, is the most advanced form of European socialism now available to study, approximates closely to the social conditions of an advanced tropical African community. The spinal column of both is a system of land tenure which ensures to the population a large measure of economic independence.

Lenin once called Morel "an honest liberal." It is evident from the above quotation that Morel was not only honest in his attitude towards the Negroes, but that he understood the revolutionary part landless races are destined to play.

And now we come back to America and the 12,000,000 Negroes in the United States and its colonies, 90 per cent of whom are workers and farmers. Oppressed as a race and as a class they have two allies—the white working class of the United States and their African kindred.

The two can be separated only at the cost of seriously hampering both. There must be no illusions in the minds of the American Negro masses that in some other capitalist nation there is freedom to be found. They are all alike and the Negro workers and peasants will have to fight the white ruling class wherever they are located.

More than that, the American Negroes will have to take the lead in uniting their race internationally, as a race, and then bringing it into line with the world struggle of the working class.

The same slogan to which the workers and peasants of Russia rallied, behind the Communists in 1917, can be used to stir the oppressed Negroes into action.

Peace, Bread and LAND—what racial or social group needs these three things more than the 120,000,000 beaten, bullied and landless African Negroes?

In the United States these same demands can be expressed in the slogan of full social, political and economic equality.

Jay Lovestone

Introduction

Jay Lovestone (1897–1990) was an American Communist Party leader who later became an anticommunist labor official in the AFL-CIO. Ascending to the leadership of the party in the late 1920s, Lovestone found himself on the wrong side of power struggles in the Soviet Union and was expelled from the party. Lovestone then led a small communist oppositional group for a time, before moving to the right and becoming an anticommunist in the 1940s.

Lovestone was born in present-day Belarus, emigrating to New York in 1907. Lovestone joined the Intercollegiate Socialist Society while a student at City College and sided with the Left Wing in the Socialist Party split. He quickly ascended to the leadership of the young Communist Party, working as an editor and writer in the party press.

In the factional battles of the early CP, Lovestone allied himself with the New York–based faction led by Charles Ruthenberg. This faction was distinguished by an emphasis on political action, arguing for a mass labor party in the United States; its opponents, led by William Z. Foster, placed more emphasis on building radical currents within the unions. Lovestone was a loyal ally of the Ruthenberg faction, and by the mid-1920s was the faction's second in command.

When Ruthenberg died in 1927, Lovestone became head of the Communist Party. In that position, he conducted the purge of James P. Cannon and other supporters of Leon Trotsky in 1928. Immediately thereafter, however, Lovestone found himself the target of a purge from Moscow. Lovestone was a supporter of Nikolai Bukharin in the USSR, and Bukharin and Stalin had come into conflict. The political roots of Lovestone's heresy

375

were in his advocacy of the theory of American exceptionalism, which held that capitalism had stabilized in the United States and insurrectionary tactics had to be abandoned. This theory came at precisely the wrong time, however, as Stalin and the Comintern had just endorsed their "Third Period" policy, which pronounced that a period of imminent revolution was on the horizon.

After his expulsion from the party, Lovestone set up the Communist Party (Opposition). Originally a loyal opposition to the official party, the CP(O) soon found its footing in alliance with various anti-CP forces within the labor movement. Though the group remained strong, it developed a cadre who would be influential beyond their numbers with both intellectuals and union activists of some talent.

As Lovestone's political activity became more and more centered on combating the Communist Party, he moved further to the right. During World War II, he turned his attention to combating Communist influence in unions internationally, working with the AFL to undermine Communist unions, often through supporting employers, organized crime, or some combination thereof. Lovestone would continue to work in this capacity until his retirement in the early 1970s. Throughout the mid-century, when the AFL-CIO conducted a covert war against communists in unions from South America to Europe to Africa, Lovestone was at the very center of it.

Lovestone's article here shows a keen insight into political developments along the color line. He argues that the Great Migration is reshaping racial politics in the United States, both in nationalizing the race question and leading to a new strength for Black workers in the North. Further arguing that the new concentration of Black workers in Northern cities is likely to yield a new Black combativeness, he urges the party to support this struggle. Lovestone's attentiveness to Black politics would continue even after his expulsion from the CP, as the CP(O) would proceed to build a base in Harlem in the 1930s, acting as a political training ground for organizers, including Ella Baker and Pauli Murray.

Further Reading

Alexander, Robert J. *The Right Opposition: The Lovestoneites and the International Communist Opposition of the 1930s*. Westport, CT: Greenwood Press, 1981.

Le Blanc, Paul, and Tim Davenport. *The "American Exceptionalism" of Jay Lovestone and His Comrades, 1929–1940*. Leiden, The Netherlands: Brill, 2015.

Morgan, Ted. *Jay Lovestone: A Covert Life*. New York: Random House, 1999.

The Great Negro Migration

As a result of the world war, the class divisions and the relation of class forces in the United States changed deeply.

A most striking phenomenon of this character is the mass migration of the Negroes, mainly from the cotton plantations of the South to the industrial centers of the northern and eastern states. John Pepper characterizes these migrations strikingly as "unarmed Spartacus uprisings" against the slavery and the oppression of the capitalist oligarchy in the Southern states. This phenomenon is of tremendous economic, political and social significance for the whole American working class.

Co-incident with such dynamic forces influencing the class relations in the United States, is the increasing world supremacy of American imperialism.

America has become the center of the economic and cultural emancipation of the Negro. Here this movement forms and crystallizes itself. Therefore it is especially important for the success of the efforts of the Comintern and the Red International of Labor Unions striving to mobilize the millions of Negro masses of Africa, Costa Rica, Guatemala, Colombia, Nicaragua, and the satrapies of American imperialism such as Porto Rico, Haiti and Santa Domingo, against the world bourgeoisie, that the movement of the Negroes in the United States should develop in a revolutionary direction.

Extent of the Negro Migration

According to the last census (January, 1920) there were in the United States 10,463,131 Negroes of whom eight million were then still in the Southern states. The recent migration of the Negroes from the South took place during two main periods. The first was 1916–1917 when, because of the entrance of

Originally published in the *Workers Monthly*, February 1926, 179–84.

America into the world war, a strong demand for skilled labor power arose and whole Negro colonies and Negro villages migrated to the northern industrial centers. This migration totaled approximately four hundred thousand. The second period, 1922–23 coincided with the peak of American industry that followed after the economic crisis of 1920–21, and is to be traced back to the great demand for unskilled labor in the Northern districts.

According to the findings of the United States Agricultural Department, the period since 1916 has seen an annual migration of 200,000 Negroes from the Southern states, as against ten to twelve thousand annually for the period before 1916. In the four years from 1916 to 1920 between 400,000 and 730,000 Negroes left for the North. In the period from 1916 to 1924 the figures reached one million. The influence of this upon the concentration of population is obvious from the following figures: In 1910 the Southern states included 80.68% of the Negro population of America, while in 1920 only 76.99%. In four of these eleven states, the decrease of the general population from 1910 to 1920 was primarily due to the migration of the Negroes.

In 1923, 32,000 or 13% of the colored agricultural workers left Georgia for the North. In the same year, there migrated from Alabama 10,000, from Arkansas, 15,000, and from South Carolina, 22,700 Negroes.

On the other hand, the Negro population of the Northern industrial city, Detroit, the greatest automobile center, increased in the period of 1910 to 1920 from 57,000 to about 90,000 and of Chicago, from 109,000 in 1919 to 200,000 in 1924. The strength of this migration from the South is evidenced by the fact that records show that in one day 3,000 Negroes passed thru a railroad station in Philadelphia. And this was not unusual. The mass of the emigrants consisted of agricultural workers and small tenants.

Because of the lack of labor power, many cotton and fruit plantations had to change to cattle breeding and dairying. According to the investigation of the Bankers Association of Georgia, there were, in 1923, in this state, no less than 46,674 deserted farms and 55,524 unplowed plots of land. Furthermore, on account of the migrations there was a loss of national wealth to the state amounting to $27,000,000.

The bourgeoisie and the big landowners in the southern states naturally at first resorted to strong measures against the mass exodus of their slaves. Thus in Georgia, for example, a law was passed according to which the "hiring of workers for other states; thru private persons or organizations is to be considered as a crime." The plantation owners in Tennessee forced their government to put all those Negroes in custody who registered themselves in unemployment bureaus. In South Carolina and Virginia, all agents who were to obtain workers for other states had to pay a special license fee of $2,500 on the pain of suffering greater fine or imprisonment.

Causes of Migration

The most important causes for the migration of Negroes from the South are the following:

1. The oppressive conditions of life and work of the Negro population, consisting mostly of tenants and agricultural workers.

2. The boll weevil plague in the cotton plantations.

3. The general agrarian crisis which forced the tenants in the South, as well as in the northern states, to look for work in the cities.

4. The deepgoing dissatisfaction among the Negroes in the South, especially after the world war.

5. The intense development of industry in the northern states, as a consequence of the world war, coupled with the immigration ban, as a result of which the demand for unskilled labor power grew tremendously.

1. Living and Working Conditions of the Southern Negroes

Most of the labor power in cotton production in the South has been Negro. In the period from 1880–1920, the percentage of plantation owners in the cotton belt sank from 62% to 49.8%. Seventy to ninety per cent of the cultivated land in the cotton districts of Georgia, South Carolina and Mississippi are rented by Negro tenants. In Mississippi 60% of all cotton farms are worked by Negroes, of whom 85% are tenants.

The tenants have not the slightest prospect of ever acquiring the possession of the land on which they work—a prospect that is still in the realms of possibility for the white farmer in the northeastern states, altho even here such prospects are now under ever growing difficulties. For the Negroes, the status of the tenant is unchangeable. Leading a miserable existence, the Negro tenant is in the rarest cases able to provide his children with an elementary education. Thus, in 1923 in the state of Georgia, the appropriations for the schools for Negroes who at that time composed 45% of the population reached the total of $15,000 as opposed to the appropriation of $735,000 for the whites. We must add to this the usurious credit system which still more diminishes the scanty earnings of the tenant. The prices of the commodities bought by Negro tenants on credit are on the average seventy percent higher but in Texas it is 81% and in Arkansas 90%.

As a rule, the Negro tenant has a claim to only a half of the product of the labor of his relatives or others whose help he can obtain. Of this, the owners are legally empowered to deduct for supposed allowances and services by the land barons for means of life, clothing, medical help, etc. Many landowners are at the same time also merchants. Since written agreements are entirely unusual, the Negro is thus further uniformly swindled in the most shameless way.

The Negro masses are exploited so intensely that they are often more miserable than under chattel slavery. The status of the Negroes, their working conditions, and their sufferings, are illustrated in the following quotation from a report of the National Association of Manufacturers, of October 7, 1920:

> The bad economic exploitation in these cases indicates a slavery many times worse than the former real slavery. Thousands of Negroes who have been working all their lives uninterruptedly are not able to show the value of ten dollars, and are not able to buy the most necessary clothing at the close of the season. They live in the most wretched condition . . . and are lucky to get hold of a worn out pair of boots or some old clothing.

Judge S. O. Bratton who was able to obtain in Little Rock, Arkansas, an accurate picture of the relations between the whites and the blacks, writes as follows: "The conditions today are worse than before the American Civil War. . . . The system of exploitation is carried to such a point that most Negroes can hardly keep themselves alive upon their earnings. The plantation owners maintain so-called 'commission businesses' in which the prices of commodities are fixed at the order of the plantation inspectors. The Negroes are prevented in every possible way from keeping an account of the wares taken by them."

Another big source of misery is to be found in the "lynch law" and the terror of the Ku Klux Klan. In the January 1924 issue of the *North American*

Review we have an illuminating report of Howard Snyder who spent many years in the plantation districts of Mississippi. Mr. Snyder says:

> If we add the cruel lynch law which is responsible for the murder of many Negroes burned alive, of whom we never hear in our great newspapers, and if we keep in mind that the Negroes working on the plantations are helpless and defenseless beings who are thrown into panic at the very mention of the Ku Klux Klan, then we will be able to understand the other causes of the mass migration. Nowhere in the world is there among the civilized peoples a human being so cruelly persecuted as the Negro in the South. Almost every day we read that some Negro was baited to death with dogs or whipped to death, or burned alive amidst the howls of huge crowds. How they could ever cherish the hope in the South that these people would suffer all this without protest when twenty dollars, the price of a railway ticket, can be sufficient to free them from this hell, passes my understanding.

2. The Boll Weevil Plague and the Agricultural Crisis

The boll weevil plague which recently visited the cotton plantations, has been a tremendous factor in changing the South. According to the approximate evaluation, the damages wrought by this pest in the years 1917–22 amounted from 1,900,000,000. As a consequence of this, cotton-cultivated land grew markedly smaller. Thus many black workers and tenants were forced to go to the North.

The World War and the Negro

This wretched system existed prior to the world war. The Negroes were dissatisfied even before the world war. Yet it was the world war with its consequent fundamental economic changes and the Negro migration as a result of the rapid industrialization in the North and East that gave special impetus and created favorable opportunities for a wave of intense dissatisfaction among the Negro tenants and agricultural workers. We must not underestimate the deep going change in the ideology of the Negro masses called forth by the world war. Whole generations were, so to speak, tied down like slaves to the soil. To them, their village was the world. And now, suddenly, hundreds of thousands of them (376,710) were drawn into military service. Over 200,000 were sent across and returned with new concepts, with new hopes, with a new belief in their people. Their political and social sphere of ideas broadened. Their former hesitancy and lack of decision was now leaving them. The Negroes were stirred en masse and set out to carry thru their aspirations, left their miserable shacks and went to look for better working and living conditions.

Simultaneously, the immigration of European workers into America was practically ended by the world war. In the post-war period, strict legal measures were taken for the same end. In this way, one of the best sources of the stream of unskilled labor was dried up. Thru the world war, however, the development of American industry made mighty steps forward and with this the demand for labor power rose. The industrial reserve army had to be filled up and the bourgeoisie of the North turned to the Southern states. In the Negro masses they saw a fitting reservoir to supply their gigantic factories of the northern and eastern states.

To illustrate how the capitalists looked upon the Negro problem in this phase of development, we have the following quotations of Blanton Fortson in a recent number of the *Forum*:

> Disregarding his low stage of development, the undesirable immigrant is characterized by all those traits which are foreign to the Negro. He is permeated with Bolshevism. He understands neither the American language nor the American employers, contracts marriage with American women, multiplies very fast, so that finally, if the door is not closed to the stream of people of his kind, the real native workers will be suppressed by them.
>
> In normal times, there always exists in the industrial centers a demand for unskilled labor. Where can the North find this? To import unskilled workers from eastern and southern Europe means to increase the number of inferior people in America (To this apologist of capitalism, the "people permeated with Bolshevism" are inferior. J. L.) If, however, we make use of the Negroes for this purpose, then we will simply redistribute the people of a lower race already existing in the United States and not increase them; in fact, diminish them.

A more open declaration as to how the ruling class in America fills up its industrial reserve army with the help of the South and in this way lowers wages could hardly be found. The Negroes who are tenants or agricultural laborers naturally seek to escape from their oppressive condition in the South. Better wage and working conditions in the North, somewhat more favorable educational facilities, and the illusory hopes of finally escaping from their difficulties are the motives of the Negroes in their migration. This phenomenon is one of the most significant in history. Today a Negro quarter can be found in nearly every one of the smallest towns of the northern states.

The Results of the Migration of the Negroes

1. The Improvement of the Standard of Living

No one can question the fact that thru this migration of the Negroes the standard of living of the colored workers and peasants has been considerably raised. In comparison with the conditions confronting them in the southern states, before 1914 the colored workers today certainly have more opportunities to dispose of their only possession, labor power. Moreover, the mass exodus from the South has forced the ruling classes in the cotton fields to ameliorate the cruel treatment of their agricultural workers and in many cases even to raise their wages. The strong demand for colored workers has raised their price.

2. The Strengthening of Race Consciousness

A further result of the mass migration of the Negroes is the development of a stronger race consciousness. Since hundreds of thousands of colored people have freed themselves from the yoke of slavery in the South, their pride and their confidence in the race have grown. The Negroes have begun to organize themselves. They are now taking up the struggle against their oppression in a more organized fashion. This is one of the real meanings of the still organizationally weak American Negro Labor Congress.

It is, therefore, no accident that in the recent years lynching has been on a decrease. For example, in 1892, there were 155 Negroes murdered in the United States; three decades later, 1922, only 61; and in 1923, only 28, while in 1924 there were only 16. This is partly to be traced to the changed attitude of the capitalists. But primarily it is to be attributed to the fact that of late Negroes have been offering more effective resistance to their oppressors.

In October, 1919, for example, the colored tenants in Phillips county, Arkansas, rose up against their oppressive exploiters. It went as far as a bloody battle in which five whites and seventeen Negroes were killed. Also in Charlestown, West Virginia, Tulsa, Oklahoma, we had similar revolts. Furthermore, the Negro uprisings in the Northern centers, Chicago, Omaha and Duluth, were in a certain sense also the evidence of a strengthened race consciousness.

3. Concentration of the Negro Proletariat

The migration of the Negro proletariat to the industrial cities of the North hastened its concentration. As evidence, we can point to the growing number of colored people living in the cities. In the last 20 years this rate of increase among the colored workers has grown much faster than among the whites. Whereas the white urban population was 43.3 per cent of the total population of the United States in 1900, 48.1 per cent in 1910 and 53.3 per cent in 1920, the following relations obtained for the colored population: 1900—22.6 per cent, 1910—27.3 per cent, 1920—34.2 per cent. In 1920 more than 50 per cent of the Negro population in 27 states was found in the cities. With the white population only fourteen states showed fifty per cent or more living in the cities.

This tendency also prevails in the South, despite of the mass migration of the Negroes. For example, in the state of Mississippi the total number of Negroes fell by 75,000 from 1910 to 1920, the colored urban population increased by 3.4 per cent. Above all, the social composition of the Negroes has changed extraordinarily. Before the migration, the overwhelming majority was employed on the cotton plantations, today the greater proportion work for the industrial concerns. In the North, the Negroes had formerly been engaged as domestic help. Now, however, they are dominantly employed in heavy industry.

The Significance of the Migration

In the South there is to be found approximately one quarter of the total population of the United States. Therefore, this migration is of tremendous economic, political and social significance for the entire country.

1. The Industrialization of the South

Up to now the operation and organization of the cotton plantations were on an extremely primitive level. It was largely because of the migration of the black workers that the bourgeoisie were forced to reorganize their cotton culture and use machinery on a larger scale. Besides, the capitalists were forced to pay more attention to the natural resources of the southern states. This also hastened the industrialization of this section of the country.

2. The Negro as a Political Factor

The mass migration of the Negroes to the North has increased their importance as a political factor. It is clear that their votes are of great importance in the elections of the northern industrial states. In the South the Negroes are very often deprived of their suffrage upon this or that pretext. In the North such disfranchisement is not so open or prevalent. From 1910 to 1920 the number of Negroes with votes (from 21 years up) increased in New York from 95,177 to 142,580; in New Jersey from 58,467 to 75,671; in Ohio from 72,871 to 126,940; in Indiana from 39,037 to 53,935 and in Illinois from 74,225 to 128,450. The Republican as well as the Democratic Party made the greatest attempts to win these voters for themselves in the northern industrial centers.

3. The Negro Question—A National Problem

Thru the migration of the Negroes to the North the Negro problem did not lose any of its significance for the United States as a whole. On the contrary, it gained importance inasmuch as it became a question of national significance. In practically every industrial center the question of the segregation of the Negroes, their segregation in separate quarters of the city, stood on the order as an acute problem in some form or other. Thus, in the last report of the American Ass'n for the Advancement of the Colored People, it said, "In 1924, the most significant question was the creation of separate schools, of separate city quarters for the colored population of the United States."

The broad masses of the Negroes migrating to the North have to a great extent recognized that the illusions which caused them to look upon the Northern states as a paradise were painfully unfounded. The apparent social and political equality of the Negro with the rest of the population of the North had only the slightest pretense to existence in fact so long as the Negroes constituted only a small minority.

The more the Negro problem takes on a national character the more important a role does the South begin to play in the economic and political life of the United States. To the working masses the Negro problem appears on first consideration as a class and racial question. But we should not forget that the basis of the class principle and not the racial principle, must serve as our point of judgement in this instance. In short, the mass migration has not solved the Negro problem in the United States. On the contrary, the great Negro migration has placed this problem before us with greater clarity.

We point to the plans to isolate the Negro population in the northern states, to the Negro revolts, as well as to the expulsion of the Negroes from the industrial city of Johnstown, Pa., in 1923.

Negro Migration and the American Proletariat

1. Racial Prejudice

Considered from the economic standpoint the Negro problem is a part of the general problem of the unskilled worker in the United States. Except for those working on the cotton plantations in the South, a large number of Negroes work in the steel industry, in the coal mines, in the packing houses, in tobacco and cigar factories. The unionization of the Negroes is made extraordinarily difficult by the artificially nourished hatred of the white worker for his colored fellow-worker. The bourgeoisie is very eager to stimulate racial prejudice.

2. The Trade Union Bureaucracy and the Organization of the Negro

The trade union bureaucracy has been consistently refusing to accept the Negro into the trade unions. We can cite the attitude and practices of the railroad workers, locomotive enginemen and firemen, the boilermakers and other trade unions. The American Federation of Labor has concerned itself with the organization of the Negroes only on paper. It is true that there was established in 1920 a special commission for this purpose. But it did nothing. At the congress of the A. F. of L. in 1923 the Executive Council reported that it was impossible to prevail upon the railroad workers and the boilermakers to change their statutes and accept Negroes into their organization. This, however, was only a gesture, since in fact nothing was undertaken to exercise any pressure upon these unions. Because of the efforts of the American Negro Labor Congress, it is said that the Executive

Council of the American Federation of Labor has put on four organizers ostensibly for special work among the Negroes.

The harmfulness of these tactics of the trade union bureaucracy is shown with special clarity in the following occurrence in the steel industry, in which at present, many Negroes are employed. From this it is clearly seen how the bosses play the reactionary leaders against the Negro workers in order to prejudice these workers against all the activities of the trade unions in the steel industry. The Negro organ, "The Crisis," made public in November, 1923, [was] a circular distributed by the Indiana Foundry Company of Muncie among the colored workers who at that time were brought in as strike-breakers. We quote from this circular which had very serious consequences for the strikers:

> "Our factory works on the open shop principle. Most of our puddlers, who are colored, have just been trained by us. The union is not in agreement with this and wants to force us to submit to its will. In our city there are four factories in which only members of the union may work and three which are open to all workers. Our factory is the only one in which the Negroes can rise to be skilled workers. Now the union demands that all colored workers who are employed as puddlers should be replaced by whites and that these must submit to the union's statutes."

The trade union bureaucrats therefore make it possible for the capitalists to split the proletarian ranks and in the above case were responsible for the capitalists being able to beat the white as well as the black workers.

3. The Possibility of Organizing the Negro

Unquestionably, the racial prejudice of the workers makes it much harder to organize the Negro proletariat. It must further be added that the Negroes on the cotton plantations of the South were working and living under an almost patriarchal system in relation to their masters. This naturally still tends to influence their minds. Yet the Negroes have many times demonstrated their organizability. In 1913 the well-known petty-bourgeois Negro leader, Booker T. Washington, attempted to determine to what extent it was possible to organize the Negro. Out of the 51 questionnaires he sent out for this purpose, only 2 were received with the answer that it was impossible to make the

Negroes good members of a labor organization. Moreover, there are already in the United States several mixed unions that include in their ranks white as well as Negro workers. Outside of that, there are 400 independent trade unions of Negroes. Then, there are hundreds of thousands of Negroes who are members of mass organizations of colored workers.

4. Necessity of Unity Between Negro and White Workers

The rapidly advancing concentration of the Negro proletariat, the increasing political significance of the Negro workers, the efforts of the bourgeoisie to stimulate the racial antagonism between the Negro and the white workers, and finally the growing racial consciousness of the Negro—all of these demand that the workers of the United States and their organizations should not allow racial prejudice to dominate in the least but should adhere only to the class principle. If the white workers follow any other tactics and permit their exploiter to split the proletariat thru racial hatred and prejudice then they will deliver themselves body and soul to their deadly enemies.

5. What Must the American Workers Do?

A solution of the Negro problem in the United States is offered only in the program of the Workers (Communist) Party. The American proletariat must at every opportunity support the Negro in his struggle against the exploiters and oppressors of all the workers—white and black. The American Negro Labor Congress is a step in the right direction for the development of a movement to unify all workers regardless of color against the bourgeoisie.

The American working class must fight for the social, political and economic equality of the Negro.

The representatives of the working class must do everything to remove the obstacles which many trade unions place in the way of the acceptance of the Negroes becoming members. Where this is not possible at the present moment, it is not out of order to form temporary organizations of Negroes, the chief task of which must be, under all circumstances, to demand unification of the American proletariat regardless of race or nationality against the exploiters, against the bourgeoisie as a whole.

William Z. Foster

Introduction

W illiam Z. Foster (1881–1961) was one of the most important union leaders of the first half of the twentieth century, later becoming a leader of the Communist Party. Foster began his long political career as an IWW member shortly after the turn of the century, later becoming a syndicalist who advocated working within existing AFL unions, finally joining the Communist Party in 1921. From then until 1957, Foster was one of the foremost leaders of the party, sidelined only by periods of illness or incarceration.

Foster first rose to national prominence as leader of the great steel strike of 1919. An attempt to force union recognition on the steel companies, the strike saw some 250,000 workers go out under Foster's leadership. Unfortunately, the determination of the striking workers was overcome by a combination of brutal repression and the use of strikebreakers. Reflecting on the defeat a few years later, Foster noted that, in particular, the union had failed to overcome divisions between Black and white workers.

Soon thereafter, Foster joined the Communist Party, won over by a visit to the USSR. In the party, Foster ran the Trade Union Education League (TUEL), a rank-and-file organization aimed at radicalizing the American union movement. Though antiracism was never a focus of the league, it did propagandize on behalf of interracialism in the unions.

Life in the CP in the 1920s was dominated by the factional struggle in the organization. Foster quickly emerged as one of the leaders of the faction most oriented to trade-union work. Work on the race question soon became a stake in the factional contest, as Foster's opponents accused the union leader and his allies, such as James P. Cannon and William F.

Dunne, of accommodating themselves to the racism of the American union movement. While there were clear weaknesses in the writings on Black oppression that Foster's group produced, on the whole, this charge is a significant distortion of their record.

These factional struggles finally ended when the Communist International, at Stalin's orders, elevated Foster above his factional opponents, who were subsequently expelled, to make him party secretary of the CP. In this capacity, Foster oversaw the transition to the Third Period line, when the CP argued that revolution was imminent, and that other progressive groups were simply reformist obstacles to be smashed. The results of this approach were decidedly mixed, particularly when it came to antiracist struggle. On the one hand, the party essentially declared war on groups like the NAACP, cutting themselves off from prospective allies and alienating the Black workers they needed to win over. On the other, the party's audacity in this period led it to take initiatives such as sending organizers into the Deep South and starting new radical unions that accepted Black workers on an equal basis, actions that would pay substantial dividends over the course of the 1930s.

Foster was the party's head until 1932, when, running for president on the CP ticket, he suffered a heart attack and had to step back from political activity. He would return to activity in 1935, but by then, the Popular Front period had begun, and the party, under the leadership of Earl Browder, was oriented to making allies with liberals. While Foster opposed this new orientation, he was careful never to let his opposition create a basis for his expulsion.

His patience paid off in 1945, when Earl Browder was removed from leadership at Moscow's behest. Foster took the reins once more, leading the party through the perilous Cold War years. Over the course of the next decade, anticommunist repression in the United States and revelations about Stalin's rule abroad wore on the party significantly, and by the time Foster retired in 1957, the party was a shadow of its former self.

Foster's article here, a report on the prospects for southern organizing, shows how seriously the party was taking the race question by the end of the 1920s. Foster argues for the necessity of organizing black workers, combating the racism of the union bureaucracy, and exposing the Democratic and Republican parties as false friends of Black Americans. Though the Black Belt Thesis, adopted by the Comintern a few months earlier in August, undoubtedly played a role in the centrality Foster ascribed to antiracist struggle, it is notable that the article contains little that derives programmatically from it. Instead, it largely builds on the previous work of CP writers such as Fort-Whiteman, Minor, and Dunne. By the time the Black Belt Thesis was published in the *Daily Worker* in early 1929, the party had already moved to make Black liberation a central strategic orientation.

Further Reading

Barrett, James R. *William Z. Foster and the Tragedy of American Radicalism*. Champaign: University of Illinois Press, 2002.

Foster, William Z. *From Bryan to Stalin*. New York: International Publishers, 1937.

Johanningsmeier, Edward P. *Forging American Communism: The Life of William Z. Foster*. Princeton: Princeton University Press, 1994.

The Workers (Communist) Party in the South

The Workers (Communist) Party has made a beginning at active work in the south. This is a fact of major importance in the development of the class struggle in the United States. For this reason, among others, the present election campaign marks an epoch in the history of our Party.

The work in the south has been begun by the sending of several organizers into the field, by touring of election speakers, by the issuance of special literature, by the placing of the Party on the ballot in a number of southern states, etc.

It was my part, in this work, to address election meetings in Louisville, Birmingham, New Orleans, Atlanta, Norfolk and Richmond. The meetings in Louisville, Birmingham and New Orleans were the first communist open mass meetings ever held in the respective states of Kentucky, Alabama and Louisiana. It is fitting that with the rapid industrialization of the south and with the developing struggle of the Negroes throughout the country, the Workers (Communist) Party, the party of the working class and the champion of the oppressed Negro race, should begin its operations in the south. These activities must be greatly increased in the future.

Manifestly, the south presents many difficult problems of a major character. These must be thoroughly analyzed, programs outlined for them, and the Party organized to solve them. To these ends it is highly important that the various organizers, speakers, and active comrades, participating in the southern work, carefully compile and present their experiences to the Party. The present article is a contribution in this sense.

Originally published in the *Communist*, November 1928, 676–81.

A Ripe Opportunity For Our Party

The industrialization of the south has been widely discussed in our press. There is no need for me to pile up, afresh, statistics to demonstrate this movement. But one is amazed in travelling through the south to see the extent of this new industrialization. Especially manifest is it in Alabama, Georgia and the Carolinas. In dozens of towns along the way one can see new factories of many kinds, either freshly built or now in course of construction. The various towns are plastered with invitations to capitalists to establish industries locally, offering them tax exemption, low-paid and satisfied labor, cheap power, etc. The respective Chambers of Commerce are carrying on nationwide campaigns of publicity along these lines. At the same time, there is widespread unemployment in the various cities of the south.

The rapid industrialization of the south increasingly develops a rich field for general class activity by our Party. Wages are very low, hours long, and working conditions bad in all the southern industries, new and old. In the great Alabama coal and steel industries, wages run as low as 15 cents per hour for unskilled workers, with 25 cents per hour top rate, with the cost of living almost as high as in northern industrial centers. The 10 to 12 hour day prevails. Similar conditions exist in the textile, lumber, railroad and other industries throughout the south. The farm workers and tenant farmers, submerged in poverty, live in a semi-feudal state.

The new proletariat in the south is being developed under conditions of hardship and poverty. It is one of the basic tasks of our Party to organize this increasingly important section of the working class and to lead it in the big struggles it is bound soon to carry on against the employers and the state. Trade unionism is weaker in the south than in any other section of the country. The great armies of workers in the coal, textile, steel, lumber and agricultural industries are completely unorganized. Only the skilled upper layers of railroad workers have unions. Even the building and printing trades workers have hardly more than a skeleton organization. Unions will be built in the southern industries and the workers' standards raised only by a militant fight against the existing terrorism, industrial and political.

It is idle to expect the ultra-reactionary southern trade-union bureaucracy to lead such a fight, or that the old unions can be used as our chief organizational basis, although we must also work in these unions. To organize the unorganized masses and lead them in struggle is the task of the left wing, led by our Party and the T. U. E. L. and its organizational program must be founded upon the establishment of new industrial unions in the basic industries. The Party and the T. U. E. L. must at once orientate themselves in this direction.

The role of the left wing as the organizer and leader of the working class of the south, is further emphasized by the increasing importance of the Negro workers in southern industry which stresses our need to organize them. Our Party is the only force that can organize and lead the Negro masses in real struggle. The Republican and Democratic Parties are manifestly the enemies of the Negroes. The trade-union bureaucracy, accepting the whole Jim Crow system of the exploiters, persecutes and oppresses the Negroes by barring them from the unions, discriminating against them in industry, and supporting their political disfranchisement and social ostracism. In Atlanta, for example, a typical situation exists. Negroes are not even allowed to come into the Labor Temple. And how little the Negroes can look to the Socialist Party for leadership is exemplified by the fact that Norman Thomas in his election tour through the south, never even mentioned the Negro question. This is in line with the general S. P. program regarding the Negroes. Only our Party speaks and fights for the Negroes and the situation in the south develops increasingly favorably for it to establish a mass following among the Negroes.

The Fight Against Jim-Crowism

The situation in the south, in addition to offering constantly more favorable opportunities for our Party to come forward as the leader of the working class, also progressively facilitates its activities as the organizer and defender of the Negro race. The bitter injustice of the Jim Crow caste system is forced upon one at every turn in the south. This outrageous thing, ranging from studied insults to the Negro race, rank discrimination in industry, political disfranchisement and social ostracism, to lynching and other forms of open terrorism, confronts one on all sides: special railroad cars for Negroes, "colored" restaurants, waiting-rooms, libraries, schools, living districts, elevators in office buildings, etc.

The hypocritical Christians do not even allow Negroes to attend the same churches with them. In one southern park a sign says: "Dogs and Negroes not admitted." In Atlanta, regarding Grant Park, a beautiful park given to the city years ago with the provision that Negroes should be entitled to patronize it as well as whites, an agitation is now on foot to close the park altogether, seeing that it is impossible, under the terms of the gift, to legally exclude Negroes. Every effort is made throughout the south to set aside the Negroes as a super-exploited class of "untouchables."

Negro life, liberty and property have no safeguards. The killing of a Negro by a white man is a minor affair. The whole Jim Crow system is enforced at the point of the gun. Negro criminals receive sentences twice as long as whites for the same crimes. Civil suits are decided as a matter of principle in favor of whites. And all this flagrant terror and injustice is perpetuated under the false, chauvinistic slogan of "white supremacy."

It is the historic task of our Party to lead the fight against this organized persecution of the Negroes. This is a revolutionary struggle. It must be carried on under the slogans of "full social, political and industrial equality for Negroes," and "the right of self-determination for the Negroes." This is necessary not only for the liberation struggle of the Negroes, but for the general revolutionary struggle of the whole working class.

The fight around the race issues will be a hard and bitter one, especially in the south. The reactionary advocates of "white supremacy" will meet the assault of our Party on their caste system with armed force as well as legal terrorism. They will seek to crush our organization with violence. Of this we may be sure when our party gets its work well under way but our Party will be equal to the situation. Overground or underground in the south, it will successfully carry on its activities.

Hoover and Smith in the South

Two basic factors now tend to facilitate our work of organizing and leading the Negroes in the south. One is the large role played by Negroes in the developing industries, which gives us a proletarian base for our Negro work in general. The other is the invasion of the "solid south" by the Republican Party, which is forcing this organization to expose its hypocritical pretenses of being the party of the Negroes. Let me speak of the latter factor.

Throughout the south one confronts widespread indications of Republican activities and sentiment. The Republican Party is making a most energetic attempt to split the solid south. Hoover buttons and automobile plates are in evidence on all sides. The Republicans will poll a large vote throughout the south, especially in Alabama, Tennessee, Kentucky,

Georgia, Virginia and the Carolinas, if they do not actually carry some or all of these states.

The industrialization of the south inevitably thrusts to the fore the chief party of big capital, the Republican Party. This party is driving to establish itself in the south by mobilizing behind it the "Protestant," dry, "American" vote. Its main instrument is the Ku Klux Klan, which, if organizationally weak, has a powerful ideological following. The Klan goes forward with a tremendous "whispering" campaign against Smith to unite all the Protestant bigotry in the south against him. This is being engineered by the republican leaders despite their public, hypocritical deprecation of such methods. The trade-union leaders, mostly Klansmen, are overwhelmingly with Hoover.

Already deep inroads have been made into the democratic organization. Splits, engineered by the republicans, have taken place in many southern states. In Virginia, "Hoover Democrats" have launched the Independent Democratic Party. In Mississippi, Democratic bolters have formed the Anti-Smith Democratic Party. Similar developments are taking place all through the south. Heflin is one of the leading spokesmen of this Anti-Smith movement which is entrenching the Republican Party in the south. On a train going through North Carolina, a party of democratic leaders, headed by Josephus Daniels, on their way to welcome Smith, occupied the same car with me and were excitedly planning how to stop all these untoward developments by "missionary work" in the districts.

To check the advance of the Republican Party, the democrats violently denounce that organization as the party of the Negroes and raise the slogan of "Vote for the Democratic Party and white supremacy." The secretary of the Democratic Party of Alabama recently declared that if the republicans break the solid south, federal troops will be used at the next election to enforce the Negro's right to vote.

Meanwhile every device of terror and duplicity is used to disfranchise the Negroes. Governor Long of Louisiana recently struck the democratic keynote in this respect when he said: "Any registrar who puts Negroes on his rolls without their coming up to the strictest requirements (which are impossible—W. Z. F.), will be removed from office and I am the man who will put them out." Violent propaganda is made on all sides that the race question is not one that can be settled by ballots but by bullets and cold steel.

But all this vigorous race prejudice propaganda fails to stop the Republican Party's progress. This is largely because that party is aggressively demonstrating that it also stands for "white supremacy." It is giving widespread assurance, by discarding its southern Negro leaders and in various other ways, that its advent to power will not disturb the Jim Crow system. It is convincing the dominant class that a vote for the Republican Party is also a vote for white supremacy and suppression of the Negro race. Thus it is compelled to throw aside its hypocritical mask as the party of the Negroes, which it has worn so unctuously for seventy years and to come out openly like the Democratic Party as a Jim Crow party.

The Workers (Communist) Party must be quick to turn to its advantage this unmasking of the Republican Party. Ever since the Civil War, the overwhelming mass of Negroes have naively supported the Republican Party as their party. But large numbers of them will be disillusioned by that party's exposure as an open supporter of Jim Crowism. We must seek to educate the Negroes generally to the true role of the Republican Party, especially in the light of the present situation, and to unite them in and around the Workers (Communist) Party as the only party that represents the interests of and fights for the Negro race.

Need of a Party Program for the South

The Workers (Communist) Party must give active and immediate attention to the development of a special program of work in the south. The Party must establish a southern district; it must get organizers in the field; it must carry through an aggressive campaign to recruit the Party membership and to establish in all the southern centers branches of our Party, the Y. W. C. L., and the auxiliary organizations. The weakness of the Party's activities generally in Negro work must be drastically overcome.

Together with this organizational program must be developed a political program for work in the south. We must have concrete demands for the Negroes, and for the workers as a whole based on the actual situation. We must outline definite campaigns to organize unions in the various industries. The decisive factor in all our work in the south is our policy on the Negro question. We must realize from the outset that it is the basic task of our Party to lead a militant struggle for and with the Negroes. All our activities there, all our successes and failures will turn around this central fact.

In the south we must be vigilantly on our guard to combat all tendencies in our Party to "soft-pedal" the Negro question, and to compromise with

Jim Crowism. This has not been done sufficiently. We must fight resolutely against white chauvinism, because it is exactly in the south, where the fire of race prejudice is the hottest and the revolutionary initiative of the Negro most repressed, that the danger of chauvinism is the greatest in our Party and in the ranks of the workers generally. We must liquidate all such tendencies as the ignoring of the Negro question in our public speeches, failure to draw Negroes into open propaganda meetings or proposals to form separate white and Negro branches, etc. Those workers who are not willing to join a common branch with the Negroes and participate with them in Party activities are not yet ready for membership in the Workers (Communist) Party.

Especially must our Party combat and liquidate the idea of building our Party in the south primarily of whites on the theory that "if you get the white workers, you've got the Negroes." This erroneous theory is simply a crystallization of white chauvinism under a mask of left phrases. It denies the revolutionary role of the Negro. It leads to the acceptance of Jim Crowism and implies the abandonment of all struggle for and with the Negroes. It is the working theory of the socialists and the A. F. of L. fakers. It has nothing in common with a communist program. Our Party must reject and eradicate it completely. The central task of our Party in the south is to unite the Negroes directly and to lead them in the struggle. Only in this way can our Party fulfill its historic task. The coming Party convention must give special attention to the general question of our work in the south.

Bibliography

Alexander, Robert J. *The Right Opposition: The Lovestoneites and the International Communist Opposition of the 1930s.* Westport, CT: Greenwood Press, 1981.

Anderson, Jervis. *A. Philip Randolph: A Biographical Portrait.* Berkeley: University of California Press, 1973.

Anderson, Kevin B. *Marx at the Margins: On Nationalism, Ethnicity, and Non-Western Societies.* Chicago: University of Chicago Press, 2016.

Arnesen, Eric. "A. Philip Randolph: Emerging Socialist Radical." In *Reframing Randolph: Labor, Black Freedom, and the Legacies of A. Philip Randolph,* edited by Andrew E. Kersten and Clarence Lang. New York: New York University Press, 2015.

Barrett, James R. *William Z. Foster and the Tragedy of American Radicalism.* Champaign: University of Illinois Press, 2002.

Basen, Neil K. "Kate Richards O'Hare: The 'First Lady' of American Socialism, 1901–1917." *Labor History* 21, no. 2 (Spring 1980): 165–99.

Berland, Oscar. "The Emergence of the Communist Perspective on the 'Negro Question' in America: 1919–1931 Part Two." *Science & Society* 64, no. 2 (2000): 194–217.

Bissett, Jim. *Agrarian Socialism in America: Marx, Jefferson, and Jesus in the Oklahoma Countryside, 1904–1920.* Norman: University of Oklahoma Press, 1999.

Blackburn, Robin. *An Unfinished Revolution: Karl Marx and Abraham Lincoln.* London: Verso Books, 2011.

Brown, Theodore M., and Elizabeth Fee. "Isaac Max Rubinow: Advocate for Social Insurance." *American Journal of Public Health* 92, no. 8 (2002): 1224–25.

Cole, Peter. *Ben Fletcher: The Life and Times of a Black Wobbly, Including Fellow Worker Fletcher's Writings and Speeches.* Chicago: Charles H. Kerr

Publishing Company, 2007.

——— . *Wobblies on the Waterfront: Interracial Unionism in Progressive-Era Philadelphia.* Champaign, IL: University of Illinois Press, 2007.

Cole, Peter, and Lucien van der Walt. "Crossing the Color Lines, Crossing the Continents: Comparing the Racial Politics of the IWW in South Africa and the United States, 1905–1925." *Safundi: The Journal of South African and American Studies* 12, no. 1 (Winter 2011): 69–96.

Cooper, Wayne. *Claude McKay: Rebel Sojourner in the Harlem Renaissance.* Baton Rouge: Louisiana State University Press, 1996.

Davenport, Tim. "Introduction to The New Review (1913–1916)." *Marxist Internet Archive.* August 2011, www.marxists.org/history/usa/pubs /newreview/index.htm.

Davies, Carol Boyce. *Left of Karl Marx: The Political Life of Black Communist Claudia Jones.* Durham, North Carolina: Duke University Press, 2007.

Dorrien, Gary. *The New Abolition: WEB Du Bois and the Black Social Gospel.* New Haven: Yale University Press, 2015.

Draper, Theodore. *The Roots of American Communism.* New Brunswick, NJ: Transaction Publishers, 2003 [1957].

Dubofsky, Melvyn. *We Shall Be All: A History of the Industrial Workers of the World.* Champaign: University of Illinois Press, 2013.

Dunne, William F. *The Struggle Against Opportunism in the Labor Movement—For a Socialist United States: A Contribution to the Discussion of Major Problems of Marxism-Leninism in Our Country.* New York: New York Continuations Committee, 1947.

Eltis, David, and Stanley Engerman. "The Importance of Slavery and the Slave Trade to Industrializing Britain." *Journal of Economic History* 60, no. 1 (2000): 123–44.

Floyd-Thomas, J.M. "Domingo, Wilfred Adolphus." In *Encyclopedia of the Harlem Renaissance.* Vol I, edited by Cary D. Wintz and Paul Finkleman, 304–5. New York: Routledge, 2004.

Foner, Philip S. "The IWW and the Black Worker." *Journal of Negro History* 55, no. 1 (January 1970): 45–64.

———. *American Socialism and Black Americans: From the Age of Jackson to World War II.* Westport, CT: Greenwood Press, 1977.

———. *Black Socialist Preacher.* San Francisco: Synthesis Publishers, 1983.

Foner, Philip S. and Sally M. Miller, eds. *Kate Richards O'Hare: Selected Writings and Speeches*. Baton Rouge: Louisiana State University Press, 1982.

Foster, William Z. *From Bryan to Stalin*. New York: International Publishers, 1937.

Gerber, David A. "Peter Humphries Clark: The Dialogue of Hope and Despair." In *Black Leaders of the Nineteenth Century*, edited by Leon Litwack and August Meier. Urbana: University of Illinois Press, 1988.

Ginger, Ray. *The Bending Cross: A Biography of Eugene V. Debs*. Chicago: Haymarket Books, 2007.

Gilmore, Glena E. *Defying Dixie: The Radical Roots of Civil Rights, 1919–1950*. New York: W.W. Norton & Company, 2008.

Glaser, William A. "Algie Martin Simons and Marxism in America." *The Mississippi Valley Historical Review* 41, no. 3 (1954): 419–34.

Green, James R. *Grass-Roots Socialism: Radical Movements in the Southwest, 1895–1943*. Baton Rouge: Louisiana State University Press, 1978.

Harley, C. Knick. "Slavery, the British Atlantic Economy, and the Industrial Revolution," In *The Caribbean and the Atlantic World Economy*, edited by Adrian Leonard and David Pretel. London: Palgrave, 2015, 161–83.

Harris, LaShawn D. "Running with the Reds: African American Women and the Communist Party during the Great Depression." *Journal of African American History* 94, no. 1 (Winter 2009): 21–40.

Heideman, Paul. "The Rise and Fall of the Socialist Party of America." *Jacobin* 23 (Fall 2016): 37–67.

Hickman, Jared. *Black Prometheus: Race and Radicalism in the Age of Atlantic Slavery*. Oxford: Oxford University Press, 2016.

Hill, Robert A. *The Marcus Garvey and Universal Negro Improvement Association Papers*. Vol. I. Los Angeles: University of California Press, 1983.

Holcomb, Gary Edward. *Claude McKay, Code Name Sasha: Queer Black Marxism in the Harlem Renaissance*. Gainesville: University Press of Florida, 2007.

Homberger, Eric. *John Reed*. Manchester: Manchester University Press, 1990.

James, Winston. *Holding Aloft the Banner of Ethiopia: Caribbean Radicalism in Early Twentieth-Century America*. London: Verso, 1998.

———. "Being Red and Black in Jim Crow America: On the Ideology and

Travails of Afro-America's Socialist Pioneers, 1877–1930." In *Time Longer Than Rope: A Century of African American Activism, 1850–1950*, edited by Charles M. Payne and Adam Green, 336–410. New York: New York University Press, 2003.

Johanningsmeier, Edward P. *Forging American Communism: The Life of William Z. Foster*. Princeton: Princeton University Press, 1994.

Johnson, Cedric. *From Revolutionaries to Race Leaders: Black Power and the Making of African American Politics*. Champaign: University of Illinois Press, 2007.

———. "Between Revolution and the Racial Ghetto: Harold Cruse and Harry Haywood Debate Class Struggle and 'the Negro Question,' 1962–1968." *Historical Materialism* 24, no. 2 (2016): 165-203.

Johnson, Walter. "The Pedestal and the Veil: Rethinking the Capitalism/ Slavery Question." *Journal of the Early Republic* 24, no. 2 (2004): 299–308.

Jones, William P. "'Nothing Special to Offer the Negro': Revisiting the 'Debsian View' of the Negro Question." *International Labor and Working-Class History* 74, no. 1 (2008): 212–24.

Kornweibel, Theodore. *No Crystal Stair: Black Life and the Messenger, 1917–1928*. Westport, CT: Greenwood Publishing Group, 1975.

Kreuter, Kent, and Gretchen Kreuter. *An American Dissenter: The Life of Algie Martin Simons 1870–1950*. Lexington: University Press of Kentucky, 2015.

Le Blanc, Paul, and Tim Davenport. *The "American Exceptionalism" of Jay Lovestone and His Comrades, 1929–1940*. Leiden, The Netherlands: Brill, 2015.

Lehman, Daniel W. *John Reed and the Writing of Revolution*. Athens: Ohio University Press, 2002.

Lewis, David L. *W.E.B. Du Bois, 1868–1919: Biography of a Race*. Vol. 1. New York: Macmillan, 1994.

Lloyd, Brian. *Left Out: Pragmatism, Exceptionalism, and the Poverty of American Marxism, 1890–1922*. Baltimore: Johns Hopkins University Press, 1997.

McDuffie, Erik S. *Sojourning for Freedom: Black Women, American Communism, and the Making of Black Left Feminism*. Durham, North Carolina: Duke University Press, 2011.

McLellan, Woodford. "Africans and Black Americans in the Comintern Schools, 1925–1934." *International Journal of African Historical Studies* 26, no. 2 (1993): 371–90.

McWhiney, Grady. "Louisiana Socialists in the Early Twentieth Century: A Study in Rustic Radicalism." *Journal of Southern History* 20, no. 3 (1954): 315–36.

Marx, Karl. *The Poverty of Philosophy* (1847), *Marxist Internet Archive*, www .marxists.org/archive/marx/works/1847/poverty-philosophy/cho2.htm.

———. "Marx to Engels in Manchester." January 11, 1860. *Marxist Internet Archive* www.marxistsfr.org/archive/marx/works/1860/letters/60_01_11.htm.

———. "The North American Civil War." *Die Press*, no. 293, October 25, 1861. *Marxist Internet Archive*. www.marxists.org/archive/marx/works /download/Marx_Engels _Writings_on_the_North_American_Civil _War.pdf.

———. "Comments on the North American Events." *Die Presse*. October 12, 1862. *Marxist Internet Archive*. www.marxistsfr.org/archive/marx/works /1862/10/12.htm.

———. *Capital: A Critique of Political Economy*. London: Penguin Books, 2004 [1867].

Makalani, Minkah. *In the Cause of Freedom: Radical Black Internationalism from Harlem to London, 1917–1939*. Chapel Hill: University of North Carolina Press, 2014.

Marti, Donald B. "Answering the Agrarian Question: Socialists, Farmers, and Algie Martin Simons." *Agricultural History* 65, no. 3 (1991): 53–69.

Maxwell, William J. *New Negro, Old Left: African American Writing and Communism Between the Wars*. New York: Columbia University Press, 1999.

Meredith, H.L. "Agrarian Socialism and the Negro in Oklahoma, 1900–1918." *Labor History* 11, no. 3 (1970): 277–84.

Miller, Sally M. "The Socialist Party and the Negro, 1901–20." *Journal of Negro History* 56, no. 3 (1971): 220–29.

———. *From Prairie to Prison: The Life of Social Activist Kate Richards O'Hare*. Vol. 1. University of Missouri Press, 1993.

Morgan, Ted. *Jay Lovestone: A Covert Life*. New York: Random House, 1999.

Mullen, Bill V. *W.E.B. Du Bois: Revolutionary Across the Color Line*. Chicago: University of Chicago Press, 2016.

Newsinger, John, ed. *Shaking the World: John Reed's Revolutionary Journalism*. London: Bookmarks, 1998.

Nimtz, August H., Jr. *Marx, Tocqueville, and Race in America: The "Absolute Democracy" or "Defiled Republic."* Lanham, MD: Lexington Books, 2003.

North, Joseph. *Robert Minor, Artist and Crusader: An Informal Biography.* New York: International Publishers, 1956.

Palmer, Bryan D. *James P. Cannon and the Origins of the American Revolutionary Left, 1890–1928.* Champaign: University of Illinois Press, 2007.

Perry, Jeffrey Babcock. *Hubert Harrison: The Voice of Harlem Radicalism, 1883–1918.* New York: Columbia University Press, 2013.

Post, Charles. *The American Road to Capitalism: Studies in Class-Structure, Economic Development, and Political Conflict, 1620–1877.* Chicago: Haymarket Books, 2012.

Reed, Adolph L., Jr. *W.E.B. Du Bois and American Political Thought: Fabianism and the Color Line.* Oxford: Oxford University Press, 1997.

Robinson, Cedric. *Black Marxism: The Making of the Black Radical Tradition.* Chapel Hill: University of North Carolina Press, 1983.

Salvatore, Nick. *Eugene V. Debs: Citizen and Socialist.* Champaign: University of Illinois Press, 1982.

Schneirov, Richard. "The Odyssey of William English Walling: Revisionism, Social Democracy, and Evolutionary Pragmatism." *Journal of the Gilded Age and Progressive Era* 2, no. 4 (2003): 403–30.

Senechal de la Roche, Roberta. *In Lincoln's Shadow: The 1908 Race Riot in Springfield, Illinois.* Carbondale: Southern Illinois University Press, 1990.

Seraile, William. "Ben Fletcher, I.W.W. Organizer." *Pennsylvania History: A Journal of Mid-Atlantic Studies* 46, no. 3 (July 1979): 212–32.

Solomon, Mark. *The Cry Was Unity: Communists and African Americans, 1917–1936.* Jackson: University Press of Mississippi, 1998.

Taylor, Keeanga-Yamahtta. *From #BlackLivesMatter to Black Liberation.* Chicago: Haymarket Books, 2016.

Taylor, Nikki M. *America's First Black Socialist: The Radical Life of Peter H. Clark.* Lexington: University Press of Kentucky, 2013.

Wedin, Carolyn. *Inheritors of the Spirit: Mary White Ovington and the Founding of the NAACP.* New York: John Wiley and Sons, 1998.

Weinstein, James. *The Decline of the American Socialist Movement, 1912–1924.* New York: Monthly Review Press, 1967.

Wetzel, Kurt. "The Defeat of Bill Dunne: An Episode in the Montana Red Scare." *Pacific Northwest Quarterly* 64(1), 1973: 12–20.

Wilkison, Kyle G. *Yeomen, Sharecroppers, and Socialists: Plain Folk Protest in Texas, 1870–1914.* College Station: Texas A&M University Press, 2008.

Woodbey, George Washington. "The New Emancipation." In *Black Socialist Preacher*, edited by Philip S. Foner, 247–250. San Francisco: Synthesis Publishers, 1983.

Zumoff, J.A. "The African Blood Brotherhood: From Caribbean Nationalism to Communism." *Journal of Caribbean History* 41, no. 1/2 (2007): 201–26.

———. *The Communist International and US Communism, 1919–1929.* Leiden, The Netherlands: Brill, 2014.

Notes

1. W.E.B. Du Bois, *New Review: A Weekly Review of International Socialism* 1, no. 5 (February 1913): 138–41.
2. Eugene V. Debs, "The Negro in the Class Struggle," *International Socialist Review* 4, no. 5 (1903): 257–60.
3. As William P. Jones points out, this image of the SP in particular often came from CP members trying to distance themselves from that party's legacy. See William P. Jones, "'Nothing Special to Offer the Negro': Revisiting the 'Debsian View' of the Negro Question," *International Labor and Working-Class History* 74, no. 1 (2008): 212–24.
4. Debs, "Negro in the Class Struggle."
5. Nick Salvatore, *Eugene V. Debs: Citizen and Socialist* (Champaign: University of Illinois Press, 1982), 227.
6. Cedric Robinson, *Black Marxism: The Making of the Black Radical Tradition* (Chapel Hill: University of North Carolina Press, 1983), x.
7. Ibid; Walter Johnson, "The Pedestal and the Veil: Rethinking the Capitalism/Slavery Question," *Journal of the Early Republic* 24, no. 2 (2004): 301. This myth is still repeated even in the most recent work on the subject. Thus, Jared Hickman argues that, even conceding that Marx wrote plenty about slavery, "it is entirely accurate to say that Marx views racial slavery as ultimately subsidiary or preparatory to his anti-Hegelian, materialist envisioning of the Absolute's movement through History in the form of the proletariat." Hickman bases this contention on Marx's argument that the anti-slavery character of the Civil War stemmed from "whether the twenty million free men of the North should submit any longer to an oligarchy of three hundred thousand slaveholders." Hickman neglects to give the date of this quote, which is from 1861, when Northern objectives in the Civil War were still manifestly not about ending slavery. Hickman treats Marx's presentation of the actual political dynamics driving the conflict as dismissive of the importance of slavery because Marx recognizes that the abolition of slavery was not yet the central issue in the war! Unfortunately, this kind of travesty of intellectual history is only too common in discussions of Marx. Jared Hickman, *Black Prometheus: Race and Radicalism in the Age of Atlantic Slavery* (Oxford: Oxford University

Press, 2016), 138.

8. Karl Marx, *The Poverty of Philosophy* (1847), *Marxist Internet Archive*, www
.marxists.org/archive/marx/works/1847/poverty-philosophy/ch02.htm.

9. For contemporary evaluations of the relationship between slavery and the
development of Atlantic capitalism, see Charles Post, *The American Road
to Capitalism: Studies in Class-Structure, Economic Development, and Political Conflict, 1620–1877* (Chicago: Haymarket Books, 2012); David Eltis
and Stanley Engerman, "The Importance of Slavery and the Slave Trade
to Industrializing Britain," *Journal of Economic History* 60, no. 1 (2000):
123–44; C. Knick Harley, "Slavery, the British Atlantic Economy, and the
Industrial Revolution," In *The Caribbean and the Atlantic World Economy*,
Adrian Leonard and David Pretel eds. (London: Palgrave, 2015), 161–83.

10. August H. Nimtz, Jr., *Marx, Tocqueville, and Race in America: The "Absolute
Democracy" or "Defiled Republic"* (Lanham, MD: Lexington Books, 2003), 61.

11. Marx, "Marx to Engels in Manchester," January 11, 1860, *Marxist Internet
Archive*, http://www.marxistsfr.org/archive/marx/works/1860/letters
/60_01_11.htm.

12. Marx, "The North American Civil War," *Die Press*, no. 293, October 25,
1861, *Marxist Internet Archive*, www.marxists.org/archive/marx/works
/download/Marx_Engels_Writings_on_the_North_American_Civil
_War.pdf.

13. Kevin B. Anderson, *Marx at the Margins: On Nationalism, Ethnicity, and
Non-Western Societies* (Chicago: University of Chicago Press, 2016), 86.

14. Ibid.

15. Ibid.

16. Marx, "Comments on the North American Events," *Die Presse*, October
12, 1862.

17. *Marxist Internet Archive*, www.marxistsfr.org/archive/marx/works/1862/10
/12.htm; Blackburn, 203.

18. Nimtz, 121.

19. Blackburn, 211–13.

20. Ibid.

21. Nimtz, 118–21.

22. Liverpool was one of the major ports for the slave trade by English ships.
Marx also wrote about this: "Liverpool 'respectability' is the Pindar of the
slave trade which—compare the work of Aikin [1795] already quoted—
has coincided with that spirit of bold adventure which has characterised
the trade of Liverpool and rapidly carried it to its present state of prosperity; has occasioned vast employment for shipping and sailors, and greatly
augmented the demand for the manufactures of the country." Marx,

Capital: A Critique of Political Economy (London: Penguin Books, 2004 [1867]), 339. www.marxists.org/archive/marx/works/1867-c1/ch31.htm.
23. Anderson, *Marx at the Margins*, 103–4.
24. Blackburn, 212.
25. Nikki M. Taylor, *America's First Black Socialist: The Radical Life of Peter H. Clark.* (Lexington, KY: University Press of Kentucky, 2013); Winston James, "Being Red and Black in Jim Crow America: On the Ideology and Travails of Afro-America's Socialist Pioneers, 1877–1930," in *Time Longer Than Rope: A Century of African American Activism, 1850–1950*, eds. Charles M. Payne and Adam Green (New York: New York University Press, 2003), 336–410.
26. Taylor, 87–106; David A. Gerber, "Peter Humphries Clark: The Dialogue of Hope and Despair" in *Black Leaders of the Nineteenth Century*, eds. Leon Litwack and August Meier (Champaign: University of Illinois Press, 1988), 184–85.
27. Taylor, 115–121; Gerber, 185–86.
28. Taylor, 124, 140.
29. Ibid., 35–37, 99–100.
30. Ibid., 135–38; Gerber, 186; James, "Being Red and Black," 342.
31. Taylor, 145; James, "Being Red and Black," 343–44.
32. Taylor, 152–54; James, "Being Red and Black," 346–47.
33. Taylor, 152–54.
34. Gerber, 187–88.
35. Taylor, 199–224.
36. Philip S. Foner, "Introduction," in *Black Socialist Preacher* (San Francisco: Synthesis Publishers, 1983), 6; James, "Being Red and Black," 356–57.
37. Foner, *Black Socialist Preacher*, 7.
38. Ibid., 8–9.
39. Foner, *Black Socialist Preacher*, 27–30.
40. Ibid., 9
41. Foner, *Black Socialist Preacher*, 25.
42. George Washington Woodbey, "The New Emancipation," in *Black Socialist Preacher*, ed., Foner, 249–50.
43. Foner, *Black Socialist Preacher*, 23.
44. James Weinstein, *The Decline of Socialism in America, 1912–24* (New York: Monthly Review Press, 1967), 65.
45. Philip S. Foner, *American Socialism and Black Americans: From the Age of Jackson to World War II* (Westport, CT: Greenwood Press, 1977), 103.
46. Sally M. Miller, "The Socialist Party and the Negro, 1901–20," *Journal of Negro History* 56, no. 3 (1971): 224.

47. Philip S. Foner, *American Socialism and Black Americans*, 95.

48. Ibid.

49. Ibid. 96.

50. Ibid.

51. Ibid, 96–97.

52. Ibid.

53. Ibid.

54. Ibid. Foner notes that the resolution was perceived as such in the black press, which turned with interest to this new party that declared its sympathy with African Americans (100–103).

55. Ibid, 105–8.

56. Debs, "The Negro in the Class Struggle"; Debs, "The Negro and His Nemesis," *International Socialist Review* 4, no. 7 (January 1904): 391–97.

57. Foner, *American Socialism and Black Americans*, 121–26.

58. Ibid.

59. Ibid.

60. Ibid.

61. Ibid., 131. On the Louisiana party more generally, see Grady McWhiney, "Louisiana Socialists in the Early Twentieth Century: A Study in Rustic Radicalism," *Journal of Southern History* 20, no. 3 (1954): 315–36.

62. Foner, *American Socialism and Black Americans*, 131–37. For more examples of the Texas party attempting to evade the race question, see Kyle G. Wilkison, *Yeomen, Sharecroppers, and Socialists: Plain Folk Protest in Texas, 1870–1914* (College Station: Texas A&M University Press, 2008), 137–41. As James Green notes, however, even in Texas, there were exceptions. See James R. Green, *Grass-Roots Socialism: Radical Movements in the Southwest, 1895–1943* (Baton Rouge: Louisiana State University Press, 1978), 95–96.

63. Foner, *American Socialism and Black Americans*, 220–21.

64. Ibid., 220–21, 238–39. As Foner notes, the Virginia socialists failed to carry through on these promises in any significant way.

65. Ibid., 223–25; Green, 100–110; H.L. Meredith, "Agrarian Socialism and the Negro in Oklahoma, 1900–1918," *Labor History* 11, no. 3 (1970): 277–84.

66. Foner, *American Socialism and Black Americans*, 226–28; Green, 102.

67. Foner, *American Socialism and Black Americans*, 230–31.

68. Ibid.

69. Ibid., 232–33.

70. Ibid.; Jim Bissett, *Agrarian Socialism in America: Marx, Jefferson, and Jesus in the Oklahoma Countryside, 1904–1920* (Norman: University of Oklahoma Press, 1999), 117–19.

71. Foner, *American Socialism and Black Americans*, 236. Unfortunately, Democratic control of the state administrative apparatus allowed them to achieve black disenfranchisement nonetheless.

72. Roberta Senechal de la Roche, *In Lincoln's Shadow: The 1908 Race Riot in Springfield, Illinois* (Champaign: Southern Illinois University Press, 1990).

73. Foner, *American Socialism and Black Americans*, 195–201; Carolyn Wedin, *Inheritors of the Spirit: Mary White Ovington and the Founding of the NAACP* (New York: John Wiley and Sons, 1998).

74. Foner, *American Socialism and Black Americans*, 254–63.

75. Ibid.

76. Weinstein, 143–45, 160–62.

77. Paul Heideman, "The Rise and Fall of the Socialist Party of America," *Jacobin* 23, (Fall 2016), 37–67.

78. Foner, *American Socialism and Black Americans*, 302–311.

79. Mark Solomon, *The Cry Was Unity: Communists and African Americans, 1917–1936* (Jackson: University Press of Mississippi, 1998), 3; Jacob A. Zumoff, *The Communist International and US Communism, 1919–1929* (Leiden: Brill, 2014), 291; Theodore Draper, *The Roots of American Communism* (New Brunswick, NJ: Transaction Publishers, 1966), 148–209.

80. "Wage Slave Riots," *Communist*, August 9, 1919.

81. Zumoff, *The Communist International*, 291–92.

82. The *Toiler*, February 13, 1920, 3.

83. Solomon, 17; "Wage Slave Riots," 1–2; Zumoff, *The Communist International*, 291–92; the *Toiler*, February 13, 1920, 3.

84. Solomon, 19.

85. Solomon, 17–19; Zumoff, *The Communist International*, 298–301.

86. For a time, the party's legal name was the Workers Party. In the interests of readability, I call it the Communist Party throughout.

87. "Theses on the Negro Question," published in the *Worker*, March 10, 1923; Solomon, 41–42; Zumoff, *The Communist International*, 308.

88. Zumoff, *The Communist International*, 306–316; William J. Maxwell, *New Negro, Old Left: African American Writing and Communism Between the Wars* (New York: Columbia University Press, 1999), 72–93.

89. Lenin, *The Right of Nations to Self-Determination* (1914). www.marxists .org/archive/lenin/works/1914/self-det/index.htm.

90. Zumoff, *The Communist International*, 312–13.

91. Solomon, 34–35; Joseph North, *Robert Minor, Artist and Crusader: An Informal Biography* (New York: International Publishers, 1956), 159.

92. Minor, "Black Ten Millions," *Liberator*, March 1924.

93. Ibid.

94. Ibid.
95. Ibid.
96. Minor, "The Negro Finds His Place—And a Sword," *Liberator*, August 1924, 205; Minor, "The Handkerchief on Garvey's Head," *Liberator*, October 1924, 17–25.
97. Solomon, 21; Zumoff, *The Communist International*, 302–3.
98. Solomon, 31–33. Glenda Elizabeth Gilmore, *Defying Dixie: The Radical Roots of Civil Rights, 1919–1950* (New York: W.W. Norton & Company, 2008), 40–42.
99. Solomon, 34–36.
100. Ibid., 43–44.
101. Zumoff, *The Communist International*, 320–21.
102. Solomon, 52–55; Zumoff, *The Communist International*, 320–24; Gilmore, 51–56.
103. Solomon, 56–58; Zumoff, *The Communist International*, 327; Gilmore, 57–59.
104. Solomon, 69–71; Zumoff, *The Communist International*, 355–60; Gilmore, 62–63.
105. Gilmore, 59–60; Zumoff, *The Communist International*, 337–40; Oscar Berland, "The Emergence of the Communist Perspective on the 'Negro Question' in America: 1919–1931 Part Two," *Science & Society* 64, no. 2 (2000): 194–217.
106. Zumoff, *The Communist International*, 348.
107. Solomon, 74; Zumoff, *The Communist International*, 348–49; Gilmore, 64–65.
108. Zumoff, *The Communist International*, 355–57.
109. Solomon 85–89; Zumoff, *The Communist International*, 360–64.
110. For more information about the CP's platform in the 30s, see Kelley, Gellman, Gilmore.
111. Johnson, "Between Revolution and the Racial Ghetto."
112. Johnson, *Revolutionaries to Race Leaders*.
113. Keeanga-Yamahtta Taylor, *From #BlackLivesMatter to Black Liberation* (Chicago: Haymarket Books, 2016).

Index

D

Daily Worker, 332, 334, 335, 338, 343, 345, 393
Dallas, Texas, 331
Daniels, Josephus, 398
Darrow, Clarence, 58, 73, 89
Davis, Jefferson, 121
Debs, Eugene V., 41–43
    on Africa, 55
    on capitalist class, 54
    on Civil War, 53
    Class Struggle and, 133
    on disenfranchisement, 23
    Domingo on, 224
    Harrison and, 104
    on immigration, 15
    IWW and, 147
    on Lincoln, 44, 48, 54
    on lynching, 42
    Messenger on, 195
    "The Negro and His Nemesis," 48–55
    "The Negro in the Class Struggle," 42, 44–48
    "nothing special to offer the Negro," 1–3, 16, 41
    on race riots, 42
    Rubinow on, 89, 90–92
    on segragation, 42
    on slavery, 55
    on socialism, 54–55
    the South and, 44, 48, 51, 204, 224
    SP and, 16, 19, 42, 43, 90–91, 95
    on the Black working class, 41, 53
    on the Negro Resolution, 19, 47, 49–50
    on the working class, 41, 46–47, 51
    on white supremacy, 52
    on working class, 90
    Woodbey and, 13

Declaration of Independence, 46, 177
The Decline of Socialism in America, 1912–1925 (Weinstein), 16
De Leon, Daniel, 57, 95
"'Democracy' and Negro Segregation" (Fraina), 131
Democratic Party, 48
    in Alabama, 327
    Bryan and, 13
    capitalist class and, 326
    in Chicago, 187
    Civil War and, 7–8
    Clark and, 12
    disenfranchisement and, 23, 317
    Foster on, 392, 396–98
    Harrison on, 111
    Lovestone on, 386
    Messenger on, 172
    Minor on, 317, 326–27
    NAACP and, 31
    O'Hare on, 97–98, 100–101
    segregation and, 130
    Simons on, 66
    in the South, 172, 327–29
    in Virginia, 398
    voters for, 97–98, 100–101
    white supremacy and, 398
Denikin, General, 193, 212, 241, 244, 261
Denmark, 204, 338
Department of Justice, 190
"Deporting Aliens and Negroes" (Briggs), 238
Detroit, Michigan, 286, 319, 356, 379
"Did Bolshevism Stop Race Riots in Russia?" (Domingo), 225–28
disenfranchisement
    Briggs on, 248
    Communist International on, 279
    Debs on, 23

Dunne on, 358
Foster on, 395, 398
Lovestone on, 380
migration from, 379–80
Minor on, 314, 316, 320, 327
Prohibition party in, 126
Republican Party and, 327
Simons on, 64
Georgia Railroad, 86, 92
German Coast Uprising, 30
Germany
  Africa and, 370–71
  Ameringer from, 21
  Brest-Litovsk treaty and, 213
  Briggs on, 261
  capitalist class of, 171
  colonialism of, 370–72
  Domingo on, 202–4, 213–14, 220, 229–30
  Dunne on, 370–71
  Fraina on, 131
  general strike in, 196
  Marx in, 4–5
  Messenger on, 192
  political parties in, 172–74
  workers in, 193–94, 196
  World War I and, 188
Ghana, 117
Giddings, Franklin H., 184
Gompers, Samuel
  Domingo on, 214
  integration and, 300
  McKay on, 300
  Messenger on, 174
Gorter, Herman, 303
Graves, John Temple, 80
Great Britain
  Briggs on, 243–44, 252, 254, 261
  colonialism of, 367, 372
  Domingo on, 204, 226, 229–32

IWW in, 204
McKay in, 297
Messenger on, 192–93, 196
workers in, 196, 230
Great Depression, 275, 349
Great Migration, 16
  Briggs on, 238, 269
  Class Struggle on, 135
  Dunne on, 355–58
  Fort-Whiteman on, 338
  IWW on, 153, 159
  Lovestone on, 34, 376, 378–89
  Minor on, 319–20
  NAACP on, 320
"The Great Negro Migration" (Lovestone), 378–89
Great Southern Lumber Company, 359
Great Uprising (1877), 11
Greeley, Horace, 217
Greenwich Village, 29, 297, 311
Green, William, 33–34
Gregorieff, General, 227
Grey, Lord, 369, 370
Guatemala, 279, 328, 378

H

Haiti, 230, 232, 251–52, 256, 280, 328, 340, 378
Haller, William, 10–12
Hall, Otto, 28, 34, 332
Hampton University, 64, 87, 185, 210
Hardie, Keir, 224
Harding, Warren G., 327
Harlem
  Briggs on, 248
  Domingo and, 199
  Harrison and, 103–4
  Lovestone and, 376
  SP in, 169

Rubinow on, 76–77, 79, 90
in schools, 137, 183–84, 189, 386
SP and, 16, 20–21, 173, 293
in St. Louis, 131
strike for, 160
Supreme Court on, 127–29
in unions, 33, 86–87, 90, 107, 109,
    136, 142, 144–45, 148, 151,
    284–85, 300, 332, 336–88, 396
in Virginia, 322
in Washington, 128, 184, 187
Wayland on, 19
Senate, 5, 96
Senegal, 231
Senussi, 268
sexual violence
against Black women, 42, 45, 80–81,
    102, 121, 322, 355
against Jews, 227
racist false accusations of, 80, 137,
    183, 354–55
slavery and, 55, 80–81
Shantung, 230
Shaw, George Bernard, 306
Siberia, 227
Simons, Algie M., 57–58
on abolitionist movement, 61
on Civil War, 62
on Democrats, 66
Hillquit and, 57
International Socialist Review and,
    57–58, 123
on lynching, 60, 66
Milwaukee Leader and, 57
"The Negro Problem," 58, 60–67
Negro Resolution and, 17
on race riots, 60, 65
on Republican, 66
on the North, 60–62
SLP and, 57

on the South, 60–64
SP and, 57
Woodbey and, 16
on World War I, 57–58
Simons, George, 226
Sinn Fein, 193, 220, 267, 303, 305–6
slaveholders
abolitionist movement and, 5
Dunne on, 354
Fort-Whiteman on, 335–36
IWW on, 153, 163
Messenger on, 177
Northern views on, 8
state power of, 5–7
US colonization and, 5–6
Woodbey on, 14
slavery. *See also* enslaved people
Briggs on, 268
churches and, 184–85
Civil War and, 4–9, 62, 178, 220,
    279, 315
as class structure, 7, 62–63
colonialism and, 370
Communist historians on, 26
Communist International on,
    278–79
Congress on, 178
Debs on, 55
Domingo on, 205
Dunne on, 353
Fort-Whiteman on, 335–36
Harrison on, 106, 108, 110
IWW on, 148, 153–54, 163–64
Lovestone on, 381, 384
Marx on, 4–9, 36
Messenger on, 177, 186
Minor on, 31, 314–16, 324
in the North, 61
O'Hare on, 102
Pemberton on, 20

About Haymarket Books

Haymarket Books is a radical, independent, nonprofit book publisher based in Chicago.

Our mission is to publish books that contribute to struggles for social and economic justice. We strive to make our books a vibrant and organic part of social movements and the education and development of a critical, engaged, international left.

We take inspiration and courage from our namesakes, the Haymarket martyrs, who gave their lives fighting for a better world. Their 1886 struggle for the eight-hour day—which gave us May Day, the international workers' holiday—reminds workers around the world that ordinary people can organize and struggle for their own liberation. These struggles continue today across the globe—struggles against oppression, exploitation, poverty, and war.

Since our founding in 2001, Haymarket Books has published more than five hundred titles. Radically independent, we seek to drive a wedge into the risk-averse world of corporate book publishing. Our authors include Noam Chomsky, Arundhati Roy, Rebecca Solnit, Angela Davis, Howard Zinn, Amy Goodman, Wallace Shawn, Mike Davis, Winona LaDuke, Ilan Pappé, Richard Wolff, Dave Zirin, Keeanga-Yamahtta Taylor, Nick Turse, Dahr Jamail, David Barsamian, Elizabeth Laird, Amira Hass, Mark Steel, Avi Lewis, Naomi Klein, and Neil Davidson. We are also the trade publishers of the acclaimed Historical Materialism Book Series and of Dispatch Books.